The presentation of poetry to auditor and reader involves a complex interaction of rhetorical, orthographical and visual mediating skills. At issue are the nature of 'authority', the creation of a readership attuned to the writer's poetic resonance, and a delicate negotiation between literary tradition and individual talent. In a series of detailed readings leading scholars focus on the presentation of work by Spenser, Herbert, Milton, Dryden, Pope, Smart, Blake, Wordsworth, Browning, Newman, Yeats, Lawrence and David Jones. The wide chronological range enables unusually extensive comparison across the boundaries of generic form, and between the varying emotional, aesthetic and rhetorical emphases of specific periods: from the creation of fictitious '*personae*' to the construction of autobiographical 'self', from the interaction of printed word and visual image to the arrangements and rearrangements of structure and sequence.

Presenting poetry

PRESENTING POETRY

COMPOSITION, PUBLICATION, RECEPTION

Essays in honour of
IAN JACK

edited by

HOWARD ERSKINE-HILL
University of Cambridge

and

RICHARD A. McCABE
University of Oxford

CAMBRIDGE
UNIVERSITY PRESS

Published by the Press Syndicate of the University of Cambridge
The Pitt Building, Trumpington Street, Cambridge CB2 1RP
40 West 20th Street, New York, NY 10011-4211, USA
10 Stamford Road, Oakleigh, Melbourne 3166, Australia

First published 1995

Printed in Great Britain at the University Press, Cambridge

A catalogue record for this book is available from the British Library

Library of Congress cataloguing in publication data

Presenting poetry: composition, publication, reception: essays in
honour of Ian Jack / edited by Howard Erskine-Hill and Richard A.
McCabe.
p.   cm.
Includes bibliographical references and index.
ISBN 0 521 47360 8 (hardback)
1. English poetry – History and criticism.   1. Erskine-Hill,
Howard.   11. McCabe, Richard A. (Richard Anthony), 1954– .
111. Jack, Ian Robert James.
PR503.P74   1995
821.009 – dc20   94-25085   CIP

ISBN 0 521 47360 8 hardback

Contents

Figures

Introduction

HOWARD ERSKINE-HILL AND RICHARD A. McCABE

> Goe little booke: thy selfe present,
> As child whose parent is unkent . . .
> And when thou art past ieopardee,
> Come tell me, what was sayd of mee,
> And I will send more after thee.[1]

Such were the words in which Edmund Spenser launched *The Shepheardes Calender* in 1579 and with it his own literary career, signing himself merely 'Immerito'. Yet this was no act of rare, personal humility but rather one of studied, rhetorical deprecation. At issue is a sophisticated concept of pastoral decorum for which the authors of genuine shepherds' almanacs had scarcely any use. The author is not 'unkent', as the mysterious 'E. K.' immediately testifies, but the book must deport itself as though he were. It is primarily a question of presentation and of anticipated 'ieopardee' – a theme which runs throughout the present volume of critical essays. The relationship between 'parent' and 'child' is almost conspiratorial. The child must pass *incognito* into the world of affairs soliciting the *imprimatur* of great persons before returning with sufficient support to secure the safe passage of its siblings. 1579 was a dangerous year, a year of close cabals, disguised departures and arrivals, ambiguous counsel and correspondence, threats of rebellion and reprisal, of desperately waiting for word of 'what was sayd of mee'. The air of mystery thrown over 'the new poet's' sudden emergence perfectly captured the spirit of the time, as did the overtly plain but actually problematic 'commentary' and the emblematic woodcuts with their ambivalent mottoes. Not only the matter of the *Calender* but its physical character, its visual and spatial dimensions, its complex interplay of text, gloss and illustration, contribute to its impact.

Surprisingly, it is the imaginative force of this engagement with immediacy, this depth of social critique, that ensures the *Calender*'s lasting relevance. As Richard McCabe demonstrates in the first essay of the present collection,

---

[1] *The Works of Edmund Spenser*, edited by Edwin Greenlaw *et al.*, Variorum Edition, 11 vols. (Baltimore, 1932–58). *Minor Poems*, I, 5.

'"Little Booke: Thy Selfe Present": the Politics of Presentation in *The Shepheardes Calender*', far from articulating a single authorial voice Spenser introduces to English verse the device of fragmented *persona* destined to achieve fulfilment in *The Faerie Queene*, and designed to evoke both the harmony and dissonance of Eliza's England, fairy land and waste land at one and the same time. Uneasily underlying such structures, however, is the Sidneian vision of the poet as *vates*, 'diviner, foreseer, or prophet', requiring an impression of authentic authorial presence such as manifests itself in the closing verses of Spenser's *Legend of Courtesie* (VI.12.40–1) or the opening lines of the third book of *Paradise Lost* (lines 1–55).[2] Not the least concern of the poet as 'maker', however 'unkent', or blind, or disaffected, is the creation of an audience attuned to his uniquely personal resonance.

Amongst England's earliest critical commentators, perhaps it is Ben Jonson who, in *Timber, Or Discoveries*, offers the most intriguing approach to the complex relationship of poet and poem. At one with Sidney in regarding the poet as a *maker*, Jonson, following Pontanus and a long critical tradition, distinguishes between poet, poesy and poem, the poem being the finished work of the poet, poesy 'his skill or Crafte of making: the very Fiction it selfe, the reason or forme of the worke. And these three voices differ, as the thing done, the doing, and the doer; the thing fain'd, the faining, and the fainer: so the Poeme, the Poesy, and the Poet' (lines 2375–8).[3] What is particularly interesting about this threefold division is that Jonson departs from his sources in claiming for each facet its own distinctive 'voice'. Thus the authorial 'voice' speaking as poet within his poem differs from the 'voice' of poetic skill and process, the voice of something coming into being, being made. This in turn differs from the 'voice' which may be ascribed to the completed work considered as a separate entity. 'Language most shewes a man', Jonson observes, slyly blending his own critical voice with that of his illustrious predecessor, Vives, 'speake, that I may see thee.'[4] But given the tenor of his critical theory, he might justly have added, 'language most hides a man, write, that you may not be seen'. Adapting Jonson's terms to, say, Spenser, the author, or 'parent unkent', is scarcely present in *The Shepheardes Calender*, but its poesy lies in the interplay of all its divergent voices, lyrical and explanatory, the total pattern of which is the poem, the thing made, the *Calender* which describes and pictorially illustrates the revolution of one year 'for every yeare'.

The visual possibilities of the printed page have intrigued poets from Spenser to e. e. cummings and David Jones. The old Horatian adage '*ut pictura poesis*' took on a new dimension with the advent of the printing press. It was not that the

[2] Sidney, *A Defence of Poetry*, edited by J. A. Van Dorsten (Oxford, 1966), pp. 18, 21.
[3] *Works*, edited by C. H. Herford and Percy and Evelyn Simpson, 11 vols. (Oxford, 1925–52), VIII, 636; XI, 282.　　[4] *Ibid.*, VIII, 625; XI, 270.

age of the illuminated manuscript could ever be said to have neglected this aspect of affairs, but that the 'monumentality' of print, as Alastair Fowler terms it, endowed the written word with 'a property of self-resembling lastingness' (p. 41). 'The new medium', he points out in '"Cut Without Hands": Herbert's Christian Altar', 'was regarded, in fact, as a form of graphic art' (p. 45) and poetry was now frequently discussed in quasi-architectural terms as being 'framed', 'raised' or 'built', while architecture itself was understood 'as an art not of masonry but of geometry and number' (p. 51). As printers rejoiced in the decorative quality of 'hands, rules, fleurons and pilcrows' (p. 41), the rediscovery of the *Greek Anthology* promoted a new vogue for figure-poems. At its deepest level, this allowed poets such as Herbert to explore the relationship between form and content in terms of profound numerological and structural coincidences of theme and pattern, mood and shape. The effect is not purely visual. In a poem such as 'Easter Wings', for example, the diminution and extension of line length is heard as well as seen, while in 'The Altar', the poem upon which Fowler concentrates, the very orthography 'unites heart and altar into a single image' until the poem becomes 'all heart' (p. 51), a total offering of self-sacrifice in return for self-sacrifice, verbal icon and visible prayer.[5]

By emphasising the effect of E. K.'s 'gloss' on Spenser, visually as well as materially authoritative, our first essay questions the nature of commentary in general whether it be in some sense authorial, as in *The Shepheardes Calender* or Pope's *Dunciad*, or so nearly contemporary as to be accorded a measure of authority on contextual grounds, or the product of modern scholarly inquiry and, therefore, supposedly detached and accurate. Here Milton and Dryden together constitute a strangely discrepant and interesting example. Each poet was at least as deeply engaged in the historical events of his time as was Spenser, though it is arguable that Milton stood in more 'ieopardee' of life and limb than either. Yet while the best modern editions of Dryden's poems regularly explicate historical and political allusion, sometimes to extraordinary degrees of complexity, the equivalent editions of Milton, at least to date, continue to present him as almost a-political: as the Renaissance humanist for whom, at his deepest level of seriousness, revolutions in affairs of state were of marginal import, as a 'timeless classic'.

Recent critical discussion, on the other hand, has been proposing a Milton of a rather different kind.[6] In 'On Historical Commentary: the Example of Milton and Dryden', Howard Erskine-Hill considers how far the discrepant nature of

---

[5] *The Works of George Herbert*, edited by F. E. Hutchinson (Oxford, 1941), pp. 26, 43.

[6] For example, Christopher Hill, *Milton and the English Revolution* (London, 1977); M. A. Radzinowicz, 'The Politics of *Paradise Lost*' in Kevin Sharpe and Steven N. Zwicker, eds., *Politics and Discourse: The Literature and History of Seventeenth-Century England* (Berkeley, 1987), pp. 204–29.

twentieth-century commentary on Milton and Dryden reflects a real difference between the two poets in the bearing of their poems upon their times. This partly involves a consideration of how far each attempted to construct a continuous authorial *persona* which could in itself be relied on implicitly to inform the matter of their poetry in historical ways. The role of prefatory matter (such as Marvell's 'When I beheld the poet blind, yet bold') and of Dryden's own rare annotations is discussed, together with two early sets of annotations by near contemporaries of the poets. These are the Traquair House manuscript of Dryden's *Hind and the Panther*, and the 'Explanatory Notes' by P[atrick] H[ume], published by Tonson in the 1695 edition of *Paradise Lost*. By way of conclusion the essay attempts to sketch the useful limits of historical commentary.

The transformation of *Paradise Lost* from the ten-book poem of 1667 to the twelve-book poem of 1674 serves to remind us of that aspect of the presentational art that concerns structure and sequence. Whereas epic poets may rely on narrative patterns to promote unity of design, others must arrange collections of disparate, if related, pieces into significant sets and sequences. *The Temple* constitutes a unified work largely because of Herbert's skill in this area, while its careful modulations of tone and attitude create an impression of the temple's priest, the 'I' who never 'appears' to relate a personal history but is everywhere present.[7] Similarly, there may be a significant order, even authorially endorsed, between extended major works. Thus Milton's introduction to *Paradise Regained* ('I who erewhile the happy garden sung . . .') not only recalls *Paradise Lost* which is thus brought into the reader's mind as the operative pre-history of the new poem, but is based upon the pseudo-Virgilian lines at the head of many manuscripts of the *Aeneid* which similarly linked the *Aeneid* with the *Georgics* in an overt claim of common authorship and latent public concern. Spenser had executed the same manoeuvre in the opening stanzas of *The Faerie Queene*. Pope, employing a similar strategy of Virgilian echo and claim, recalled the opening of his *Pastorals* at the end of *Windsor Forest*, as Virgil had echoed the opening of his *Eclogues* at the end of the *Georgics*. Pope thus sought to imply that he wished to exemplify that expanding pattern of the great *opus* constituted by Virgil's move from Eclogue to Georgic, and from Georgic to Epic.

Pope's Virgilian programme was fulfilled in no very straightforward sense. Even if we allow his mock-epics and his Homer translations to stand in his canon in the place of the *Aeneid*, it is clear that by the early 1730s he was producing epistles and satires which, if they required a larger structure, could not derive one from the works of Virgil. Pope's own sense of the required larger order of poems took him first to his concept of an *opus magnum*, into which epistle, satire, mock-epic and even, perhaps, epic (the *Brutus* project) might fit.[8] All too soon,

---

[7] Ian Jack, 'A Choice of Orders: The Arrangement of "The Poetical Works"', in Jerome McGann, ed., *Textual Criticism and Literary Interpretation* (Chicago, 1985), pp. 127–43.

[8] Miriam Leranbaum, *Alexander Pope's 'Opus Magnum' 1729–1744* (Oxford, 1977).

however, this notional structure failed, leaving Pope to deal with a problem somewhere between, say, Herbert's ordering of his poems in *The Temple*, on the one hand, and the shaping of the Virgilian canon on the other. There is evidence that Pope now began to consider arranging some of his epistles and satires into significant groups, chronological, formal or thematic. And yet, as Pat Rogers argues in 'Sequences of Reading: Pope's *Moral Essays* and *Imitations of Horace*', it is sometimes necessary to deconstruct long-standing authorial and editorial groupings in order to see the verse afresh. In the case of Pope the traditionally 'arranged' text 'supplies a kind of template for our critical judgements' (p. 91) which precludes satisfactory awareness of 'the sequence of events within the poetry' (p. 90). We may, therefore, attribute to both of the groups in question 'a solidity and distinctness which owes more to editorial sleight of hand than to Pope's original creative urges' (p. 86). Read in chronological order the poems, 'in their raw state, unmediated by subsequent editorialising, undistracted by the *Opus Magnum*, and unfiltered by abstract schemes or ulterior purposes' unleash poetic energies repressed in subsequent reorganisations (p. 94). The effect is certainly to 'defamiliarise' a great classic in a way that many readers will find disconcerting but, as Rogers concludes, 'we may need to resist the poet to gain our fullest sense of the poetry' (p. 94).

Our second section, 'The Self Presented and Revised', examines the shift from ostensibly fictional '*personae*' to deceptively autobiographical 'selves'. In various ways Smart, Blake and Wordsworth attempted to shape their readers' response not merely to their poetry but also to themselves, to their peculiar sense of their own 'authority' as visionaries, prophets and seers. Reacting for different reasons against what they regarded as the tyranny of 'reason' in aesthetic matters, they sought to reclaim for poetry and its makers something of the ancient mystique of divine inspiration – Druidic and Hebraic as much as Greek – which necessitated a conscious entanglement of text and context, an abandonment not merely of 'Augustan' detachment but of the very notion of detachment as an artistic ideal. The poet was to make visible in his works the source of his own poetic talent, the medium would become the message, the text be the man. It never can, of course, as Tristram Shandy discovers to his cost. The notion of total involvement is every bit as chimerical as that of total detachment, yet both provide enabling ideologies for those who espouse them if only because their very contradictions may prove aesthetically stimulating. *The Prelude* is a great autobiographical poem precisely because it depends so heavily upon fictional techniques, upon strategies of detachment and self-distancing, upon the ability to interpret oneself in the light of retrospect and revise one's interpretations in the prospect of new personal and professional ambitions.

In 'Presenting Jeopardy: Language, Authority and the Voice of Smart in *Jubilate Agno*', Tom Keymer examines this struggle for 'authority' through a figure central to the myth of poetic enlightenment, the figure of the 'mad' poet.

Dismissed as insane by some of his contemporaries and subject to the persistent 'jeopardy' of incarceration, Smart laboured to establish within the private world of a work written for himself and God the criteria of its public justification – and his own. Like Spenser in 'ieopardee' before him, he too sought to articulate his vision through the revival of an authoritative language, in this case a form of Hebraic diction known as 'Mashal', peculiarly expressive 'of power, or supreme authority'. Since madness was popularly perceived to destroy the integrity of the personality, Smart's adoption of biblical style, Keymer asserts, 'is not merely a matter of liturgical reform, but of urgent expressive need' (p. 110). His voice blends with the voice of Job and Christ to become that of suffering innocence, of spiritual sanity beset by crassly insane comforters. Thus, Keymer concludes, Smart 'at once survives and proclaims his jeopardised state' (p. 115). But in so far as the defence of the poet's personal sanity is made through poetry, it constitutes a defence of poetry's sanity also, of alternative ways of seeing and responding to the phenomena of experience to those approved of from on high.

Like Smart, Blake too was intensely conscious of the potential 'jeopardy' of defying the canons of acceptable utterance, and also like Smart he struggled to create a form of poetic diction expressive of his prophetic insight. A prophetic 'self', however, is a more complex entity than a rhetorical *persona* and certainly more liable to misconstruction. Blake's radical credentials are sometimes challenged and with them the validity of his self-proclaimed stance as prophet against the empire. But what were Blake's politics? Did self-interest lead him to temporise with the 'Beast and the Whore' (church and state), or even 'to become a political "apostate" like Wordsworth, Coleridge, and Southey?'[9] In 'Did Blake Betray the French Revolution? A Dialogue of the Mind with Itself', Jerome McGann appropriately explores the ambivalence of the poet's image – and, indeed self-image – through the mechanisms of critical dialogue. Much of the resulting debate centres upon Blake's sojourn at Felpham from 1800 to 1803 during the course of which his sense of 'self-division', evident, for example, in *The Four Zoas*, prompted 'a profound critique of what he came to see as his own self-delusions' (p. 122). At the heart of the issue lies our understanding of 'political consciousness' and the nature of political acts. During his period of greatest overt sympathy with the French Revolution, Blake's name appears on no police record yet, it is argued, the *Poetical Sketches* themselves constitute an alternative sort of 'patriotic rising' (p. 131), and, perhaps, the most effective kind for someone determined to undermine 'the imperialism of established art, matching the imperialism of the state it supports' (p. 124). The extent to which Blake succeeded in this project is questionable and the possibility remains that 'his "politics of vision" spun into another dance of those famous Shelleyan

9 *The Complete Poetry and Prose of William Blake*, edited by David V. Erdman, with commentary by Harold Bloom, revised edition (Berkeley, 1982), p. 611.

reciprocals, beauty and ineffectuality', and that the prophetic 'self' suffered accordingly.

Wordsworth is, perhaps, the supreme self-inventor, and self-reviser, of English poetry, and one whose self-revision entails, from the radical outlook, the supreme example of political revisionism. It is, therefore, fitting that the essay devoted to him should consider not merely the complexion of the various 'selves' he endeavoured to express at different times, but the very concept of the 'self' and the manifold emotional and intellectual discontinuities it entails. The 'self' in revision is, paradoxically, a potentially alien creature. Wordsworth had to contend with this potential self-estrangement while at the same time lending to idiosyncratic memories and Hartleian 'associations' some sense of general human relevance. Somehow the poet, as 'man speaking to men', had to secure for his particular, even unique, development the authority of representative experience.[10] In 'Presentation of the Self in the Composition of *The Prelude*', Robert Woof explores such dichotomies by focussing attention upon 'the Lyric spirit of philosophy' without which the 'egotistical' element of Wordsworth's vision would never have achieved any form of sublimity. To study the poem's various drafts this closely is to become aware of a process of 'growth' and self-definition in no sense organic like the elemental forces supposed to operate upon it, but painstakingly constructed and reconstructed in response to successive phases of political and emotional revisionism. No less is involved than the appropriation of epic weight to lyric voice, and the effect upon the reader – first Dorothy, then Coleridge, then humankind – is meticulously calculated to create the impression that refusal of the poet's insight is tantamount to an admission of inhumanity.

Or tantamount, as Robert Langbaum would argue, to a refusal of 'epiphany', a psychological phenomenon he defines in *The Poetry of Experience* as 'a manifestation in and through the visible world of an invisible life'.[11] It was Browning's paradoxical contribution to the art of self-presentation to refract the 'pure white light' of subjective lyrical vision into the 'prismatic hues' of dramatic monologue. 'What I have printed', he told Elizabeth Barrett Browning in 1845, 'gives *no* knowledge of me . . . I never have begun, even, what I hope I was born to begin and end – "R. B. a poem".'[12] And yet, what he printed did give *some* knowledge of him. In his contribution to the present volume, 'The Epiphanic Mode in Browning's Poetry', Langbaum explores the complex relationship between the apparently confessional 'I' of romantic lyric and the deceptively fictitious 'I' of dramatic monologue. Under the right circumstances, masks may facilitate

---

[10] *The Prose Works of William Wordsworth*, edited by W. J. B. Owen and J. W. Smyser, 3 vols. (Oxford, 1974), I, 138.

[11] *The Poetry of Experience* (Harmondsworth, 1974; first pub. 1957), pp. 39–40.

[12] *The Letters of Robert Browning and Elizabeth Barrett Browning 1845–1846*, edited by Elvan Kintner, 2 vols. (Cambridge, Mass., 1969), I, 7, 17.

confessions.[13] 'In Browning's poems', Langbaum argues, 'the author seems to have disappeared; yet he remains present in the intellectual and spiritual force of the dramatised character' (p. 163). But precisely because 'the text never quite equals the epiphany', the poetry lies 'in the jumps the reader is forced to make for himself', in the infinite mental space between words on the page and words in the mind (p. 164). In a poem such as 'Childe Roland', which Browning claimed to have come upon him 'as a kind of dream', 'the epiphany of his own spiritual development breaks upon the speaker, but the epiphany of character breaks upon the reader' (p. 174). 'In the epiphany of character', Langbaum remarks, 'the speaker's development not through concession but through a steady line of self-intensification is perceived through the intensification and finally transformation of the reader's consciousness' (p. 174). But if the reader's response is crucial to the poet's plan, the plan itself is to that extent uncertain – even amongst the select coterie of the Browning societies. Because the 'men and women' who read the volume so entitled are every bit as diverse and fragmented as the characters they encounter, it is always possible that sympathy may displace irony to defeat moral judgement. As Yeats also discovered, audience response is a perilous rock upon which to build one's art: 'All day I'd looked in the face / Of what I hoped 'twould be / To write for my own race / *And the reality*.'[14]

Our third section, 'Readerships Inherited and Invented', further explores the complex relationship between poets and their audiences upon which Langbaum's essay necessarily impinges and the later writings of Ian Jack have tended to focus.[15] Not at issue here are the sociological or demographic aspects of the book-trade, although the results may well have implications in those areas, but the cultural principles and contradictions invested in an author's concept of his readership and a reader's concept of 'authority' in its manifold forms, whether the 'text' in question be a royal proclamation publicly posted or a radical satire circulated surreptitiously. Six centuries ago, Chaucer's Goodwife of Bath threw down the theoretical gauntlet in preferring immediate 'experience' before its censoriously edited record, and still central to the issue are those very patterns of moral and emotional relevance disputed in her tirade – the relevance an author imagines his personal experience will have for others and the often quite contrary relevance his readers actually find there.[16] Could Milton have anticipated a reader such as William Blake, or Blake a reader such as William Empson?

Reading is not a passive activity but involves an ongoing and frequently hostile reassessment of authorial values amounting, in extreme cases, to a total rewriting

[13] See E. Warwick Slinn, *Browning and the Fictions of Identity* (London, 1982), pp. 37–75; L. D. Martin, *Browning's Dramatic Monologues and the Post-Romantic Subject* (Baltimore, 1985), pp. 33–81.   [14] *The Poems*, edited by Richard J. Finneran (London, 1984), p. 148.
[15] Ian Jack, *The Poet and his Audience* (Cambridge, 1984).
[16] *The Riverside Chaucer*, edited by Larry D. Benson *et al.* (Boston, 1987), p. 105.

of the original. The passage from Milton's God to Empson's atheism *via* Blake's deification of Satan is merely one case in point.[17] According to Emerson, ''tis the good reader that makes the good book' but the value judgements inherent in these twin varieties of 'goodness' remain doubly problematic.[18] The quest for an ideal readership constitutes a major theme of English poetry from Spenser to Yeats, frequently involving the actual, unideal readership in traumas of self-definition and self-appraisal. If the poetic 'self' longs to prove representative, even paradoxically in its most idiosyncratic expressions, it struggles ever harder in an increasingly fragmented age to find its cultural constituency. The ambiguity of the lyric 'I' is greatly compounded by its attempted expansion into an authorial 'we'. The poet too, no less than his creations, is a 'character' in development constantly altering his political and intellectual stance in response to changing circumstances. And as he changes he revises his text.

The significance of such revisions is explored by Eric Griffiths in 'Newman's Leading' with reference to the changing titles of the poem popularly known, and more popularly sung, as 'Lead, Kindly Light' but which first appeared, anonymously and enigmatically, as 'Faith'. 'As it ages', he observes, 'the poem draws to itself depths of experience not all harmonious with each other in implication or tone' (p. 193). At the same time the public perception of Newman himself was altering 'beyond recognition' (p. 182), and if 'the poem's first title had said quickly what the poem meant' its successor 'admitted that the poet had spoken too soon' (p. 194). Definitive exegesis is always premature even when undertaken by the author in that it presumes an impossibly complete control over the medium of poetic communication and, more questionably still, over the media of poetic reception. The success of Browning's dramatic monologues largely resides in their demonstration of the opposite, in the limitless possibilities for 'infelicitous' self-betrayal inherent in the use of language and the mistaking of one's audience. In Newman's case, the very theme of the poem is a surrendering of control, 'lead thou me on . . . one step enough for me', amounting if not to a disowning of authority, at least to an acknowledgement of external dictation.

If, as Griffiths argues, editorial practice 'concerns not dead lines on paper but the application that living beings make of such lines' (p. 195), then the poet's conception of his audience, however ill-judged or even perverse, may prove essential to an understanding of his personal and public aesthetic. In 'The Politics of Genre and Audience in Yeats', Seamus Deane locates his subject squarely within the Burkeian tradition 'in which the act of writing itself is construed as the act by which an audience is formed (or re-formed) and in which the success of such a formation depends upon the suasive powers of the author in

---

[17] William Empson, *Milton's God* (Norfolk, 1961).
[18] *The Complete Works of Ralph Waldo Emerson*, edited by Edward Waldo Emerson, 10 vols. (Boston, 1903–4), VII, 296.

discriminating between what is real and what is phantasmal' (p. 202). Aspiring to write for a nation rather than a coterie, Yeats employed 'mythological, occult and historical figures . . . to perform the double function of being both voices that address an audience and the voices of the audience that he himself wishes to address' (p. 205). The epic poet searches for a heroic people, the lyric poet searches for a representative individual – a fisherman, perhaps, in grey Connemara clothes – until the heroic is found within the ordinary and 'Yeats's poems, constituted as volumes, perform an epic, twelve-volumed gesture' (p. 208). Yet 'the reality' resists its idealisation. About the figure of Maud Gonne, and the Ireland of 'eroticised violence' she came to symbolise, Yeats constructed an epic of heroic deprivation, a second Iliad without a second Troy, 'an epic composed of lyric sequences in which she is the subject of and audience for the poem' (p. 210), and ultimately an 'incompetent audience' (p. 212). The sixty-year-old smiling public man was destined to become an Irish school text, but not necessarily to refashion the schoolchildren's perception of Irish history nor supplant 'the reality' of post-colonial commercialism with his own vision of ancestral nationhood.

If, then, the public apologias of the eminent cardinal, the Victorian seer, and the first Irish Nobel-laureate were destined to find appreciative audiences only within the select circles of their personal devotees, perhaps the answer lay in the treatment of less public themes, perhaps in the common experience of the emotional and sexual life. D. H. Lawrence turned his attention to the patterns of emotional autobiography only to discover, as Wordsworth had discovered before him, how intensely fictional a genre autobiography is. As Mark Kinkead-Weekes illustrates in 'The Shaping of D. H. Lawrence's *Look! We Have Come Through!*', the fashioning of a poetic sequence, even one so overtly bound to the circumstances of lived experience, was no less a matter of painstaking revision, rewriting and relocation for Lawrence than it was for Pope. The result is no longer drama or autobiography 'because it is both' (p. 233). And yet, from the reader's viewpoint, lack of precise biographical information may render certain sections emotionally 'opaque' (p. 224). As is the case with Pope, alternative patterns of ironic awareness emerge as the carefully ordered context is undone and individual poems are returned to their chronological position, or reread in earlier drafts. In other words, the very artistry that makes the sequence 'representative' obscures the thing it represents. The 'I' and 'we' of Lawrentian lyric, while inviting a measure of identification, also invite such detachment as Kinkead-Weekes himself adopts, forcing every reader to question 'what it might mean to "come through"' (p. 234). Not merely the 'epiphany' is located in the reader but the cold emotional and sexual comings that may eventually lead to it.

Continuing this theme in the final essay of the volume, 'Presentation and Self-Presentation in *In Parenthesis*', Colin Wilcockson demonstrates how the subtle interplay of the pronouns 'he' and 'I' indicate varying relationships both of author and reader to the text. Like Spenser and Blake, David Jones is deeply concerned with the integration of word and picture, with raising typography and typographical layout to a higher power within the total text. On one level, the project of a self-annotated poem is distinctly Spenserian except that 'in the notes of *In Parenthesis*, there is a tentativeness that strongly contrasts with the authoritative voice of the text' (p. 238). Now it is as though the poetry illuminates the commentary, transforming mere personal incident into a type of public myth. Through the character of John Ball, a modern-day Colin Clout, Jones mediates his experiences upon the Western Front during such battles as Mametz Wood, but both the heroic and anti-heroic potential of this unassuming *persona* are themselves mediated through subtextual reminiscences of Malorian romance deftly evoked by an elaborate pattern of apparently trivial Arthurian references which 'impregnate the work with that tradition of moral dilemma which is to be found in many of the greatest epics' (p. 255). And just as there was for Yeats no second Troy, there is for Jones no second Camelot. *In Parenthesis* is dedicated not only to John Ball's British comrades but also to their German 'brothers' who shared the common experience of warfare and the common stigma of fratricide. Thus from the very outset, the reader is invited to find the 'I' in the 'he', the self in the Other. The process is apparently complete in *The Anathemata* where the dominant pronoun is an inclusive 'we'. Paradoxically, however, as Wilcockson argues, this constitutes a form of 'retreat towards anonymity' (p. 236). But anonymity, too, has powerful presentational uses, not the least of which is the avoidance of the varied forms of 'jeopardy' which bore so heavily upon Spenser, Smart, Blake and even, perhaps, the anonymous authors of the first edition of the *Lyrical Ballads*.

Tom Keymer notes how the vertical and horizontal patterns of *Jubilate Agno*, as preserved in Smart's manuscript, serve to elucidate different aspects of that work's design (p. 99). Something similar might be said of the present volume since the wide chronological range of the essays, an essential feature of the anthology's design, tells one story, the sectional groupings another. All of our poets were concerned with the nature of their readership – it is, after all, a principle of classical rhetoric – and not just those in section three, just as all were concerned with problems of sequence and structure. In some senses the chosen authors defy chronology: Malory is, quite literally, a part of David Jones's text, just as Chaucer is a part of Spenser's. And yet, the very act of quotation combines a genuflection to tradition with an assertion of individuality, a sense of continuity with a sense of disjunction. The tenor of poetic response to issues such as *persona*, self and reader alters over the centuries as the perception of literature's role comes under renewed scrutiny. Our sectional groupings are not, therefore, intended to identify exclusive areas of concern but rather to highlight changing patterns of approach and attitude. By and large, the poets of our first section operated within a broad tradition which regarded poetry as a branch of rhetoric, an authoritative art which prided itself upon its ability to persuade through the manipulation of proven linguistic techniques. Those of section two sought new forms of suasive authority in theories of 'natural' expression and individual appeal. Their rhetoric was no less elaborate, but attuned to different needs. Those of the third section experienced a fragmentation of values so acute as to render all concept of a single audience untenable, and to necessitate radical reassessments of the relationship between poet and reader. Yet these divisions are in no sense absolute. Anticipations of later methods may be found in earlier writers, just as modern authors may, in a self-conscious fashion, adopt the techniques of classical rhetoric for unclassical ends. Indeed the notion of modernity may be understood only within the sort of twofold structure which a volume such as this affords.

It will be seen that the present work owes a debt to some recent critical theory relating bibliography and criticism.[19] The conception of a poem that emerges is certainly not that of a discrete intellectual entity, abstracted from books, context and authorship. However surviving texts may relate to a historical author they carry with them in some measure the literary *idea* of an author. The fragmentation of the authorial image in works such as *The Shepheardes Calender*, or even *The Waste Land*, is a sophisticated variation but not necessarily an exception. The traditional poem bears a myth of its own origin. *Poema* and *poeta* can rarely be separated. Rarely, again, can a single poem be abstracted from its literary context without loss of some kind, even when it does not belong to some larger sequence. Rarely, finally, can the forms of material presentation in typography, layout, illustration and picture be regarded as incidental. And when poets set an example in supplying prose commentary to their own verse, as they sometimes do, the modern scholarly commentator may be forgiven for regarding his *rôle* as less categorically subordinate, and more co-operative, than used to be the case. In the delicate negotiation between tradition and the individual talent, the personal self and the literary self, in which both poets and their editors are perpetually engaged, the art of presentation is paramount.

[19] Jerome J. McGann, *A Critique of Modern Textual Criticism* (Chicago and London, 1983); *The Textual Condition* (Princeton, 1991); D. F. McKenzie, *Bibliography and the Sociology of Texts*, The Panizzi Lectures (London, 1986).

PART ONE

Personae, sequence and commentary

1

'Little booke: thy selfe present': the politics of presentation in *The Shepheardes Calender*

RICHARD A. McCABE

Et in Arcadia Ego: the famous inscription on Poussin's Arcadian tomb mutely voices not merely the objective fact of mortality but the pervasive, subjective melancholy of pastoral complaint. In this sense it may be said to speak for all who encounter it, to characterise the 'I' of pastoral elegy. 'Winter is come', observes Colin Clout, 'that blowes the balefull breath, / And after Winter commeth timely death' (*December*, lines 149–50).[1] He might more properly have said, 'Winter is come again', for Spenser's decision to begin *The Shepheardes Calender* with January rather than March ensures a certain circularity of lament, an elegiac coherence to the entire collection premised upon the irreversible effects of entropy. Death is 'timely' not merely because it affords Colin a release from its miseries but because it constitutes the ultimate product of time's passage. For all its 'recreative' beauty the Arcadian landscape is seldom 'idyllic' in the popular sense. In Poussin's *Landscape with a Man Killed by a Snake*, for example, the natural splendours of the backdrop prove impervious to the terrible tragedy enacted in the foreground. As Alain Merot comments, 'fear touches a small core of people directly, but its impact decreases with distance. The world moves on, regardless, steered by a stoical *logos* that metes out the good and the bad indiscriminately.'[2] It is largely a matter of perspective: only from the viewpoint of the onlooker does the fact of mortality lend sinister connotations to the shadows of the canvas.

Spenser himself had poetically interpreted a similar scene. The sixth woodcut in Jan van der Noot's *Theatre for Voluptuous Worldlings* depicts, by way of illustration of a Petrarchan sonnet lamenting the death of Laura, a fair lady suddenly stung to death by a hidden serpent while walking pensively in a pastoral landscape, 'wherewith she languisht as the gathered floure' (Fig. 1).[3] The graphic style is very similar to that of *The Shepheardes Calender*, juxtaposing visions of the lady in her splendour and her fall. These woodcuts would be of particular

---

[1] All quotations are from *The Works of Edmund Spenser*, edited by Edwin Greenlaw *et al.*, Variorum Edition, 11 vols. (Baltimore, 1932–58).

[2] Alain Merot, *Nicolas Poussin* (London, 1990), p. 153.

[3] Jan van der Noot, *A Theatre for Voluptuous Worldlings* (London, 1569; rpt, New York, 1939), sig. Bviiʳ.

1 'Lady Stung by a Snake' from Van der Noot's *A Theatre for
Voluptuous Worldlings* (1569).

interest to Spenser in preparing for the publication of his own work since the
translations were made not from the original Italian but from the French versions
of Clement Marot, the pastoral elegist who inspired the *November* and *December*
eclogues and whose influence, according to E. K.'s initial gloss, confirmed the
choice of 'Colin' as the name for the central *persona*. Within the *Calender*
elaborate rhetorical strategies of poetic fallacy enable Colin Clout to 'proportion'

his life to the seasons of the year even though the two remain radically disproportionate. The seasons are cyclical, the individual is not. The divergent preoccupations of Thenot, Hobbinol, Cuddie and the rest afford contrasting visions of pastoral life and the tenor of individual eclogues is correspondingly argumentative, dystopian and problematic.

Despite its escapist potential, literary pastoral had long been recognised as a confrontational mode, politically as well as otherwise. The *Idylls* of Theocritus begin with a lament for the death of Daphnis while Virgil's *Eclogues* begin with the problems of dispossession and exile. Neither opted to insulate their Arcadian settings from the miseries of contemporary existence. As in the case of the two Poussin landscapes, the shock of pastoral frequently arises from the conflict between expectation and experience, a conflict acutely sharpened in neoclassical authors such as Petrarch, Boccaccio, Mantuan, Sannazaro, Barclay and Marot.[4] In England, the gradual convergence of Hebraic and classical eclogue, manifest as early as the Wakefield Master's *Shepherds' Plays*, strengthened the perception of pastoral as a mode of social and political critique – if not necessarily of social and political realism – artificially devised 'not of purpose to counterfait or represent the rusticall manner of loves and communication: but under the vaile of homely persons, and in rude speeches to insinuate and glaunce at greater matters, and such as perchance had not bene safe to have beene disclosed in any other sort'.[5] Apparent rusticity was recognised to be a device of actual sophistication. As even the most cursory comparison with the rough diction of the Wakefield Master demonstrates, the conscious archaism of Spenser's language was as much an artificial convention as the supposedly 'antique' costumes of Poussin's shepherds. Not surprisingly, therefore, *The Shepheardes Calender* marks the beginning of Spenser's complex engagement with the *realpolitik* of the Tudor regime through the medium of allegory. At a time when various conflicting ecclesiastical and political factions claimed to represent the 'Good Shepherd', pastoral allegory provided a very inviting means of exploring the contemporary malaise. This is not to deny Spenser a factional interest of his own, but rather to distinguish the authorial 'I' from that of its creature Colin Clout, and to acknowledge in the conflict of competing voices a critical response to the complexity of contemporary issues coupled with an aesthetic determination to create lasting images from transient materials, 'a Calender for every yeare' from the materials supplied by one.

[4] S. K. Heninger Jr has argued that the pattern of illustration, argument and annotation adopted in *The Shepheardes Calender* is modelled upon that of the 1571 edition of Sannazaro's *Arcadia* as a compliment to Sir Philip Sidney. 'The Typographical Layout of Spenser's *Shepheardes Calender*' in *Word and Visual Imagination*, edited by Karl Josef Holtgen, Peter M. Daly and Wolfgang Lottes (Erlangen, 1988), pp. 33–71.

[5] George Puttenham, *The Arte of English Poesie*, edited by Gladys Doidge Willcock and Alice Walker (Cambridge, 1970: first pub. 1936), p. 38.

The visual impact of *The Shepheardes Calender* reinforces this emphasis for, as Ruth Luborsky well observes, 'only poetry is illustrated consistently'.[6] In one respect, however, the observation is not entirely accurate. The single most consistent preoccupation of the woodcuts is the passage of time and, when viewed in sequence, they serve to reinforce the reader's illusion of progress through the four seasons of a calendrical year, an original feature which differentiates them from the illustrations appended to Sebastian Brandt's edition of Virgil (1503) or from those supplied to Barclay's *Egloges* (1515?).[7] In many respects they hark back, in a manner as self-consciously archaic as that of the poetic diction, to older forms of manuscript illustration of the sort found, for example, in *Les Très Riches Heures du Duc de Berry*, or in early printed form in the original *Kalender of Shepherdes* from which Spenser borrowed his title. In depicting the months it was traditional to illustrate representative occupations, sometimes incorporating the appropriate zodiacal signs. The celebrated sequence of months in *Les Très Riches Heures*, for example, supplies detailed astrological material in the celestial hemispheres which crown the vignettes. But *The Shepheardes Calender*, equally deprived of the subtle nuances of colour and the intricacies of fine graphical design, adopts the simpler pattern found in Renaissance editions of Bartholomaeus or Bede which entails the allocation of one zodiacal sign per month, suggestive of a false synchronism of sidereal and terrestrial time, instead of the more accurate distribution of months between signs.[8] Nevertheless, the overall effect is to establish the strictly sequential nature of the eclogues and the vulnerability of human agents to celestial influence. The zodiacal signs together with their conventional glyphs are in all cases segregated from the human world in a canopy of cloud. Year by year the scenes beneath them change while they remain perpetual. The cyclical passage of human time is thus rendered strictly subordinate to greater cycles of revolution and the events chosen for depiction are, therefore, of a typical nature, representative scenes from the recurrent drama of human life. The seasonal appropriateness of the various backdrops corroborates this impression. In *Februarie*, for instance, the traditional occupation of woodcutting is skilfully coalesced with the needs of the fable. In *Iune*, *Iulye* and *August* the annual activities of mowing, raking, cutting and harvesting continue undisturbed despite the various political and theological rivalries of the shepherds. Pathetic fallacy to the contrary, the natural world continues on its course irrespective of personal fate. Rosalind, the supreme object

[6] Ruth Samson Luborsky, 'The Illustrations to *The Shepheardes Calender*', in Patrick Cullen and Thomas P. Roche Jr, eds., *Spenser Studies*, 2 (Pittsburg, 1981), 3–53 (p. 26).

[7] *Ibid.*, pp. 14–17.

[8] S. K. Heninger Jr, *The Cosmographical Glass: Renaissance Diagrams of the Universe* (San Marino, 1977), pp. 113–15.

of Colin's affections, never once appears in the woodcuts – nor anywhere else – and the theme of frustrated love gradually broadens into the vanity of human wishes.

Recent concentration upon the poetics of self-aggrandisement or courtly factionalism have unduly narrowed and misrepresented the aesthetic goals of *The Shepheardes Calender*. Attempts to understand the politics of the pastoral genre have tended to subordinate the form to the politics by the simple expedient of ignoring eclogues of no apparent political content in favour of those which allow of precise factional application.[9] All too often, 'public' eclogues are accounted more significant than 'private' eclogues and attract proportionately more attention. It seems to me, however, that the challenge of the form as Spenser employs it was to integrate the private and the public. Regarded as source materials rather than political determinants, the events of 1579 were certainly intriguing: a proliferation of sermons and pamphlets opposing the French match until the subject was officially banned; Alençon's surreptitious arrival in August 'in a masque', closely followed by Simier's disclosure of Leicester's clandestine marriage; John Stubbs's publication in September – when 'the Westerne winde bloweth sore' – of *The Discoverie of a Gaping Gulf Whereinto England is Like to be Swallowed* followed later the same month by its condemnation as a piece of seditious libel and in November by the savage punishment of the author and bookseller despite pathetic pleas for mercy.[10] 'Stubbs and Page', relates Camden,

had their Right hands cut off with a Cleaver, driven through the Wrist by the force of a Mallet, upon a Scaffold in the Marketplace at Westminster. The Printer was pardoned. I remember (being there present) that when Stubbs, after his Right hand was cut off, put off his Hat with his Left, and said with a loud voice, 'God save the Queen'; *the Multitude standing about was deeply silent.*[11]

Perhaps at no time since her accession did Elisa's England seem less like Arcadia and the decision to explore its internal dynamics through the medium of pastoral allegory was, to say the least, richly ironic. All too easily, Stubbs feared, might England be transformed into another 'landscape with a woman stung by a snake': 'they have sent us hither, not Satan in body of a serpent, but the old serpent in shape of a man, whose sting is in his mouth, and who doth his endeavor to seduce

9   See, for example, Louis Adrian Montrose, '"Eliza, Queene of shepheardes", and the Pastoral of Power', *English Literary Renaissance*, 10 (1980), 153–82; 'Of Gentlemen and Shepherds: The Politics of Elizabethan Pastoral Form', *ELH*, 50 (1983), 415–59; Richard Helgerson, 'The New Poet Presents Himself: Spenser and the Idea of a Literary Career', *PMLA*, 93 (1978), 893–911.
10 J. E. Neale, *Queen Elizabeth I* (St Albans, 1979: first pub. 1934), pp. 240–59; Wallace T. MacCaffrey, *Queen Elizabeth and the Making of Policy, 1572–88* (Princeton, 1981), pp. 251–66.
11 William Camden, *The History of Princess Elizabeth*, edited by Wallace T. MacCaffrey (Chicago, 1970), p. 138. See H. J. Byrom, 'Edmund Spenser's First Printer, Hugh Singleton', *The Library*, fourth series, 14 (1933), pp. 121–56.

2 'Januarye' from *The Shepheardes Calender* (1579).

our Eve, that she and we may lose this English paradise'.[12] And Spenser's printer was none other than Hugh Singleton, the very man pardoned on 3 November for daring to publish *A Gaping Gulf*. The mere appearance of his name upon the anonymous title-page of *The Shepheardes Calender* was enough to dispel any lingering fantasies of Utopian pastoralism. Appropriately enough, the first woodcut shows a disconsolate Colin Clout, his broken bagpipes lying at his feet, gazing away from the countryside to the town in a pose that constitutes a bleak, parodic anticipation of Hilliard's *Young Man amongst Roses* (Fig. 2).[13] The poetic impact of *The Shepheardes Calender* derives to a large extent from its subtle interplay of *personae*, illustrations and gloss, and it is to this innovative and complex form of pastoral presentation that I now wish to turn my attention.

The *Aprill* eclogue is famous for its eulogy of 'fayre *Elisa*, Queene of shepheardes all', but arguably the single most significant aspect of that eulogy's presentation is the conspicuous absence of Colin Clout, now grown too 'alienate and with drawen' to perform a panegyric composed in happier times. In other words, the context of the celebration is alienation and it is only when taken out of that context, as for example in the Latin translation produced in 1600 in honour of the aged Queen Elizabeth, that it can be interpreted as a simple hymn to sovereign virginity.[14] In particular, the word 'alienate' rings heavily for it is simultaneously traditional and topical – traditional in the sense that it evokes the powerful ethos of political and social alienation evoked by Virgil's first eclogue, and topical in that it also evokes the prevalent mood of contemporary England. John Stubbs, for example, objected to the proposed French marriage because 'it agreeth not with this state or frame of government to deliver any trust of undergovernment to an alien . . . the place of an alien is far from such trust by the judgment of our natural laws'.[15] According to the royal proclamation, however, it was Stubbs's own purpose, 'to alienate the love and estimation which [Elizabeth's] people have of her for her godly, Christian, and peaceable government'.[16] Sir Philip Sidney, to whom Spenser dedicated *The Shepheardes Calender*, and whose name accompanies that of Singleton on the title-page, agreed substantially with Stubbs. Writing to the queen at Leicester's behest at more or less the same time as the *Calender* appeared, he warned of how her subjects' hearts might be 'galed, if not aliened, when they shall see you take to husband a frenchman and a

---

[12] *John Stubbs's 'Gaping Gulf' with Letters and Other Relevant Documents*, edited by Lloyd E. Berry (Charlottesville, 1968), pp. 3–4. Hereafter *Gaping Gulf*.

[13] For the political dimension of this miniature see Roy Strong, *The Cult of Elizabeth* (London, 1977), pp. 56–83.

[14] *Spenser Allusions in the Sixteenth and Seventeenth Centuries*, edited by William Wells, 2 Pts, *Studies in Philology*, Texts and Studies, 68, 69 (Chapel Hill, N.C., 1971–2), Pt 1, p. 71.

[15] *Gaping Gulf*, p. 34.   [16] *Ibid.*, p. 147.

3 'Aprill' from *The Shepheardes Calender* (1579).

papist'.[17] Acknowledging the problem, Elizabeth herself warned Alençon that his demand for joint sovereignty 'could not but breed a dangerous alienation of our subjects' goodwill from us'.[18] Because the rhetoric of alienation had come to pervade the tone of public debate in the spheres of both domestic and international politics, the use of the term 'alienate' strikes a very ominous note at the outset of a supposed encomium. Colin's song was not composed in, or for, the April of the *Calender*'s year of concern, but 'once' upon a time, perhaps in some happier April past. In April 1579 Sir George Talbot wrote that, 'the Preachers ... are somewhat too busy to apply their Sermons to tend covertly against this Marriage: many of them inveighing greatly thereat', and Elizabeth in turn ordered that 'none should hereafter preach upon any such Text as the like might be inferred'.[19]

The *Aprill* eclogue celebrates Elizabeth's virginity at the very moment she seemed most determined to abandon it. To this extent it seeks to imprison her in her own image, or 'stereotype' as Wallace MacCaffrey terms it, to compel her continuing fidelity to the mystical marriage with England to which she was understood to have committed herself as early as 1560.[20] It constitutes a perfect demonstration of Sir Ralph Sadler's dictum that, 'it is easier for subjects to oppose a Prince by applause than by armies'.[21] The depiction of April in *Les Très Riches Heures* has young lovers exchanging vows but the corresponding woodcut in *The Shepheardes Calender* excludes all male companionship in accordance with the emphasis of the verse (Fig. 3):

> Let none come here, but that Virgins bene,
> to adorne her grace. (lines 129-30)[22]

The message, as Shakespeare later phrased it, is 'come not near our fairy queen', but that was in the 1590s and it is well to remember that the image of the virgin queen bequeathed to history by annalists such as John Stowe and William Camden is largely a retrospective rationalisation of haphazard events, events

---

[17] *Works*, edited by A. Feuillerat, 4 vols. (Cambridge, 1912–26), III, 52. See Katherine Duncan-Jones, *Sir Philip Sidney, Courtier Poet* (London, 1991), pp. 162–3.

[18] *The Letters of Queen Elizabeth*, edited by G. B. Harrison (London, 1935), p. 132. The Earl of Sussex warned of the dangers incident to a potential 'alienating of the Low Countries to the French'. See *Memoirs of the Life and Times of Sir Christopher Hatton*, edited by Nicolas [Sir Nicholas Harris] (London, 1847), p. 87.

[19] John Strype, *Annals of the Reformation and Establishment of Religion*, 3 vols. (London, 1735–37), II, 560–1.

[20] *Queen Elizabeth and the Making of Policy*, p. 266. Camden, *History of Princess Elizabeth*, edited by MacCaffrey, pp. 29–30. For Stubbs, Elizabeth is simply 'goodwife of England', *Gaping Gulf*, p. 15.

[21] John Nichols, *The Progresses and Processions of Queen Elizabeth*, 2 vols. (London, 1788), II, 10.

[22] *Les Très Riches Heures du Duc de Berry*, edited by Jean Longnon and Raymond Cazelles, with preface by Millard Meiss (London, 1969), sig. F4ᵛ.

which led directly to the termination of the Tudor dynasty.[23] Throughout the first twenty years of her reign, Elizabeth was ceaselessly petitioned to abandon virginity in the interests of the succession. Indeed, as she wryly points out in the proclamation issued against Stubbs, the very factions that now showed themselves most hostile to her marriage had previously been amongst its foremost promoters. The prevalent 'alienation' was occasioned by a perceived conflict of image and reality. The so-called 'cult' of Elizabeth was not so much the product of a consistent body of opinion, let alone a semi-religious movement, as a series of deft political accommodations to changing political circumstance. Much of the evidence suggests that Elizabeth seriously considered marriage in 1579, partly no doubt because a genuine attraction to Alençon (and his factor Simier) was buttressed by the encouragement of two of her most trustworthy advisers, Burleigh and Sussex, but only partly. There is also a sense of urgency, if not desperation, about the whole affair, a sense that the courtly game of proposal and refusal played out since her accession had reached its crisis. During her coronation procession she had identified herself as the favoured child of time, but time that gave did now that gift confound.[24] Elizabeth was in her forty-sixth year and the Alençon marriage represented her last hope of producing an heir of her own body. Thus the apparently 'timeless' quality of Colin's panegyric stands in acutely ironic relation to its subject's intimations of mortality and to the *Calender*'s general insistence upon transience. E. K.'s gloss upon 'the Redde rose medled with the White yfere' (line 68) presents Elizabeth not as a timeless icon but as the product of a particular historical process, that of 'the uniting of the two principall houses of Lancaster and of Yorke', a process which must of necessity continue through her or perish in her. In any case, an April eclogue can hardly be timeless although the choices made in a moment of time may entrap the chooser in an 'eternal' image.

From the outset, the *Calender*'s treatment of love is infused with a peculiarly sour quality. In *Januarye*, Colin's love-longing is responsible for the 'ill governement' of his sheep (line 45) at a time when the 'Queene of shepheardes' and her flock were popularly perceived to be suffering from a similar malady. E. K.'s gloss on the etymology of 'couthe' ('to know or to have skill') associates it with that of 'king' by directing our attention to 'the worthy Sir Thomas Smith in his booke of goverment' (line 10), the relevant passage following hard upon criticism of selfish monarchs who 'were not shepheardes as they ought to be'.[25] Significantly, E. K. credits his acquaintance with this work to the kindness of Sir

[23] John N. King, 'Queen Elizabeth I: Representations of the Virgin Queen', *Renaissance Quarterly*, 43 (1990), 30–74. See also Robin Headlam Wells, *Spenser's 'Faerie Queene' and the Cult of Elizabeth* (London, 1983), pp. 14–21.

[24] Raphael Holinshed, *Chronicles of England, Scotland, and Ireland*, 6 vols. (London, 1808), IV, 166.

[25] Sir Thomas Smith, *De Republica Anglorum*, edited by Mary Dewar (Cambridge, 1982), pp. 55, 56.

Thomas's 'kinseman', Gabriel Harvey, whose *Gratulationes Valdinenses*, celebrated in the gloss to *September*, opposed the French match and ineptly
championed a marriage with Leicester – who would, unknown to Harvey, marry
the Countess of Essex in September. From this point onwards images of
unrequited, spoilt or unsatisfactory love are juxtaposed with images of political
mischance, so that the very texture of the verse reflects its emotional discontents.
In *Februarie*, the ambitious young briar beloved of 'shepheards daughters' (line
120) and 'dyed in Lilly white, and Cremsin redde / . . . Colours meete to clothe a
mayden Queene' (lines 130–2) is responsible for the destruction of the ancient oak,
one of the husbandman's greatest 'trees of state' (line 146). 'The prince's fall',
Stubbs had warned, 'is like that of a mighty oak which bears down with it many
arms and branches.'[26] Love, it would seem, invariably spells political disaster.

In the *March* eclogue, Cupid becomes entangled in a 'fowling net' laid to
entrap 'carrion Crowes' intent upon despoiling a fruitful 'peeretree' (lines 109–
10), and the goddess Flora is interpreted by E. K., in one of his most studied
disintegrations of the pastoral mood, as 'a famous harlot which with the abuse of
her body having gotten great riches, made the people of Rome her heyre' (line
16). Here, immediately prior to the *Aprill* eclogue, the very notion of deification
is rendered suspect while the nature of love is progressively degraded. Indeed the
story of the unfortunate Thomalin 'who scorned Love and his knights so long, till
at length him selfe was entangled, and unwares wounded with the dart of some
beautifull regard, which is Cupides arrowe' subtly interweaves the topical and
the traditional – as does Willy's conclusion that 'to be wise and eke to love, / Is
graunted scarce to God above'. In its use of the word 'Gaule', Thomalin's reply
may well harbour a political pun: 'Of Hony and of Gaule in love there is store: /
The honye is much, but the Gaule is more.' During the Norwich progress of 1578
Cupid was ignominiously driven off, in the presence of Alençon's ambassadors,
and his bow delivered into Elizabeth's keeping.[27] As a poem within a poem – a
structure divergent from any of its literary models – Colin's *Aprill* panegyric,
written in happier times but now recited on his behalf by an equally unhappy
friend in a disabling moment of alienation and withdrawal, attains a new and
sombre resonance. Yet the *Aprill* queen is largely oblivious to the anxieties of her
subjects: 'shee is my goddesse plaine, / And I her shepherds swayne, / Albee
forswonck and forswatt I am' (lines 97–9). There is little here of the 'beautiful

---

[26] *Gaping Gulf*, p. 15. Whatever the precise application of Spenser's allegory, for England's 'mayden
Queene' his imagery is replete with disquieting personal and political innuendo. The fall of Lord
Admiral Seymour, for (*inter alia*) reputedly intriguing to wed the young Princess Elizabeth was
lamented by John Harington the elder, at one time her fellow prisoner in the Tower, as that of a
'hospitable' oak 'erst in Arcadia's londe much prais'd' but brought to ruin by envy and 'despight'.
Nugae Antiquae, edited by Henry Harington, 2 vols. (London, 1804), II, 330–3.

[27] Thomas Churchyard, *A Discourse of the Queenes Majesties Entertainment in Suffolk and Norffolk* in
Nichols, *The Progresses*, II, 63–73.

relation between rich and poor' which William Empson regarded as the essential fabrication of courtly pastoral.[28] The shepherd's boy serves the shepherds' queen 'albee' the burdens of pastoral bondage which she does nothing to ease. Though she moves in green pastures, she does not share them with her flock. Rather, the true 'God of shepheards *Tityrus* is dead' and, as the *October* eclogue makes clear, Elisa's England affords no proper patronage to his successors.

As passages such as this demonstrate, it is not merely the context that mutes *Aprill*'s 'recreative' mood. Within the song itself are clear indications of a studiously qualified response to the queen. 'Like *Phoebe* fayre' (line 65) Elisa may well be, but she is not a real goddess nor will Colin risk blasphemy in so presenting her:

> I will not match her with *Latonaes* seede,
> Such follie great sorow to *Niobe* did breede (lines 86–7)

The point was again topical to the extent that the 'cult' of Elisa had already begun to spawn its heretics. Not long after the publication of *The Shepheardes Calender*, Robert Wright, chaplain to Lord Rich, was arrested on the grounds that 'he had spoke some Time ago against keeping the Queen's Day. Which, he said, was, *To make her an Idol*. Which she heard of, and was very angry.'[29] Hobbinol's emblem 'O dea certe' thus constitutes a questionable response to Thenot's inquiry 'O quam te memorem virgo?' since the Virgilian incident they both recall is that of Venus, goddess of sexual indulgence, masquerading as a nymph of Diana.[30] It was about this time, as Sir Roy Strong notes, that Elizabeth began to be depicted as the vestal virgin Tuccia complete with the emblematic sieve in which she carried water to the temple to demonstrate her integrity. What he does not note, however, is the implication of doubt underlying the image in that Tuccia's actions constituted a response to allegations of impropriety.[31] As adopted by Elizabeth, the iconography is as much defensive as assertive. Yet the same Virgilian incident that inspired the *Aprill* emblems serves to remind us that Venus was also the mother of Aeneas and, in that capacity, progenitor of empire. In the third book of *The Faerie Queene* she leads Amoret into the prolific gardens of Adonis and away from the solitary, barren state of Belphoebe in whom Spenser 'shadows' the frustrated private life of Elizabeth Tudor. But *Aprill* cannot allow any positive images of maternity, as its reference to Niobe indicates, because pride in offspring merely breeds 'sorow'. Apropos 'the uncertainty of succession', Sidney pointed out that 'many Princes have lost their Crownes, whose

---

[28] William Empson, *Some Versions of Pastoral* (Harmondsworth, 1966: first pub. 1935), p. 17.

[29] John Strype, *Annals of the Reformation*, III, 123. See also John Strype, *Historical Collections of the Life and Acts of the Right Reverend Father in God, John Aylmer* (Oxford, 1821), pp. 54–6.

[30] *Aeneid*, I, lines 314–410 (lines 327–8). See Richard A. McCabe, *The Pillars of Eternity: Time and Providence in 'The Faerie Queene'* (Dublin, 1989), p. 132.

[31] Roy Strong, *Gloriana: The Portraits of Queen Elizabeth I* (London, 1987), pp. 95–107.

owne children were manifest successours, and some . . . had their owne children used as instrumentes of their ruine'.[32] The only other 'mother' to figure in the *Calender* is the unfortunate she-goat of *Maye*.

A deep-seated objection to the veneration of graven images was felt by many of Elisa's subjects yet the tradition of Colin's *Aprill* song is essentially messianic, being that of Virgil's fourth eclogue. But Colin's insistence upon Elizabeth's virginity enforces the radical disparity between Spenser's poem and its classical antecedent which concerns itself with the birth of a child destined to continue a royal dynasty or initiate a golden age.[33] The result is that the aging Elizabeth, in whose face 'the Redde rose medled with the White yfere' (line 68), must herself be presented in the role of miraculous child even though the uniting of the Houses of York and Lancaster properly occurred in the person of her father. In her virginity, by contrast, the process came to an abrupt end. Supporters of the match such as the Earl of Northampton pointed out that failure to produce an heir could well lead to a renewal of the Wars of the Roses, a violent unravelling of red and white flowers.[34] He also objected to the paternalistic attitude of those who would keep Elizabeth 'in wardship at forty years of age and above' rather than allowing her to play the natural roles of wife and mother. The point is perceptive: Stubbs had argued that in directing the queen's choice of consort her counsellors should 'learn of every parent . . . that hath a loving care of their daughter', and Sidney wished her to remain 'the most excellent frute of all [her] progenitours, and the perfect mirroir to [her] posterity' – even though she was to have none.[35]

To those of Northampton's outlook, it was time for the miraculous child, over whose birth Raphael Holinshed and John Foxe had cast such an aura of providential mystery, to enter the adult world.[36] They thus objected to the whole paradoxical business upon which Sidney and Spenser were engaged. For example, Colin's song employs the imagery of an epithalamion while precluding all possibility of actual marriage so that the very form of the work comes to encapsulate the irony of its subject's situation: 'The pretie Pawnce / And the Chevisaunce, / Shall match with the fayre flowre Delice' (lines 142–4).[37] 'Flowre delice', comments E. K., is properly 'flos delitiarum' with all the sensual connotations that implies. But there was to be no match with the fleur-de-lis. Union with Alençon, Stubbs argued, could bring no gain to England for 'we who already bear the *fleur-de-lis* quarterly receive no honor by joining with it *par pale*.

---

[32] *Works*, III, 58.   [33] Compare Theocritus, *Idylls*, XVII.

[34] *Gaping Gulf*, pp. 164–5.   [35] *Ibid.*, pp. 69, 171; *Works*, III, 60.

[36] Foxe, *The Acts and Monuments*, edited by George Townsend, 8 vols. (London, 1843–9), V (1846), pp. 61–2; VIII (1849), pp. 600–25 (p. 602). Holinshed, *Chronicles of England, Scotland, and Ireland*, III, 787–8.

[37] L. Stanley Johnson, 'Elizabeth, Bride and Queen: A Study of Spenser's April Eclogue and the Metaphors of English Protestantism', in *Spenser Studies*, 2 (1981), 75–91 (p. 82).

And sith our Queen rightfully bears it, as King of France, and he occupieth it as actual French king [in the event of his succession], I believe it will pose the king of heralds of either realm to make a loving agreement and in one escutcheon well to marshal, according to their rules, the selfsame coat of the usurper with the selfsame kingly coat of the right heir.'[38] Never before had the conventional bridal imagery of floral adornment been infused with such deep political tension.

The positioning of Colin's song in *Aprill*, fourth month of the calendrical year, may well have been influenced by Virgil but in other respects represents a most unusual choice. Elizabeth was born in September under the appropriate natal sign of Virgo, and the month most closely associated with the celebration of her 'cult' was that of her accession, November. Either of these would have made a most appropriate choice for Colin's eulogy. As it is, however, 'fayre *Elisa*' appears under the zodiacal sign of Taurus whose associations are with Venus rather than Diana. According to the old *Kalender of Shepherdes* (1506), a person born under Taurus is apt 'to leave his freendes and live among straungers'.[39] In this capacity, Taurus is three times identified in *The Faerie Queene* with the bull from the sea that carried off the virgin Europa.[40] And April, as Chaucer reminds us in the 'Prologue' to *The Canterbury Tales*, is the month when 'longen foulk to goon on pilgrimage' (line 12). Stubbs warned that in the event of Alençon's accession to the French throne, 'either must our Elizabeth go with him out of her own native country and sweet soil of England ... or else she must tarry here ... as an eclipsed sun diminished in sovereignty': it is unclear from the *Aprill* woodcut whether the sun behind Eliza is rising or setting.[41] Perhaps in fearful anticipation of such a loss, the virgin queen is displaced from her rightful position under Virgo and the month of her accession is reserved for the elegy of 'Dido', an unfortunate queen who lost life and power through infatuation with a foreign prince, sung by a shepherd 'lulled a sleepe through loves misgovernaunce' (line 4). Thus it would appear that for Colin Clout, as for T. S. Eliot, April is the cruellest month and both the alienated character of the *persona* and the distanced manner of poetic presentation serve to undermine the paeons of unqualified praise expected of a formal panegyric.

If the insulated landscape of Colin's *Aprill* song reflects, at least in theory, the royalist ideal of social harmony through hierarchical control that of the ensuing

---

[38] *Gaping Gulf*, p. 67. In *The Faerie Queene* the fleur-de-lis embosses Mercilla's throne (v.9.27) yet, despite her own ancestral claims, she assists Bourbon (Henry IV) to regain the Lady Flourdelis (v.11.49).

[39] *The Kalender of Sheepehardes (1585)*, edited by S. K. Heninger, facsimile edition (Delmar, N.Y., 1979), p. 191. Incongruously for Spenser's purposes, women born under this sign are likely to have 'many Husbands and many children' and to prove to be 'great lyers'. See J. Michael Richardson, *Astrological Symbolism in Spenser's 'The Shepheardes Calender'* (Lewiston, 1989), p. 270.   [40] *The Faerie Queene*, III.11.30; v Proem 5; VII.7.33.   [41] *Gaping Gulf*, p. 49.

moral eclogues reflects by contrast the volatile, perilous state of contemporary politics.[42] Here amidst fallen backdrops subject to all the vicissitudes of temporal mutability Spenser charts England's derogation from idealism in terms of the 'coloured deceipt' of 'dissolute shepheards and pastours', of contempt for 'Poetrie and pleasaunt wits'. The subject is no longer Edenic innocence – 'no mortall blemishe may her blotte' – but fall: the fall of the innocent but foolish kid in *Maye*, Colin's exclusion from 'Paradise' in *Iune*, the destruction of the 'good' shepherd Algrind in *Iulye*, the decline of the church in *September* and the neglect of poesy in *October*. 'Mixed with some Satyrical bitternesse', the world-vision of these eclogues seems remote indeed from that of Colin's eulogy. The Elisa of the *Aprill* eclogue is 'Queene of shepheardes *all*', and Colin's song makes no overt acknowledgement of the divisions incident to the realm, 'for shee is *Syrinx* daughter without spotte, / Which *Pan* the shepheards God of her begot' (lines 50–1). Officially, her history is subsumed into her myth or rather supplanted by it. As the child of Pan and Syrinx, Elizabeth is effectively equated, through the Ovidian poetics of metamorphosis, with the reed 'pipe', and by implication, in view of popular Neo-Platonic interpretations of the myth, with cosmic harmony.[43] But in *Januarye* disillusionment with 'rude Pan' and his 'unlucky Muse' causes Colin to break 'his oaten pype' as though the metamorphic spell had now been broken, as though the 'Queene of shepheardes' no longer possessed the ability to transmute dissonance into harmony or to inspire others to do so.

The argument of the *Maye* eclogue qualifies the title of 'Queene of shepheardes all' by introducing us to 'two formes of pastoures or Ministers, or the protestant and the Catholique' perpetually at odds with each other and potentially antagonistic to Elisa herself.[44] Catholics by and large appear to have favoured the Alençon match, except for a select band of 'commonweal Papists' too 'civilly-wise' to undermine the country's 'safety' for religious reasons.[45] Protestants generally opposed the match and expressed their opposition in a deluge of sermons, pamphlets and belligerent popular ballads which afford striking contrasts to the subtler semantics of Spenserian opposition:

> The kinge of ffrance shall not advance his shippes in English sande
> Ne shall his brother ffrancis have the Ruleng of the lande:
> Wee subiects trwe untill oure queene, the forraine yoke defie,
> Where too we plight oure faithefull hartts, our lymes, our lyves
> and all,

---

[42] See Philippa Berry, *Of Chastity and Power: Elizabethan Literature and the Unmarried Queen* (London, 1989), p. 76.   [43] See Natalis Comes, *Mythologiae* (Venice, 1567), fols. 137ᵛ–140ᵛ.

[44] Elizabeth is alleged to have told the French ambassador in 1579, 'that she would maintain the Religion that she was Crowned in, and that she was baptized in: and would suppress the Papistical Religion, that it should not grow. But that she would root out Puritanism, and the Favourers thereof.' Strype, *Annals of the Reformation*, II, 568.

[45] See *Memoirs . . . of Sir Christopher Hatton*, p. 165.

thereby to have our honor rize, or tak our fatall fall.
Therefore, good ffrancis, Rule at home, resist not our desire;
for here is nothing else for thee, but onely sworde and fyer.[46]

The ritual marriage of Flora (whore goddess of the March eclogue) to May
attended by 'a fayre flocke of Faeries' (line 32), glowingly described by the
Catholic Palinode, is curtly dismissed by the Protestant Piers whose fable of the
fox and the kid may be intended to suggest an unnerving correspondence
between D'Aubigny's baleful influence on Scotland and Alençon's probable
effect upon Elisa.[47] The application is worked out in greater detail in the
concluding section of *Mother Hubberds Tale*, often dated to the same period. The
burden of both arguments is candid: 'it is daungerous to mainteine any
felowship' with Catholics 'or give too much credit to their colourable and feyned
goodwill'. '*Timeo Danaos vel dona ferentes* [I fear the Greeks bearing gifts]',
commented Stubbs, 'and well may a simple Englishman say, *Timeo Gallos* [I fear
the French], namely *Valesios nuptias ambientes* [the Valois proposing mar-
riage].'[48] By proffering gaudy gifts, the fox induced the kid to open the door.
Palinode's infectious joy in the rites of May, however attractively versified, is
irreconcilable with Piers's moral vigilance. They inhabit two conflicting imaginative worlds, Palinode responding to the immediate pleasures of the pastoral
landscape, Piers to its allegorical significance.

Iune introduces an increasingly despondent Colin Clout, forever exiled from
Hobbinol's 'Paradise' of 'frendly Faeries, met with many Graces, / And lightfote
Nymphes' destined to prove equally elusive on the slopes of Mt Acidale (lines
25–6). His condition, E. K. assures us, 'is no poetical fiction' whereas 'the
Opinion of Faeries' is a rank vestige of Catholic superstition deliberately
'feigned' to 'nousell the comen people in ignoraunce, least . . . they woulde in
tyme smell out the untruth of theyr packed pelfe and Massepenie religion', very
reminiscent of the 'packe' of worthless baubles carried by the fox. The imagery of
May Lady and Faery Queen had already begun to attach themselves to the
celebration of Elisa (particularly through Sidney's *Lady of May* and the Suffolk
and Norfolk progresses of 1578), but Piers and E. K. seem determined to debunk
it through a series of provocatively prosaic glosses corrosive of, and inimical to,
the royalist ethos of the *Aprill* eclogue.

The *Iulye* eclogue 'made in the honour and commendation of good shepheardes' drives home this dichotomy. As in *Maye*, Pan is now Christ, not the
monarch, and 'good' shepherds serve the higher authority. Catholics account the

---

[46] *Ballads from Manuscripts*, edited by F. J. Furnivall and W. R. Morfill, 2 vols. (London, 1868–73),
II, 114. See also Edmund Lodge, *Illustrations of British History*, second edition, 3 vols. (London,
1838), II, 149–50.

[47] Paul E. McLane, *Spenser's 'Shepheardes Calender': A Study in Elizabethan Allegory* (Notre Dame,
1961), pp. 71–91.   [48] *Gaping Gulf*, p. 40.

Pope 'theyr Pan' (line 179) and define their own spiritual limitations in the bogus apotheosis this entails. There are no mortal gods. Representative of 'bad' shepherds is the mythical Paris 'that left hys flocke' for 'love he bought to deare' (lines 147–8), thereby occasioning through the subordination of duty to desire 'tenne yeares warre in Troye' and the 'sack' of the 'moste famous citye of all Asia'. Whereas the proud and ambitious pastor Morell tends to confound merely poetic paradises with their biblical counterpart, almost to the extent of equating Parnassus with Mt Olivet, the good shepherd Thomalin sharply distinguishes them, 'thou speakes lyke a lewde lorrell, / of Heaven to demen so' (lines 93–4). Paradoxically, as in *Maye*, the more unguardedly imaginative of the two pastors has the worst of the moral argument, as though Spenser has not found a way, or allowed his shepherds to find a way, of reconciling the biblical with the classical. The poetic medium bucks the moral message. Thomalin's mentor is not Virgil's Corydon but Algrind, alias Archbishop Grindal, 'a shepheard great in gree' whose destruction by a *female* eagle he bitterly laments: 'So now astonied with the stroke, / he lyes in lingring payne' (lines 227–8).[49]

It was three years since the archbishop had dared to defy the queen, nominally on the issue of unauthorised 'prophesyings' but more crucially upon the vexed problem of ecclesiastical and spiritual authority arising from exaggerated notions of the spirituality of secular power primarily intended, in the first instance, as counterblasts to the temporal claims of the papacy: 'So sprong her grace / Of heavenly race' (*Aprill*, lines 52–3). Bishop Jewel had asserted that 'in civil government a king is a king . . . but, after that wee be once come to the reverence and obedience of God's will, there God only is the king; and the king, be he never so mighty, is but a subject.'[50] Nevertheless, Jewel recognised the *de facto* primacy of the temporal power and there remained to the end a radical contradiction at the heart of his theology. In theory the church was the guardian of unalterable doctrine, in practice ecclesiastical doctrine could be determined by the prince. In 1576 in his famous letter to Elizabeth, provocatively modelled upon St Ambrose's excommunication of Theodosius and tactlessly dispatched to a Protestant monarch already excommunicated from Rome, Grindal warned against the dangers of 'flattery' seeing that 'in God's causes the will of God, and not the will of any earthly creature, is to take place'. When she dealt in 'matters of

---

[49] Grindal had employed the same classical anecdote in a sermon of 1564 on the death of the Emperor Ferdinand. Thus it comes to demonstrate the common mortality of poet, prince and prelate. See *The Remains*, edited by William Nicholson (Cambridge, 1843), p. 8. Appended to John Dove's Latin translation of the *Calender* is an elegy for 'Archbishop Algrind, many times mentioned in that work'. See Leicester Bradner, 'The Latin Translations of Spenser's *Shepheardes Calender*', *Modern Philology*, 33 (1935–6), 21–6 (p. 22).

[50] *The Works of John Jewel*, edited by John Ayre, 4 vols. (Cambridge, 1845–50), IV (1850), p. 670. See W. M. Southgate, *John Jewel and the Problem of Doctrinal Authority* (Cambridge, Mass., 1962), pp. 201–16.

faith and religion' she might not 'pronounce so resolutely and peremptorily, *quasi ex auctoritate*', as she might do 'in civil and extern matters'.[51] *Aprill*'s Elisa 'sits upon the grassie greene / . . . Yclad in Scarlot like a mayden Queene' (lines 55–7), but 'Algrind' exhorts her to 'look not only (as was said to Theodosius) upon the purple and princely array, wherewith ye are apparelled; but consider withal, what is that that is covered therewith. Is it not flesh and blood? Is it not dust and ashes? Is it not a corruptible body, which must return to his earth again, God knoweth how soon?' Elizabeth has 'done many things well' but 'cannot be blessed' unless she determines to persevere to the end. 'Reverence to the word of God' is 'the only rule of faith and religion' whatever 'strange opinions' may enter the head of a mere woman.[52] The issue of authority is therefore clear: 'bear with me, I beseech you, Madam, if I choose rather to offend your earthly majesty, than to offend the heavenly majesty of God'.[53] Service of the shepherds' God, it would seem, dictates disobedience to the shepherds' queen. So intense and denigrating are Grindal's criticisms that Colin's *April* song may be seen to constitute a tentative reconstruction of a discredited image in a sequence of poems subversively redolent of Algrind's praise, to be 'recreative' in a revisionist sense. *Iulye*'s female eagle mistakes appearance for reality and consequently paralyses the best shepherd in the land.

Grindal's sequestration severely hampered the administration of the church, played into the hands of Catholics, and dismayed the more radically minded of Elizabeth's Protestant subjects. On either side of the royal arms in the parish church of Bury St Edmunds there appeared surreptitiously two well-known verses from the Book of Revelation originally directed to the Laodiceans and richly indicative of popular feeling: on the left, 'I know thy Works, that thou are neither cold nor hot. I would thou wert cold or not'; on the right, 'Therefore because thou art lukewarm, and neither cold nor hot, it will come to pass, I will spew thee out of my Mouth' (3: 15–16).[54] The ultimate responsibility for the appalling state of the English church outlined in the *September* eclogue by Diggon Davie, alias Richard Davies, Bishop of St Davids, rested with its supreme governor and the despoiling prelates she apparently encouraged. Bishop Cox, who wrote a treatise opposing the Alençon match, was alleged to have termed her a 'harpy' in relation to the progressive alienation of diocesan properties.[55] Since Davies had served on Grindal's commission into ecclesiastical abuses, the generalised complaints of *September* are intimately related to the treatment of Algrind in *Iulye*.[56]

---

[51] *Remains*, p. 389. See Patrick Collinson, *Archbishop Grindal 1519–1583: The Struggle for a Reformed Church* (London, 1979), pp. 233–52.   [52] *Remains*, pp. 378, 389, 390.

[53] *Ibid.*, p. 387.   [54] Strype, *Annals of the Reformation*, III, 123.

[55] See James Jackson Higginson, *Spenser's 'Shepherd's Calender' in Relation to Contemporary Affairs* (New York, 1912), p. 134.   [56] McLane, *Spenser's 'Shepheardes Calender'*, p. 223.

In view of all this, it is perhaps not surprising that the eclogue for *November*, the month most closely associated with Elizabeth's accession, should take the form of an elegy for Dido, 'the great shepehearde his daughter sheene' (line 38). 'The great shepheard', comments E. K., 'is some man of high degree, and not as some vainely suppose God Pan. The person both of the shephearde and of Dido is unknowen and *closely buried* in the Authors conceipt' (my emphasis). In terms of poetic form and structure the poem is designed as a counterpart to *Aprill*, but its principle literary model is Marot's stately pastoral elegy for Queen Louise of Savoy, that 'shepherdess of Peace' ('la Bergere de Paix') whose influence occasioned the elegist so much pain and disquiet.[57] The closest Virgilian equivalent is the elegy for Daphnis often interpreted in the Renaissance, in accordance with the commentary of Servius, as a lament for Julius Caesar.[58] In other words, both of Spenser's closest literary models are, or were perceived to be, elegies of state. Because Dido is the Virgilian queen who destroyed herself through infatuation for a foreign prince, the poem has been interpreted by Paul McLane and Roy Strong as symbolically presaging the death of Elisa's virginity and all it had come to represent in the political sphere.[59] The association between *Aprill* and *November* is all the stronger in that Dido is also referred to in the *Aeneid* as Elissa, most notably at the outset of book five in relation to her 'sad funeral' (lines 3–4). Elizabeth is frequently referred to as 'Elissa' throughout the *Gratulationes Valdinenses*, a work implicitly hostile to Alençon in its apparently gratuitous attack upon the Machiavellian politics of the Medici, his mother's family. We are given to understand that the white cliffs of Albion and their queen must be preserved from such evil influences. The satiric irony is merely compounded by Innocent Gentillet's dedication of the *Anti-Machiavell* to Alençon just two years previously.[60] In any case the names Eliza, Elisa and Elissa seem to have been interchangeable: Marlowe refers to Dido as 'Eliza'.[61] Such a political reading of Spenser's elegiac imagery is by no means unlikely. At the Accession Day tilt of 17 November 1590 the Earl of Essex employed the device of a funeral cortège to express his temporary alienation from the queen, a type of

---

[57] Clement Marot, *Œuvres*, edited by George Guiffrey and Jean Plattard, 5 vols. (Geneva, 1969; first pub. 1911), IV, 399–407 (p. 406). See Annabel Patterson, 'Re-opening the Green Cabinet: Clement Marot and Edmund Spenser', *English Literary Renaissance*, 16 (1986), 44–70.

[58] *Servii Grammatici qui feruntur in Virgilii Carmina Commentarii*, edited by G. Thilo and H. Hagen, 3 vols. (Leipzig, 1881–1902), III (1887), Pt 1, pp. 56–7.

[59] McLane, *Spenser's 'Shepheardes Calender'*, pp. 47–60; Strong, *Gloriana*, pp. 96–7. Helen Cooper notes that John Lane's *Elegie Upon the Death of the High Renowned Princesse, Our Late Soveraigne Elizabeth* borrows from both *Aprill* and *November* thereby confirming their association, *Pastoral: Mediaeval into Renaissance* (Ipswich, 1977), p. 209.

[60] Gabriel Harvey, *Gratulationes Valdinenses* in Nichols, *The Progresses*, II, 35–7. See also T. H. Jameson, 'The "Machiavellianism" of Gabriel Harvey', *PMLA*, 56 (1941), 645–56.

[61] *The Tragedy of Dido, Queen of Carthage*, (IV.2.10), edited by C. F. Tucker Brooke (London, 1930), p. 194.

symbolic 'death'.[62] There were those who believed that, in the event of pregnancy, Elizabeth could not survive childbirth, but Sir Philip Sidney delivered the more potent warning that by marrying Alençon she would accomplish merely 'the manifest death' of her 'estate' for 'as in bodies naturall any soudain change is not without perill, so in this body politick wherof you are the onely head, it is so much the more as there are more humours to receave a hurtfull impression'.[63]

In *A Gaping Gulf* Spenser may have encountered for the first time the theory of the queen's 'two persons or bodies' destined to play such a vital role in his imaginative response to Elizabeth: 'the one her natural body, such as other private ones have, the other her body politic or commonweal body, which is her body of majesty'. Stubbs detected imminent danger to the health, and indeed the life, of both, regarding feigned love as the final and most potent weapon in the arsenal of her enemies.[64] The problem was that possession of Elizabeth's private body threatened usurpation of the body politic – a problem entirely arising from the monarch's sex. It is perhaps significant in this light that the most famous of the 'sieve' portraits, representing Elizabeth as Tuccia, painted sometime between 1580 and 1583 incorporates a symbolic pillar inset with a series of medallions depicting the story of Dido and Aeneas and implicitly celebrating the fortunate escape of the still virgin queen.[65] Personal virginity ensures political autonomy. It thus appears that the association between Elisa and Dido established itself as a powerful contemporary motif. But having said all this, one has still not registered the single most important aspect of the *November* eclogue, namely that it constitutes one of the finest poetic achievements in the *Calender*, and one of the best of its kind in the English elegiac tradition. The foreground of the *November* woodcut has Colin crowned with laurel leaves: Dido's cortège is a mere detail in the distance. For all its political resonance, the *Calender* is not a political treatise, nor was Spenser endeavouring to weave abstruse factional allegories into the texture of pastoral lament so much as drawing poetic inspiration directly from contemporary events. If his theme is political alienation, he has discovered within it the poetry of personal alienation. He appears to have been fascinated by Elisa's use of her own paradoxical public image, by that strangely erotic combination of virginity and seductiveness only her chosen *persona* seemed able to reconcile.

Yet he was writing at the precise moment when the lady herself seemed intent upon dismantling her own reputation, upon violating the sacred motto of *semper*

[62] Strong, *The Cult of Elizabeth*, p. 152.

[63] *Works*, III, 52, 59. Marriage to Alençon might blur the popular distinction between Elizabeth and her sister who made an 'odious mariage with a stranger which is now in question whether your Majesty should doe or no' (p. 58).   [64] *Gaping Gulf*, pp. 68, 79.

[65] Roy Strong, *Gloriana*, pp. 106–7.

eadem adopted at the outset of her career.[66] He was at one with Sir Philip Sidney in recognising that, in the final analysis, only Elisa herself could disillusion her supporters: 'so if any thing can staine so true a forme it must be by bringing your self not in your owne likenesse, but in new colours unto them'.[67] The deepest 'political' theme of the *Calender* is the role of images in society, the relationship between icons and believers, between Arcadian ideals and actual conditions, and the necessary consignment of all human aspirations to fragile and vulnerable agents. Despite *Aprill's* visions of natural order, *November* demonstrates the mortality of ideals themselves. Like Poussin's painting, the great elegy is resonant far beyond the circumstances of any particular bereavement. It turns to celebration – 'O heavie herse' / 'O happye herse' – only upon its substitution of the Elysian fields for the turbulent landscapes of 'Elizian' England: 'no daunger there the shepheard can astert / . . . The fieldes ay fresh, the grasse ay greene' (lines 187–9). Only the good shepherd of the Psalms can guarantee 'green pastures', and the apparently indiscriminate use of 'Pan' for both king and monarch ultimately enforces their disparity. The celebratory sections of *November* are, to this extent, more detrimental to royalist aspirations than the dirge that precedes them. The 'good place' is not within the monarch's gift. 'Although ye are a mighty prince', Grindal had warned, 'yet remember that He which dwelleth in heaven is mightier.'[68] The friends of Colin Clout seem very mindful of this.

But who is Colin Clout? The question is important because the complex meanings of *The Shepheardes Calender* emerge through the interaction of its *personae*. Indeed the creation of such *personae* is fundamental to the allegorical conception of the work and was perceived to form an integral part of the classical tradition: 'for under these personnes, as it were in a cloake of simplicitie, they would eyther sette foorth the prayses of theyr freendes, without the note of flattery, or enveigh grievously against abuses, without any token of bytternesse'.[69] So far as subject-matter is concerned, it is political complexity which masquerades under the 'cloake' of rural simplicity. Ten of the eclogues take the form of pastoral debates or contests during the course of which are discussed various contemporary problems of political, social or aesthetic concern. The only exceptions are *Januarye* and *December* where Colin Clout delivers doleful monologues, but in both cases the *persona* is introduced by a detached authorial voice and is hereby distinguished from the 'I' of the envoy and epilogue. Whatever the truth of E. K.'s assertion that the poet 'shadows' himself under the

[66] Camden, *History of Princess Elizabeth*, edited by MacCaffrey, p. 35.   [67] *Works*, III, 59.
[68] *Remains*, p. 389. See also D. M. Rosenberg, *Oaten Reeds and Trumpets* (London, 1981), pp. 85–7.
[69] William Webbe, *A Discourse of English Poetrie* (1586), in *Elizabethan Critical Essays*, edited by G. Gregory Smith, 2 vols. (Oxford, 1904), I, 262.

'name' of Colin Clout, the fact remains that in the few instances where Spenser's voice might have blended with that of his creature the two are formally set apart. This is not surprising in view of the varying connotations of the verb 'shadow' as used by Spenser's contemporaries: to protect or shelter from the sun, to screen, to obscure, to conceal, but also to represent, to typify, to portray. Colin Clout is a complex product of the need to conceal and reveal simultaneously, obscurely delineated to screen his creator from the power described in *Aprill* as 'another Sunne belowe' (line 77). Furthermore, the general contribution of E. K. often serves to emphasise the complexity of apparently straightforward symbolism – as, for example, in the case of *Februarie* where he enforces the opinion that the superstition of 'popishe' priests occasions the final decay of the ancient oak thereby rendering it vulnerable to the ambitious briar. By ascribing a habitual godlessness to old age, E. K.'s comment upon the eclogue's emblems further qualifies Thenot's evident sympathy for the supposed victim since 'olde men are muche more enclined to such fond fooleries, then younger heades'.

Thus to integrate the magisterial authority of the annotator into the imaginative force of the poem was possibly the greatest innovation of the *Calender*'s composition, and this remains true whether 'E. K.' is Edward Kirke, Gabriel Harvey or Edmund Spenser. The manner of the commentary's presentation, immediately following each eclogue and vital to the comprehension of their respective emblems, enables it to influence the reader's emotional response to the poetry while seeming to offer purely informative assistance. So successful is the overall effect that one of the most difficult tasks of Spenserian editing is the attempt to achieve an objective standpoint from which to assess the dialectical interaction of gloss and verse. Rosemond Tuve once argued for the strictly limited applicability of Elizabethan imagery amounting to an exclusion of all connotations deemed logically inappropriate to any given context, but time and again E. K. provokes the opposite response either by advancing startling associations of his own, such as the comparison of Colin Clout (and/or Edmund Spenser) to Narcissus in *September*, or by provoking the reader to do the same by the simple expedient of claiming to have disclosed 'all the meaning' of difficult emblems (*Iune*).[70] More subtly, the glosses interact upon the imaginative effect of Spenser's imagery as, for example, when Hobbinol's love for Colin Clout is gratuitously denied to be of the 'disorderly' kind 'which the learned call paederastice', or the goddess Flora is degraded to the status of philanthropic whore, or the fairies to figments of popish superstition. Because the surrounding glosses are in other respects so prosaically explanatory, it becomes well-nigh impossible to reread the poems without reference to E. K.'s more provocative suggestions. The homosexual issue, for instance, appears from Webbe's

[70] Rosemond Tuve, *Elizabethan and Metaphysical Imagery* (Chicago, 1947), p. 293.

comments to have exposed the *Iune* eclogue to allegations of 'unsavery' love 'skant allowable to English eares'.[71] The effect is to render Hobbinol's private 'paradise' no less questionable than its various public counterparts. Indeed, E. K.'s glosses persistently function to elicit the intricate interaction of private and public affairs central to the outlook of the work as a whole.

Colin Clout's relationship to the reader is as problematic as his relationship to the other *personae*. The Skeltonic expectations of the name are simply not borne out.[72] Instead, Piers, Thomalin and Diggon Davie fulfil the roles of social satirist and Christian counsellor. Indeed Colin himself is conspicuously absent from all eclogues of overt social complaint and remains equally distanced from the praise of Elisa as from her blame. Even in the October eclogue, where the subject is society's responsibility for the decline of poetry, Cuddie speaks out on his behalf although in this case E. K. concedes 'that some doubt, that the persons be different'. It is a moot point for the elaborate gloss upon this eclogue (amounting to a series of short essays on the nature of poetry) has fuelled doubts that the persons of E. K. and Spenser 'be different'. So significant is this material from the viewpoint of critical history that even those who argue for Edward Kirke's authorship of the gloss postulate his use of the lost treatise, 'The English Poete', mentioned in the argument.[73] In other words they extrapolate Spenser's voice from that of the glossator, denying independence of attitude even as they assert independence of identity. In terms of pastoral characterisation, however, Colin Clout, if not exactly Narcissus, is certainly self-absorbed. Commenting upon the woodcuts in which he appears, Ruth Luborsky observes that 'when the poet has an audience and a theme other than himself, he succeeds, the subject of his poetry is represented, and he plays an unbroken instrument, as in *Aprill*, *August*, and *November* . . . when no one listens or he has only a solipsistic subject, he fails, and a broken pipe lies at his feet, as in *Januarye*, *Iune*, and *December*'.[74] Alienation and distraction are integral to the *persona* from the outset.

Under the name of Colin Clout, E. K. informs us, 'this Poete secretly shadoweth himself, as sometimes did Virgil under the name of Tityrus' but the contrast here is more germane than the comparison. Tityrus appears in Virgil's first eclogue as a contented, generously patronised poet, but Spenser has chosen

---

[71] *Elizabethan Critical Essays*, I, 264. See Jonathan Goldberg. *Sodometries: Renaissance Texts, Modern Sexualities* (Stanford, 1992), pp. 63–101.

[72] Robert S. Kinsman, 'Skelton's *Colyn Cloute*: The Mask of Vox Populi', in *Essays Critical and Historical Dedicated to Lily B. Campbell* (Berkeley, 1950), pp. 17–26.

[73] See *Minor Poems*, Variorum Edition, I, 645–50. See also D. T. Starnes, 'Spenser and E. K.', *Studies in Philology*, 41 (1944), 181–200; Raymond Jenkins, 'Who is E. K.?', *South Atlantic Bulletin*, 20 (1945), 22–38, 82–94; Robert W. Mitchner, 'Spenser and E. K.', *Studies in Philology*, 42 (1945), 183–90. S. K. Heninger contends that Harvey was E. K., 'The Typographical Layout of Spenser's *Shepheardes Calender*', 43–51.

[74] *The Spenser Encyclopedia*, edited by A. C. Hamilton *et al.* (Toronto, 1990), p. 655.

4 'December' from *The Shepheardes Calender* (1579).

in his first eclogue to characterise Colin Clout more in terms of the dejected Meliboeus thereby signalling a wholly different stance *vis-à-vis* the political establishment. Attempting to develop the implications of this decision, Paul McLean has argued that Rosalind should, for the purposes of political allegory, be interpreted as Elizabeth.[75] To some extent it is true, as in *Colin Clouts Come Home Againe*, that Colin's private ills reflect wider social discontents and that the frustrated relationship between lady and lover corresponds to that between queen and would-be laureate.[76] Both ladies perpetually disappoint the devotion of their admirers and both are perceived to move upon distant horizons of pastoral contentment, apparently oblivious to the suffering around them. The least one may say is that the complaints of Piers, Thomalin, Diggon Davie, Cuddie and the rest publicly contextualise Colin's private grief, but there is a further sense, I would suggest, in which Colin's lamentations subsume all others without cryptically encoding their diverse concerns in some deep allegory. Colin's is the supreme expression of pastoral discontent, the supreme rejection of Arcadia as the good place, and by implication of the 'Queene of shepheardes all' as the provider of 'green pastures'.

For Spenser's Colin, as for Marot's, the pastoral idiom functions as the diction of disquiet. The anxieties of Colin Clout frame *The Shepheardes Calender*: the *December* eclogue 'even as the first beganne is ended with a complaynte of Colin to God Pan'. But *December* goes beyond Marot whose *Eglogue au Roy soubz les noms de Pan et Robin* constitutes its closest literary model and informs its content to an unprecedented degree. In the first place it is not directed to the monarch. It neither invokes her present aid nor commemorates past service. Though addressed to 'soveraigne *Pan*' it proceeds to doubt his divinity – 'perdie God was he none' (line 50) – and to elevate Colin himself to semi-divine status, 'to *Pan* his owne selfe pype I neede not yield' (line 46). The broken pipes have been restored but without recourse to politicised Ovidian myth. Throughout the 'complaynte' there emerges a self-reliance, even in decline, quite at odds with that of Marot's poem. At the end of the *Eglogue au Roy* Robin believes that Pan, in his green mansion, has had the goodness to entertain his petition ('desia Pan, de sa verte maison, / M'a faict ce bien, d'ouyr mon oraison').[77] But Colin Clout ends as he began; as he was not Tityrus in eclogue one, he is not Robin in eclogue twelve. The monarch cannot, or will not, help him. Rather, *December* serves to recapitulate the ills attendant upon every season of human life thereby establishing Colin's personal mood of alienation and withdrawal as the defining mood of the poem's pastoral consciousness. According to Sir Philip Sidney, pastoral is the form 'which somtimes out of *Mælibeus* mouth, can shewe the miserie of people,

---

[75] *Spenser's 'Shepheardes Calender'*, pp. 27–46.

[76] David R. Shore, *Spenser and the Poetics of Pastoral: A Study of the World of Colin Clout* (Kingston, 1985), p. 129.   [77] Marot, *Œuvres*, II, 285–98 (p. 298).

under hard Lords, and ravening souldiers . . . And again by *Titerus*, what blessednesse is derived, to them that lie lowest, from the goodnesse of them that sit highest.'[78] By associating Colin Clout with Meliboeus rather than Tityrus, however, Spenser seems to have determined upon fulfilling one of these functions but not the other. Colin's absence from the *Aprill* eclogue serves to remind us that Marot's adaptation of Virgil's fourth eclogue (honouring the birth of the Dauphin's son) was written in political exile by one who styled himself 'l'infortune Berger'.[79]

More important to *The Shepheardes Calender* than any specific complaint or series of complaints is the mood of alienation pervading the sequence as a whole and so accurately reflecting the mood of Elisa's England in December 1579. Annabel Patterson has argued that Spenser demanded from his readers 'an ability to translate one metaphorical system into another, a personal explanation of Colin's melancholy into a national one'.[80] But perhaps it is the other way around. Perhaps it is the private dimension of public grief that is characterised in Colin's melancholy. His praise of Elisa is the effort of carefree youth, but time has doomed that image as surely as it has frustrated his love. No longer can the private dimension of his life draw solace from the public. Instead, they feed upon each other's malaise. The personal, subjective realm of the poem subsumes all others and remains the most resonant and enduring. The final woodcut affords a simple portrayal of personal desolation, a stark image of the despondent 'ego' that haunts Arcadia (Fig. 4).

[78] *Works*, III, 22.
[79] Marot, *Œuvres*, II, 479–84. See Patterson, 'Re-opening the Green Cabinet', p. 57.
[80] 'Re-opening the Green Cabinet', p. 63.

2

'Cut without hands': Herbert's Christian altar

ALASTAIR FOWLER

So far as the seventeenth century is concerned, numerical composition is often thought of as a medieval inheritance: a survival, or perhaps a hangover that the aspirins of the Enlightenment were soon to dispel. That is very far from true. Numerology seems in fact to have been more widely practised than ever in the Renaissance – certainly more assiduously elaborated. In the seventeenth century, particularly, a new excitement burned for everything mathematical. Mathematics seemed to hold the key to nature's mysteries. But science was not the only new excitement with a bearing on literary form. Writers were also greatly excited by the new medium of print. It now began – in Britain only just began – to displace script as the preferred medium for serious writing. These two excitements combined to affect the forms of poetry profoundly. It was not just that reading print had become easier than reading script, so that more pondering beyond surface meanings was in order. (For early blackletter could actually be *less* legible than a good scribal italic.) Nor was it merely that texts, and the positions of individual passages within them, had become relatively stable. (For in the cheirographic tradition, a standard modulus of thirty lines per page often allowed fairly easy line-counting and finding.) It was rather that print had a property of self-resembling lastingness that for want of a better word may be called monumentality. Poetry was now often described, significantly, as 'framed', 'raised', 'built' – 'he knew / Himself to sing, and build the lofty rhyme'. *Ut architectura poesis*. For this and other reasons, the visual appearance of writing was more considered. The written (and printed) word was often visually emblematic, in one way or another, of the meaning it communicated.

The early effects of print on literature were in some ways quite surprising. One might have expected writing to become steadily more like our own – or, at least, more like Victorian writing – to be, as it were, 'forward-looking'. Specifically, one might have expected the written word, as it donned the decent uniform of print, to become less noticeable. Surely it would seem more transparent, so that readers would read more directly for the content, as we tend to do. But not a bit of it. By the seventeenth century, typographers were using a thick impasto of italics and full capitals, to say nothing of hands, rules, fleurons and pilcrows, in such a way as to make the printed page a thoroughly opaque medium. The poem on the page now looked less like a modern poem than early Tudor scribal scribbles had ever done. Professor Donald McKenzie suggests that the early ostentatiousness of 'setting forth' was an attempt to limit the difference of print from script.[1] But that does not explain the increased opacity in the seventeenth century. Rather should one think in terms of aesthetic preferences.

The repercussions of print on memory art seem to have been equally contrary to expectation. The assumption has been that as the printed word came in, the need to memorise declined, and the arts of memory went out. But, as Frances Yates, Mary Carruthers and others have shown, memory art thrived into the late seventeenth century and beyond. In so far as texts were used primarily as memory prompts, print may positively have assisted memorising, since it facilitated rapid skimming to supply forgotten details. For memory art worked chiefly with *res* rather than *verba*. When Richard Baxter speaks, as he often does, of his congregations 'repeating' sermons, he hardly means learning them by heart, word for word.[2] On the other hand, Milton had reasons for using memory art to keep the words of *Paradise Lost* in mind, in their proper locations.

I am not thinking, here, only of Milton's blindness. There is also the reason that *Paradise Lost* was to be organised numerologically. Notoriously, when Messiah ascends the throne of his cosmic chariot to begin the triumphal alchemic work of creation, he does so at the numerical centre of the poem's 10,550 lines (1667 edition): 'He . . . Ascended, at his right hand Victory / Sat, eagle-winged' (VI. 760–3). (Recently, a confirming intertextuality has been found, with Michael Maier's seminal alchemic treatise *Atalanta Fugiens* (1618), where Jupiter sends *eagles* east and west to 'establish Earth's centre' – *medium explorare locum*.)[3] Numerology was closely bound up with memory art; since, at the simplest level, verse was memorised in relation to a numerical grid.[4] Symbolic associations of a line-number, moreover, could often supply a useful additional link to fix an elusive passage.[5] It is not very surprising, therefore, to find that in *Paradise Lost* the content of a verse sometimes agrees quite strikingly with the symbolic value of its line number.

A glance at the opening of the *principium*, book one, lines 1–5, may make clear what I mean:

> Of man's first disobedience, and the fruit
> Of that forbidden tree, whose mortal taste

[1] Donald F. McKenzie, 'Speech – Manuscript – Print', in *New Directions in Textual Studies*, edited by D. Oliphant and R. Bradford (Austin, 1990), p. 101.

[2] See *OED*: *Repeat* vb 2 'to recount': e.g. Shakespeare, *II Henry IV*, IV.1.201–4: 'therefore will hee ... keepe no Tell-tale to his Memorie, / That may repeat and Historie his losse, / To new remembrance' ; and 2b 'to hear lessons': 'to repeit with the studentis' (1579).

[3] Epig. xlvi. I am indebted for this reference to Paul Cheshire.

[4] See Mary Carruthers, *The Book of Memory: A Study of Memory in Medieval Culture* (Cambridge, 1990), Index: *Numbers, Numerology*. [5] *Ibid*.

Brought death into the world, and all our woe,
With loss of Eden, till one greater man
Restore us, and regain the blissful seat . . .

One, the monad, was a form of the Pythagorean sacred *tetraktys*, the fountain of all creation, and by a universally understood syncretism identified with God and Christ.[6] In the 'fruit' of the forbidden tree, Milton refers to the evil consequences of disobedience, further described in the lines that immediately follow. But he also refers to the *felix* fruit of that *culpa*, in Christ's incarnation. Before even the consequences are spelt out, Christ is previeniently present in the poem, metaphorically, to redeem them. The first line also contains the word *first* itself; and Milton places other occurrences of 'first' with similar appropriateness, for the word occurs again in line 8 ('That shepherd who first taught the chosen seed') and line 27 ('Say first, for heaven hides nothing from thy view'); 8 being 2^3, the first cube of a female number, and 27 being 3^3, the first male cube.[7] In the same way, 'one' occurs in line 4 because 4 is the first square number. In line 2, 'mortal taste' introduces the earliest suggestion of death, which in number symbolism was regarded as a manifestation of the evil dyad, interrupting the unity of life.[8] Line 4 aptly has 'Eden' and 'one greater man', for the four rivers of paradise (Genesis 2: 10) were the basis of a strong association of paradise with this number.[9] The tetrad was also the number of the human body with its four humours and complexions.[10] 'One' may pointedly recur in this line because in Pythagorean and Christian number symbolism tetrad and monad were both forms of the *tetraktys*, besides being identified with Christ, the 'greater man', *vinculum* of matter and spirit, and the 'unknown god'.[11] Finally, the 'blissful seat' or throne occurs aptly in line 5, because five occupied the central place of sovereignty among the nine digits, and hence symbolised triumph or sovereignty.

The opening lines thus suggest, through their number-symbolic associations, many of the themes of the poem at large. Of course, not every image and word is apt in this way – that would be insufferable *dirigisme*. But other striking examples

---

[6] Pietro Bongo, *Numerorum Mysteria* (Bergamo, 1591) pp. 13–61 (p. 18). For convenience I give references to this authoritative work, but most of the symbolisms can be found in the Venetian Francesco Giorgio's *Harmonia Totius Mundi* (Paris, 1545), in biblical commentaries, or in popular writers such as Thomas Lodge and John Taylor the Water Poet. Among a great many scholarly and critical works on the application of number symbolism to poetical composition, there is room only to mention two of general application – Vincent Foster Hopper, *Medieval Number Symbolism* (New York, 1938: rpt Norwood, Pa., 1977); Ernst Robert Curtius, *European Literature and the Latin Middle Ages*, translated by Willard Trask (London, 1948) – and two primers – I. Christopher Butler, *Number Symbolism* (London, 1970); John MacQueen, *Numerology: Theory and Outline History of a Literary Mode* (Edinburgh, 1985). [7] See Bongo, pp. 322, 355.
[8] See *ibid.*, p. 49: 'regnum mortis, in odio, quae est divisio . . . vita praesens est unio: mors, divisio'.
[9] See *ibid.*, 244–5. [10] *Ibid.*, p. 193. [11] *Ibid.*, p. 235.

come to mind, such as the traditionally nine 'heavens' in line 9, and the 'sea-beast' Leviathan in line 200.[12] The point may seem sufficiently obvious. It is not exactly an obvious one, either, though. For not every such instance can be taken as proving Milton's conscious intention. Some may wish to suppose that we have stumbled, here, on the mechanics – or merely the scaffolding – of composition. But in my own view these are not real alternatives. Conscious or not at the time of publication, the numerical associations had been in Milton's mind and would be in the minds of some of his fit readers. They are meanings of what he has written. Besides, against the 'unconscious' theory may be set the many instances, studied by Gunnar Qvarnström and others, of verse-paragraphs in the poem with symbolic line-totals.

Fewer problems of intentionality arise with figure- or pattern-poems. These too were a new, or renewed, phenomenon. Certainly there are many striking examples from the Carolingian period and earlier, such as the astronomical manuscripts of Julius Hyginus, in which painted heads or limbs emerge out of bodies shaped from sprinkled letters; or the pious grids of Hraban Maur, who deploys every cheirographic resource of coloured ink and outline drawing, to signalise multiple acrostics and complex hypograms.[13] But figure poems were actually far more popular in the late Renaissance than in the Middle Ages.[14] The rediscovered *Greek Anthology*, which in this as in other ways profoundly influenced the development of Renaissance lyric throughout Europe, offered, in its many *technopaegnia* or art-games the principal models for figure-poetry.[15] A neglected subsidiary factor, here, is the simultaneous development of print as a medium of communication. The new possibilities are visibly played with in the forms given to colophon and bastard titles. There is a striking transition from the simple colophons of early incunabula, through centred inverted cones (as in the bastard title to the Venice 1502 Statius) to more elaborate forms like the lozenge or diamond in Guyart's *Compendium* (Bordeaux, 1524), and the drinking-glass in J. Schoeffer's edition of Trithemius (Mainz, 1515). Italy is in the forefront of this particular avant-garde: there was already a drinking-glass in a Paduan edition of Petrarch in 1472.[16]

---

[12] *Ibid.*, p. 595: the number is often taken 'in malam partem'.

[13] See Massin, *Letter and Image*, translated by Caroline Hillier and Vivienne Menkes (London, 1970), with many illustrations.

[14] For figure-poetry treated as a Renaissance phenomenon, see Margaret Church, 'The First English Pattern Poems', *PMLA*, 61 (1946), 636–50; Bart Westerweel, *Patterns and Patterning: a Study of Four Poems by George Herbert* (Amsterdam, 1983); Ian D. McFarlane, 'The Renaissance Epitaph'. Presidential address of the MHRA. *MLR*, 81 (1986), 1–11.

[15] See Westerweel, *Patterns and Patterning*, Index: *Greek Anthology*.

[16] These and other examples are illustrated in Theodore Low de Vinne, *A Treatise on Title-Pages* ... (New York, 1902); *cf.* Alfred W. Pollard, *An Essay on Colophons with Specimens and Translations* (Chicago, 1905; rpt New York: Franklin n.d.), pp. 103–5 (inverted cone from Gasparo Visconti, *Rithmi* (Milan, 1493) and verse in the form of a rhombus displayed, or hourglass, from *Journal Spirituel* (Paris, 1505)).

It is no exaggeration to say that the emblem vogue and the figure-poetry vogue had a common origin in printers' devices, among which almost all their components are to be found, decades before Andrea Alciatio's *Emblemata* (1531) – although not, to be sure, assembled in quite the same constellation.[17] The new medium was regarded, in fact, as a form of graphic art: the art of print was not unlike the art of prints. About the same time, for reasons that also had to do with the *Greek Anthology*, the emblem was establishing itself as a dominant form, again throughout Europe. *Ut pictura poesis*: it was almost inevitable that the emblem should colonise poetry, and that poets should take up the device of printed shapes. The extent of the figure-poetry vogue is nonetheless remarkable. There were editions of the *Greek Anthology* pattern poems by Crispinus, Henricus Stephanus, J. C. Scaliger, and Fortunio Liceti;[18] they reappeared in arts of poetry; and virtually every early seventeenth-century poet attempted one or two. Poets seem to have taken a special pleasure in the visual aesthetics of print. As John Kerrigan has remarked of Carew, the seventeenth-century poet 'seems to welcome print – its definite, almost emblematic disposition, but also leaden-type fixedness'.[19] George Herbert seems to feel this delight in printedness when he adds letters in 'Iesu', rearranges them in 'Ana-{MARY/ARMY}-gram', or prunes them one by one in 'Paradise', from GROW through ROW to OW. The erstwhile University Orator was naturally *au fait* with the vogue for emblems and figure-poems. But I should not like to give the impression he was merely in the grip of a fashionable craze. As the work of George Wither and Francis Quarles shows, emblems could also be conceived as sincere, naive, even demotic. And for Herbert himself, as we shall see, the figure-poem was anything but a toy – or, at least, anything but a trivial toy.

In the revived Hellenistic tradition, several set shapes reliably recur, such as wings, the pyramid, Simias' egg, and the column. Neo-Latin arts of poetry from J. C. Scaliger's and Richard Willes's to Dionysius Ronsfertus', and arts in the vernacular like George Puttenham's *The Arte of English Poesie* and King James's *Essayes of a Prentise* give more or less detailed specifications for constructing some of the shapes (not usually all).[20] In a chapter (II. xii) on 'Ocular Representation', Puttenham includes the lozenge, rhombus, triangle, square, egg, sphere or roundel, pilaster or column, and pyramid, together with the same forms 'reversed' and 'displayed'. It may seem an otiose business for poets to have repro-

---

[17] For a definition of the printer's device, and many illustrations, see Hugh William Davies, *Devices of the Early Printers 1457–1560: Their History and Development* . . . (London, 1935).

[18] See Westerweel, *Patterns and Patterning*, p. 67.   [19] 'Thomas Carew', *PBA*, 74 (1989), 346.

[20] J. C. Scaliger, *Poetices Libri Septem* (Lyons, 1561), facsimile ed. August Buck (Stuttgart, 1964); Dionysius Ronsfertus, Notes to Fr. Mario Bettini's *Rubenus* (Parma, 1614); Richard Willes, *Poetum Liber* (London, 1573); *The Arte of English Poesie*, edited by Gladys Doidge Willcock and Alice Walker (Cambridge, 1936), p. 97; James VI and I, *The Essayes of a Prentise in the Divine Art of Poesie* (1584).

duced set forms like these; but of course all depended on the relation of content to form, on details, and on modulations of the tradition. Thus, the altar poems of Dosiadas (*c.* 150 BC) and Vestinus (*c.* 100 AD) in the *Greek Anthology* have the shape of pagan altars, complete with sacrificial slabs on top.[21] Absence of this slab in the altar poems of most Christian poets may be taken to mean that Christ's crucifixion has done away with sacrifice; a point neglected by Westerweel when he speaks of Herbert's slabless altar as the Mosaic altar of Exodus 20: 25.

Without the sacrificial slab, however, the altar shape becomes indistinguishable from a column:

5 Templates for shaped poems: Dosiadas (*left*) and Davison (*right*).

Such columns (sometimes called altars, as by Francis Davison and Herbert)[22] are very common, in sacred and secular poetry alike. Undoubtedly the form implies an architectural analogy to poetry. This is particularly clear where several columns are used liminally, as a kind of porch (as in Joshua Sylvester's 1605 Du Bartas), or as division markers (as by Robert Herrick, to mark the division between *Hesperides* and *Noble Numbers*) – a well-known convention that may be

[21] For illustrations see Westerweel, *Patterns and Patterning*, p. 69.
[22] Richard Willes, 'Ara'; Francis Davison, 'An Altare and Sacrifice to Disdaine, for freeing him from Love'.

compared to the *metae* or turning-posts of the ancient Roman circus, or the limiting pillars of Hercules in Charles V's PLUS ULTRA *impresa*. The substitution of column for altar – indeed, their virtual identification – may be puzzling at first. But it is illuminated by John Onions in *Bearers of Meaning*, where he explains how columns (sometimes used as altars in the early Christian church) came to be seen as symbolising Christ and his apostles.[23] Particularly when forming a sequence of eleven or twelve (as in the Sainte Chapelle), columns were taken to allude to the apostles. The same probably applies to Sylvester's twelve column-poems, which Westerweel (p. 79) calls altars of praise, but which might be described more precisely as the columns of virtue on which crowns or wreaths were hung in triumph. Herbert's altar-column, assimilating all these traditions, performs a liminal function, coming at the beginning of *The Temple* proper, immediately after 'The Church-porch' and 'Superliminare':[24]

The Altar

A broken ALTAR, Lord, thy servant reares,
Made of a heart, and cémented with teares:
    Whose parts are as thy hand did frame;
    No workmans tool hath touch'd the same.
        A   HEART   alone
        Is   such   a   stone,
        As   nothing   but
        Thy pow'r doth cut.
        Wherefore each part
        Of my hard heart
        Meets in this frame,
        To praise thy name.
    That if I chance to hold my peace,
    These stones to praise thee may not cease.
O   let   thy   blessed   SACRIFICE   be   mine,
And   sanctifie   this   ALTAR   to   be   thine.

Herbert's poem has rightly been discussed in relation to emblems in Daniel Cramer's *Emblemata Sacra* and Benedict van Haeften's *Schola Cordis*, and others by their English imitators Christopher Harvey and Patrick Carey. In all these the contrite heart is laid for sacrifice on an altar.[25] Herbert, however, unites heart and

---

[23] John Onions, *Bearers of Meaning: The Classical Orders in Antiquity, the Middle Ages, and the Renaissance* (Princeton, 1988), pp. 70, 75, 79, 88 etc.

[24] On the position in the volume, see Westerweel, *Patterns and Patterning*, pp. 58–9, 66, 138; on Herbert's use of Sylvester, *ibid.*, pp. 79–82.

[25] See Westerweel, *Patterns and Patterning*, p. 89 with illustrations; Rosalie L. Colie, *The Resources of Kind: Genre-Theory in the Renaissance*, edited by Barbara Kiefer Lewalski (Berkeley, 1973), pp. 58ff. See also Hans Sebald Beham's two emblems, of a flaming heart upon a pagan and on a squared altar, illustrated in Albert F. Butsch, *Handbook of Renaissance Ornament . . .*, edited by Alfred Werner (New York, 1969), p. 154.

altar into a single image.[26] The stony heart has been broken by attrition, it is implied; contrite, its parts can be framed by God into an altar for the offering and sacrifice. It might be wrong to assume that this change is made simply in the interest of compression, or unity, or economy; for such differences often had a theological value. Joseph Summers comments:

Herbert's conceptions that the broken and purged heart is the proper basis for the sacrifice of praise and that even stones may participate in and continue that praise were firmly biblical. In his psalm of repentance (Ps. 51) David had stated that the true sacrifices of God are 'a broken and a contrite heart'; Christ had promised that 'the stones' would cry out to testify to Him (Luke 19: 40); and Paul had stated that 'Ye also, as lively stones, are built up a spiritual house . . . to offer up spiritual sacrifices.' (I Peter 2: 5)[27]

But Herbert, a Protestant, would be very careful with the term 'sacrifice', and may have wished to convey the inherence of the believer in the once-only sacrifice of Christ. Perhaps for that reason he makes the heart itself the altar, for an inner sacrifice that is Christ's alone, although appropriated by the believer's true repentance.

If this point has been approached often enough in recent criticism, there has not been any recognition at all of the brilliant numerological content of Herbert's poem, which applies its metaphors so fitly as to make them movingly immediate. To the broad notion of the column in such as Puttenham ('In architecture he is considered with two accessarie parts, a pedestall or base, and a chapter or head, the body is the shaft')[28] Herbert adds a more detailed prosodic proportioning that eloquently accompanies the sense. Verbal resemblances suggest that Herbert may have taken a hint, in this, from the 'Ara' of Publius Optatianus Porfirius, a celebration of his own poetic art. Porfirius minutely describes his slabbed altar as shaped by significant variations of metre: 'I force each edge to be drawn in, line by line, by tiny steps, in lines turning in . . . regulated everywhere by the measure'.[29] Possibly Herbert may have noticed an 'Ara' by the Jesuit Richard Willes, with a body of 8 lines.[30] However that may be, Herbert's poem is numerologically articulated to a far greater extent.

Metrically, first, it comprises: 2 pentameters | 2 tetrameters | 8 dimeters | 2 tetrameters | 2 pentameters. That is,

---

[26] See Westerweel, *Patterns and Patterning*, p. 111.

[27] Joseph H. Summers, *George Herbert: His Religion and Art* (Cambridge, Mass., 1968), p. 142. *Cf.* the imagery of Henry Vaughan, 'Regeneration', lines 55–6, also drawing in I Peter 2: 5.

[28] *The Art of English Poesie*, p. 97.

[29] Translated by Westerweel, *Patterns and Patterning*, p. 71.

[30] *Poematum Liber* (1573), No. 4. The altar is slabbed: presumably Willes keeps the pagan form out of decorum, since his poem refers to the slaying of Troilus at the altar of Apollo.

$$2 \times 5$$
$$2 \times 4$$
$$8 \times 2$$
$$2 \times 4$$
$$2 \times 5$$

— altogether 16 lines, or 4^2. This is in consonance with the human referent; for, as Puttenham says, 'so is the square for his inconcussable steadinesse likened to the earth, which perchaunce might be the reason that the Prince of Philosophers in his first booke of the *Ethicks*, termeth a constant minded man, even egal [equal] and direct on all sides, and not easily overthrowne by every litle adversitie, *hominem quadratum*, a square man'.[31] (One might contrast Davison's 20-line altar, with its probable allusion to the twenty of woe.)[32] More specifically, Herbert's 16 refers to the double octave of passions that in an integrated soul sounds as the music of a harmonious diapason. Then its 'parts are as thy hand did frame' (line 3).[33] 'This frame' (line 11) of the heart, moreover, belongs to an architectural *allegoria* ('mixed' or discontinuous), in which 'stone', 'parts', and 'cémented' besides 'frame' itself, figure as vehicle items, all being terms of art in building. And the general sense of all this is visibly confirmed by the contrast of the 8 very short lines of the column shaft and the 4 longer lines of capital and base. For the 4 | 8 | 4 pattern repeats the 1 : 2 ratio of the diapason, a ratio held to signify harmonious control of passion.[34] The shaft or body has 8 lines, as in Willes and Samuel Speed, for the same reason as baptismal fonts commonly had 8 sides: because 8 was the number of regeneration.[35]

Not only has Herbert ordered the metrical parts of his poem eloquently, but also the very distribution of its words. For, in the column shaft, the numbers of words per distich are: 7 | 7 | 7 | 8. Thus, the stoniness and hardness of the heart is the burden of distichs with 7 words each. But when its parts 'Meet in this frame / To praise thy name', this seven of mutability is raised to the eight of regeneration.

Herbert's interest in the aesthetics of print shows also in his use of capitalised words. In 'The Altar' four words are printed in full capitals: ALTAR, HEART, SACRIFICE and ALTAR, in that order. They number four, clearly, because four is the sacred *tetraktys*. As we saw, this was the number of virtuous man, and

---

[31] Puttenham, *The Arte of English Poesie*, p. 100. *Cf.* Bongo, *Numerorum Mysteria*, pp. 413–14: the number 16 is 'quadratus quadrati quaternarii, quattuor in lateribus continens unitates'.

[32] See Bongo, *Numerorum Mysteria*, pp. 424–6 with many classical examples.

[33] See Alastair Fowler and Douglas Brooks (now Brooks-Davies), 'The Structure of Dryden's *Song for St Cecilia's Day, 1687*', in *Silent Poetry*, edited by Alastair Fowler (London, 1971), p. 196; *cf.* Spenser's 'goodly frame of Temperaunce', *The Faerie Queene*, II.12.1.

[34] Pico della Mirandola, *Opera Omnia*, 2 vols. (Basle, 1573), I, 79.

[35] See Hopper, *Medieval Number Symbolism*; MacQueen, *Numerology: Theory and Outline History*, p. 80; Bongo, *Numerorum Mysteria*.

identified by Christian authors with Christ as *vinculum*.[36] The sequence of
Herbert's four capitalised words forms a chiasmic pattern – itself often symbolic
of reconciliation – that closely links the two middle terms 'HEART' and
'SACRIFICE'. Most eloquent of all, though least obvious, is the decorum of the
capitalised words' placement in their respective lines. 'ALTAR' comes in third
place, and again in fourth; 'SACRIFICE' comes in fifth place; but the stony
'HEART' in second place. The praise this silently offers, through the disposition
of the poem's physical members – 'these stones' – is celebration of Christ's
triumph over the hard heart. For 'a HEART alone' is in the second position of the
evil dyad; but when the broken heart becomes a broken altar, it moves to fourth
place, the position of the *tetraktys*. The third, fourth, and fifth places of the
'good' capitalised words indicate the Pythagorean 3–4–5 triangle of moral
proportion. (Herbert elsewhere uses this as the main structural motif of another
poem of regeneration and sanctification, 'Aaron'.)[37] Finally, in the first line of
'The Altar', the word standing fourth of seven, in the sovereign central place, is
'Lord'. Christ thus rules the apostolic column as its head or capital. And, in a
visible *imitatio Christi*, the regenerate 'HEART' occupies an answering central
position in the base. It, too, occupies the fourth place, that of the *tetraktys*, and so
is *en khristo*.

If this is more or less on the right lines, it creates something of a critical
problem. It is a problem of alterity, or distance. Herbert's consonant form is not
quite that of a modernist process-poem; still less can it be called an 'organic'
form, like that sometimes attributed to Romantic poems. Again, how serious is
one to think of a figure-poem as being? Some have regarded Herbert's patterns as
pious trifling. But in view of the above, many will surely now recognise that
precipitate dismissal as having proceeded from ignorance – certainly that was
true in my own case – of how much art was devoted to framing such devices.
Perhaps we can now begin to glimpse how comprehensively Herbert strove to
offer to God his poetic gift. The visual pattern was for him an opportunity for
further and further restatements, ever more intimately close to God and his
reader.[38] 'The Altar' is in this way not far removed from Gabriel Rollenhagen's
altar with a laurel wreath of praise, in *Nucleus Emblematum* (1611).[39] Herbert
wanted his whole art to be an offering.

---

[36] For documentation see Alastair Fowler, *Spenser and the Numbers of Time* (London, 1964),
pp. 275–8.
[37] For the symbolism of the Pythagorean triangle, see *ibid.*, Index: *Zoogonic Triangle*.
[38] The logical sequel was realisation in print. But Herbert's pattern-poems were never printed in his
lifetime.
[39] Emblem II. 1. *Cf. The Poems of Patrick Carey*, ed. Sister Veronica Delany (Oxford, 1978), p. 103,
citing also Camerarius. Rollingen's emblem is modified by Wither (illustrated in Westerweel,
Patterns and Patterning, Fig. 19) who has a burning heart on the altar.

In 'The Altar', Herbert represents his art through the metaphor of architecture. And naturally he conceives architecture according to its Renaissance understanding – as an art not of masonry but of geometry and number, 'all material stuff being excluded'.[40] It is this concept that allows Herbert's architectural pattern-poem to convey with touching aptness his sense of the altar prophesied by Daniel: 'a stone . . . cut without hands'.[41] The poem is all heart – contrite, unstony. There is to be nothing merely artificial about it: 'no workman's tool hath touched the same' (line 4).

In describing 'The Altar' objectively, I have left aside a question as to how Herbert intends its pronouns. Whose heart is hard? Clearly 'The Altar' is not a confessional poem: no poem so full of art could be that. Nevertheless I do not think it merely dramatises the thought-processes of some hard-hearted, recently repentant, new believer. In fact, it seems closer to figuring an act of repentence of just such a sinner as Herbert himself, renewing his vocation and confessing the incompleteness of previous repentances. To all except antinomian Calvinists, a believer's heart was always relatively or potentially hard. Thus, the poem's shaping may be thought of as shadowing Herbert's shaping of his own nature, as he puts on Christ. That is to say, it figures his sanctification, a constructive process commonly formulated by the architectural metaphor of 'edification'. Herbert was so far from being antinomian, indeed, that for him edification would certainly have involved frequent attempts to be virtuously four-square. At the same time, the poem also concerns processes of craftmanship; so that it may reasonably be seen as figuring Herbert's renewal of his art's dedication. Perhaps one may even see a new dedication, to the degree that he may have looked towards a printed version of his poems, and with that a new phase of his art. From this point of view, it is striking that in the Williams Manuscript version of 'The Altar' the four words full-capitalised in the print are not yet distinguished as such. Preparation for print appears to have occasioned a reconsideration of the poem's numerological structure.

[40] John Dee, Preface to *The Elements of Geometrie* . . ., translated H. Billingsley (1570).
[41] Daniel 2: 34 and 45; *cf.* Mark 14: 58.

3

On historical commentary: the example of
Milton and Dryden

HOWARD ERSKINE-HILL

A reader new to seventeenth-century English poetry might reasonably be puzzled by modern editions of these two major poets. Ever since Walter Scott, scholarly editions of Dryden have glossed his poems with copious historical explanation, extending in some recent instances to elaborate critical hypothesis.[1] Editions of Dryden's elder contemporary display a complete contrast. While Milton's political sonnets and certain earlier poems have attracted historical commentary by editors, the major poems have not, and it might seem that in his last seventeen years Milton lived in a different age from that of Dryden. Yet their lives overlapped; each served under the Lord Protector in the 1650s, each published a new kind of epic poem in 1667, and each was deeply involved with the historical crises of his time. These circumstances, I suggest, are sufficient warrant for us to suspend experimentally the orthodox belief that the two poets are different in kind (Milton the last poet of the Renaissance, Dryden the first of 'the Augustan Age') and consider the question of commentary afresh.

To take an example from each poet, consider the two following instances of the institution of a false authority. The first is the enthronement of Satan at the beginning of *Paradise Lost*, book two, the second the coronation of 'King *Buzzard*' in the Hind's Fable of the Pigeons, at the end of part three of *The Hind and the Panther*.

> High on a Throne of Royal State, which far
> Outshone the Wealth of *Ormus* and of *Ind*,
> Or where the gorgeous East with richest hand
> Showrs on her Kings *Barbarick* Pearl and Gold,
> *Satan* exalted sate, by Merit rais'd
> To that bad eminence . . . (II. 1–6)[2]

---

[1] *Cf.* Earl Miner's description of Dryden's *The Hind and the Panther* as 'a discontinuous fable or intermittent allegory' and his proposal that the Buzzard, in that poem, is a double allusion to two historical originals (*The Works of John Dryden*, vol. III, *Poems, 1685–1692*, edited by Earl Miner and Vinton A. Dearing (Berkeley and Los Angeles, 1969), pp. 341, 449–52. This volume is hereafter referred to as *Works*, III.)

[2] In quoting from *Paradise Lost* I use the text of *The Poetical Works of Mr John Milton* . . . published by Jacob Tonson (London, 1695) since the commentary I discuss was included in this edition.

Alastair Fowler, in the distinguished Carey-Fowler edition (London, 1968), has nothing historical or political to say about this moment, save to note that Satan has already been referred to as an 'eastern tyrant' at 1. 348. Douglas Bush (1966) had no very different emphasis, though writing of the 'realistic verisimilitude' of the council which is about to begin. Merritt Y. Hughes (1957) valuably referred to Fulke Greville's *Alaham*: 'Is this Ormus? Or is Ormus my hell . . .' which, if recalled, would carry the implication that Satan is not just a tyrant but a usurper.[3] Even Patrick Hume in Tonson's 1695 Milton, the fountain-source of commentary on *Paradise Lost*, sees no historical allusion here though, in glossing '*Barbarick*' with reference to Lucan's *Pharsalia* (as well as to Lucretius and Virgil), he may remind us of Julius Caesar's barbaric troops, and that from Lucan's republican viewpoint Caesar was a usurper. None of these commentators pauses at: 'by Merit rais'd / To that bad eminence', a paradox which tells us more precisely what kind of a monarch Satan was in Renaissance terms. Jean Bodin, in his *Six Livres de la République* (1576) distinguished between royal monarchs, lordly monarchs and tyrants. Lordly monarchs did not owe their crown to inheritance and law but to their own efforts, usually military conquest. They did not necessarily rule like tyrants (against the law of nature and nations). Lordly monarchs were often the founders of dynasties. The words 'bad eminence' tell the reader not to take the word 'Merit' on trust: nevertheless the seven words emphasise the basis on which the devils acclaim and follow their ruler.[4] He is to them a lordly monarch naturally deserving a throne. At this point intimations of tyranny and the fact of a failed conquest never come through into direct statement. To have called Satan tyrant directly would have broken the balance of presentation.

'King *Buzzard*', in Dryden's poem, is chosen from several candidates. In the 'grave Consult' of the Pigeons he emerges as their preferred solution, recommended in the leading speech:

> On this high Potentate, without delay,
> I wish you would conferr the Sovereign sway:
> Petition him t'accept the Government,
> And let a splendid Embassy be sent.
> This pithy Speech prevail'd, and all agreed,

Page references after quotations from the commentary are to its independent pagination within that volume.

[3] *The Poems of John Milton*, edited by John Carey and Alastair Fowler (London, 1968), pp. 508–9; Milton, *Poetical Works*, edited by Douglas Bush (London, 1966), pp. 232–5; *John Milton: Complete Poems and Major Prose*, edited by Merritt Y. Hughes (New York, 1957), p. 232.

[4] This aspect of Bodin has been discussed in Howard Erskine-Hill, *The Augustan Idea in English Literature* (London, 1983), pp. 58–64; see also the fuller discussion by Quentin Skinner, *The Foundations of Modern Political Thought*, 2 vols. (Cambridge, 1978), II, *The Age of Reformation*, pp. 284–301.

Old Enmity's forgot, the *Buzzard* should succeed . . .
He came, and Crown'd with great Solemnity,
God save King *Buzzard*, was the gen'rall cry.
A Portly Prince, and goodly to the sight . . . (III. 1130–40)[5]

Again, something might have been said about kinds of kingship, for Dryden's understated irony in line 1131 makes it clear that this is in effect, though not theory, an elective king. The Pigeons do not, like Milton's Devils, confront a monarch likely to prove a tyrant, they *choose* one. Commentators have, however, been concerned with an even more specific question: what historical figure does the Buzzard represent? James Kinsley, following a lead from Scott, supported Gilbert Burnet, popular preacher and now *protégé* of the Prince and Princess of Orange, while Earl Miner in the Clark Library edition argues for a double allusion, to both Burnet and William of Orange. Perhaps rightly, neither editor has questioned the sense of seeking an original. Certainly, when we start to look, some features of the Buzzard point one way, some another. Thus his physical description applies well to Burnet and not at all to William (lines 1140ff.) while of line 1135 the reverse is true. And naturally the fact that William was soon invited over to England and crowned tends to sway our judgement.

It is interesting that in this instance the difficulty of identifying a single original has led, not to the abandonment of the search for originals, but to the more subtle critical hypothesis of multiple allusion. Had the editorial commentators on Milton entertained such a possibility, they might have had more to say about the enthronement of Satan. At this point, however, it is useful to go behind *Paradise Lost* to the choosing of Saul as King of the Hebrews in Cowley's *Davideis*, book four, since a pre-Miltonic example will serve to test the fairness of considering Milton and Dryden together. Published in 1656, *Davideis* may have been composed in the earlier 1650s.[6] In book four the priest and judge Samuel responds as follows to the Tribes' request for a king:

> You're sure the first (said he,)
> Of *Free-born* men that begg'd for *Slavery*.
> I fear, my Friends, with Heav'nly *Manna* fed,
> (Our old Forefathers crime) we lust for *Bread*.
> Long since by God from *Bondage* drawn, I fear,
> We build anew th' *Egyptian Brickiln* here.
> Cheat not yourselves with *words*, for tho' a *King*
> Be the mild *Name*, a *Tyrant* is the *Thing*.[7]

On the face of it this passage is a warning against kingship as an institution, and so its source in I Samuel 8:11 was used by Milton when in *The Tenure of Kings and*

[5] Quotations from Dryden's poems are drawn from *The Poems of John Dryden*, edited by James Kinsley, 4 vols. (Oxford, 1958) – hereafter referred to as *Poems*.
[6] Frank Kermode, 'The Date of Cowley's *Davideis*', *Review of English Studies*, 25 (1949), pp. 154–8.
[7] *The Works of Mr Abraham Cowley . . .*, ninth edition (London, 1700), p. 86.

Magistrates (1649) he defended the execution of Charles I.[8] However, Cowley is among those poets who comment on their own poems. His commentary on the quoted passage is balanced and circumspect. The biblical source is not to be regarded as defining 'the *right* of *Kings*', now to be established among the Hebrews with Saul. On the contrary, the Hebrews continued to live and be governed by laws. Samuel's words (he implies) warn of what kings may do, not what by definition they will do, and this interpretation is borne out by the Westminster Assembly *Annotations Upon All the Books of the Old and New Testament*, (second edition, 1651).[9] Cowley's collocation of texts is of great interest, the verse narrative being linked, often by the biblical references which are shoulder notes on the same page, to the biblical and classical commentary at the end of each Book. In the present instance a double effect is achieved, the verse expressing some of the impetuous and intransigent republicanism of the Independents of the time, while the commentary, fairly interpreting Scripture by the latest lights, keeps the idea of monarchy in play. It is no surprise that twentieth-century commentators have been divided as to Cowley's intention. A. H. Nethercot, in *The Muse's Hannibal* (1931), followed the longer narrative of book four and I Samuel, together with Cowley's Commentary, to suggest that this part of *Davideis* recommends a restoration of the Stuart monarchy. David Trotter, in *The Poetry of Abraham Cowley* (1979), rejected the 'political allegory' which he considered such an interpretation entailed, and saw Cowley as having moved away from an absolutist royalism found in his unfinished earlier poem *The Civil War* (c. 1643).[10] Nethercot's analysis seemed to involve two contemporary allusions: Saul reminded of the young Charles II, Samuel, perhaps, of Oliver Cromwell. There is, however, a further possibility, not mentioned by either critic. This is that Cromwell himself might be the new Saul. The possibility of a Cromwellian monarchy was much discussed in the mid-1650s, and seems to have been envisaged as early as 1651 by Andrew Marvell in his *Horatian Ode*.[11] Authorial text and commentary together thus suggest multiple allusion. They explore the concept of monarchy afresh, together with the sentiments that ran against it, implying but never suggesting specific contemporary originals. This lack of specific intimations (which seems to point to both Burnet and William of Orange in *The Hind and the Panther*) is likely to have been the result not only of political caution, but of the genuine uncertainty of the political future in the 1650s.

While these three examples show the three poets working differently, Cowley

---

[8] *Revolutionary Prose of the English Civil War*, edited by Howard Erskine-Hill and Graham Storey (Cambridge, 1983), pp. 124–5.

[9] Volume I (no pagination), under I Samuel 8, especially verses 9 and 11.

[10] *The Poetry of Abraham Cowley* (London, 1979), pp. 84–92.

[11] Marvell's structural allusion to Horace, *Odes*, I. 37, intimates a parallel between Cromwell and Augustus: see Howard Erskine-Hill, *The Augustan Idea in English Literature*, pp. 194–8.

is not so different from Dryden in his handling of political implication that he cannot, with Dryden, form an interesting context for the interpretation of Milton. Most important, however, is the way in which Cowley's commentary reveals his lively awareness of how a vigilant contemporary reader might respond to the implications of the poem.

Authorial comment does not demand a formal commentary of the kind Cowley supplied. Opportunity is offered in other features of prose apparatus, such as prefaces, subtitles and shoulder notes, usually printed in closer association with the verse and, when able to link with the presentation of the poet within the poem, capable of crossing the prose/verse frontier to merge with the poetic text itself. Before proceeding to discuss two seventeenth-century commentaries on Milton and Dryden by hands other than theirs it is necessary to consider such other forms of authorial comment.

Here nothing is more striking than to compare the two 1667 epic poems already mentioned: *Paradise Lost* in ten books, and Dryden's *Annus Mirabilis*. The latter is a fine example of an extended poem well integrated with an elaborate authorial prose apparatus. This apparatus consists of five components. 1. *Annus Mirabilis* are merely the opening words of a long descriptive title the very typeface of which emphasises the form of the work (more precisely 'AN HISTORICAL Poem' than an epic) which will set forth 'our Naval War with *Holland*' and THE FIRE OF LONDON' (I. 42). 2. The dedication 'TO THE METROPOLIS OF GREAT BRITAIN' is a short historical and religious meditation on the subject of the poem. 3. The Letter to Sir Robert Howard supplies a copious critical essay on the character and models of the poem, and includes '*Verses to her* Highness *the* DUTCHESS . . .' (I. 42–51). 4. A system of concise footnotes (contrasting with Cowley's copious endnotes) is supplied to accompany the narrative. 5. A further system of explanation, a series of interspersed subtitles, helps to pace the poem, and clarify, at certain points, the narrative development behind a verse meditation. 4 and 5 particularly concern us here. Like Cowley Dryden uses notes to explain historical points as well as literary echoes and allusions. Stanza 198, for example:

> Repenting *England* this revengeful day
> ʸTo *Philip*'s Manes did an off'ring bring:
> *England*, which first, by leading them astray,
> Hatch'd up Rebellion to destroy her King.

is immediately followed by this note: '(y) *Philip*'s Manes: Philip *the* second, *of* Spain, *against whom the Hollanders rebelling, were aided by Queen* Elizabeth' (*Poems*, II, 87), a significant reflection in view of Dryden's future religious and political development. The subtitles, for their part, not only clarify the specific subject-matter but, as here, emphasise the causal and symbolic structure of the poem:

> *Burning of the Fleet in* the Vly *by Sir* Robert Holmes . . .
> Transitum *to the Fire of* London . . .
> *King's Prayer* . . .
> *Cities request to the King not to leave them.* (*Poems,* I, 88–102)

In stark contrast *Paradise Lost* had on its first appearance in print no prose apparatus whatsoever: no comment in either verse or prose. Only the title-page tersely announces: 'Paradise lost. / A / POEM / Written in / TEN BOOKS / by JOHN MILTON . . .' Even the prose Argument to each book, together with the accompanying printer's note, was not added until 1668. If we postulate a reader in 1667 with no knowledge at all of Dryden or Milton, he would be able to learn much from the apparatus of Dryden's poem, which was indeed presented in a matrix of loyal sentiment and critical opinion. Of Milton this reader would be able to learn nothing save from the poem itself – but this was of course a good deal. The self-presentation of the poet within the poem, when as at the beginning of books three, seven and nine, it conveys certain circumstances and values, is itself a comment on the poem as a whole. Before considering this, however, it is worth briefly reviewing Milton's earlier presentational practice.

Lycidas is a significant example. When in 1638 it first appeared, the collection in memory of Edward King which it concluded carried a Latin preface explaining, among other things, that the drowned King had knelt and prayed on the deck of the sinking ship while others tried to save themselves.[12] This was surely significant information for the reader of Milton's poem. But when it was republished in Milton's *Poems,* 1645, it carried for the first time an explanatory headnote with a different emphasis: 'In this Monody the Author bewails a learned Friend, unfortunatly drown'd in his Passage from *Chester* on the *Irish* Seas, 1637. And by occasion foretels the ruine of our corrupted Clergy then in their height' (p. 57). This authorial comment is much in the tradition of Spenser's *Shepheardes Calender.* It shows Milton was not always averse to spelling out the political and religious tendency of his poetry. On the contrary, it suggests he was prepared to say more when the times seemed to have turned in his direction. *Lycidas* was originally published in the time of Charles I's single rule; in 1645 the 'corrupted Clergy' have in Milton's view been challenged in the Civil War and, as he may have hoped, vanquished. This headnote connects with other features of the 1645 *Poems.* For example, two dramatic and political sonnets in this collection, 'Captain or Colonel, or Knight in Arms . . .' and 'Daughter to that good Earl, once President . . .' begin to give clear intimations of the political and religious character of Milton, consistent with what he now says about

---

[12] *The Poems of John Milton,* edited by Carey and Fowler, p. 232.

Lycidas. 'Ad Patrem' further fills out the picture. From these works the character of that 'Mr. *John Milton*', whose 'POEMS . . . BOTH ENGLISH and LATIN, / Compos'd at several times' are proclaimed on the 1645 titlepage, begins to be composed: a man devoted to learning and the Muse, hostile to the Laudian Church, with republican strains beginning to be heard in sonnets on public themes. Such an image is consonant with what could be gathered from a more declamatory title-page from the year before: *Areopagitica; a Speech of Mr. John Milton | For the Liberty of Unlicens'd Printing* (1644).

These two books begin to form the main lines of Milton's authorial character. This character was most prominently developed by his defences of the people of England for executing their king. These became famous, or notorious, and many who had not read them would know of them. In a passage in *The Second Defence* (1654), perhaps his internationally best-known work in his lifetime, Milton includes a personal passage which brings together his defence of regicide and his blindness.[13] He does the same in very different form in the public and personal sonnet 'To Cyriack Skinner on his Blindness', never printed in his lifetime, though possibly circulated in manuscript in the mid-1650s. Here we have the lasting features of Milton's authorial character in the public mind. If we may change the hypothetical reader of the 1660s who knew nothing of Milton and Dryden for a reader who knew at least some of the more obvious things about the elder man, we may say that the appearance of John Milton's name on title-page alone would have been enough to raise and point expectation. This in itself suggested an authorial character and seemed to propose a context for the new work. In a sense this constituted an incipient commentary. It is worth noting that, in what was probably the most courageous work Milton ever published, *The Readie and Easie Way to Establish a free Commonwealth . . .* (1660), where the title-page only bore the words: 'The author J. M.', the epigraph from Juvenal, I. 15–16, '—*et nos | consilium dedimus Syllae, demus populo nunc*' seems to inform the reader of the author's previous achievement: he who has advised Sulla now advises the people.[14] The allusion to Sulla, taken with Milton's phrase in the tract: 'those unhappie interruptions', is more likely to refer to Cromwell than Monck (in addition the last three words of the epigraph will not be found in Juvenal) and, altogether, the logic of this title-page is to direct the attention of the reader to the fact that the author who once advised the Lord Protector has now turned his attention to the people. The political point, though of great interest, is less important for the purposes of the present essay than the fact that, in a pamphlet so dangerous that Milton allowed only his initials to appear on the title-

[13] John S. Diekhoff, *Milton on Himself* (London, 1939; second edition 1965), p. 99. W. R. Parker, *Milton's Contemporary Reputation . . .* (Columbus, 1940), pp. 72–119, especially pp. 99–119, demonstrate what Milton's name on a title-page might have been expected to evoke.
[14] *Revolutionary Prose of the English Civil War*, pp. 203–4.

page (or acquiesced in such a proposal from the nameless printer) he nevertheless directed the reader's attention to his previous record. Milton's title-pages, which as the years go by and the political circumstances change against him, grow more terse, always, I believe, are meant to remind the reader who the author was, what he stood for, and what he did.

There can hardly be a more important point than this for the interpretation of Milton's major poem. The unelaborated title-page of the 1667 *Paradise Lost* links, once the reader has got there, with the opening of book three:

> Thee I re-visit safe,
> And feel thy sov'reign vital Lamp; but thou
> Re-visit'st not these Eyes, that rowle in vain
> To find thy piercing Ray . . . (III. 21–4)

and the opening of book seven where Urania is invoked:

> More safe I sing with mortal voice, unchang'd
> To hoarse or mute, though fall'n on evil days,
> On evil days though fall'n, and evil tongues;
> In darkness, and with dangers compass'd round,
> And solitude . . . (VII. 24–8)

Such moments are effective metaphors for much in the human condition, but it is clear that they also ask the reader to think about the identity of the author. An additional comment was supplied in 1668 when, at the printer's request, Milton added the prose Argument and his note on 'The Verse'. Not only is the note helpful commentary on the form of the poem but, drawing a legitimate analogy, it unmistakably reminds the reader of the author's political record: '*This neglect then of Rhime so little is to be taken for a defect, though it may seem so perhaps to vulgar Readers, that it rather is to be esteem'd an example set, the first in* English, *of ancient liberty recover'd to Heroick Poem from the troublesome and modern bondage of Rhiming.*' Perceiving the parallel between liberty and bondage in verse, and liberty and bondage in the state, we remember something of what liberty and bondage had meant to Milton in earlier times. This note may be the first example of a practice used by Dryden after 1688, and by Pope after him: to seem to be talking about the kingdom of poetry when they are also talking about the kingdom itself. It is a form of coded expression available to writers who see themselves in internal opposition to the powers that be.

1671 and 1674 see a further presentational development in Milton's authorial character. In the 1671 volume, the Proem to *Paradise Regained* uses the pseudo-Virgilian Proem to the *Aeneid* to assert the continuity of authorship between *Paradise Lost* and *Paradise Regained*: 'I Who e're while the happy Garden sung . . .'. In a graceful and intelligent imitation Milton affects to see the former poem as pastoral or georgic compared with the real epic now to come. This is not merely an apt Virgilian gesture, since the implications of the intimated parallel are confirmed by the radical view of epic expressed at the opening of book nine of *Paradise Lost* (1–47). Thus the 1671 title-page with its announcement: 'The Author / JOHN MILTON.' links at once with the opening lines of the first poem, in consequence of which other salient associations of Milton's reputation are brought into play. This title-page, of course, also bore the enigmatic words: 'To which is added / *SAMSON AGONISTES.*' The author now follows his precedent from the note to *Paradise Lost* to 'epistle' rather than prologue his poetic drama with some explanation of his concept of tragedy. Enough has already been said about the salient features of Milton's self-created authorial character to suggest the implications of this drama of heroic blindness. While there are evident limitations to any merely biographical approach to a literary text, later seventeenth-century readers were not new critics. I suggest that Milton's drama, first appearing in 1671, invited the reader to find, at a certain level, the poet in the poetic text. And this, surely is what Milton's best-placed and most intelligent reader did. Andrew Marvell's remarkable commendatory poem, which prefaced the twelve-book 1674 version of *Paradise Lost*, takes up all the salient features of Milton's authorial character linking them felicitously with the history of Samson:

> When I beheld the poet blind, yet bold,
> In slender book his vast design unfold –
> Messiah crowned, God's reconciled decree,
> Rebelling angels, the forbidden tree,
> Heaven, hell, earth, chaos, all – the argument
> Held me awhile misdoubting his intent,
> That he would ruin (for I saw him strong)
> The sacred truths to fable and old song
> (So Samson groped the temple's posts in spite),
> The world o'erwhelming to revenge his sight. (lines 1–10)

Notice how Marvell puts his first thoughts on record; he does not in the end think that Milton, any more than Milton's Samson, ruins for revenge, and the image of Samson is eventually replaced by that of Tiresias. Yet the first lines show how readers probably responded to Milton at this time, and the words 'blind, yet bold' say it all.

In the presentation of Milton's poetry, I suggest, the constraint of hostile times deflected him from the kind of authorial commentary supplied by Cowley for *Davideis* in the 1650s, or even the sort of comment he had written for the 1645 republication of *Lycidas*. Instead he was able to assert his authorial presence by the combination of title-page and poetic self-portrayal, though powerfully assisted by, first, his 1668 note on 'The Verse' and, secondly, Marvell's perceptive commendatory poem, which he must have allowed his publisher to include. Restoration times, by contrast, positively invited Dryden to be expansive: he had small reason to fear giving hostages to fortune. His presentation of *Annus Mirabilis* sets the general pattern of copious critical and personal discussion in the apparatus, little or no self-presentation in the work itself. Then with the Exclusion Crisis of 1681 Dryden's practice begins to change. With *Absalom and Achitophel* he published for the first time a major poem without his name on the title-page. A year later, *The Medall* is declared only to be by 'The Author of *Absalom and Achitophel*'. That this locution was by now as much an incentive to the buyer as a mask of the author is suggested by its use on the title-page of the probably unauthorised publication of *Mac Flecknoe* in 1682. With this exception his name returns to his title-pages until *The Hind and the Panther* in 1687, though the preface to this poem rapidly makes it clear who the author is. During this period Dryden begins, sparingly but deliberately, to introduce himself into his own poetic texts. 'To the Memory of Mr. *Oldham*' (1684) starts this trend which continues with the *Ode to the Pious Memory of . . . Anne Killigrew* (1686), *The Hind and the Panther* and, after the Revolution, 'To My Dear Friend Mr Congreve . . .' (1693). Varied specific motives, no doubt, combined to produce this turbulence in Dryden's presentational practice (for example, in 1681, the court may not have wished to announce his new form of poem with its new political voice as a laureate performance) but it seems certain that political instability was one factor. Indeed political and religious uncertainty contribute directly to the strange form of *The Hind and the Panther*, part three, where the two inset fables offer pessimistic alternative visions of the future, even though this is a Roman Catholic poem in a Roman Catholic reign. These circumstances offer no clear parallel to Milton's experience, but it is notable that after the Revolution, when from Dryden's point of view almost the worst had happened, his resort to poetic self-presentation and coded poetic obliquity became more marked.

Still in pursuit of an explanation of the different commentary-treatment of Milton and Dryden, I now turn to two late seventeenth-century commentaries, one on *Paradise Lost*, one on *The Hind and the Panther*. I call them both commentaries only in the broadest sense of the term. The first I shall consider, Patrick Hume's 'Annotations' on *Paradise Lost*, published in Tonson's edition of Milton's *Poetical Works* (1695), hardly could be a more learned, serious and extended commentary. As it is often said, it supplies *Paradise Lost* with the kind of attention expected hitherto only for the great classics of antiquity. No English poem had been accorded this kind of scholarly attention before.[15] The second

---

[15] Hume's '*Annotations*' has been discussed by Ants Oras, 'Milton's Editors and Commentators from Patrick Hume to Henry Todd (1695–1801): A Study in Critical Views and Methods' in *Eesti Vabariigi Tartu Ülikooli Toimetused: Acta et Commentationes, Universitatis Tartuensis (Dorpatensis)*, B, Humaniora, XIX (Tartu, 1930), pp. 22–49. Oras hardly considers the aspects of Hume's commentary discussed here.

commentary I shall discuss, probably produced in 1689, is part of a manuscript of *The Hind and the Panther*, based on the printed editions of 1687, and supplying a full marginal gloss to all the mysterious figures and allusions in Dryden's strange beast fable. It is at present at Traquair House, in the Scottish Borders, and was probably produced for some member of the family of the Roman Catholic and Jacobite Earls of Traquair, in the late seventeenth century.[16] Only to a certain extent is one comparing like with like.

Hume's commentary on *Paradise Lost* is well known to editors of Milton at least, and may be summarised briefly. It is linguistic and literary. The standard distinction between *Interpretatio* and *Notae*, in contemporary editions of the great Latin classics, is not here distinguished on the printed page, but accounts for the large amount of space devoted by Hume to meticulous paraphrase in prose of Milton's verse. A remarkably high proportion of Milton's words are etymologically explained. Then, allusions and analogues are presented, from English, Italian, French, Latin, Greek and Hebrew literature. Hume also seems to be at home, by late seventeenth-century standards, in Old English. The greater part of Hume's commentary is devoted to these matters. If that were all, it would be a stunning achievement on Hume's part, but his commentary has some other features, minor in his eyes perhaps, but interesting for the purposes of the present essay.

My chief concern with Hume's 'Annotations' will be with the question of historical allusion, but his remarks on the visual presentation of Milton's poem are worth noticing. Hume's notes were published with Tonson's text of *Paradise Lost* which had, since 1688, been adorned '*with Sculptures*' by J. B. Medina. He comments on the illustration to book one (Satan contemplating his fallen followers in Hell) and to book twelve (the expulsion of Adam and Eve from Eden) (see Figs. 6 and 7). These remarks help, as it happens, to date the probable composition of the 'Annotations' to 1688–94, but more critically interesting is the way they highlight Milton's innovations in biblical and emblematic representation. Medina has Michael, a sword in his right hand, his left hand on Adam's shoulder, thrust 'Our lingring Parents' out of Eden, not, as Milton has it, catch them 'In either hand' (XII. 637). Hume complains: 'The Angel led our Parents, loath to depart from their beloved Seat, in each hand, which the Designer of the Copper Plate has not well exprest, representing him *shoving them out*, as we say, *by Head and Shoulders*' (p. 321). Marcia R. Pointon, *Milton and English Art* (Manchester, 1970), notes that Medina follows the great tradition of Masaccio,

---

16 The Traquair Manuscript has been discussed, its textual readings collated with the early editions of Dryden's poem, and its commentary reproduced, by Richard L. Eversole, 'The Traquair Manuscript of Dryden's *The Hind and the Panther*', in *The Papers of the Bibliographical Society of America*, 75 (Second quarter, 1981), 179–90. I am grateful to Professor Eversole for enabling me to check my own transcription of the commentary against his article.

6 J. B. Medina's 'sculpture' for *Paradise Lost*, book twelve; first published in Tonson's
edition (1688). 'The Angel . . . *shoving them out*, as we say, *by Head and Shoulders*'
(Patrick Hume).

63

7 J. B. Medina's 'sculpture' for *Paradise Lost*, book one; first published in Tonson's edition (1688). 'He might have spared his Horns and Asses Ears, so unsuitable to the Description of the Arch-Angel' (Patrick Hume).

Raphael and Guilio Romano in depicting the expulsion; she considers the Plate a failure (p. 15) but not for Hume's reason, which surely emphasises the parental and providential way in which our 'Parents' are made to leave Eden. They are led forth rather than thrown out, and by an angel without a sword. Yet more significant is Hume's comment on Medina's illustration to book one: 'he might have spared his Horns and Asses Ears, so unsuitable to the Description of the Arch-Angel . . .' (p. 39). As Pointon says (pp. 4–6), Medina was pictorially traditional and demonologically correct even in seventeenth-century terms. But Hume rightly perceives that such a depiction betrays the very human way in which Milton's text presents Satan in the earlier books of the poem. The being with 'Horns and Asses Ears' is no very subtle temptation to the reader, though not without an aspect of expressive grief. As we shall see at the end of this essay, there may have been yet other reasons why Hume resisted the traditional iconology of Satan.

At first sight, Hume's 'Annotations' have nothing to do with historical commentary. His authority seems to support the view that *Paradise Lost* was not a political or historical poem, or at least that readers in the 1690s did not think so. A connected matter is that he might easily appear uninterested in Milton's career. The question which should be asked is: how far does Hume's 'Annotations' recognise what has been proposed, in the preceding section of this article, as the self-created authorial character of Milton?

It is clear that to Hume the concept of an author was alive and significant. His note on *Paradise Lost*, I. 16, '. . . unattempted yet in Prose or Rhime', identifies learnedly and passionately with Milton's attitude to rhyme as expressed in his 1668 note on 'The Verse' (itself included in Tonson's 1695 Milton). 'Poetry', Hume says,

(of which Rhime is a Modern part) is tied up to certain Measures and Quantities, which, among the *Greek* and *Latin* Poets, (till the times of Monkish Ignorance) consisted in an Harmonious Modulation of Numbers, that implyed nothing less than the inconvenient gingle and chime at the ends of Verses, which we falsly call Rhime; so deservedly disdained by our Author, for the shackles it puts upon Sense; no Comparison better suiting such Poetasters than that of Tagging of Points in a Garret (p. 4).

Obviously Hume has remembered Marvell's prefatory poem in the 1674 *Paradise Lost*, taking up his joke about 'points' and 'tags' (lines 49–50), and it is hard to see that Marvell's 'Town-Bayes', i.e. Dryden, is not here contemptuously alluded to among 'such Poetasters'. Aubrey's tale of Milton's giving Dryden leave 'to tag his verses' seems to lurk behind Hume's note.[17] The word 'shackles' seems to respond to Milton's word 'bondage', and the location of this tagging and gingling to 'a Garret' gives the whole matter a 1690s Grub-Street air, familiar

---

[17] Milton, *Poetical Works*, edited by Bush, p. 210.

from *A Tale of A Tub* (1704). Hume, however, hardly enhances the political implication of Milton's note. The poet's words '*ancient liberty recover'd*' are not made to resonate in the language of the commentator.

If we turn to the first of Milton's famous personal passages in the poem, that in the opening of book three, which alludes to his blindness, we find Hume responding to the poet's words less as to an eloquent metaphor than a medical condition. He writes of 'a thick and continual dropping from the Head, by which the Optick Nerve is stopt and choak'd' and comments on 'the Mildew, or hurtful Dew that falls in the Evening sometimes, to which our Author compares the noxious Distillation that from his Head fell down into the Optick Nerve . . .' Hume's recitation of medical hypotheses on blindness in his notes to III. 25–6 implies a biographical concern with Milton the blind poet, before he turns to analogues with blind poets of classical antiquity. Milton's life is, for the moment, in the commentator's view, but he does not strike the same note as Marvell, when he speaks of 'the poet blind, yet bold'. Once again, there is a feature of Milton's self-portrayal (as suggested above) to which the commentator does not respond. This is clearly confirmed by Hume's commentary on the opening sequence of book seven. There, Milton's words in lines 25–8, 'On evil days though fall'n, and evil tongues . . .' might have seemed the best opportunity in the poem to comment on what Milton had been, historically and personally, before the Restoration, and what he had done and undergone since. Hume has nothing to say about Milton's allusion to himself here though, in keeping with his general procedure, he gives the etymology of the word 'Solitude' (line 28). It is a significant silence. More might have been said about Milton in commentary on the beginning of book nine, though the opportunity was less clear than in book seven. Again the opportunity was passed over. A final point of the same kind remains to be noted. It is Mary Ann Radzinowicz who has pointed out in XII. 216–19: 'not the readiest way, / . . . / War terrifie them inexpert, and fear / Return them back to *Egypt* . . .' a direct recall of *A Readie and Easie Way* . . . and the collocation of two relevant verbal echoes makes the allusion certain.[18] The seventeenth-century commentator, whom one might normally prefer to a twentieth-century one, does not however register this allusion, though he correctly notes the allusion in line 219 to Exodus 14: 11–12. Hume would never say, with Radzinowicz, anything to the effect that 'Milton's spokesman Abdiel, shows clearly that he has read Milton's prose tracts' (see V. 772–7).[19] The prose tracts hardly figure in this commentary at all.

At this point one might conclude that Hume, while ready to feature Milton as 'our Author' in regard to literary opinion and some biographical matters, saw no

---

[18] Mary Ann Radzinowicz, 'The Politics of *Paradise Lost*' in *Politics of Discourse: The Literature and History of Seventeenth-Century England*, edited by Kevin Sharpe and Steven N. Zwicker (London, 1987), pp. 218–19.   [19] *Ibid.*, p. 221.

reason why the political history of his author's life or affairs of state in general should enter into the first serious commentary upon a classical English poem. As it turns out, however, this would be an incorrect conclusion. At several points Hume conveys historical and political opinions, apparently his own. For example, at I. 87 he glosses Milton's 'mutual league' with: 'A Confederacy or siding of Factious Subjects against their Sovereign, of which the Holy League in *France*, and its Spawn the Solemn League and Covenant in our Country, are two abominable Instances' (p. 9). This comment might seem to achieve a high royalist association of recent historical rebellions and the original revolt of Satan, though Milton too had detested the Presbyterians of the Solemn League. A more striking historical comment still is Hume's response to 'close Ambition varnish'd o're' at II. 486: 'A noble Verse, and highly expressive of those zealous Hypocrites our Author's Contemporaries, an Age so impiously Godly, and so zealously Wicked, that Prayer was the Prologue to the Murder of a Monarch at his own Gate . . .' (p. 68). Within a few days of its taking place Milton had defended this 'Murder' in print. From a modern view it seems extraordinary that Hume should thus slide over the part played by 'our Author' in historical events which need not, perhaps, have been mentioned. A final example from Hume is more political than historical. Glossing the word 'Patriarchs' at IV. 762, the commentator, having explained the Greek roots of the word, adds: 'All Government took its Original Power and Authority from that of Fathers over their Children; and *Adam* was the first grand universal Patriarch and Monarch of Mankind' (p. 161). This is a round statement of the patriarchal origins of government, consistent with Robert Filmer in his *Patriarcha* (published in 1680 though composed before the Civil War), and the chief counter-argument to contractual theories of government of the kind invoked by Milton. Hume repeats the point more fully in his gloss on XII. 26 (p. 310).

Hume's strategy now seems clear. He is not unconcerned with Milton's life. He is very much concerned with political and historical matters, but not to the extent of featuring Milton's record or views on them. Where, as at I. 87, he can find a co-incidence between his own views and those of the poem he will register the point; but generally his aim is to detach 'our Author' and his poem from the historical events of the century's middle decades. He does not, as Marvell did, pick up all the features of Milton's implied authorial character after the Restoration. Hume's 'Annotations' is, perhaps, the first attempt to accomodate Milton to later times, and take the political sting out of his metaphysical epic. Yet Hume should not be utterly condemned as sanitising *Paradise Lost* from its political taint. The poem itself makes a move, not to evade but to touch with delicacy the roots of recent, tragic, political argument. Milton himself had in his poem obvious opportunities to express what were, or had been, his openly expressed political views. Patriarchalism is neither denied nor affirmed in

Milton's account of the unfallen Adam. No mention of any 'original contract' is to be found. Book twelve offers no discussion of the choice of Saul as King of the Hebrews: the episode is not even mentioned. The political challenge of the Restoration is here ignored. But that is not to say that the poem does not eventually affirm a political view consistent with Milton's earlier writings. Michael speaks of the 'fair equality, fraternal state' of man before the 'Dominion' of Nimrod (XII. 24–32) and Adam concludes of God that 'Man over Men / He made not Lord' (XII. 69–70). The matter then turns on 'Dominion', lordly rule which in book twelve is associated with tyranny, while monarchy in a positive sense is appropriated to God and the Son. That Hume's political emphasis is consciously out of key with that of Milton is seen from the fact that his longest affirmation of the patriarchal origin of government is not in response to the words 'paternal Rule' (XII. 24) but to 'fair equality' (XII. 26). It is as if he wishes to block off the poem's political line of thought.

For the modern historical commentator on *Paradise Lost* Hume ought not generally to be trusted. While in other ways a rich resource, he seeks to occlude Milton's political career and principles and, with perhaps one salient exception, to detach the poem from its historical matrix. Recent critics, notably Christopher Hill, have begun to look for historical references in the text, albeit loosely and speculatively.[20] The fact that Hume offers virtually no encouragement for such a search should in reality be no discouragement. For in his presentation of *Paradise Lost* Hume dehistoricises the poem, even using it as an occasion for expressing his own un-Miltonic political views. He is likely to have had a profound effect on the subsequent reception of Milton.

The Traquair House commentary on *The Hind and the Panther* (hereafter: 'T.H.C.') is part of a manuscript of the whole poem. It announces itself, in the first of its two hands, as: 'The Hind and Panther / a Poem in 3 parts / By Mr Dryden / – Antiquam exquirite matrem / Et vera, incessu patuit Dea. / Your ancient Mother Church if you wou'd find / Her Mark of Truth and Majesty well mind / A Msst. from the printed Edition – London / with notes on the Margion. /

---

[20] Christopher Hill, *Milton and the English Revolution* (London, 1977), pp. 365–402.

[21] Traquair House, Socrates 5th 32. The MS. is in two hands, in that a second, later, hand retraced almost the whole original, as well as occasionally adding to the commentary. It is in this hand, on the front endpaper, that a statement of provenance is given: 'Quondam / Ex libris Gulielmi Stuart / Sed nunc Comitis de Traquaire 1729'. This William Stuart may have been the younger son of Charles, Fourth Earl of Traquair (1659–1741). If so the MS. cannot have been produced for him, for he was born on 2 February 1698. Given the Roman Catholic and Jacobite record of the Stuarts of Traquair at this time, it seems probable that the MS. was produced for some member or connection of the family with a particular interest in Dryden's poem. See R. L. Eversole, 'The Traquair Manuscript of Dryden's *The Hind and the Panther*', *Papers of the Bibliographical Society of America*, 75 (1981), 179–90. I acknowledge with gratitude the kindness of the late Peter Maxwell Stuart of Traquair who allowed me to examine the MS. at Traquair House in 1980 and to transcribe the commentary.

1689'.[21] The 'notes on the Margion' are more precisely a key than a commentary, and are an integral part of a manuscript book prepared for a reader likely to have shared the poet's religion and politics at the time the poem was composed. They offer identifications which could, perhaps, hardly have been printed after 1689. By contrast with Patrick Hume, T. H. C. wishes to share its poem's more intimate historical life. Taken generally, it certainly endorses the practice of Dryden's editors in finding countless historical references in this text.

Turning to the specific features of T. H. C. we may first consider the modest apparatus Dryden himself provided for his poem: its preface 'TO THE READER' and its six shoulder-notes. At once a deficiency appears. Though present in all the 1687 printings and the Bodleian manuscript designated 'M' by the Clark Library editors, the preface does not appear in T. H. C. One of the places where Dryden speaks personally is thus lost to this version. Further, though T. H. C. incorporates all the poet's other shoulder-notes, the important one at the end of part two where a portent marking James II's 'late nocturnal victory' – 'I saw myself the lambent easie light' (line 658) – receives the marginal endorsement 'Poeta loquitur.', is omitted. (It is also omitted from M.)[22] This might seem almost a studied unconcern with the poet's self-presentation, but there is in fact no consistent pattern. At part one line 72, 'My thoughtless youth was wing'd with vain desires . . .' T. H. C. adds the gloss: 'Mr Dryd. of himself', thus affording contemporary confirmation of that critical tradition which has found confessional passages in the poem (Works, III, 346). However, the third confessional and personal passage now generally recognised, that ending at III. 289–97, receives the comment: 'The Cath. Church Speaks to her Child' with these lines set in quotation marks. The second hand in T. H. C. – it is a later hand – expands the last word to: 'Children for their good'. The original gloss should not be readily dismissed. Formally, at least, the Hind is speaking here, which is not the case with the 'I' designated as: 'Mr Dryd.' in I. 72–99. No doubt the speech of the Roman Catholic Church in part three may be thought to modulate into that of one of her children to himself, but is it not better to accept the gloss, and conclude that the personal dimension of this moving speech lies less in the speaker than in the person addressed : the poet who is now the Church's 'Child'?

Poetic self-presentation having been considered, the contribution of T. H. C. may be further explored under three heads: 1. where it confirms the accumulated critical tradition as represented in Works, III; 2. where it adds to modern commentary; and, 3. where it disagrees with it.

1. The broad reference of the beast-fable is confirmed: the Hind is (as we have seen) the Roman Catholic Church, the Panther the Church of England, the Bear the Independents, the Hare the Quakers, the Ape the Latitudinarians, the Boar the Baptists, the Wolf the Presbyterians (many references in both cases), the Fox

---

[22] Works, III, 545.

the Arians, the Dog the Atheists, and the Lion King James II, lions kings in general: 'a *Lyon* old' (I. 351) is glossed: 'K. Henry 8'. Less basic, often more subtle confirming identifications are too numerous to list here, and too diverse to summarise. However, an instance where Earl Miner in the Clark Dryden proposes a new correction, affecting interpretation of an extensive and important passage, may be significantly compared with the presentation of T. H. C. In I. 235–90 the poet seems to plead for 'pity' to persecuted Protestants providing the civil power can curb their 'malice to destroy' and denounces 'that which persecutes the mind' (I. 235–40). Miner's corrective gloss proposes that 'the pious Pastor' in the triplet: 'Such pity now the pious Pastor shows, / Such mercy from the *British* Lyon flows, / That both provide protection for their foes' (I. 288–90) is Pope Innocent XI, 'a moderate and reforming pope', rather than another epithet for James II ('the *British* Lyon'). If both epithets alluded to the king, then the general 'protection' might seem to refer to his measures of partial toleration in Scotland in February 1687, which then involve problems of dating (*Works*, III. 368). If Dryden alludes first to the pope, and then to his own Catholic king, he is writing of the policy of his Church, not merely the manoeuvrings of his monarch. T. H. C. confirms Miner's correction. The 'pious Pastor' is: 'The Pope', the '*British* Lyon': 'K. James 2'.

Turning to 2 (additional identifications proposed by T. H. C.) we may first note one from the passage just discussed. At I. 283, 'the mighty hunter' is not commented on by either Miner or Kinsley. T. H. C. glosses: 'Nimrod' who is then contrasted with the agreed identification in the next line, 'the blessed *Pan*': 'Christ'. Dryden's thought is nearer to *Paradise Lost*, book twelve, here, than we might have supposed.

Here is a short selection of T. H. C. annotations additional to those preserved in Kinsley and Miner. I. 67: 'forbids the sight': 'Natural Reason'; 70: 'here alone': 'The Cath. Church'. I. 129: 'Along the coast': 'Humane Reason'. I. 171: '*Cambria*': 'England'; 'last of all the litter': 'Calvin'; 178: '*Helvetian* kind': 'Switzers'; '*Leman lake*': 'near Geneva'; 183: '*Sanhedrin*': 'Synagogues Vid Heyl. pref to Ye Hist. of presb'. I. 434: 'Stedfast in various turns of state she stood': 'Cromwell's days'. I. 515: 'sylvan subjects': 'Dissenters'. II. 262: 'garble' [T. H. C. reads 'gurble']: 'Purge'. III. 260: 'perjur'd murtherer': 'Dr Oates'. III. 441: 'Sad auguries of winter': 'Persecution'. III. 703: our Sovereign Lord': 'K. Ja. y^n D. of york' [this equally applies to 'dis-heir' in the next line]. III. 776: 'fair *Lavinia* for your bride': 'Liberty of Conscience'. III. 993: 'Another Farm': 'a Catho. Chappell.' III. 1051: 'Monster': 'Popery'. III. 1167: 'hospitable Foes': 'the Pope & Cardinals'.

3. A brief final selection from T. H. C. concentrates on differences from Miner's commentary. Many of them will be found compatible with his emphasis. II. 419–22, on '*Curtana*', correctly explained by Miner as '"the sword of mercy,

which wants a point"'', contrasted with the sword of justice, is glossed by T. H. C.: 'Excommunication', neglected by the Anglican Church in favour of legal penalties. 11. 640–1, 'long lost sons' welcomed back by the Roman Catholic Church, is referred by Miner to the Parable of the Prodigal Son (Luke 15: 11–32). T. H. C. glosses the words: 'Engd.', merely pointing the application. At 111. 160: 'Your sons of Latitude' Miner has a long note on Cambridge Platonists and 'broad-way' divines; T. H. C. gives a different emphasis with its single word 'Trimmers', applying a current political term to theological controversy. This is closer to Scott's comment on these words, who wrote of 'the juggling designs of [a] faction' (Kinsley, *Poems*, IV, 1980). At 111. 550–65, the line 'New blossoms flourish, and new flow'rs arise' (line 553) describes the false Spring which deceives the Roman Catholic Swallows in the Panther's fable of the Swallows, one of the two inset fables which conclude the poem. Miner outlines three possible precise times: Spring 1687, November 1686, and Autumn 1685, preferring the second application. T. H. C. cuts through the detailed pros and cons with: 'K. Ja. 2^{d}'s time' and it may be thought that this at least accommodates the finer points of detail set forth by later commentary. At 111. 613, 'The latter brood' of the Swallows causes Miner to hesitate between young Catholics, or recent Catholic converts. T. H. C. glosses: 'late Converts'.

The Hind's fable of the Pigeons returns us to the problem of the Buzzard already glanced at in the first part of this essay. At 111. 899, 'the *Pigeons*, and the *Buzzards* Love', T. H. C. offers the following comments in order: 'High Church' and 'Presbyter'. No identification is proposed by Miner or Kinsley for these birds at this point. When T. H. C. next comments on the Buzzard, at 111. 1121, he co-incides with Kinsley, but not (or not wholly) with Miner, in finding the reference to 'D^{r}. Burnet'. At this stage Miner, casting his eye forward over the next fifty lines, advances his case for a double allusion in the Buzzard to Gilbert Burnet and the Prince of Orange (*Works*, III, 450–51). We note that while the 1689 commentator does not support the 1969 one, this is not because the former is tied to a one-to-one system of interpretation: for T. H. C. the Buzzard is both 'Presbyter' and 'D^{r}. Burnet' though Burnet was of the Established Church. It seems improbable that the author of a commentary designed for a Roman Catholic circle would hold back from acknowledging an allusion to William III. And indeed at a later point he does not. In the final major difference between T. H. C. and Miner, Willam is mentioned in a context more damning even than that of an invited and usurping monarch. Towards the end of the Hind's character of the Buzzard the following lines occur:

> But he, uncall'd, his Patron to controul,
> Divulg'd the secret whispers of his Soul:
> Stood forth th'accusing *Sathan* of his Crimes,
> And offer'd to the *Moloch* of the Times. (111. 1179–82)

71

Where Kinsley and Miner find, in 'his Patron', allusion to Burnet and the Duke of Lauderdale, T. H. C. glosses: 'K. Jam. 2'. Where Kinsley is silent on '*Moloch*' and Miner glosses: 'God of the Amorites . . .', T. H. C. identifies him as: 'Pr.^ce of Orange'.

The reader accustomed to reading Dryden's poem in the light of Miner's copious and subtle commentary may feel that in these identifications T. H. C. simply goes astray. I would not argue that a seventeenth-century commentary *must* be more accurate than a twentieth-century one, but it is worth considering what kind of sense it makes. One might have expected that in 1689, when Dryden's story of King Buzzard must have seemed a pretty accurate prophecy, T. H. C. would have been tempted to find direct allusions in the Buzzard to William of Orange. It is then significant that these are never suggested. William, however, is not banished from the picture: he is elevated above the bird of prey to become his bloodthirsty god. Further, on T. H. C.'s reading, there is a pointed contrast between two potentates, James and William, the paternal prince vulnerable to betrayal, and the warlord who becomes the object of idolatry. (Such an interpretation of line 1179 does, of course, slide over much significant biographical detail concerning Burnet and Lauderdale which can only be harmonised by the reflection that Lauderdale had represented James in Scotland.) Meanwhile, Buzzard/Burnet is indeed the false king in the Hind's fiction, and represents the possible future he hoped his master would achieve. The two commentators have the same political world in play, but at this important stage of the poem, where Miner proposes a compound portrait, T. H. C. is inclined to separate out and stratify the allusions he finds. This is not a foolish presentation of the poem, and can stand as a viable alternative to the approach of Miner.

Some conclusions may now be proposed. Political circumstance explains a good deal. Cowley commented copiously but with circumspection on his own poem because the political future looked so uncertain: a continuation of the Commonwealth, a Cromwellian monarchy, even a Stuart monarchy? Verse text and comment together explore the principles that would be involved in change. Milton after the Restoration refrained from all but the briefest comment, and especially the sort he had added to *Lycidas* in 1645, not because it was superfluous, but because it would have been dynamite. Milton found other ways of manifesting his authorial presence, so as to raise expectation and direct the reader's thought. Dryden, with so much less to live down, on the Restoration, and so much more to hope for from the new order, supplied an elaborate prose apparatus for his poems, not because they required so much more explication than Milton's, but because, in the earlier decades at least, he felt politically secure in expanding on the issues that interested him. Commentaries more or less contemporary with the poems they consider need to be measured against such poetic self-presentation, and vice versa. Such commentaries cannot be used as simple touchstones of historical truth. They too need to be read in context and, when reliable historical commentary is our goal, they too must be explored for their own political orientation.

In the case of the two poems and the two commentaries discussed above, the situation is the opposite of what it might seem at first sight. We cannot assume that an earlier, a-historical, poem invoked a (slightly) earlier a-historical commentary, while a later, densely historical poem invoked a later, heavily historical key. The salient contrast between the two commentators is that while T. H. C. identifies with the ethos of the later Dryden, Hume deliberately resists the ethos of Milton, distancing the commentary from the poet's context, and affirming, more than once, a patriarchal hypothesis on the origin of government which there is no evidence Milton ever supported, and which he violently repudiated in his middle years. The general absence of historical allusions in Hume's commentary comes, one may suppose, less from his not seeing any in the poem than from his resolve not to mention any he saw. We are thus left with the example of Dryden and T. H. C. which, from 1689, suggests a later seventeenth-century readiness to read poetry containing such names as '*Sathan*' and '*Moloch*' as involving contemporary historical allusion. Further, it is easy to assume that Hume somehow represents an earlier mode of reading poems than does T. H. C. But Hume probably compiled his commentary between 1688 and *c*. 1694.[23] Hume, in fact, is the more modern of the two, pointing ahead to Addison, T. H. C. more imbued in seventeenth-century practice and preoccupation. It may not therefore be quite anachronistic to wonder whether *Paradise Lost* does not, to some degree, operate like *The Hind and the Panther*, and whether T. H. C. may not be, sometimes, a suggestive example for readers of Milton's poem.

In the light of all this, let us turn for the last time to Dryden's King Buzzard and Milton's Satan. The Buzzard/Burnet, the accusing Satan to his true king, worshipper of his warlord god, Moloch the Prince of Orange, suddenly reminds us, in its intensity of contemporary political awareness, that a modern commen-

---

[23] Since Hume's 'Annotations' are so extensive, learned and detailed, one might think that he began work on them soon after the first publication of the poem. As we have seen, however, his disapproving comments on J. B. Medina's illustrations to book one and book twelve of the poem, first published in 1688, suggest that the 'Annotations' were composed between 1688 and 1694. (Conceivably, though, Hume inserted his comments on Medina into his commentary at a late stage.) There is other evidence suggesting a late date: Hume's remarks about Hog's Latin translation of Milton's poem, e.g. on 11. 906 (p. 88). On balance, it seems unlikely (though not impossible) that Hume began to work on *Paradise Lost* much before 1688. If so, his patriarchal opinions on the origin of government cannot be thought a prudent deference to the powers that be. Hume's commentary was published six years after Locke's *Two Treatises on Civil Government* (1689), composed around the time of the Exclusion Crisis, but not printed until after the coming of William III.

tator on *Paradise Lost*, J. B. Broadbent, has described Satan as 'the devils' Cromwell'.[24] We may then return to Patrick Hume, reflecting that an allusion from Satan to Cromwell would not be inconsistent with Hume's politics, and we may then reconsider what Hume says about Milton's words in *Paradise Lost*, II, 486, 'close Ambition varnish'd o'er with zeal': 'highly expressive of those zealous Hypocrites our Author's Contemporaries, an Age so impiously Godly, and so zealously Wicked, that Prayer was the Prologue to the Murder of a Monarch at his own Gate . . .' (p. 68). Against Hume's general strategy of detaching the poem from its time, and the more notable for that, do not these words invite the reader to link the enthroned Satan with Cromwell, regicide and lordly monarch?[25] We may distrust Hume's words because they fit in with his political views, or we may trust them as the one exceptional reference in his commentary to the political events of Milton's life. It comes at a point in the poem (II. 430–505) when the enthroned Satan seems to prove his inherent capacity to reign the Bodinian lordly monarch of Hell and perhaps of some further land. As a brilliant young Miltonist, David Armitage, has recently proposed, Satan's flight to discover the Earth may well recall Cromwell's western design to the new world of the Caribbean in 1654–5.[26] On balance, I think these words of Hume may reveal a long-neglected Miltonic allusion.

Sustained historical commentary has, hitherto, hardly been written about *Paradise Lost*. When it is, the new presenter of the poem will need to consider the possibility of a Cromwellian dimension to that famous poetic scene which opens with the words:

High on a Throne of Royal State, which far
Outshone the Wealth of *Ormus* and of *Ind* . . .
Satan exalted sate . . .

[24] J. B. Broadbent, *Some Graver Subject* (London, 1960), p. 115. See also Northrop Frye, *Five Essays on Milton's Epics* (London, 1966), p. 115.
[25] It is mistaken to suppose that Independents such as Milton were necessarily unqualified admirers of Cromwell: see, for example, Lucy Hutchinson, *Memoirs of the Life of Colonel Hutchinson . . .*, edited by James Sutherland (Oxford, 1973), p. 208. Milton's early praise of Cromwell may be thought to modulate into warning through praise in the *Second Defence*, and from that to clear if inconspicuous repudiation in *A Readie and Easie Way* in 1660.
[26] David Armitage, 'Cromwell's Western Design and the Idea of Empire', unpublished article kindly communicated to the present writer. See David R. Armitage, 'The British Empire and the Civic Tradition, 1656–1742', Ph.D dissertation (Cambridge, 1992), pp. 91–123.

4

Sequences of reading: Pope's *Moral Essays* and
Imitations of Horace

PAT ROGERS

It is strange that the order in which poets collect their verses, and the volumes they make out of their individual poems, should have been so little explored until quite recently. We should not feel any surprise that Ian Jack was amongst the very first to devote careful attention to this issue. He is a scholar whose originality can be overlooked by those who remark simply that he has worked principally on traditional mainstream authors – dead white males and females – and that much of his work has appeared in standard series, such as the Oxford editions of Charlotte Brontë and Browning, or the Oxford History of English Literature. In fact, the Browning edition exemplifies his concern for the issue I mentioned at the outset, whilst his (again) standard-looking study of *Browning's Major Poetry* (1973) shows how the poet planned and shaped his collections of shorter poems.[1] The approach has now been taken up by other scholars, including Neil Fraistat and Jerome McGann.[2] But Ian Jack deserves recognition for his pioneering insights, which form part of that lasting contribution he has made to our understanding of major British writers.

Thus far, the emphasis in this area of study has been on the Romantic and Victorian periods, mainly no doubt because the lyric then stood so high on the poetic scale, and collections of shorter poems were a prime agency of dissemination. Palgrave, after all, compiled an anthology of 'the best songs and lyrical poems in the English language', and set the taste of two or three generations. The approach Jack helped to initiate has been used much less in respect of eighteenth-century verse. But he began his career with work of enduring value on the age of

I wish to thank Donald Nichol for kindly reading a draft of this essay, and putting me straight on Warburton editions in particular – an area in which he holds high authority.

[1] See for example Ian Jack, *Browning's Major Poetry* (Oxford, 1973), pp. 77ff, 96ff, 195ff.
[2] See Neil Fraistat, *The Poem and the Book: Interpreting Collections of Romantic Poetry* (Chapel Hill, N.C., 1985); and Fraistat, ed, *Poems in their Place: The Intertextuality and Order of Poetic Collections* (Chapel Hill, N.C., 1986). The second volume contains an important essay by Vincent Carretta, '"Images Reflect from Art to Art": Alexander Pope's Collected Works of 1717', pp. 195–233. This is the best study to date of Pope's fashioning of his career, but it naturally does not look ahead to the work of the 1730s. Also included in this volume is Jerome J. McGann, 'The Book of Byron and the Book of a World', pp. 254–72.

Pope and Johnson: and this gives rise to the thought that the volumes by these writers, to which we have grown so accustomed, may prove less innocent than they appear. Pope is, as it happens, a particular case in point. We seem to have assumed that his collections rose out of the sea, already clad in their natural raiments.

The way we read Pope's work of the 1730s has been partly determined by a series of historical accidents. It is by now a familiar fact that the author had planned a vast assemblage of poems, generally known as his *Opus Magnum*. This was a project Pope tinkered with throughout the decade but never brought to anything resembling full realisation. The surviving portions which would have formed part of the scheme include the *Essay on Man*, the four 'ethic epistles' (otherwise *Moral Essays*), and perhaps some sections of the last book of *The Dunciad*. These comprise merely the torso of a greater whole, rather as *The Prelude* survives, along with *The Excursion* and smaller works, as a hint of what the overarching master-poem entitled *The Recluse* would have contained. Moreover, the Horatian imitations on which Pope embarked in the same decade have an oblique relation to the scheme of the *Opus Magnum*, although they were never intended to form an actual part of that scheme. This last fact already suggests one of the complications which affect our historical placing of Pope's output in the 1730s. Not to anticipate my conclusions, there is straightaway a doubt raised as to whether the Horatian items make quite as distinct and coherent a group as we generally take them to do.

    F. W. Bateson was one of the first commentators to appreciate the manner in which Pope's abandoned plans for his *Opus Magnum* have distorted our reading of his work. In his introduction to the Twickenham edition of the 'moral essays', Bateson wrote some cogent and still pertinent things about the matter. (Of course, the very title of this volume, designating the four poems as *Epistles to Several Persons* rather than 'moral essays' was itself an attempt to go back beyond Warburton to an earlier, 'authentic' ordering of the material.) Bateson remarks that the order in which we customarily read the poems was that fixed in the *Works* in 1735 – an artificial order, he implies, which has been preserved ever since. The items are invariably printed in the sequence, to list by addressee, Cobham, Martha Blount, Bathurst, Burlington. The order of composition was rather Burlington, Bathurst, Cobham, Blount – it is worth adding that this was also the order of publication, since these things do not always go together. Further, Bateson offers the perhaps gratuitous suggestion that the order of merit is different again: that is, Blount, Burlington, Bathurst, Cobham. The normal printed sequence – in which according to Bateson 'most of us still tend, perhaps wrongly, to read them – was entirely determined by requirements of the almost non-existent "Opus Magnum"'.[3] Two terms seem to me debatable here – the *Opus Magnum* was inchoate and ultimately unrealisable, but it was not yet in 1735 'non-existent', especially if we consider what was going on in Pope's head, the most important locus of his collected works at this stage. More important is the question as to whether the placing was 'entirely' determined by the *Opus Magnum* scheme in its narrowest application. That is a matter which will become clearer as we consider the detailed publishing history a little later.

The fullest study of the grand master-plan is that of Miriam Leranbaum, published in 1977. Her contention is that we may find it rewarding to read the poems of the 1730s 'within the system', and that in particular the *Moral Essays* (a label I shall use for convenience and clarity) will benefit if they are seen within this framework, whereas they are 'often read with great pleasure as wholly independent units – as if they were, in fact, separate Horatian adaptations.'[4] For Leranbaum's own immediate purposes, this was a helpful strategy, and the outcome is a satisfying study which has increased our understanding of Pope's later career. However, the angle of approach adopted in this book precludes consideration of matters which are germane to my present discussion, and which are naturally raised by any consideration of the full picture of composition and publication. To take a single example, Leranbaum nowhere mentions the *Epistle to Arbuthnot*, whose placing in early editions of Pope's works, as we shall see, is a matter of some interest and importance.

The third principal work of scholarship which deserves mention in this preliminary survey is David Foxon's study of *Pope and the Early Eighteenth-Century Book Trade* (1991). It hardly needs saying that this is a book with a range of concerns which goes well beyond the issues treated in this essay. However, one of its most significant findings (not unduly stressed by the author himself) relates to the opportunistic methods Pope employed to stitch together an acceptable volume. Indeed, Foxon hints that Pope may even have postponed composition or revision of his poems to fit the needs of the *Works* then in preparation.[5] Since he

---

[3] *Epistles to Several Persons (Moral Essays)*, edited by F. W. Bateson, The Twickenham Edition of the Poems of Alexander Pope, vol. III.ii, second edition (London, 1961), p. xx. Future references in the form '*TE*, III.ii'.

[4] Miriam Leranbaum, *Alexander Pope's 'Opus Magnum' 1729–1744* (Oxford, 1977), p. 130.

[5] David Foxon, *Pope and the Early Eighteenth-Century Book Trade*, edited by J. McLaverty (Oxford, 1991), especially pp. 117–31. Foxon sees the contriving of the 1735 *Works* as ' tragi-comedy' (p. 117). He uses bibliographical evidence to reach an intriguing conclusion: 'It looks as though Pope started to print the three epistles previously published, *Bathurst*, *Burlington*, and *Cobham*, in that order, and that the inclusion of the new *Epistle to a Lady* (Gilliver paid him £50 on 4 January 1735) was an afterthought.' The 'balancing' of the volume became problematic with the new addition, since the *Works* were made up of items partly under Pope's control and partly under Gilliver's. Note especially that the original running order, as suggested by the evidence of the physical bibliography, had begun not with *Burlington* but with *Bathurst*.

was able to use only certain poems (depending on which copyrights he had retained to himself or to Lawton Gilliver), it follows that what we should regard as his 'creative' career may have been dictated in part by legal and commercial constraints. Next winter Pope might go off and write more *Essays on Man*, if the grand scheme required that, but only if the terms were right and the contracts did not limit the ways in which the poem could be released to the world. Foxon had shown earlier in his book how Pope contrived with Lintot to get the two-canto *Rape of the Lock* into an advantageous final position within a miscellany volume of 1712.[6] He leaves it in no doubt that it was Pope, rather than Gilliver, who fixed the running order for the works in 1735. But again there are ways in which the evidence could be taken further, if we confine ourselves to the make-up of Pope's *Works* in his final decade.

If we view the publication history of the key items in the 1730s and onwards in the context which Foxon's findings provide, then we may be able to see more freshly what happened to Pope's *œuvre* as it began its long process of transmission to us two hundred and fifty years later. By 'key items' here, I mean a group of poems including the *Moral Essays* and the *Imitations of Horace*. Although the *Essay on Man* is always hovering on the edge of the story, it is never at the centre of my attention. The imitations of Donne provide another minor complication. But certain poems which do not belong to the groupings I have just named, at least in our modern conception of these things, need to come into reckoning: these include the earlier epistles addressed to figures such as Addison, Jervas, Oxford and the Blount sisters. For the sake of accuracy it should also be stated that the *Epistle to Arbuthnot* has been taken as belonging to the Horatian group listed above; that is where we should expect to find it today, but it is prejudging matters to make that an unspoken assumption, since its positioning in that location is precisely one of the *post facto* decisions which we shall need to review.

To facilitate discussion, we shall need to work through some rather laborious tabulations, first with regard to the epistles and second with regard to the imitations of Horace. This involves going over some ground familiar to all students of Pope, but it cannot be evaded.

The initial tabulation covers the publishing history of ten poems which were commonly included in Pope's *Works* from 1735 in a group variously designated but always labelled 'Epistles' in some fashion. Not all of them were present in this way on each printing of the collected *Works*. The information listed includes the date of composition (which is usually a minor consideration in my later

---

[6] Foxon, *Pope and the . . . Book Trade*, pp. 34–8.

Table 1

Title	Date of composition	First publication	Griffith no.
1 Epistle to Cobham	1730–3	January 1734	329
2 Epistle to a Lady	1732–4	February 1735	360
3 Epistle to Bathurst	1730–2	January 1733	280
4 Epistle to Burlington	1730–1	December 1731	259
5 Epistle to Oxford	1721	December 1721	130
6 Epistle to Arbuthnot	1731–4	January 1735	352
7 Epistle to Addison	c. 1713–19	September 1721	128
8 Epistle to Jervas	c. 1715	1716	46
9 Epistle to Miss Blount with works of Voiture	c. 1710	1712	6
10 Epistle to Miss Blount on her leaving the Town	1714	June 1717	79

argument, but cannot be entirely forgotten), and the date of first publication, with the item number for that publication in Griffith's *Bibliography*.[7]

A few details may be disposed of before we look at the broader conclusions prompted by the data presented here. The titles are those in familiar use, in a short form; they do not necessarily correspond to those used on first publication or within successive editions of the *Works*. Secondly, the date of composition is often approximate, and is based on that established by the Twickenham editors. Thirdly, a given item sometimes appeared more or less simultaneously in different formats; where no other basis for priority is clear, I have arbitrarily chosen one printing to enter here, normally the one with the earlier Griffith number. Fourthly, it is worth recalling that the *Essay on Man* was issued in four instalments between February 1733 and January 1734, quite apart from the Horatian poems appearing in the same period – these will be considered shortly.

Permutations of some or all of these ten poems were printed as 'epistles' in a group throughout the last portion of Pope's life. Where the items to Oxford, Arbuthnot and Addison are present, a common order is 7, 5, 6 (that is, Addison, Oxford, Arbuthnot). Thus Gilliver's small folio *Works*, volume two (Griffith no. 370), published in April 1735, contains a set of 'Epistles' comprising 1, 2, 3, 4, 5, 6. As Bateson reminded us, the canonical order of 1, 2, 3 and 4 was set from the beginning; but we must add that they were at this stage merely the outriders in a longer retinue. In the octavo edition of volume two published in July 1735

---

[7] 'Griffith' numbers refer to R. H. Griffith, *Alexander Pope: A Bibliography*, one volume in two parts (Austin, Tex., 1922–7), citing the item number of each publication.

(Griffith no. 388), we have 'Ethic Epistles. The Second Book', containing the canonical four, split off from 'Epistles. The Third Book', containing 5, 7, 8, 9, 10 and 6.[8] By 1739 in the Dodsley–Cooper edition of the *Works*, the list has been reduced to items 1 to 7, and these 'Epistles to Several Persons' no longer comprise the second book of 'Ethic Epistles'. In other words the epistles have been partially freed of the overall grip of the *Opus Magnum*, by now a dwindling hope on Pope's part. Leranbaum observes that 'After 1735 Pope published no more epistles having a direct connection with his system', but he refused to abandon the scheme as far as his published works went.[9] It was only in 1739 that the project was in effect repudiated with the presumed connection between items 1 and 2 and the second epistle of the *Essay on Man* no longer maintained, since further items which were to have corresponded to other parts of that *Essay* would not be written.[10] I omit from consideration here made-up volumes, such as Griffith no. 514 (1739), which may have been put together simply on the basis of whatever stock a bookseller chanced to have on hand.

We can look forward briefly to Warburton's edition in 1751 (Griffith no. 645). Here volume two is devoted to the 'Moral Essays', including the canonical items 1–4 plus 7. (The half-title reads 'Moral Essays in Four Epistles to Several Persons', despite the fifth item.) Bateson made strenuous objections to the new title but said virtually nothing about the addition of the item to Addison. We might also have forgotten that this grouping of five rather than four ever existed, had not Herbert Davis reprinted the *Poetical Works* in 1966 with a text primarily based on Warburton; he thus preserved the five-part layout. But his actual text for the poems came from the 1744 deathbed edition, so that we have the widely preferred and implicitly Popeian title, 'Epistles to Several Persons', along with the five-item grouping which has been abandoned by every other modern

---

[8] Leranbaum, *Pope's 'Opus Magnum'*, p. 36, points out the omission of the word 'ethic' in the half-title for this latter group, as a sign that the group is 'carefully marked off' – presumably as not belonging to the *Opus Magnum* scheme. She also notes that the quarto and folio editions of the same year do not make any such division, and print 1, 2, 3, 4, 5 and 6 with no break. Leranbaum acknowledges that this is 'anomalous', and indicative of the fact that 'Pope was still very indefinite about the scope of his system', but it may suggest a more radical indecision than her argument allows.

[9] Leranbaum, *Pope's 'Opus Magnum'*, p. 183. The same author takes issue with W. J. Courthope's view that the *Moral Essays* were never properly integrated into the larger design (pp. 128–9); she makes some valid points, but does not perhaps reckon sufficiently with the fact that the clear cut four-poem grouping only established itself after the larger plan had fallen into abeyance.

[10] As late as the 'Advertisement' to the deathbed edition in 1744, Pope was giving a (now retrospective) account of what the masterwork would have looked like, and repeats the statement that 'the four following Epistles [the *Moral Essays*] were detached portions' of the great scheme: 'the *two first* [*Cobham* and *To a Lady*] . . . being the introductory part of this concluding Book' (quoted by Leranbaum, *Pope's 'Opus Magnum'*, p. 178). Leranbaum also has interesting comments on the disappearance of the scheme in the layout of the 1739 volume (p. 139), admitting that the 1735 arrangement may only have been 'a makeshift one'.

edition. Volume four of Warburton's edition contains 'Satires, &c.', where the Horatian items appear. A similar pattern is found in other mid-century editions. It should be remarked that Bateson had noted the importance of the deathbed edition of *Four Ethic Epistles*, supposedly prepared by Pope and Warburton in 1744 but not published, and eventually brought out by Knapton in 1748 (Griffith no. 591). But Bateson much preferred the title 'Epistles to Several Persons', employed by Pope in the *Works* of 1739, 1740 and 1743, and in his depreciation of Warburton's influence he tended to use the deathbed edition selectively in his own editorial decisions.[11]

What does this potted history reveal? It is clear that the group of epistles was a fluctuating entity. It had no assured title, and its individual components likewise sometimes bore titles different from those they had formerly carried. Its size went up and down, and the order of items varied. The modern canonical grouping never appeared as a separate set prior to the deathbed edition. The most favoured modern title for the whole group did not appear until 1739, and the most durable label, that of Warburton, only made its appearance in 1751. For some time an attempt was made to relate the group to the larger design of the *Opus Magnum*, and to underline a special relationship between some of the individual items and other parts of that scheme, notably the *Essay on Man*. But even whilst this was going on, as in the 1735 octavo, another group of 'Epistles' was also in place, which included a work (the *Epistle to Arbuthnot*) we take to belong, if anywhere, to quite another grouping. Finally, and most striking, we see that this extended group of 'other' epistles, tied or not into the larger grouping which was given this title, included poetry written long before and in very different circumstances. The label equally covers the familiar 'Moral Essays' of the 1730s, all of which had appeared between 1731 and 1735, and items such as the 'Verses Occasioned by Mr Addison's Treatise on Medals', which had come out in Addison's *Works* in 1721, or the poem to the Earl of Oxford, which had come out in Pope's edition of Parnell's *Poems on Several Occasions* in 1721. The earliest item goes back to around 1710, and reached the world in a collection bearing Griffith's item number 6 – almost like the Köchel number for one of Mozart's infant compositions.

These non-canonical 'epistles' have very little to do with the later foursome which became known as the *Moral Essays* – or at least, with those latter poems in the way we customarily approach them today. The non-canonicals are much more disparate; they include, as we have seen, the *Epistle to Arbuthnot*, which would soon be shifted to what evidently seems to most people a better home within the Horatian group. Most of the others go back many years, and appeared as occasional verse on their début. Crucially, they are generally much shorter

---

[11] See *TE*, III.ii, ix–xx: compare Leranbaum, *Pope's 'Opus Magnum'*, pp. 177–81.

than the canonical items. They have no broad moral subject such as the use of riches. They had never had anything to do with the *Opus Magnum*, which was still hanging on as the putative basis of some of these groupings. They seem not to belong in this category at all, by modern lights. But that is because we have inherited a special set of preconceptions about the shape of Pope's *œuvre*. We imagine that the distinction between canonical Burlington and non-canonical Jervas was fixed from the start. We forget that when Pope addressed Burlington in 1731, all he had was a vague plan relating to the much bigger *Opus Magnum* scheme. The four-movement series of *Moral Essays* or *Epistles to Several Persons* (it does not matter for the moment how we identify the collection) had as yet no independent existence. And even when the foursome was in place, in 1735, Pope still did not know that this would be the full production line. We have naturalised the grouping into an inevitable sequence, and we silently delete the Addison item from the run of poems if we are using Warburton, or the Warburton layout as with Herbert Davis. We have, I think, no modern edition in which Burlington precedes Bathurst. An arbitrary arrangement on which Pope belatedly settled (if he ever did – we do not precisely know Warburton's share in the deathbed edition) has come to dominate our sense of this grouping.

Things are not all that different when we turn to the imitations of Horace. Again it is necessary to tabulate the publishing history. Here I omit *Satire II.vi* (Griffith no. 479), appearing in 1738, which is mostly Swift; and *One Thousand Seven Hundred and Forty*, a non-Horatian Horatian poem in the same vein, unpublished till Warton included it in 1797. The odes are also left out of account. This leaves us with the main run of imitations, including for completeness the *Epistle to Arbuthnot* once more together with the two dialogues of *Epilogue*, and also the Donne imitations which tend to hang on to the coat-tails of the versions of Horace. On this occasion items are listed in order of publication. Again there were numerous reprints of individual items in different formats, not taken account of here. Once more the dates of composition are approximate. And again the titles of certain items are different in earlier versions from that with which we are most familiar: Donne's fourth satire originally appeared as *The Impertinent*. Such shifts in nomenclature are broadly relevant to my argument, but they are not the primary matter to which we should give our attention.

It will be a defamiliarising experience to most readers of Pope to scan this list. Virtually all editions of his poetry present the imitations in clearcut groups, based on division between the satires and epistles, with Donne as a separate pairing. The familiar order, using the numbers found in Table 2 above, runs as follows: 5, 1, 3, 10, 9, 8, 7, 13, 4, 6, 2, 11, 12. This involves removal of *Sober Advice* to a later position, although strictly it belongs earlier, between 3 and 10, since it is based on Horace's *Satire I.ii*. The only place in which the chronological order of publication is observed is in the volume devoted to these poems in the

Table 2

Title	Date of composition	First publication	Griffith no.
1 Satire II.i	1733	February 1733	288
2 Donne Satire IV	[1713],1733	1733	317
3 Satire II.ii	1733	July 1734	341
4 Sober Advice from Horace	1734	December 1734	347
5 Epistle to Arbuthnot	1731–4	January 1735	352
6 Donne Satire II	[1713],1733	April 1735	370
7 Epistle II.ii	1736	April 1737	447
8 Epistle II.i	1736	May 1737	458
9 Epistle I.vi	1737	January 1738	476
10 Epistle I.i	1737	March 1738	480
11 Epilogue Dialogue I	1738	May 1738	484
12 Epilogue Dialogue II	1738	July 1738	494
13 Epistle I.vii	1738	?May 1739	507

Twickenham edition, edited by John Butt, although here the final four items are printed in the order 13, 10, 11, 12, which implies an earlier date for publication of item 13 (in the octavo *Works*, Griffith no. 507) than the facts seem to warrant. And of course the Twickenham volume does not interlard the sequence with other poems appearing in the same period of time. The one-volume Twickenham version of the entire *œuvre*, also edited by Butt (1963), reverts to the sequence I have given above as 'the familiar order'. Once more, then, the Horatian poems are sealed into a category of their own, and arranged according to an arbitrary scheme which bears no relation to the circumstances in which they originally appeared.

It is instructive to contemplate the evolution of this category. The Horatian poems were slower to reach a critical mass; in the *Works* of 1735 there are only two satires, items 1 and 3, plus the two Donne items, and even when the epistles started to appear they were not immediately grouped with the satires. Indeed, it was not until the *Works*, volume two, part 2 (1740), Griffith no. 524, that the two genres were so much as brought together in a single volume. In the early days, as we have seen, the *Epistle to Arbuthnot* belonged in a quite different bracket, that is with the poems we know as the *Moral Essays*. The poem was only moved to the head of the Horatian group, with a subtitle, 'being a Prologue to the Satires', when Warburton made his new layout in 1751. In fact it was probably Warburton's organisation of the poems which underlies the 'familiar order', though we have long abandoned one of his inclusions, a version of Donne's third satire, written probably by Parnell, which was placed between items 7 and 6 – Warburton naturally omitted the scabrous item *Sober Advice*, which was excluded as late as the Elwin and Courthope edition in the late nineteenth century. (*Sober Advice* had however entered the collected works in 1738 (Griffith no. 507), and remained there in Pope's lifetime. It was also included in the *Supplement to Mr. Pope's Works*, published by Mary Cooper in 1757.)

Most of Warburton's editorial decisions have been controversial. There has been surprisingly little discussion of his procedures here: for example, Butt does not comment on the moving or retitling of the *Epistle to Arbuthnot*. Even some of those who may regard this as an impertinence on the editor's part seem to have become used to the *placing* of the poem, that is (regardless of whether it can properly be regarded as a 'prologue' to the group) its mere inclusion among the imitations. Readers of Pope naturally look for the *Epistle* in the Horatian sequence, not in the category allotted to the *Moral Essays*, and certainly not in a group embracing the epistles to Jervas or the Blount sisters. This might well have surprised Pope. The Horatian category was only beginning to take shape in the very last years of his life, and *Arbuthnot* was not within that category.

The way in which the series came into being is a matter of solid record. Pope's remarks to Spence have often been quoted, but they need to be repeated here if we are to understand the full pattern of developing events. This is what Pope told Joseph Spence in 1744:

Lord Bolingbroke came to see me, happened to take up a Horace that lay on the table, and in turning it over dipped on the First Satire of the Second book. He observed how well that would hit my case, if I were to imitate it in English. After he was gone, I read it over, translated it in a morning or two, and sent it to press in a week or a fortnight after. And this was the occasion of my imitating some other of the Satires and Epistles afterwards.[12]

This was in January 1733, when Pope was confined to his room at Lord Oxford's house with a fever. The opportunistic nature of the undertaking is self-evident; one is tempted to insert a tacit adverb '[eventually]' between Pope's words in the last sentence, 'this was . . . the occasion.' The poem was published about 15 February, so no time was wasted as regards the particular imitation Bolingbroke had drawn to Pope's attention. The poet could not then have known that the series would finally run to something like ten to fifteen items, depending on exactly which items are included in the tally. There is no hint in the exchange, as reported by Spence, that either Pope or Bolingbroke saw the opportunity for an extended set of Horatian poems. Nor is there any indication at this early stage that versions of Donne, which Pope had originally essayed some twenty years back, might be incorporated into the scheme. There really was not a scheme at all at this point. The integrity of the design owes much to *post facto* manipulation: the grouping by satires and epistles, the suppression of chronological ordering,

---

[12] *Imitations of Horace*, edited by J. Butt, Twickenham Edition, vol. IV, second edition (London, 1953), p. xiii: see also the source in Joseph Spence, *Observations, Anecdotes, and Characters of Books and Men*, edited by J. M. Osborn (Oxford, 1966), I, 143. Butt's edition is cited as '*TE*, IV'.

the addition of the epilogue and (posthumously) the creation of a prologue by diverting the *Epistle to Arbuthnot* from its original position in the *Works*. It should be noted here that the first dialogue of what we know as the 'epilogue' came out as *One Thousand Seven Hundred and Thirty Eight; A Dialogue Something Like Horace*, on its original appearance in May 1738. The second dialogue, two months later, had the same main title as its predecessor. It was only in the *Works* (1740), Griffith no. 524, that the idea of an 'epilogue' was suddenly plucked from the air. We might perhaps have a better sense of the immediacy of these two dialogues if their original title was restored – but that would be to undo two hundred and fifty years of gradually accumulating expectations and presuppositions.

It is almost equally curious that we should so readily have accepted the Donne poems as 'imitations' in exactly the same sense as those of Horace, although in the one case there is an entire transposition of language and in the other merely a form of modernisation from a not-very-remote English. As remarked, Pope had first attempted to update Donne's satires in 1713, at a time when his Scriblerian colleague Swift was busy on versions of Horace. By 1735 Pope was confident enough to print his text of the second Donne satire, on its very first appearance, in a small group including the two Horatian satires and the fourth satire by Donne. He also prepared an introduction to this group (which was still bereft of the epistles) which aligned the two sets of imitations in a single coherent plan. We have been content to take Pope's word for it ever since. Every augmentation to the original small group has served to make the category more coherent and natural in appearance, that is in a manner to reify the notion of 'imitations' collectively.

I have just mentioned the 'Advertisement' which Pope set at the head of the relevant section in the *Works* of 1735, a form of words he retained in subsequent editions (as did Warburton). It will be worth inspecting the opening of this statement:

The Occasion of publishing these *Imitations* was the Clamour raised on some of my *Epistles*. An Answer from *Horace* was both more full, and of more Dignity, than any I could have made in my own person; and the Example of much greater Freedom in so eminent a Divine as Dr *Donne*, seem'd a proof with what Indignation and Contempt a Christian may treat Vice or Folly, in ever so low, or ever so high, a Station.[13]

This must originally have been intended as a localised defence against threats prompted by the early satires alone. But it survived, like much else, when the group was swelled by the more numerous epistles, not to mention the artificial addenda of prologue and epilogue. Once more, our sense of these things has been

---

[13] *TE*, IV, 3.

Pat Rogers

clouded by our failure to appreciate the situation as it was in 1735, as opposed to 1740 or 1751.

In the preceding discussion, we have looked separately at the group of poems corresponding to the modern 'moral essays' and at those we regard as the 'imitations of Horace'. In both cases we found that the group did not begin as a coherent category of its own; the former group evolved out of Pope's plan for the *Opus Magnum*, and only took its present form very gradually, whilst the second accumulated by stages towards the form in which we know it today. In both cases it is apparent that the chronological order of composition and publication was quickly effaced in the new arrangements which are found in the works, and it is these later arrangements which constitute the poems and the groups for us today. As a result, we may attribute to both groups a solidity and distinctiveness which owe more to editorial sleight of hand than to Pope's original creative urges. However, there is a larger issue still to consider, and this hinges on the interrelation of these two apparently separate 'groups'. Imaginatively, they may be cut more from the same cloth than our habitual reading, based as it is on the editorial reordering, easily allows us to see.

A good way to focus the issues is to look back at something Miriam Leranbaum says in her study of the *Opus Magnum*. She was, of course, writing from the specific angle implied by that last phrase, and this may have coloured her judgement; but her views still deserve the closest consideration. Her study up to this point has considered the original conception of the masterwork, and has analysed in detail the eight epistles which had actually emerged by 1735 – the only parts of the scheme ever to achieve any finality in print. These were of course the four parts of the *Essay on Man* and the four 'ethic epistles', or *Moral Essays*. She continues:

In the process of composing these, Pope had begun another, related to the project, the 'Imitations of Horace'. Although he speaks of these rarely in his letters, when he does so he consistently distinguishes them from those epistles that are within his 'system'. In accordance with Pope's own division of these poems into two distinct categories, there are a number of observable differences between the two. Most conspicuously, the poems that were eventually collected and published as the 'Imitations of Horace' almost all have specific Horatian antecedents, adversaries who play an active role in the lively dialogue form, a more obvious focus upon the contemporary political or literary scene, and a much more central concern with the role of the poet and a clear sense of the poet in *propria persona*. One may with ease make exceptions of individual poems or parts of poems in either category for which this group of distinctions does not hold true, and one can certainly find many of the serious philosophical and moral concerns, themes, and allusions we have studied in preceding chapters [of Leranbaum's book] also present in the 'Imitations', but the general distinction is, I hope, both useful and valid. It derives in part from the fact that many of Pope's 'Imitations' are of Horace's satires rather than his

86

epistles, and modern students of Horace distinguish Horace's own epistles from his satires in a way that parallels this distinction between Pope's epistles within the system and the Horatian poems he was writing concurrently.[14]

The last argument may be taken briefly at the outset. Its validity is impaired to some degree by the fact that the items based on Horace's satires all came early in the sequence, that is at the same time when the *Opus Magnum* was still a live option. It is from 1736 onwards, that is after the gradual breakdown of the master-plan, that Pope turns to rendering the epistles of Horace. In other words, Pope began to write epistles 'outside the system' only after he stopped writing what Leranbaum calls 'epistles within the system'. We might fairly conclude that the impulse to concentrate on Horatian epistles has something to do with the slow abandonment of the *Opus Magnum*. Put speculatively, this might mean that, though the Horatian poems came into being after the scheme was planned, and form no part of its intellectual design, Pope's poetic practice was such that what we might term masterwork plasma continued to help compose the fabric of his work in the later 1730s.

This is to delay the larger issue, however. How 'valid' is the 'general distinction' Leranbaum makes? To answer that question we need to look with some care at the two groups of poems, and naturally Leranbaum was not bent on that exercise – this is the only section of her book where the imitations of Horace receive any sort of frontal attention. A specialised monograph will necessarily abstract its key material from the general mass of surrounding materials. The problem here is that this is to re-enact a manoeuvre we perform unconsciously all the time. We have grown up reading Pope within the established categories, and there is at present no easy way of reintegrating our response to the poetry of the 1730s. It is not just an aberration on the part of the Twickenham editors, or other modern scholars such as Herbert Davis and Aubrey Williams. We get exactly the same result if we go back to Elwin and Courthope, or even to Bowles, Warton, Warburton – indeed, to Pope himself. There has never been a major edition (if one at all) which commingled the poems of this phase in the way that they appeared, disparate, initially homeless, unarranged. Only by an effort of will can we remember that the *Epistle to Arbuthnot* is a floater which has undergone a fundamental change in its generic loyalties, or that there were five moral essays for a long time, or that a few poems predate the *Essay on Man* whilst the majority postdate it, or that the title 'Epistles to Several Persons' favoured by Bateson once included a poem written before the Hanoverian accession.

---

[14] Leranbaum, *Pope's 'Opus Magnum'*, pp. 129–30. In fact, of course, only three of Pope's imitations derive from satires by Horace (items 1, 3 and 4 in Table 2 above); the greater number relate to epistles by Horace, and the division between the two categories is sharper in the arrangement of the *Works* than it might have been to contemporaries encountering the separate poems for the first time as they appeared.

The vital statement in Pope's advertisement is the one at the outset: 'The Occasion of publishing these *Imitations* was the Clamour raised on some of my *Epistles*.' This remark was originally made in application to the two first versions of Horace and the two versions of Donne, that is items 1, 2, 3 and 6 in Table 2. In other words, these were response by way of *satires* to a clamour raised by *epistles*. But Pope's counter-offensive was launched before the four ethic epistles had been completed. The retort through Horace and, to a slightly lesser extent, through Donne began before the epistles to Cobham and to Martha Blount had been written. Once more, this is a case where printing the entire series of poems in chronological order would reveal the nature of Pope's intentions more clearly than is possible if we read the poems in their usual arrangement.

We can be more particular still, however. The response was spearheaded by the imitations of Horace *Satire II.i*, published on 15 February 1733. At its heart this poem deals with the fallout from the two *Moral Essays* already published. (Of course this last grouping did not exist in that form.) In other words, the series of Horatian items was initiated by matters relating to the 'other' series, that of the ethic epistles. As we have just seen, Pope can have had no idea at this stage that other answers from Horace would be necessary or possible. It was at the start no more than an *ad hoc* gesture, occasioned by the public reception of the *Epistle to Bathurst* in particular. The satire turns out to be dense with allusion to the epistles which had already been written, as well as to the material of later satires *and* epistles. This suggests that we should not be too preoccupied by the generic distinction. In one way the poet moved over the 1730s from 'Popeian' familiar epistles to 'Horatian' satires and epistles, and again the distinction is blurred when we take account of the considerable overlap in theme and material. It can be argued that a kind of *Stiltrennung* operates, by which the satires demand a more urgent and colloquial use of language – that view might be supported by the very first of the Horatian sequence, but it tends to break down with the comparatively decorous *Satire II.ii* and the racy immediacy of *Epistle II.ii*.

The opening poem in the series, addressed to William Fortescue, alludes directly to the controversies aroused by the two *Moral Essays* which had so far appeared. Its theme, indeed, is the possibilities of free speech in satire:

> There are (I scarce can think it, but am told)
> There are to whom my Satires seem too bold,
> Scarce to wise *Peter* complaisant enough,
> And something said of *Chartres* much too rough.
>
> (lines 1–4)[15]

Now Pope could easily have been thinking of *The Dunciad* in writing of his satire as 'too bold'; but despite the huge public upheaval his mock-epic had caused, that

---

[15] The text follows that of *TE*, IV, 5. Other citations are from this edition.

work is never really in evidence here. The poem addresses the matter of the emerging series of familiar epistles, rather. This is indicated by the mention right at the start, not of prominent dunces, but of Peter Walter and Francis Charteris; the next name to enter the text in 6, is 'Lord *Fanny*', that is John Baron Hervey. Pope is referring back directly to passages such as *Bathurst*, line 125, for Walter, and *Bathurst*, line 20, for Charteris.[16] The names of these two primary villains are combined again in the poem to Fortescue, line 89: and of course both men were to figure repeatedly in work of every description through the 1730s. Walter, for example, would crop up in combination with the swindler John Ward in *Epistle 11.i*, line 197; here Pope was harking back to another figure pilloried in *Bathurst*, line 20: 'To Ward, to Waters, Chartres, and the Devil.' Equally, as will appear, the Fortescue poem alludes to men like Denis Bond, who had been specified in a note to *Bathurst* line 102 as underlying the character of Harpax. The unidentified 'Shylock' from *Bathurst*, line 96, is recalled by the friend in the Fortescue poem, line 103. There are other echoes of names, real or generic.

Pope's friendly interlocutor makes some of his most explicit references to the earlier poems in the middle of the imitation:

> *F.* Better be *Cibber*, I'll maintain it still,
> Than ridicule all *Taste*, blaspheme *Quadrille*,
> Abuse the City's best good Men in Metre,
> And laugh at Peers that put their Trust in *Peter*.
> . . . A hundred smart in *Timon* and in *Balaam*:
> The fewer still you name, you wound the more;
> *Bond* is but one, but *Harpax* is a score.
>
> (lines 37–40, 42–4)

The opening line here looks forward to the satire on Cibber as laureate in the *Epistle to Augustus* and the revised *Dunciad*. But then we are back in the *Moral Essays*: Pope had deigned to ridicule the entire world of taste in *Burlington*, but he had then gone actually to 'blaspheme' quadrille in *Bathurst*, line 64. The last-named work is little short of a sustained onslaught on the City, involving its allegedly 'good Men' in the process, with John Blunt at their head. Peter Walter we have already dealt with. Then Pope brings up one of the noisiest of all the controversies his poetry had provoked, that is the scandal set up by his portrayal of 'Timon' in *Burlington*, lines 99–168. A corresponding type-figure in *Bathurst*, lines 339–402, Sir Balaam, had evoked less debate – indeed the arguments over his real-life model (if any) have been more vigorous in the years after Pope's death. Bond has already been mentioned; the Harpax lines in *Bathurst*, lines 93–4, have eluded any firm identification, though the 'robber' in question has

[16] For Walter, Charteris, Crook and other villains, see Howard Erskine-Hill, *The Social Milieu of Alexander Pope* (New Haven, 1975).

qualities which align him with named individuals such as Walter, Crook, Charteris and Bond.

These are some of the echoes. But there are also pre-echoes and foreshadowings. The famous lines on Lady Mary Wortley Montagu in the Fortescue poem, lines 83–4, 'From furious *Sappho* scarce a milder fate, / P--x'd by her Love, or libell'd by her Hate', prefigure *Epistle to a Lady*, lines 24–6 ('Sappho at her toilet's greazy task . . .') as well as *Epilogue to the Satires I*. 15 ('In *Sappho* touch the *Failing of the Sex*'). Equally there are links with the still unpublished *Epistle to Arbuthnot*. The Fortescue poem has this:

> Whether the darken'd Room to muse invite,
> Or whiten'd Wall provoke the Skew'r to write,
> In Durance, Exile, Bedlam, or the Mint,
> Like *Lee* or *Budgell*, I will Rhyme and Print.
>
> (lines 97–100)

This is comically transposed in the picture of obsessive writers in *Arbuthnot*, with the mention of one who 'lock'd from Ink and Paper, scrawls / With desp'rate Charcoal round his darken'd walls' (lines 19–20). Even closer is the hint of *Arbuthnot*, lines 155–6, 'If want provok'd, or madness made them print, / I wag'd no war with *Bedlam* or the *Mint*'. Here we have identical rhyme-words and precisely the same phrase in the same metrical position. Finally it is worth noting the glimpse into the world of *Arbuthnot* in the Fortescue poem at lines 123–4: 'Know, all the distant Din that World can keep / Rolls o'er my *Grotto*, and but sooths my Sleep.'

Naturally this does not exhaust the list of parallels and interconnections which could be drawn out: the archetypal reference to Charteris in *Bathurst*, with its long note citing the epitaph on this rogue which Arbuthnot had composed, is but the herald of numerous other damaging references, in the Fortescue poem, the *Epistle to a Lady*, and the second *Epilogue to the Satires*.[17] But enough ought to have been said to make the point. A whole congeries of satiric material had been set up in *Bathurst* and *Burlington*. The imitation addressed to Fortescue is the first and most explicit passage of recollection, but in truth the entire series of satiric poems in the 1730s draws on that body of material. In its turn the Fortescue item does more than look back in the earlier epistles, though that is its chief mode of operation; it also supplies hints for later poems, either Popeian or Horatian epistles. Some of the echoes are obvious enough, and will have been noted by attentive students of Pope's work; what we are *not* usually alive to is the sequence of events within the poetry. Who, offhand, can reconstruct the pattern

---

[17] Leranbaum, *Pope's 'Opus Magnum'*, pp. 34–5, lists some of the connections between the *Moral Essays* and the *Essay on Man*, as signalised by Pope's own notes – a parallel use of interfusion between the poems, but not centrally germane to my argument here.

of allusions to Lady Mary? We forget which references came first, and which were provoked by a counter-blow from Pope's adversary. Subliminally we probably make the assumption that the *Epistle to a Lady*, for instance, is earlier than the Fortescue satire, because in collections of Pope we nearly always get them in that order. The 'arranged' text supplies a kind of template for our critical judgments, one might say a programme for reading Pope.

It would be wearisome to go through all the separate items in the sequence and show their interdependence. A few brief summaries of the position may suffice. Thus, *Satire 11.ii* looks back to the peroration of *Burlington* at line 120, 'Make Keys, build Bridges, or repair White-hall': its mention of Lord Fanny at line 101 anticipates allusions in several places, including Donne *Satire IV*. That last-named poem echoes *Bathurst* on the Charitable Corporation at line 142, and looks forward to *Arbuthnot* at line 61. Donne *Satire II* has another barb directed at Peter Walter (line 66). *Epistle I. VI* brings up Timon once again at line 85. *Epistle II.i* picks up 'slashing Bentley' (line 104) from *Arbuthnot*, line 164. Most obviously, the two dialogues of *Epilogue to the Satires* perform a resumptive function. They naturally recall details from the Horatian poems, at whose close they invariably stand in editions of Pope. There are even a few hints of *The Dunciad* this time (for example, 1.66). But something we might easily overlook is the fact that both dialogues also revert to the primary material that derived originally from *Bathurst*, e.g. the passage listing Ward, Japhet Crook, Bond and Walter at lines 119–21 – all this line of attack is ultimately dependent on positions set up in *Bathurst*. Blunt (line 14) is another point of reference established in the dialectic of the ethic epistle. In the second dialogue, we are given a recollection of the Man of Ross, again from *Bathurst* (line 250). In short, the *Epilogue* does indeed serve as a summation of 'the satires', but this term must be extended to include the *Moral Essays* along with the *Imitations of Horace*. In our reading, we forget that the two dialogues have no direct basis in Horace. They are always annexed to the Horatian group, and that is where they have rooted themselves in our mind. The habitual arrangement conceals from us the fact that they ought to be read into the sequence of *Moral Essays*, too.[18]

This leaves the question of the placing of *Arbuthnot*. In view of the many

---

[18] I have left out separate printings of the Horatian imitations as a group outside the *Works*, since these did not have the same lasting influence. It may, however, be worth adding that *Epistles from Horace* (1738) and *Poems and Imitations of Horace* ('1738', for 1739), offer quite new combinations and arrangements. For the first, which despite its title includes one of the odes, we find that the items included were set out in 'precisely the reverse order' to that in which they had first been published (see Foxon, *Pope and the ... Book Trade*, p. 141). The second of these volumes adds the dialogues still known as *One Thousand Seven Hundred and Thirty Eight*, subsequently rechristened the *Epilogue to the Satires*. Note that in this edition there were no 'satires' in the strict generic sense, merely four epistles and an ode.

overlaps we have noted (and others that have not been noted, such as the renewed engagement with Timon's villa and Cannons at lines 299–300), it will not be a surprising conclusion if I say that the poem does not belong organically in the Horatian group. Of course, mere cross-references cannot settle a question of generic loyalty; but when we consider other factors, the case against retaining its transferred position grows stronger. It is after all an 'epistle' to a friend, without a Horatian model, just like the four *Moral Essays*. It enlists the same conventions of the familiar epistle, and incorporates along with its obloquy of contemporary life some tributes to admired friends. It is true that there are certain differences; the culminating lines of compliment to Arbuthnot are brief, partly because Pope himself has arrogated some of the rhetorical space usually reserved for the addressee, and partly perhaps because Arbuthnot was on the brink of death. But these differences do not align *Arbuthnot* with the Horatian poems in any particular way. It may be relevant that the work was under way earlier than any of the imitations, indeed at the same period as the first *Moral Essays*: we are now aware that it derived from an abortive poem addressed to William Cleland, planned around 1732. And, as is well known, it incorporates an unusual amount of earlier snatches of writing, such as the Atticus portrait, perhaps going back in part as far as 1715.[19] One could understand why Pope's initial impulse was to allot it the same site in his *œuvre* as that occupied by the other 'familiar' epistles. A last consideration is that the poem has nothing about it which especially merits the title of a prologue. (It is something of a surprise that Bateson, who dislikes most things Warburton did, fails to draws attention to this fact.) It does not announce general themes, certainly not to the extent that *Bathurst* set the agenda for the poems of the 1730s. It does in some measure characterise satire and the satirist, but in more autobiographical terms than a generally applicable overview would perform this function. It only joined the Horatian group, one suspects, for two reasons. First, symmetry demanded a balance to the epilogue which had been created. Second, Pope had come to feel that the earlier epistles to friends no longer sat easily with his mature foursome of epistles, which were to be marked off as 'ethic epistles' and posthumously as 'moral essays'. Such labels would never really have fitted the short poems addressed to Martha and Teresa Blount or Jervas. Once the group had been destabilised and broken up, *Arbuthnot* too needed to find another home within the *Works*. Warburton's decision to move it to the head of the imitations was at least a bold step, with a show of logic to it. But almost one quarter of a millennium has now passed, and we have given our passive assent too long.

---

[19] See Maynard Mack, *The Last and Greatest Art: Some Unpublished Manuscripts of Alexander Pope* (Newark, 1984), pp. 410–54.

The evidence reviewed here suggests that the familiar arrangement of Pope's works may distort the shape of his poetic career. It imposes artificial groups and occludes links. There is a simple and radical means of solving some of these problems; it does not solve them all, but no means is likely to achieve that. We shall, then, get the clearest sense of Pope's development in the 1730s if we read the poems in more or less strict chronological order. This will allow the reader to see the intimate commerce between the two series of epistles and imitations, and will bring together topical like with like, as with the controversy over the Charitable Corporation. It permits the Horatian poems to be read as an evolving and almost organic growth, rather than within a set of arbitrary boxes prescribed by Horace's works. It will enable us to view Pope's output between *The Dunciad Variorum* and the *New Dunciad* as a sustained and richly interconnected body of satire, flexibly responsible to the tide of external events.

One has to say 'more or less strict chronological order', since a very minor adjustment is needed in the case of the *Essay on Man* – it is a further advantage of the revised layout that we can now see precisely where this item belongs. The fourth epistle of the *Essay* did not appear until 24 January 1736, eight days after the *Epistle to Cobham*. But unlike the other works we have been considering, the *Essay* was planned from the start as a cohesive four-part composition. It can therefore be inserted into the sequence as a unit prior to *Cobham* and Donne *Satire IV*. The result will be a mixed series of poems, starting with *Burlington* and ending with *Epistle I.vii*. Adopting the numerical scheme of Tables 1 and 2 (1.1 = *Cobham*, etc.), we arrive at the following arrangement: 1.4; 1.3; 2.1; *Essay on Man* I–IV; 2.2; 1.1; 2.3; 2.4; 2.5 (= 1.6); 1.2; 2.6; 2.7; 2.8; 2.9; 2.10; 2.11; 2.12; 2.13 (or if it is desired to end with the *Epilogue*, 2.13; 2.11; 2.12). It can be seen straight away how Burlington and Bathurst are brought to the front, how the Fortescue poem is drawn right up against them, and how *Arbuthnot* is put back into the middle of things. (The poems written earlier, 1.5 and 1.7–10, are omitted.)

Some might argue that this is to lose a possible piece of careful aesthetic placing on Pope's part, when he reordered the *Moral Essays*. But I agree with Bateson that 'the order in which these poems was printed' was at least *primarily* determined by the requirements of the *Opus Magnum*. Bateson went on, with a sound instinct, to remark that 'the fact is a striking example of the way the *Essay on Man* has cast its distracting shadow over what are essentially four Horatian satires' – but he did not develop this line of thought.[20]

It will be a jolting experience for many readers of Pope to view the prospect of

---

[20] *TE*, III.ii, xx.

such a destabilisation of the familiar pattern. I can only point to the evidence assembled, and stress once more that the patterning was very largely retrospective.[21] Pope's satire has lost some of its immediacy today because of its dense topical reference, and we may need to use what look at first sight like desperate remedies if we are to recapture the freshness of his vision. The best way to do that, in my submission, is to encounter the poems in the order and in the collocations of their original appearance. If so, we shall no longer be the slaves to a generic tyranny. We shall be able to jettison distinctions which are often without a difference, and come face to face with the poems in their raw state, unmediated by subsequent editorialising, undistracted by the *Opus Magnum*, and unfiltered by abstract schemes or ulterior purposes.

The arrangements which poets choose to make of their own works naturally hold a measure of authority. Even the categories into which Wordsworth divided his collected verse, such as 'Moods of My Own Mind', have a genuine interest, although sometimes a quaint one. As Stephen Gill observes, Wordsworth 'was determined to control the image of his own intellectual development that emerged from the poetry.'[22] In the case of Pope this management of an image was even more marked, and sometimes we may need to resist the poet to gain our fullest sense of the poetry.

[21] Fraistat, *The Poem and the Book*, p. 17, suggests that 'English poets as diverse as Spenser, Jonson, Milton, Pope, and Byron were all adept at using the poetic volume as a form of self-fashioning and self-advertisement', but only Carretta's essay, mentioned in note 2, above, has really documented this claim for Pope. What is at stake is not chiefly self-fashioning as such, but – so far as the poetry of the 1730s is concerned – a sustained attempt to direct the manner in which the poems should be read.

[22] Stephen Gill, *William Wordsworth: A Life* (Oxford, 1990), p. 405. See also other passages in Gill which illuminate Wordsworth's care to present a particular view of his poetic career (e.g. pp. 258, 367, 415).

PART TWO

The self presented and revised

5

Presenting jeopardy: language, authority and the voice of Smart in *Jubilate Agno*

TOM KEYMER

To write of one Fellow of Pembroke in honour of another is apt enough. Perhaps Smart's memory is less prominent in the College than that of his contemporary Thomas Gray; possibly he has not been forgiven for his jest that Gray *'walks* as if he had fouled his small-clothes, and looks as if he *smelt* it'.[1] Yet there is little doubt of the formative influence of Smart's studies there on his growth as a poet, even if this influence is oddly shown. Contesting allegations 'that the ideas in [*Jubilate Agno*] . . . are the product of Smart's period of insanity', A. D. Hope has argued that 'in fact they probably go back to Smart's residence in Cambridge as a student and later as a fellow of Pembroke Hall'.[2] How the effects of insanity could so easily be confused with those of a Cambridge education is not explained by Hope; probably there is no clue in one of *Jubilate Agno*'s more blatantly satirical combinations of versicle and response: 'Let Ithream rejoice with the great Owl, who understandeth that which he professes. | *For I pray God for the professors of the University of Cambridge to attend and to amend.*'[3]

Jubilate Agno will seem a perverse choice, however, for an essay about the presentation to the reader of the poetic text, and of the poet's voice within it. For there is no knowing that Smart ever intended the work for any eyes other than his own – apart, of course, from '*the eyes of the Lord*' (B131). It is true that *Jubilate Agno* invokes the largest implied (if not actual) audience, a universal community embracing ancient Hebrews, primitive Christians, modern Britons, and all the species of Creation, undivided by time or place. And if (as is often argued) Smart initially envisaged the poem as his opening gambit in a campaign of liturgical reform influenced by the literary principles and values of Robert Lowth's *De sacra poesi Hebraeorum* (1753), it seems fair to assume that at least part of his thinking must have involved the idea of public attention, and even of public performance. 'The Lord magnify the idea of Smart singing hymns on this day in

---

[1] Attributed to Smart in *Facetiae Cantabrigienses* (1825), p. 45; cited by Christopher Devlin, *Poor Kit Smart* (London, 1961), p. 37.

[2] 'The Apocalypse of Christopher Smart', in *Studies in the Eighteenth Century: Papers Presented at the David Nichol Smith Memorial Seminar*, edited by R. F. Brissenden (Canberra, 1968), p. 273.

[3] *Jubilate Agno*, B69. This and all future references (unless otherwise identified) are to Karina Williamson's edition of the poem, *The Poetical Works of Christopher Smart*, vol. I (Oxford, 1980).

the eyes of the whole University of Cambridge' (D148) may be mere self-consolation, but the line combines with Smart's notorious relish for '*loud prayer*' (B225) to support W. H. Bond's view that, though he cannot be proved to have intended printing or public performance and must certainly have relinquished such thoughts long before ending *Jubilate Agno*, Smart first devised the poem in the form of a celebratory public ritual and may even have 'visualized an actual performance of *Jubilate Agno* . . . with himself as the second reader or responder'.[4] Yet the fact remains that the poem never was presented to the public of the poet's own day, either in print or in performance, and Smart cannot have failed to see its unacceptability to an audience unready even for the far more measured and lucid *Song to David* (which for William Mason showed its author 'as mad as ever', and which Smart's own nephew omitted from the collected edition of 1791, regretting the 'melancholy proofs' it bore 'of the recent estrangement of his mind').[5] It was not until 1939 that *Jubilate Agno* reached print, having survived in autograph fragments that represent probably less than half of the original text.[6]

Yet it is this very history of non-publication that gives critical importance to the smallest details of presentation, both in the manuscript to which Smart daily committed the poem during the period of his confinement and in the printed editions in which its surviving parts have more recently been assembled. The poem's fragmentary state is compounded by its opaque language and wayward development to make close knowledge of its appearance on the page vital not only for editors seeking to reconstruct the poem but for anyone seeking to read it. At the most general level, one need only recall how nineteenth-century views of *A Song to David* as divinely deranged scribble thrived on talk of its being 'scratched . . . on the wall of a madhouse by a madman during a lucid interval'[7] to see the significance of *Jubilate Agno*'s manifestly painstaking preparation: its rigorous textual ordering vividly contradicts those views of the poem as mere mad jotting to which its disruption of conventional poetic language and form might otherwise seem to lead. More local signals serve to clarify the poem's alternative modes of development, the relations between its constituent parts, and the intricate patterns of horizontal and vertical association on which the whole depends. An enlarged script picks out the key transitional lines at B123, for example; a

---

[4] *Jubilate Agno*, edited by W. H. Bond (Cambridge, Mass., 1954), pp. 17, 21, 20.

[5] *The Poems of the Late Christopher Smart*, 2 vols. (Reading, 1791), I, xliii n.; William Mason to Thomas Gray (28 June 1763), *The Correspondence of Thomas Gray*, edited by Paget Toynbee and Leonard Whibley, 3 vols. (Oxford, 1935), II, 802.

[6] *Jubilate Agno*, edited by Bond, p. 17. For Bond's fuller account of the manuscript and his conjectures on its original length, see 'Christopher Smart's *Jubilate Agno*', *Harvard Library Bulletin*, 4 (1950), 39–52.

[7] *Athenaeum*, 3095 (19 February 1887), reviewing Browning's *Parleyings*; cited by Sophia B. Blaydes, *Christopher Smart as a Poet of His Time* (The Hague, 1966), p. 25.

prominent catchword at the foot of each page insists on the distinctness as sequences of 'Let' from 'For' lines.

The variable success of editors in registering these textual signals (and it must be said that the ideal edition of *Jubilate Agno* would have to incorporate the manuscript in facsimile) makes a critical scrutiny of the various editions in which the poem has been mediated to a modern audience just as important as detailed knowledge of the fragments from which they begin. Mid-century attitudes were conditioned by the editorial decisions of William Force Stead, whose annotations on the intellectual contexts of *Jubilate Agno* can only have been undone by his fanciful decision to subtitle it *A Song from Bedlam*, and whose failure to detect and represent the antiphonal relations between 'Let' and 'For' lines obscured another important aspect of the poem.[8] The limits thus imposed on early responses are demonstrable: one wonders, for example, what use Britten would have made of this antiphonal structure in his cantata *Rejoice in the Lamb* (1943), had he had access instead to the Bond edition of 1954 in which it was first revealed. Even a general endorsement of Bond's discovery in subsequent scholarship has not resulted, however, in final consensus on the precise direction in which lines should be combined or read. Bond's recognition of the concurrent and parallel relation between 'Let' and 'For' sequences led him to present corresponding passages from each sequence on facing pages; the Oxford edition prints 'Let' and 'For' lines as pairs alternating down the page, thus highlighting horizontal relations but at the same time interrupting (as has recently been complained) the vertical relations equally stressed in the organisation of the manuscript itself.[9]

Editorial presentation is only the start of the problem, however. Still more vexed is the question of how to understand a work so private in its forms of encoding, so recalcitrant in its disclosure of meaning. The cryptic character of the text combined with critical fashion in the period following Bond's edition to encourage ingenious interpretations and totalising readings, often illuminating of aspects of the poem but rarely capacious or flexible enough to explain it fully. Now that openness and discontinuity have come to enjoy the critical prestige once reserved for notions of organic unity, it is perhaps easier to see the violence done by such efforts to a work identified by Smart's habits of daily composition as a flexible process, not a finished artefact; to a work that is fragmentary in the most literal and obvious sense; and to a work explicitly committed to fragmentation and diversity as the nearest possible approach to valid expression. 'Let Observation with extensive View, / Survey Mankind, from *China* to *Peru*', Johnson

---

[8] *Rejoice in the Lamb: A Song from Bedlam*, edited by William Force Stead (London, 1939).
[9] Harriet Guest, *A Form of Sound Words: The Religious Poetry of Christopher Smart* (Oxford, 1989), p. 125 n.

13. Let Elizur rejoice with the Partridge, who is a prisoner of state and is proud of his keepers.

Let Shedeur rejoice with Pyrausta, who dwelleth in a medium of fire, which God hath adapted for him.

Let Shelumiel rejoice with Olor, who is of a goodly savour, and the very look of him harmonizes the mind.

Let Jael rejoice with the Plover, who whistles for his live, and foils the marksmen and their guns.

Let Raguel rejoice with the Cock of Portugal — God send good Angels to the allies of England!

Let Hobab rejoice with Necydalus, who is in Greek of a Grub.

Let Zurishaddai with the Polish Cock rejoice — The Lord restore peace to Europe.

Let Zuar rejoice with the Guinea Hen — The Lord add to his mercies in the WEST!

Let Chesed rejoice with Strepsiceros, whose weapons are the ornaments of his peace.

Let Hagar rejoice with Gnesion, who is the right sort of eagle, and towers the highest.

Let Libni rejoice with the Redshank, who migrates not but is translated to the upper regions.

Let Nahshon rejoice with the Seabreeze, the Lord give the sailors of his Spirit.

Let Helon rejoice with the Woodpecker — the Lord encourage the propagation of trees!

Let Amos rejoice with the Coote ———— prepare to meet thy God, O Israel.

Let Ephah rejoice with Buprestis, the Lord endue us with temperance & humanity, till every cow have her mate!

Let Sarah rejoice with the Redwing, whose harvest is in the frost and snow.

Let Rebekah rejoice with Iynx, who holds his head on one side to deceive the adversary.

Let Shuah rejoice with Boa, which is the vocal serpent.

Let Ehud rejoice with Onocrotalus, whose braying is for the glory of God because he makes the best musick in his power.

Let Shamgar rejoice with Otis, who looks about him for the glory of God, & sees the horizon completest at once.

Let Bohan rejoice with the Scythian Stag — he is beef and breeches against want & nakedness.

Let Achsah rejoice with the Pigeon who is an antidote to malignity and will carry a letter.

Let Tohu rejoice with the Grouse — the Lord further the cultivating of heaths & the peopling of deserts.

Let Hillel rejoice with Ammodytes, whose colour is deceitful and he plots against the pilgrim's feet.

Let Eli rejoice with Leucon — he is an honest fellow, which is a rarity.

Let Jemuel rejoice with Charadrius, who is from the HEIGHTS the sight of him is good for the jaundice.

Let Pharaoh rejoice with Anataria, whom God permits to prey upon the ducks to check their increase.

Let Lotan rejoice with Sauterelle. Blessed be the name of the Lord from the Lote-tree to the Sutlers.

Let Fishon rejoice with the Landrail, God give his race to the society for preserving the game.

Let Hushim rejoice with the King's Fisher, who is of royal beauty, tho' plebeian size.

Let Machir rejoice with Convolvulus from him to the ring of Solomon, which is the gift of God to the sight of God.

Let Shad bless with Eleos, the nightly Memorialist ΕΛΕΟΣ ΟΡ ΚΥΡΙΕ

Let Japhim rejoice with the Bittern blessed be the name of Jesus for Denver sluice, Ruston, & the draining of the fens.

Let Ohad rejoice with Byturus who eateth the vine and is a minister of temperance.

Let Zohar rejoice with Cychramus who cometh with the quails on a particular affair.

Let Serah the daughter of Asher, rejoice with Cinx, who makes his cabin in the Halcyon's hold.

Let Magdiel rejoice with Ascarides, which is the life of the bowels — the worm hath a part in our frame.

Let Becher rejoice with Oscen who terrifies the wicked as trumpet and alarm the coward.

Let Shaul rejoice with Circus, who hath clumsy legs, but he can wheel it the better with his wings.

Let Harnal rejoice with the Crystal, who is pure and translucent.

Let Ziphion rejoice with the Tit-Lark who is a groundling, but he raises the spirits.

Let Mibzar rejoice with the Cadess, as is there number, so are their names, blessed be the Lord Jesus for them all.

Let Jubal rejoice with Cecilia, the woman and the slow-worm praise the name of the Lord.

Let Arodi rejoice with the Royston Crow, there is a society of them at Trumpington & Cambridge.

Let Areli rejoice with the Criel, who is a dwarf that towereth above others.

Let Shuvah rejoice with Physeteres, whose weapons of defence keep them innocent.

Let Shimron rejoice with the Kite, who is of more value than many sparrows.

Let Sered rejoice with the Wittal. a silly bird is wise unto his own preservation.

Let Elon rejoice with Attelabus, who is the Locust without wings.

Let Jahleel rejoice with the Woodcock, who liveth upon suction and is pure from his diet.

Let Shuni rejoice with the Gull, who is happy in not being good for food.

Let Ezbon rejoice with Musimon, who is from the ram and the she-goat.

Let Barkos rejoice with the Black Eagle, which is the least of his species and the best-natured.

Let Bedan rejoice with Ossifrage — the bird of prey and the man of prayer.

Let Naomi rejoice with Pseudosphece, who is between a wasp and a hornet.

Let Ruth rejoice with the Tumbler — it is a pleasant thing to feed him and be thankful.

Let Sham rejoice with the Fieldfare, who is a good gift from God in the season of scarcity.

Let Manoah rejoice with Cerastes, who is a Dragon with horns.

Let Talmai rejoice with Alcedo, who makes a cradle for its young, which is rocked by the winds.

Let Bukki rejoice with the Buzzard, who is clever, with the reputation of a silly fellow.

Let Michal rejoice with Leucocruta who is a mixture of beauty and magnanimity.

Let Atriah rejoice with Morphnus who is a bird of passage to the Heaven.

Let Jair rejoice with the Water-wag-tail, who is a neighbour, and loves to be looked at.

Let Dodo rejoice with the purple Worm who is cloathed sumptuously, tho' he fares meanly.

Let Ahio rejoice with the Merlin who is a cousin german of the hawk.

Let Joram rejoice with the Water Rail, who takes his delight in the river.

Let Chileab rejoice with Ophion who is clean made, less than a hart and a Sardinian.

Let Shephatiah rejoice with the little Owl, which is the winged Cat.

Let Ithream rejoice with the great Owl, who understandeth that which he professes.

Let Abigail rejoice with Lethophagus God be gracious to the widows indeed.

Let.

8a and b Holographs (reduced) of 'Let' and 'For' passages from Fragment B of Christopher Smart's *Jubilate Agno*.

9. For I am not without authority in my jeopardy, which I derive inevitably from the glory of the name of the Lord.

For I bless God whose name is Jealous — and there is a zeal to deliver us from everlasting burning.

For my enthusiasm is good even amongst the slanderers and my memory shall arise for a sweet savour unto the Lord.

For I bless the PRINCE of PEACE and pray that all the guns may be nail'd up, save such as are for the rejoicing days.

For I have abstained from the blood of the grape and that even at the Lord's table.

For I have glorified God in GREEK and LATIN, the consecrated languages spoken by the Lord on earth.

For I meditate the peace of Europe amongst family bickerings and domestic jars.

For the HOST is in the WEST — the Lord make us thankful unto salvation.

For I preach the very GOSPEL of CHRIST without comment & with this weapon shall I slay envy.

For I bless God in the rising generation, which is on my side.

For I have translated in the charity, which makes things better & I shall be translated myself at the last.

For he that walked upon the sea, hath prepared the floods with the Gospel of peace.

For the merciful man is merciful to his beast, and to the trees that give them shelter.

For he hath turned the shadow of death into the morning, the Lord is his name.

For I am come home again, but there is nobody to kill the calf or to pay the musick.

For the hour of my felicity, like the womb of Sarah, shall come at the latter end.

For I should have avail'd myself of waggery, had not malice been multitudinous.

For there are still serpents that can speak — God bless my head, my heart & my heel.

For I bless God that I am of the same seed with Ehud, Mutius Scaevola, and Colonel Draper.

For the word of God is a sword on my side — no matter what other weapon a stick, or a straw.

For I have adventured myself in the name of the Lord, and he hath mark'd me for his own.

For I bless God for the Post-master general & all conveyancers of letters under his care especially Allen & Shelvock.

For my grounded in New Canaan shall infinitely compensate for the flats & maynes of Staindrop Moor.

For the praise of God can give to a mute fish the notes of a nightingale.

For I have seen the White Raven & Thomas Hall of Willingham & am myself a greater curiosity than both.

For I look up to heaven which is my prospect to escape envy by surmounting it.

For if Pharaoh had known Joseph, he would have blessed God & me for the illumination of the people.

For I pray God to bless improvements in gardening till London be a city of palm trees.

For I pray to give thy grace to the poor of England, that Charity be not offended & that benevolence may increase.

For in my nature I quested for beauty, but God, God hath sent me to sea for pearls.

For there is a blessing from the STONE of JESUS which is founded upon hell to the precious jewel on the right hand of God.

For the nightly Visitor is at the window of the impenitent, while I sing a psalm of my own composing.

For there is a note added to the scale which the Lord hath made fuller, stronger & more glorious.

For I offer my goat as he browses the vine, bless the Lord from chambering & drunkenness.

For there is a traveling for the glory of God without going to Italy or France.

For I bless the children of Asher for the evil I did them & the good I might have received at their hands.

For I rejoice like a worm in the rain in him that cherishes and from him that tramples.

For I am ready for the trumpet & alarum to fight, to die & to rise again.

For the banish'd of the Lord shall come about again, for so he hath prepared for them.

For sincerity is a jewel which is pure & transparent, eternal & inestimable.

For my hands and my feet are perfect in the sublimity of Naphtali and the felicity of Asher.

For the names and number of the names are, & at the felicity of Asher.

For I pray the Lord Jesus to translate my MAGNIFICAT into verse and number, & represent it.

For I bless the Lord Jesus from the bottom of Horizon Cave to the top of the stars.

For I am a little fellow, which is intitled to the great mess by the benevolence of God my father to the top of King's Chapel.

For I this day made over my inheritance to my mother in consideration of her infirmities.

For I this day made over my inheritance to my mother in consideration of her age.

For I bless the thirteenth of August, in which I had the grace to obey the voice of Christ in my conscience.

For I bless the fourteenth of August, in which I was willing to run all hazards for the sake of the name of the Lord.

For I kept my flocks and my nevers and my lauds at merc... for the sake of Christ.

For nature is more various than observation tho' observers be innumerable.

For Agricola is Ingeniosus.

For I pray god to bless POLLY in the blessing of Naomi and assist her to the house of DAVID.

For I am in charity with the French who are my foes and Moabites because of the Moabitish woman.

For my Angel is always ready at a pinch to help me out and to keep me up.

For CHRISTOPHER must slay the Dragon with a PYTHON's heel.

For they have separated me and my bosom, whereas the right comes by setting us together.

For silly fellow! silly fellow! is against me and belongeth neither to me nor my family.

For he that scorneth the scorner hath condescended to my low estate.

For Abiah is the father of Joab and Joab of all Romans and English men.

For they pass by men their tour and the good Samaritan is not yet come.

For I bless God in the behalf of TRINITY COLLEGE in CAMBRIDGE & the society of PURPLES in LONDON.

For I have a nephew CHRISTOPHER to whom I implore the grace of God.

For I pray God bless the CAM — Mr HIGGS & Mr & Mrs WASHBOURNE at the drops of the dew.

For I pray God bless the king of Sardinia and make him an instrument of his peace.

For I am possessed of a cat, surpassing in beauty, from whom I take occasion to bless Almighty God.

For I pray God for the professors of the University of Cambridge to attend & to amend.

For the Fatherless Children and widows are never deserted of the Lord. For.

writes in *The Vanity of Human Wishes* (1749);[10] '*For nature is more various than observation tho' observers be innumerable*' (B53), writes Smart in a line that may well express a sceptical response. The superficial authority of the lofty, magisterial, truth-telling stance on which Johnson's poem depends is here contested; instead one must rely on a more mobile and fractured mode of utterance, responsive to variety and of a piece, perhaps, with the expressive flexibility that Lowth had detected in the structure of Hebrew prophecy. Here, Lowth writes, the reader who expects 'an artificial and methodical arrangement of the general subject, a regular disposition of the parts, a perfect connexion and orderly succession in the matter, and with all this, an uninterrupted series of eloquence and correctness . . . will really expect what was foreign to the Prophet's design'. Such writing is better seen instead as a kind of vehement patchwork, 'a number of plaintive effusions . . . uttered without connexion as they rose in the mind', 'so that the whole bears rather the appearance of an accumulation of corresponding sentiments, than an accurate and connected series of different ideas, arranged in the form of a regular treatise'.[11]

As for the interpretation of these 'accumulated sentiments', one might apply to the text itself another of its own lines: '*For the phenomenon of dreaming is not of one solution, but many*' (B371).

In this spirit, the present essay is offered as no more than one of many 'solutions' to *Jubilate Agno*, and not as an effort to establish the poem's unity by means of a single explanation. My purpose is to suggest ways of adapting and extending a familiar approach to the poem – the approach established by scholars who have seen in *Jubilate Agno* Smart's '*MAGNIFICAT*' (B43) and the expression of his ambition to be '*the Reviver of ADORATION amongst ENGLISH-MEN*' (B332) by means of a work in which all Creation is called to the utterance of a universal prayer. In thematic terms, this reading describes the obviously devotional motives of the poem; in formal terms, it describes the vigour with which, his ear trained by the orientalism of Lowth, Smart sought to reanimate the language of Hebrew verse and adapt it to ends of his own.[12] My purpose here, while recognising this abiding concern with prayer and also the influence of biblical models, is to refocus our sense of both. For it is clear that Smart's interest in sacred discourse lies not only in the public acts of communal adoration and prophetic announcement but also in the far more personal and private acts of

[10] Johnson, *The Vanity of Human Wishes*, lines 1–2, *The Poems of Samuel Johnson*, edited by David Nichol Smith and Edward L. McAdam, second edition (Oxford, 1974).

[11] *Lectures on the Sacred Poetry of the Hebrews*, translated by G. Gregory, 2 vols. (1787), II, 131–2 (discussing the Lamentations of Jeremiah).

[12] *Jubilate Agno* as a Magnificat registering the influence of Lowth is first discussed in the editions of Stead (1939) and Bond (1954), and in Bond's article of 1950. See also Allan J. Gedalof, 'Smart's Poetics in *Jubilate Agno*', *English Studies in Canada*, 5 (1979), 262–74; *The Poetical Works of Christopher Smart*, II, xxiv–xxviii; Guest, *A Form of Sound Words*, pp. 123–66.

lamentation and complaint. In fulfilling these latter concerns, I would suggest, Smart finds in biblical verse not merely a new and powerful language through which to work out a blueprint for liturgical reform; he also finds a language ready to serve more urgent rhetorical and expressive purposes specific to his predicament in the madhouse. In the first place, such sources supply a spare unjaded language, giving the complaint that is voiced an unusual plangency and force. Beyond this, they lend the poem a significant resonance, a structure of typological echoings through which the poet's own complaint borrows status and meaning from the pious precedents inevitably invoked by his words. It is in these ways that Scripture provides for the construction of a distinctive and necessary voice, a voice in which Smart is able to define his condition and press his complaint in the sanctified contexts of biblical suffering and endurance.

It is useful to approach this act of self-presentation and the linguistic means through which it is attempted by comparison with another work, in progress simultaneously with *Jubilate Agno* and sharing its fragmented and experimental character – Sterne's *Tristram Shandy* (1759–67). For both works are profoundly concerned with the difficulties of self-definition, especially in so far as they involve the elusiveness of any adequate and stable language in which to attempt the task. 'There is not a more perplexing affair in life to me, than to set about telling any one who I am', writes the Yorick of *A Sentimental Journey*, and Tristram is similarly perplexed: 'Don't puzzle me', he replies to the seemingly simple query 'And who are you?'[13] Yet it is not simply the lack of a coherent and stable identity that foxes Tristram. Missing, above all, is any unambiguous and infallible language in which even the most provisional sense of self, once established, may be safely conveyed to the reader. Endlessly defeated by what he calls (citing Locke) 'the imperfections of words', Tristram shares the failure of his characters to communicate unmistakable meanings. A fuller allusion to Locke comes in the novel's first instalment, where Tristram describes the similar 'perplexities' of his Uncle Toby, 'the almost insurmountable difficulties he found in telling his story intelligibly'. Drawing with wry pedantry on book two of Locke's *Essay*, he attributes 'the cause of obscurity and confusion, in the mind of man' to three phenomena: 'Dull organs, dear Sir, in the first place. Secondly, slight and transient impressions made by objects when the said organs are not dull. And, thirdly, a memory like unto a sieve, not able to retain what it has received.'[14] He then plays wittily on Locke's illustration of the point, which in the *Essay* runs as follows:

If the Organs, or Faculties of Perception, like Wax over-hardned with Cold, will not receive the Impression of the Seal, from the usual impulse wont to imprint it; or, like Wax

<hr>

[13] Sterne, *A Sentimental Journey*, edited by Ian Jack (Oxford, 1968), p. 85; *The Life and Opinions of Tristram Shandy, Gentleman*, edited by Ian Campbell Ross (Oxford, 1983), p. 421.
[14] *Tristram Shandy*, pp. 288, 67, 70.

of a temper too soft, will not hold it well, when well imprinted; or else supposing the Wax of a temper fit, but the Seal not applied with a sufficient force, to make a clear Impression: In any of these cases, the print left by the Seal, will be *obscure*.[15]

But here Tristram has a distinction of his own to add (closer to the subject of Locke's third book) between questions of perception and prior questions stemming from the obscurity of language itself. '[T]he true cause of the confusion in my uncle *Toby*'s discourse', he asserts, is at root linguistic, arising from 'the unsteady uses of words which have perplexed the clearest and most exalted understandings'. However clear the minds of Uncle Toby and his audience, communication between them is perpetually sabotaged by the instability of the language they use: '"Twas not by ideas, – by heaven! his life was put in jeopardy by words.'[16]

To return from Sterne and Locke on the difficulty of fixing impressions on the mind through language is to find new resonance in one of *Jubilate Agno*'s best-known lines (and one written shortly after the publication of Sterne's first instalment):[17] '*For my talent is to give an impression upon words by punching, that when the reader casts his eye upon 'em, he takes up the image from the mould which I have made*' (B404). Here Smart tackles related problems, and through a closely related image. The line has been linked with Berkeley's theories of perception, but it also suggests a direct engagement with Locke (named in B396) and with the particular causes of obscurity that he discusses in the *Essay* – 'dull Organs; or very slight and transient Impressions made by the Objects; or else a weakness in the Memory, not able to retain them as received'.[18] Relating these problems specifically to communication between poet and reader, Smart gives Locke's imagery a presumptuous twist. Sure transmission of meaning will result from more emphatic kinds of impression than those described by Locke, whose analogy with sealing is transformed into a complex metaphor suggestive simultaneously of type-founding and coining. The impression punched by Smart makes a mould from which the reader casts an image – an image, following the logic of the metaphor, that is solid, enduring, perfectly retaining the shape of the poet's utterance. Smart's later preface to Horace maintains the same hope of escaping the Shandean dilemma. Praising 'the beauty, force and vehemence of

[15] Locke, *An Essay Concerning Human Understanding*, edited by Peter H. Nidditch (Oxford, 1975), pp. 363–4.   [16] *Tristram Shandy*, p. 71.
[17] The dating of lines in *Jubilate Agno* is notoriously difficult, not least because of the inconsistency with which Smart held to his dictum that '*the old account of time is the true*' (B367). The most likely date for B404 (and the date that follows from the assumptions of Arthur Sherbo, 'The Dating and Order of the Fragments of Christopher Smart's *Jubilate Agno*', *Harvard Library Bulletin*, 10 (1956), 201–7) is 14 February 1760. The first two volumes of *Tristram Shandy* were on sale in London on 1 January (*Tristram Shandy*, p. vii).
[18] Locke, *An Essay Concerning Human Understanding*, p. 363. On Smart and Berkeley, see Geoffrey Grigson, *Christopher Smart* (1961), pp. 28–9; Gedalof, 'Smart's Poetics', 262–7.

Impression' which he finds the peculiar strength of Horatian poetry, Smart explains: '*Impression* then, is a talent or gift of Almighty God, by which a Genius is impowered to throw an emphasis upon a word or sentence in such wise, that it cannot escape any reader of sheer good sense, and true critical sagacity.'[19] The 'talent' that is the common currency of both Horace and his present translator, Smart suggests, again secures the elusive goal of true communication.

In what, though, does this 'talent' consist? Clearly it has much to do with idiosyncratic language: Smart's praise for 'the lucky risk of the Horatian boldness', for the 'unrivalled peculiarity of expression' and 'curiosity of choice diction' that distinguish his poetry, makes clear that what he prizes above all is a flouting of poetic norms.[20] His illustrations confirm the point, as when he singles out the penultimate stanza of Book IV Ode 3, translating it as follows:

> O mistress of the golden shell!
> Whose silence you command, or break;
> Thou that canst make the mute excel,
> And ev'n the sea born reptiles speak;
> And, like the swan, if you apply
> Your touch, in charming accents die.[21]

Yet the ode highlighted here is as significant for its meaning as for its diction, for it addresses Melpomene, the tragic muse, and attributes entirely to her the poet's success. 'Impression', it would seem, is a divine gift, one granted by the muse to the pagan Horace and by God to the Christian Smart. 'O thou muse . . . who canst immediately bestow, if thou pleasest, the notes of the *dying* swan upon the mute fish!', as Smart had earlier rendered the passage;[22] and this wording is recalled when, in *Jubilate Agno*, he implicitly attributes the soaring of his own poetic voice to his shift in the madhouse from the *vers de société* of previous years to a new devotional mode: '*For the praise of God can give to a mute fish the notes of a nightingale*' (B24).

There thus emerges a dual explanation of the 'beauty, force and vehemence of *Impression*' that enables the poet to fix meanings in the reader's mind with clarity and power. On one hand this quality results from unconventional habits of lexical choice and combination (the Horatian *curiosa felicitas*); on the other it is attributable, if not directly to God, then at least to the poet's focus on devotional themes and forms. A further idea may be added when we gloss B24 with reference to the meanings implied by the imagery of fish in the poem as a whole – an idea that closely associates poetic success with suffering and its articulation.

That Smart draws here on traditional Christian symbolism is clear enough. A

---

[19] *The Works of Horace, Translated into Verse*, 4 vols. (1767), II, xii.   [20] *Ibid.*, I, vii–ix.

[21] *Ibid.*, I, xviii–xix; II, 83.

[22] *The Works of Horace, Translated Literally into English Prose* (1756), sixth edition, 2 vols. (1790), I, 185.

later allusion to God's capacity *'to fish up men to their salvation'* (B131) recalls the ancient identification of fish as Christian souls. This, together with an earlier reference to the nightingale as 'musician of the Lord! and the watchman of the Lord!' (A105), enables us to see in B24 the transformation of the passive soul, awaiting salvation, into God's earthly spokesman – *'the Lord's News-Writer – the scribe–evangelist'*, as Smart is later to put it (B327). There is yet further resonance, however, in Smart's presentation of his own role by analogy with 'a mute fish'. Later comes the following pair of lines:

LET PETER rejoice with the MOON FISH who keeps up the life in the waters by night.
For I pray the Lord JESUS that cured the LUNATICK to be merciful to all my brethren and sisters in these houses. (B123)

The complex links between Peter, the moon fish and night are central here. Peter and his brother, originally fishers, become by following Jesus 'fishers of men' (Matthew 4:19); 'night' recalls the hours of literal and spiritual darkness in which Peter despairs of, and denies, his redeemer. The nocturnal moon fish, then, picks up from Peter a plainly religious connotation, but the link is as much one of contrast as of likeness – for in the dark and hostile environment in which it alone stays moving its capacity to 'keep up the life' suggests that of the pious Christian who continues even in adversity to trust in Christ, 'the way, the truth, and the life' (John 14: 6). This theme of patience in adversity is carried across the page. Christ's care for a boy who is 'lunatick, and sore vexed' (Matthew 17: 15) again gives special status to the afflicted, and the etymological link between 'MOON FISH' and 'LUNATICK' ('Mad; having the imagination influenced by the moon')[23] is reinforced by Smart's emphatic capital script to pick out both as parallel emblems of endurance in adversity. The effect is to give lunatics, *'my brethren and sisters in these houses'*, a status normally denied them; they themselves become types of suffering patience, who like the moon fish 'keep up the life in the waters by night'. The poet himself is one of their number; but he, marked out by his nightingale voice, is able not only to endure night but also to sing in its depths. The implication is plain. What gives Smart his voice is not simply the kind of affliction later stressed in the line *'For stuff'd guts make no musick; strain them strong and you shall have sweet melody'* (B307); nor is it simply the poet's Christian faith. It is the combination of the two, his unique condition as moon fish and nightingale at once.

Various passages combine to describe, then, a poetic voice that owes its power to three things – strange diction, the praise of God, a suffering condition. It is in the meeting of these three qualities that we may find the key to *Jubilate Agno*'s 'impression'; and here Smart's turn to the Hebrew model is central. Combining

---

[23] Samuel Johnson, *A Dictionary of the English Language*, 2 vols. (1755): 'Lunatick'.

as it does a language remote from the conventions of modern verse with an inherent leaning towards both devotion and complaint, it provides for the construction of the distinctive, impress-ive, poetic voice that Smart so urgently seeks.

Nowhere is this point more fully evident than in the opening lines of Fragment B:

Let Elizur rejoice with the Partridge, who is a prisoner of state and is proud of his keepers.
For I am not without authority in my jeopardy, which I derive inevitably from the glory of the name of the Lord. (B1)

These rich and complex lines give voice to one of the poem's most pressing purposes – the daily articulation of the poet's suffering condition, not only as a means of expressive release or sustaining purpose throughout the drudgery of confinement, but also as a means of endowing this confinement with the hallowed shape and status of Christian trial. Through the daily ritual of writing, Smart is able to give 'authority' to his 'jeopardy', redefining it not as hopeless or meaningless affliction but as a recapitulation of sacred history that is at once the test and affirmation of his holy status.

'Jeopardy' is a word to dwell on here. Johnson was wrong to dismiss it in his *Dictionary* of 1755 as 'not now in use': setting aside Uncle Toby's jeopardy of 1759, Smart would have encountered the word in the first part of Butler's *Hudibras* (1663), sections of which he had translated into Latin. Swift uses it in a Horatian translation of 1714; it reappears in volume four of *Tristram Shandy* (1761), Churchill's *The Times* (1764) and Blackstone's *Commentaries* (1768).[24] What is true, however, is that no eighteenth-century writer uses the word so emphatically or oddly as Smart.

Already the word is complex. Johnson defines it simply as 'Hazard; danger; peril', noting its supposed derivation 'from *j'ai perdu*, or *jeu perdu*'; he follows Nathan Bailey, who suggests 'Danger, Hazard, Risk' and the same origin in the French for 'a lost Game'.[25] *OED* establishes a more interesting derivation, from *parti* not *perdu*, so that the underlying idea of 'divided play or game, even game' gives rise to the definition 'A position in a game, undertaking, etc. in which the chances of winning and losing hang in the balance; an even chance; an undecided state of affairs; uncertainty; chance'. (Hence the legal term *jocus partitus*, 'when two Proposals are made to a Person, and he hath Liberty to chuse which he

---

[24] Butler, *Hudibras*, edited by John Wilders (Oxford, 1969), First Part, Canto I, line 690; Swift, 'The First Ode of the Second Book of Horace Paraphras'd', line 30, *Poetical Works*, edited by Herbert Davis (London, 1967); *Tristram Shandy*, p. 205; Churchill, *The Times*, line 580, *Poetical Works*, edited by Douglas Grant (Oxford, 1956); Blackstone, *Commentaries on the Laws of England*, 4 vols. (1765–9), III, xxii, 326.

[25] Johnson, *Dictionary*: 'Jeopardy'; Bailey, *An Universal Etymological English Dictionary* (1721): 'Jeopardy'.

pleases'.)[26] Only then come more familiar definitions: 'Risk of loss, harm, or death; peril, danger', and 'A deed involving peril; a daring exploit'.

'Jeopardy' comes to mean, then, not simply danger and the risk of loss: it implies a hazardous state of balance, an open and uncertain process in which triumph and disaster are equal and opposite prospects, each as real as the other. So much is clear from biblical cases that Smart clearly knew – Zebulun and Naphtali, who 'jeoparded their lives unto the death in the high places of the field' (Judges 5: 18); the three mighty men who braved the Philistines 'with the jeopardy of their lives' to draw water from the well of Bethlehem (I Chronicles 11: 19); even the disciples on the lake who, before Christ calms the storm, 'were filled with water, and were in jeopardy' (Luke 8: 23). All undergo a trial, in which the chances of winning and losing do indeed hang in the balance; all are divinely protected, in ways that make clear that jeopardy is a route not only to loss but also to providential favour. It is perhaps with this in mind that Zebulun, Naphtali and Abishai (drawer of the Bethlehem water) are given unusual prominence in *Jubilate Agno*.[27] So is the less fortunate Eleazur, surnamed Savaran, who 'put himself in jeopardy, to the end he might deliver his people, and get him a perpetual name' (I Maccabees 6: 44): his noble death is recalled in A80.

Smart's emphatic recollection of these jeopardised predecessors already establishes a context in which his own jeopardy is to be understood. Beyond this, his idiosyncratic use of the word elsewhere works not simply to associate but actually to *equate* his own condition in the madhouse with that of jeopardy in the abstract. For the word is, in Smart's usage, if not synonymous with confinement, then clearly inclusive of it. *A Translation of the Psalms of David* (1765) gives several examples. In Psalm 18, the Prayer Book's 'He brought me forth also into a place of liberty' becomes 'He saw my jeopardy discharg'd, / And freedom's ample walk enlarg'd', as the Psalmist is set by God 'in a spacious place' (a typically longing expansion, in Smart's writing of this period, of the idea of release). In Psalm 53, an appeal 'that the Lord would deliver his people out of captivity! Then should Jacob rejoice' becomes an appeal that God should 'break our chains' and 'make his people free': 'Then Jacob should lift up his voice, / And from his jeopardy rejoice'. Again, in Psalm 105, 'the prince of the people let him go free' becomes 'And Egypt's fierce despotic prince / His jeopardy discharg'd.' Only in Psalm 119 does the word denote a less specific state of adversity and trial, during which the Psalmist vows to keep his faith: though 'In daily jeopardy', he will 'not forget a clause / Of what is written in thy laws / Through error or offence.'[28]

[26] Giles Jacob, *A New Law-Dictionary*, third edition (1736): 'Jocus partitus'.

[27] See B453, B611 (Zabulon); A14, B41, B433, B607 (Naphtali); A35, B187, B442 (Abishai).

[28] *The Poetical Works of Christopher Smart*, III, edited by Marcus Walsh (Oxford, 1987), Psalm XVIII, lines 109–112; Psalm LIII, lines 40–44; Psalm CV, lines 79–80; Psalm CXIX (Nun), lines 25–30.

'Jeopardy' is thus closely involved for Smart with the idea of captivity, an emphasis that is clearly personal in meaning. Later in Fragment B he defines himself forthrightly as a *'prisoner'* (B519), then praying: *'the Lord direct me in the better way of going on in the Fifth year of my jeopardy June the 17th N.S. 1760'* (B560). Annotating this line, Karina Williamson supposes (in the absence of any record of confinement before 1757) that Smart here extends his usual definition of the word to include his illness of 1756. But the recent discovery of a letter lamenting 'Seven years in Madhouses' (from which we know him to have been finally released early in 1763) shows that his use of the word in fact remains constant here: his jeopardy and his confinement are one and the same.[29]

This same connotation of captivity is clear in B1 itself. 'The Partridge, who is a prisoner of state and is proud of his keepers', may well recall the 'Quail, / Confin'd within its wiry jail' of 'The English Bull Dog, Dutch Mastiff, and Quail' (1758), an ironic attack on myths of British liberty.[30] But the most obvious allusions are to two passages of Scripture. As 'prisoner of state', the partridge is linked with the royal David, who likens his persecution to that of 'a patridge in the mountains' (I Samuel 26: 20); as an emblem of pride, the bird recalls an Apocryphal proverb: 'Like as a partridge taken and kept in a cage, so is the heart of the proud' (Ecclesiasticus 11: 30). These combined echoes carry across from versicle to response the implication not simply of incarceration, then, but of incarceration as a noble condition.

In what sense, however, is Smart *'not without authority'* in this state of confinement or jeopardy – an authority *'derived inevitably'* from God? Clearly he lacks the worldly authority or power of the biblical Elizur, head of the house of Reuben, and indeed *Jubilate Agno* repeatedly identifies Smart as a victim of such power. One superbly precise and controlled line describes how *'the officers of the peace are at variance with me, and the watchman smites me with his staff'* (B90). Later he suggests that it is not *'of man to make laws'* (B299), and frankly appeals: 'The Lord obliterate the laws of man!' (B291). Whatever authority Smart has in his jeopardy, then, is clearly not human but divine; and here he is more at one with Elizur, whose Hebrew name means 'God is rock'.[31] *'For the Lord is my ROCK and I am the bearer of his CROSS'*, he writes (B94): in his faith, in his affliction, even in his very name (Christopher, bearer of Christ), his sufferings at the hands of worldly authority are also a mark of his godly status. 'Great sufferings claim applause divine', as he puts it (of 'King Charles the Martyr') in

[29] *The Poetical Works of Christopher Smart*, I, 79 n.; Smart to Charles Burney (26 April 1770), *The Annotated Letters of Christopher Smart*, edited by Betty Rizzo and Robert Mahony (Carbondale, 1991), p. 132.
[30] *The Poetical Works of Christopher Smart*, IV, edited by Karina Williamson (Oxford, 1987), 301.
[31] W. Moelwyn Merchant, 'Patterns of Reference in Smart's *Jubilate Agno*', *Harvard Library Bulletin*, 14 (1960), 24; Guest, *A Form of Sound Words*, p. 131.

Hymns and Spiritual Songs,[32] and the point is often repeated in *Jubilate Agno*: '*For tall and stately are against me, but humiliation on humiliation is on my side*' (B112); '*For I have adventured myself in the name of the Lord, and he hath mark'd me for his own*' (B21).

More important for our understanding of the poem, however, is the way in which this God-given authority is confirmed by authority of a more strictly literary kind – authority in the sense of a source invoked to give weight to one's own contention. For the authority that Smart derives in his jeopardy has to do above all with language, and it stems directly from his appropriation of a biblical style of complaint – a style that gives lapidary expression to his suffering condition and links it with the sufferings of sacred exemplars. '*For the word of God is a sword on my side – no matter what other weapon a stick or a straw*' (B20): against the watchman's staff of B90, or the '*harping-irons*' of B124, Smart sets the word of God, his spiritual and scriptural weapon. Here is a supreme authority in both poetic and religious terms, lending the poet a way of presenting his complaint that at once dignifies it with sublime poetry and asserts its place in a tradition of pious suffering that reaches back through Christ himself to such models as David and Job. It is thus that Smart's adoption of biblical style is not merely a matter of liturgical reform, but of urgent expressive need. Such language serves crucial functions, sustaining him in his jeopardy, supplying him with a potent language of complaint and bringing with it a host of allusions that mark him, like the pious exemplars of his sacred sources, with the distinction of the holy martyr.

This linguistic and literary 'authority' is precisely described in Lowth's *Praelectiones*, and it is likely that Smart has his analysis in mind when using the word in B1. Lowth uses the term '*Mashal*' to describe the Hebrew style now often associated with Smart's writing, and he notes that the word is 'expressive of power, or supreme authority, and when applied to style, seems particularly to intimate something eminent or energetic'. *Mashal* thus has two distinct senses: '*he likened, he compared, he spoke in parables; he uttered proverbs, sentences grave and pointed*, a *composition ornamented with figures* and *comparisons*: also he *ruled*, he *was eminent*, he *possessed dominion* and authority'. Noting an evident relation 'between the two interpretations of this root', he goes on to define the *Mashal* style in terms that suggest its authoritative, forceful characteristics. '*Mashal* is therefore a composition elevated and grave, weighty and powerful, highly ornamented with comparisons, figures, and imagery; such is the style of the Psalms, the Prophets, and the Book of Job . . . it is in fine, any sentence or axiom excellently or gravely uttered, concise, and confined to a certain form or

---

[32] *The Poetical Works of Christopher Smart*, II, edited by Marcus Walsh and Karina Williamson (Oxford, 1983), 41.

manner'.[33] Later lectures identify the salient features of this certain form. One is its 'studied brevity', a characteristic combining great expressive power with (to readers unversed in the metaphorical codes of the style) a certain obscurity of meaning. Typically, such brevity is fostered by tight syntactical patterning:

The Hebrew poets frequently express a sentiment with the utmost brevity and simplicity, illustrated by no circumstances, adorned with no epithets (which in truth they seldom use); they afterwards call in the aid of ornament; they repeat, they vary, they amplify the same sentiment; and adding one or more sentences which run parallel to each other, they express the same or a similar, and often a contrary sentiment in nearly the same form of words . . . Frequent and laconic sentences render the composition remarkably concise, harmonious, and animated; the brevity itself imparts to it additional strength, and being contracted within a narrower space, it has a more energetic and pointed effect.[34]

A second feature defining the style is its metaphorical intensity. 'The word *Mashal*, in its most common acceptation, denotes resemblance, and is therefore directly expressive of the figurative style, as far as the nature of figures consists in the substitution of words, or rather of ideas, for those which they resemble.' Setting out 'to exhibit objects in a clearer or more striking, in a sublimer or more forcible manner', it depicts 'the obscure by the more manifest, the subtile by the more substantial', finding (in a judgement reminiscent of *Jubilate Agno*, B53) that 'The whole course of nature . . . offers itself to human contemplation, and affords an infinite variety, a confused assemblage, a wilderness, as it were, of images, which being collected as the materials of poetry, are selected and produced as occasion dictates.' These two aspects of *Mashal* verse, terseness and metaphor, meet in the characteristic Hebrew concentration of imagery into an unextended, unexplained and rapidly shifting form, 'condensing and compressing every exuberance of expression, and rendering it close and pointed. Thus, in the very parts in which other poets are copious and diffuse, the Hebrew, on the contrary, are brief, energetic, and animated . . . for it is not so much their custom to dilate and embellish each particular image with a variety of adjuncts, as to keep together a number of parallel and analogous comparisons, all of which are expressed in a style of the utmost brevity and simplicity.'[35]

The great example of *Mashal* verse, repeatedly cited by Lowth, is the Book of Job. Here he finds 'that force of composition . . . which strikes and overpowers the mind, which excites the passions, and which expresses ideas at once with perspicuity and elevation; not solicitous whether the language be plain or ornamented, refined or familiar'. Lowth knows 'nothing more poetical' than Job's opening complaint, and the terms in which he describes it hint always at the origin of '*Mashal*' in notions of authority or power. Its 'concise and abrupt form',

---

[33] Lowth, *Lectures on the Sacred Poetry of the Hebrews*, I, 304; I, 77 n.
[34] *Ibid.*, I, 98; I, 100–2.   [35] *Ibid.*, I, 104; I, 111; I, 118; I, 116–17; I, 275.

its 'spirited, vehement, and perplexed form of expression' are such that 'to make it more copious and explanatory' would be to attenuate this expressive power: he cites by contrast a related passage in Jeremiah, who 'fills up the ellipses, smooths and harmonizes the rough and uncouth language of Job', so weakening its force.[36] This force depends precisely on the roughness of Job's language, and on a recurrent disregard for clarity and pattern – points evident where 'anger and vexation dissipated the order of his ideas, and destroyed the construction of this sentence', or where 'a violent and sudden transition' takes place, 'the force and boldness of which is incomparable'. Job's disruptions of structure, indeed, are central to a larger success, in which 'the agitated and disordered state of the speaker's mind is not more evidently demonstrated by a happy boldness of sentiment and imagery, and an uncommon force of language, than by the very form, conduct, and arrangement of the whole'.[37]

To show how closely Smart himself echoes in *Jubilate Agno* the kinds of sublimity described by Lowth, 'that vivid and ardent style, which is so well calculated to display the emotions and passions of the mind',[38] would be a task as unoriginal as lengthy. My point is not to perform it here, although it would be perfectly possible to find in almost any of the lines (or pair of lines) cited in this essay a close observation of the formal qualities described by Lowth – the abruptness, the density, the figures of parallelism and contrast, the welter of terse and unexplained metaphorical substitutions. My point is simply to suggest that it is to this widely acknowledged characteristic of *Jubilate Agno* – to the spare, rigorous, yet intensely plangent style of the poem – that Smart alludes when he talks of being '*not without authority in my jeopardy*' – the authority of the *Mashal* style, and the forceful language by which it lifts his complaint to a new expressive plane.

There is one further point to be made about this authority. By appropriating for his own expressive purposes the *Mashal* style, Smart does not simply supply himself with a stylistic power otherwise unavailable in the more conventional range of poetic voices deployed in his earlier work. For the Hebrew models from which *Jubilate Agno* grows necessarily bring with them not only the force of impression celebrated in B404, but also the force of allusion. The effect is to link the poet with the exemplars of sacred literature, so that his own plight comes to assume something of the status and meaning of theirs. Implicitly (and at times not so implicitly), the style links him in typological fashion with the pious sufferers of the Old Testament – notably with David (a model invoked throughout his poetic career, and often discussed in criticism),[39] but equally

[36] *Ibid.*, I, 307; I, 313; I, 314; I, 315.   [37] *Ibid.*, I, 318–19; I, 320; I, 321.   [38] *Ibid.*, I, 321.

[39] See Thomas F. Dillingham, '"Blest Light": Christopher Smart's Myth of David', in *The David Myth in Western Literature*, edited by Raymond-Jean Frontain and Jan Wojcik (West Lafayette, 1980), pp. 120–33; Allan J. Gedalof, 'The Rise and Fall of Smart's David', *Philological Quarterly*, 60 (1981), 369–86.

notably with Job. By taking on the words of these exemplars he gains their authority in the most powerful and immediate of senses; his life comes to seem a modern re-enactment of theirs, radiant with the same meanings.

Job is in this sense a strikingly apposite text, offering not only a style of complaint but also a model of pious fortitude and endurance (together even with the prospect of the restitution and reward to which the poet looks, in '*New Canaan*' if not in '*Staindrop Moor*' (B23)). It cannot be known whether Smart knew the view put forward in Cambridge during his studies there that the Book of Job was itself an allegory of imprisonment, representing in the hero's trial the sufferings of the Jewish people during 'the crisis of all its affairs, the Babylonish captivity'.[40] But he will have known Lowth's more orthodox account of a work presenting 'the example of a good man, eminent for his piety, and of approved integrity, suddenly precipitated . . . into the lowest depths of misery and ruin'. Throughout this trial, Job remains '(as far as is consistent with human infirmity) an example of perfect virtue . . . He is holy, devout, and most piously and reverently impressed with the sacred awe of his divine Creator; he is also upright, and conscious of his own integrity; he is patient of evil, and yet very remote from . . . insensibility.' And the potential analogy goes on, the specific nature of Job's affliction offering Smart rich opportunity for borrowing and allusion. As one bereft of his property, family, wife, friends and health, Job seems almost to prefigure a poet who meditates peace '*amongst family bickerings and domestic jars*' (B7), and who ruefully commemorates sacrificing '*my flocks and my herds and my lands*' (B52). When Job is subjected to 'the unjust suspicions, the bitter reproaches, and the violent altercations of his friends, who had visited him on the pretence of affording consolation' and who then 'reproach him . . . with pride, impiety, passion, and madness', the prefiguration seems complete.[41] The result is that Job's complaint – 'appeals to the Almighty, asseverations of his own innocence, earnest expostulations, complaints of the cruelty of his friends, melancholy reflections on the vanity of human life, and upon his own severe misfortunes' – provides Smart with the perfect resource. This is by no means simply a vague feature of style; often the echoes are highly pointed. Perhaps the most striking instance comes in B74 ('*For my brethren have dealt deceitfully as a brook, and as the stream of brooks that pass away*'), which quotes, with little change, Job's rebuke to his comforters: 'My brethren have dealt deceitfully as a brook, and as the stream of brooks they pass away' (Job 6: 15). The line's force will have been impressed on Smart by Lowth, who comments in detail on it at least three times. He finds it the perfect example of compressed comparison, glossing it as follows: the verse,

---

[40] John Garnett, *A Dissertation on the Book of Job* (1749), p. 93.
[41] Lowth, *Lectures on the Sacred Poetry of the Hebrews*, I, 371; II, 407; II, 372; II, 374.

impeaches the infidelity and ingratitude of his friends, who in his adversity denied him those consolations of tenderness and sympathy, which in his prosperous state, and when he needed them not, they had lavished upon him: he compares them with streams, which increased by the rains of winter, overflow their borders, and display for a little time a copious and majestic torrent; but with the first impulse of the solar beams are suddenly dried up, and leave those, who unfortunately wander through the deserts of Arabia, destitute of water, and perishing with thirst.[42]

The link between abandonment and drought that Lowth finds here is interestingly converted when Smart adds: '*For being desert-ed is to have desert in the sight of God and intitles one to the Lord's merit*' (B333). But what is most significant is the analogy implicitly proposed by Smart's adoption of the image: now his brethren became latterday comforters, compounding his own existing afflictions by calumny, abandonment and fraud.

Elsewhere Smart elaborates on the verse 'Yet man is born unto trouble, as the sparks fly upward' (Job 5: 7) in a way characteristic of *Mashal* synonymy. The flying sparks of the verse seem to prompt in his mind an image that may be from smelting: '*For man is born to trouble in the body, as the sparks fly upwards in the spirit. | For man is between the pinchers while his soul is shaping and purifying*' (B431–2). A further passage identifies this Job-like state of purification '*between the pinchers*' as a mark of personal election. '*[P]atience is the child of strength*' (B405), he proclaims in one of three surviving verses that explicitly name Job; earlier comes another: 'Let Job bless with the Worm – the life of the Lord is in Humiliation, the Spirit also and the truth' (A51). The worm is that of Job 19: 26 ('Though after my skin worms destroy this body, yet in my flesh shall I see God'); and though the response to this line does not survive, the versicle itself is enough to suggest a quiet prediction of the reward which, like the restoration of Job's riches, awaits Smart at his '*latter end*' (B16).

Job could offer one further rhetorical weapon. Paul J. Korshin has shown how the Job story was seen in the period as 'one of the most dramatic typological accounts in the Old Testament' – as a story not only providing 'the type of true Christian fortitude and faith in adversity' but also predicting the pious suffering of Christ himself.[43] As Smart himself writes in 'Patience' (from *Hymns for the Amusement of Children*), Job is the 'type of our Emmanuel Christ', who, 'With all the gems he had in store, / None half so bright as Patience wore'.[44] His patience in adversity prefigures his redeemer's; and Smart has no qualms about following the association to its logical end. If in some respects he is himself a Job, in others he resembles Christ; and the link between all three emerges most clearly with the

[42] *Ibid.*, II, 375; I, 273 (see also I, 134; I, 278).
[43] Paul J. Korshin, *Typologies in England, 1650–1820* (Princeton, 1982), p. 249.
[44] *The Poetical Works of Christopher Smart*, II, 345.

allegation of madness. '*For silly fellow! silly fellow! is against me and belongeth neither to me nor my family*' (B60), Smart writes, perhaps recalling Eliphaz's rebuke to Job that 'envy slayeth the silly one', whose 'children are far from safety' (Job 5: 2–4). Switching to the language of the New Testament, Smart then echoes Mark 3: 21 ('And when his friends heard of it, they went out to lay hold on him: for they said, he is beside himself') to associate himself, as one unjustly deemed mad, with the suffering Christ: '*For I am under the same accusation with my Saviour – for they said, he is besides himself*' (B151). Fortified by this dual precedent, the poet himself, '*willing to be called a fool for the sake of Christ*' (B51), enjoys authority indeed.

To note such connections as these is merely to scratch the surface of the habits of typological thinking through which Smart finds meaning and status in an otherwise deplorable condition. The poem's analogies are rich, complex and shifting, and they require more sustained exploration than space allows here; for it is in the expression of such links that much of *Jubilate Agno*'s 'authority' – its power both of style and of allusion – lies. What is already clear, however, is that by turning to scriptural models Smart finds not only an innovative medium, well adjusted to the liturgical ambitions that the poem occasionally announces; more immediately, he finds his poetic voice in a language that makes sense of his suffering by articulating it with clarity and force, and by interpreting it through analogy with the righteous sufferers of Scripture. It is thus, through the different kinds of authority that stem from the *Mashal* style, that Smart at once survives and proclaims his jeopardised state, presenting himself as a sufferer in whom the different trials of Job, David and Christ meet and find their echo. From these sources he constructs his voice, presents his complaint, and lends it (to return to his critical writing) that 'beauty, force and vehemence of *Impression*' through which he claims that meaning may be surely conveyed.

This feat of forceful self-presentation reaches its wry climax in one of the first poems that Smart wrote following release from his jeopardy in the madhouse and his simultaneous suspension of the poem that documents it. Celebrating his release in *An Epistle to John Sherratt, Esq.*, Smart risks a pun that he seldom allowed himself, but for which the perfect place was now offered. Looking back on the seven friendless years of his jeopardy, he finds in Sherratt and his wife a noble contrast to *Jubilate Agno*'s deceitful brethren:

> Well nigh sev'n years had fill'd their tale,
> From Winter's urn to Autumn's scale,
> And found no friend to grief, and *Smart*,
> Like Thee and Her, thy sweeter part.[45]

[45] *Ibid.*, IV, 345.

Coming as the line does from a poet who saw in language a divine revelation,[46] we must take seriously what might otherwise seem mere verbal play. With this conclusive gesture the poet presents himself, not as Job, David or Christ, but simply as 'Smart' – the fellow of grief, the very embodiment (in Johnson's definition) of 'Pain, corporal or intellectual'.[47]

[46] See Guest, *A Form of Sound Words*, pp. 167–95.   [47] Johnson, *Dictionary*: 'Smart'.

6

Did Blake betray the French Revolution?
A dialogue of the mind with itself
Interlocutors: Anne Mack and J. J. Rome

JEROME J. McGANN

JJR: But why drag in Blake's critique of Wordsworth's poetry? It's nothing but a red herring. The issues there are aesthetic and perhaps religious, but not political. Don't complicate a simple question: did Blake become a political apostate like Wordsworth, Coleridge and Southey?

AM: But his critique of Wordsworth *is* pertinent. One cannot, in Blake's case, make so sharp a distinction between politics, art, and religion. 'Are not Religion & Politics the same thing' is a rhetorical question posed in *Jerusalem* (57: 10) that calls for an affirmative response. Besides, Blake was outspoken in thinking that an artist's work is an index of a person's political and ideological convictions.

JJR: Even accepting that general characterisation of Blake, I don't see the relevance of the critique of Wordsworth. Unlike Byron's, or even Shelley's, Blake's critique is equivocal: 'I see in Wordsworth the Natural Man rising up against the Spiritual Man Continually & then he is No Poet but a Heathen Philosopher at Enmity against all true Poetry or Inspiration' (E666).[1]

AM: The problem is your absurdly narrow conception of politics. You simply don't grasp the *political* significance of Blake's Christian antinomianism.[2] What he says about Wordsworth recalls his early critique of Richard Watson's *An Apology for the Bible* (1797) and his late denunciation of Dr Robert Thornton's *The Lord's Prayer, Newly Translated* (1827). In each case he attacks what he sees as a 'heathen' philosophy masking itself as something 'spiritual' or even Christian. The attack on Watson, the Bishop of Llandaff, is especially telling, in the context of the Wordsworth comparison. Wordsworth's political apostasy involved a total retreat from his early radicalism, when he attacked the conservative politics of the same Bishop of Llandaff; for

---

[1] Unless otherwise indicated, all quotations are taken from David V. Erdman, ed., *The Complete Poetry and Prose of William Blake*, with commentary by Harold Bloom, revised edition (Berkeley and Los Angeles, 1982); citations are given in the text as E plus the page number.

[2] If JJR has not grasped that significance, Michael Ferber has with great clarity; see his *The Social Vision of William Blake* (Princeton, 1985), especially chapters 2, 3.

117

Wordsworth would eventually embrace ideological views that were at least the equivalent of the worthy bishop's. This Blake never did. Blake was not a political apostate because he always saw institutional religion and its authoritative spokesmen as the defenders and transmitters of wicked and cruel ideas. For him they were nothing but apologists of state power and exploitation – and Blake knew very well that the exploitation was a material, a social and an economic, crucifixion. This is why he says of Thornton's book that 'I look upon this as a Most Malignant & Artful attack upon the Kingdom of Jesus By the Classical Learned thro the Instrumentality of Dr Thornton' (E667), and why his irony at Thornton's privileged piety is so savage, and so class conscious: 'Give us the Bread that is our due & Right by taking away Money or a Price or Tax upon what is Common to all in thy Kingdom' (E668). And again: 'Christ & his Apostles were Illiterate Men Caiaphas Pilate & Herod were Learned' (E667).

These are the antinomian ideas of the urban working class, and they remain at the core of Blake's thought from the beginning to the end of his life. His critique of Reynolds proceeds from exactly the same awareness of class-based exploitation:

The Enquiry in England is not whether a Man has Talents. & Genius? But whether he is Passive & a Virtuous Ass: & obedient to Noblemens Opinions in Art & Science. If he is; he is a Good Man: If Not he must be Starved (E642)

Blake has no illusions about the reasons some succeed as artists whereas others do not. For there are 'Artists who live upon Assassinations of other Men' precisely because 'The Rich Men of England form themselves into a Society. to Sell & Not to Buy Pictures.' This is the society where 'Commerce settles on every Tree', killing art as well as life by forcing everyone to 'live upon Gold'. To Blake's mind, where Mammon reigns, as it does in England, 'all are Born Poor', including those covered with material riches (E642).

JJR: No one doubts Blake's radical consciousness, or that (like his prophet Los) he kept a humane vision through his times of trouble. But there is a problem you simply won't face, and which I can best get at by supplementing your Blakeian texts with a few more that move to much the same spirit. In the 'Public Address' Blake drafted for his 1809 exhibition he says that 'The wretched state of the Arts in this Country & in Europe originat[es] in the Wretched State of Political Science which is the Science of Sciences' (E580). When he attacks Reynolds he urges the artist of integrity to 'throw his Contempt on such Trading Exhibitions' (E642) as those supported by 'Sr Joshua & his Gang of Cunning Hired Knaves' (E636), but in the 'Public Address' he goes even further and indicts the entire political structure of England:

I am really sorry to see my Countrymen trouble themselves about Politics. If Men were Wise < the Most arbitrary > Princes could not hurt them. If they are not Wise the Freest Government is compelld to be a Tyranny[.] Princes appear to me to be Fools Houses of Commons & Houses of Lords appear to me to be fools they seem to me to be something Else besides Human Life (E580)

A M: I know these texts, but they only support my original point – that Blake, like Byron's Milton but unlike Southey, Wordsworth and Coleridge, 'closed the tyrant-hater he begun' (*Don Juan*, 'Dedication' st. 10). He went further than Byron's Milton because he included the entire parliamentary system in his vision of England's exploitative society.

J J R: Went beyond? Well, I recall Byron's mordant, even nihilist, 1814 epigram on the political condition of England, and it seems to me a fair equivalent of Blake's wholesale repudiation:

> 'Tis said *Indifference* marks the present time,
> Then hear the reason – though 'tis told in rhyme –
> A King who *can't* – a Prince of Wales who *don't* –
> Patriots who *shan't*, and Ministers who *won't* –
> What matters who is *in* or *out* of place
> The *Mad* – the *Bad* – the *Useless* – or the *Base*?[3]

But that by the way, and I want to return to the Blake texts – which I quoted not so much to underscore *your* views as to expose more clearly a pair of Blakeian contradictions. In the first place, Blake's unhappiness that his 'Countrymen' should be concerned about politics immediately follows a remark about the pre-eminent importance of political science as 'the Science of Sciences'. Blake's sense that this science is badly conceived in his own day seems to have driven him to a position of political quietism and acquiescence in the status quo. This fact is emphasised by the form that these pronouncements take. That is to say, Blake never transmitted these words to the public: despite the fact that they appear in a text he titled a 'Public Address' they remained as private as his remarks on Thornton and Reynolds and Watson. What he actually published was only his *Descriptive Catalogue*, where he is very careful to suppress his offensive political views.

A M: Be serious. You cannot mean to suggest that Blake kept his opinions to himself. Those who knew him repeatedly comment on the fact that his worldly unsuccess was partly due to his impolitic and candid habits. He was an opinionated man and he didn't hide his views.

J J R: True, this is our received view of Blake, but it may be a more accurate portrait of Blake before the treason trials of 1794–5 than of the later Blake. His comments on Watson's *Apology for the Bible* are telling: 'To defend the Bible

---

[3] *Lord Byron. The Complete Poetical Works*, edited by Jerome J. McGann (Oxford, 1981), III, 91.

in this year 1798 would cost a man his life. The Beast & the Whore rule without controls' (E611). In his private notes on Watson's biblical interpretations Blake defends Paine because Blake reads the Bible in the tradition of the Everlasting Gospel.[4] In that antinomian language 'The Beast & the Whore' are code terms for the established state and church, who pervert the true redemptive meaning of the Bible into a text that supports policies of wicked governance. But in the year 1798 Blake shrinks from speaking openly of such matters, as he wouldn't have done earlier. In 1798 Blake has been 'commanded from Hell not to print this as it is what our Enemies wish' (E611).

A M: And yet how interesting that Blake should still be following, in 1798, the commands of 'Hell', as he followed them earlier when he was producing his Bible of Hell. But to keep the divine vision in a time of trouble meant for Blake the 'expedient' of what David Erdman has called 'a split personality'.[5] Blake's self-division emerges most clearly in the work of *The Four Zoas*, which he wrote in the dark years between the treason trials and the Peace of Amiens. 'Much of the epic is taken up with the Tongue's plight in exile and under censorship, an aspect of Blake's own predicament after 1795. His tongue clamors to speak out; his reason seeks to enforce silence. The conflict is uneasily resolved by a compromise *which is this poem*. The tongue has its way, for Blake does not write. But reason wins too, for he writes in ambiguous words and does not print'.[6]

J J R: But it's only too clear that Blake pays a dear price for this 'compromise'. Even he recognised this. *Milton* is the work he undertakes after the collapse of the false Peace of Amiens, and it is in many ways an explicit critique of the

---

[4] See A. L. Morton, *The Everlasting Gospel. A Study in the Sources of William Blake* (London, 1958). For further information on Blake's connections with figures like Richard Brothers and Joanna Southcott see Morton D. Paley, 'William Blake, the Prince of the Hebrews, and the Woman Clothed with the Sun,' in Paley and Michael Phillips, eds., *William Blake: Essays in Honour of Sir Geoffrey Keynes* (Oxford, 1973), pp. 260–93. See also David V. Erdman, 'Terrible Blake in His Pride: An Essay on *The Everlasting Gospel*', *From Sensibility to Romanticism: Essays Presented to Frederick A. Pottle*, edited by Frederick W. Hilles and Harold Bloom (New York, 1965), pp. 331–56; and Jeanne Moskal, 'Forgiveness, Love, and Pride in Blake's *The Everlasting Gospel*,' *Religion and Literature*, 20 (Summer 1988), 19–39.

[5] David V. Erdman, *Blake. Prophet Against Empire* second edition (Princeton, 1969), p. 305. See Marilyn Butler's treatment of this Blakeian self-division as a crisis between his 'English [political] radicalism' and his 'Protestant sectarianism', in *Romantics, Rebels, and Reactionaries: English Literature and its Background 1760–1830* (Oxford, 1982), p. 49. In an excellent (and as yet unpublished) essay, Robert Essick also argues that Blake's 'split personality' (a) represents the tension between his commitments to radical and antinomian Christian ideas, on one hand, and his sympathy with certain strains of a secular radicalism on the other; and (b) that these tensions persisted throughout his life, or at least since his involvement with the Mathew circle in the early 1780s: see his 'William Blake, Thomas Paine, and Biblical Revolution', when it finally appears in print.   [6] *Ibid.*, p. 298.

'compromise' worked out in *The Four Zoas*.[7] The entire poem pivots around Satan's 'soft dissimulation' (8: 35), which Los explicitly denounces in general terms, and directly to the character of Satan at the outset of the work:

> If you account it Wisdom when you are angry to be
> silent, and
> Not to shew it: I do not account that Wisdom but Folly.
> (4: 6–7)

Milton is an accounting of the cost of Blake's adherence to a Satanic model – in Blake's personal terms, of following hell's command to be silent. Blake's situation, according to the poem, is a repetition of John Milton's, Blake's precursor and *alter-ego* 'who walked about in Eternity / One hundred years... / Unhappy tho in heav'n, he obey'd, he murmur'd not. he was silent' (2: 16–18). Milton's silence *is* his unhappiness, according to Blake, and the great Puritan is 'mov'd' to break his silence by 'A Bard's prophetic Song' – which is, in fact, the very 'song' constituted in and through Blake's own poem, *Milton*. And the latter represents Blake's renunciation of a silence begun in 1795 and climaxing in his years at Felpham, that 'heaven' into which William Hayley plunged Blake between 1800 and 1803.

The story is well known – that Hayley tried to rescue Blake both from his radical London ideological environment, on one hand, and from his extremely difficult financial circumstances on the other; and that Blake, though at first happy in this simulated heaven, gradually came to feel the curse of Hayley's benevolence. 'The meer drudgery of business', Blake ultimately realised, was interfering with his visionary projects, for 'I should be Employd in Greater Things' than doing portraits, miniatures and illustrations for Hayley. 'Such [Greater] things', Blake observed, 'depend ... on the Spiritual & not on the Natural World.' Besides, these spiritual 'Talents [should] be properly exercised in Public' (E724), and not in the sequestered vales of Sussex.

AM: I don't disagree with any of that. Blake's sojourn at Felpham *was* in certain respects a kind of spiritual retreat and backsliding, but in the end Blake felt his stay at Felpham worked to his benefit:

---

[7] The fact that neither party to this debate discusses the meaning of the late additions to *The Four Zoas* suggests an uncertainty about how to interpret those additions. Passing comments by this dialogue's interlocutors indicate that they are both in agreement with, for example, Erdman's general position set forth in *Blake. Prophet Against Empire* (see especially pp. 377–83): that 'The coming of peace demonstrates that Christ lives' (p. 378), and that this living Christ brings a message not of 'human [political] struggle' but of divine mercy and mutual forgiveness. Though these matters are agreed upon, the dialogists cannot agree upon what these matters signify in terms of the larger issue at stake here: the political significance of Blake's antinomianism.

all our three years trouble Ends in Good Luck at last & shall be forgot by my affections
& only remembered by my Understanding to be a Memento in time to come & to speak
to future generations by a Sublime Allegory which is now perfectly completed into a
Grand Poem[.] (E730)

Most useful was how the Felpham sojourn clarified his mind on certain
imperative matters, and pushed him to the composition of a work that would
be able to speak of these issues 'to future generations'. That 'Grand Poem' is
Milton, which Blake here tells us stands completed in a draft version (the date
is 6 July 1803).

Of course Blake did initially speak of the contradictions of his life at
Felpham very differently.

I labour incessantly & accomplish not one half of what I intend because my Abstract
folly hurries me often away while I am at work, carrying me over Mountains & Valleys
which are not Real in a Land of Abstraction where Spectres of the Dead wander. This I
endeavour to prevent & with my whole might chain my feet to the world of Duty &
Reality. (E716)

At Felpham Blake forced himself to subordinate his historical visions to the
quotidian tasks Hayley was setting for him. This struggle eventually seemed to
Blake a kind of agony in a garden, so that by January 1803 he came to the
'determination . . . To Leave This Place' and return to London (E725), where
he could resume his 'great task! / To open the Eternal Worlds, to open the
immortal Eyes / Of Man inwards into the Worlds of Thought: into Eternity'
(*Jerusalem* 5: 17–19).

The return to London, in other words, involved two momentous (and
related) changes in Blake's intellectual life. In the first place, his Felpham years
drove him to a profound critique of what he came to see as his own self-
delusions. These began when he agreed to follow Hayley, that is, when he
agreed to give priority to his worldly interests rather than his spiritual 'duty'.
He went there in September 1800, but by the following September he already
felt torn between his quotidian tasks and his 'Abstract folly', as he told his
friend Thomas Butts. He stayed at Felpham for two more years, however
(until September 1803), and he seems to have suppressed his anxieties and
sense of uneasiness – to have followed the satanic path of silence – for over a
year after he first told Butts about the war in his members. Finally, however, in
November 1802, his own conspiracy of silence is broken in a letter to Butts:

You will Justly enquire why I have not written All this time to you? I answer I have
been very Unhappy & could not think of troubling you about it or any of my real
Friends (I have written many letters to you which I burnd & did not send) (E719)

Thus Blake begins to utter that litany of sorrows he will tell in letters over the next several months, until his decision to return to London has been made and agreed to by everyone concerned.

But he might well have returned much earlier had it not been for the promise held out by the Peace of Amiens. Though the actual treaty was not signed until March 1802, news of a peace with France came in October 1801, and Blake was moved to celebrate the event in a letter to his and Hayley's friend, the mild Swedenborgian artist John Flaxman:

The Kingdoms of this World are now become the Kingdoms of God & his Christ, & we shall reign with him for ever & ever. The Reign of Literature & the Arts Commences. Blessed are those who are found studious of Literature & Humane & polite accomplishments . . . I hope that France & England will henceforth be as One Country and their Arts One, & that you will Ere long be erecting monuments In Paris – Emblems of Peace. (E718)

The treaty was signed in March 1802, but by the following November – when Blake told Butts of his unhappiness – the dark promise of a return to war was already in the air, and England in fact reopened hostilities in May 1803.

It is in this context of ruined political hopes that Blake's Pyrrhonist attitude toward secular politics has to be understood. One of his deepest convictions was that war and 'corporeal' violence were unequivocal evils. In this respect Blake was a member of that otherwise wildly heteroglot group known as the Friends of Peace, whose members included dissenters, both secular and religious, of all stripes – from pietists like Flaxman to intellectuals like Price and Priestley to Jacobins like Hardy.[8]

Like them Blake held England responsible for the war with France, and his critique of Bishop Watson is one battle in his 'Mental Fight' against the ideologues who articulate and promote state militarist policies. When Watson attributes 'the *guillotine-massacres*' of the Terror to '*the principles of your book* [i.e., Paine's *Age of Reason*]', Blake denounces the bishop's hypocrisy: 'To what does the Bishop attribute the English Crusade against France. is it not to State Religion. blush for shame' (E613).

So when England re-declared war with France in 1803, Blake had already decided it was time to reassume his spiritual duties. Foremost of these was the necessity of opposing the corporeal wars of the state with the intellectual wars of vision. Between 1795 and 1804 England's 'Crusade' against France had not

---

[8] See J. E. Cookson, *The Friends of Peace. Anti-War Liberalism in England, 1793–1815* (Cambridge, 1982); Albert Goodwin, *The Friends of Liberty: The English Democratic Movement in the Age of the French Revolution* (London, 1979); James E. Bradley, *Popular Politics and the American Revolution in England* (Macon, Ga., 1986).

merely condemned England's open political dissenters to jail, transportation, and even death, it had wounded society at what was for Blake its critical intellectual centres: 'The Arts & Sciences are the Destruction of Tyrannies or Bad Governments Why should A Good Government endeavour to Depress What is its Chief & only Support' (E636). That question, laid down at the beginning of Blake's marginalia to Reynolds's *Discourses*, is of course rhetorical, and it indicates the close relation Blake observed between state policy and an (ostensibly 'private') ideological apparatus like the Royal Academy. The 'Crusade' against France found its domestic analogues, not merely in the treason and sedition trials, but in the neglect of England's most important artists: 'Reynolds & Gainsborough Blotted & Blurred one against the other & Divided all the English World between them Fuseli Indignant < almost > hid himself – I [was] < am > hid' (E636). The imperialism of established art, matching the imperialism of the state it supports, drives the country's true spiritual leaders into obscurity and silence. So Blake left Felpham in 1803 determined to break that silence.

JJR: Your narrative is accurate enough, in general. I only insist that we not forget the circumstances under which Blake's sojourn at Felpham was originally imagined by those most concerned about it: that is, by Hayley, Blake himself and Blake's other patron Thomas Butts. Hayley brought Blake to Felpham, initially, to do a drawing and engraving of Hayley's beloved illegitimate son Thomas Alphonso, who had just died. Hayley quickly took a fond paternal interest in Blake, who reminded him of the poet William Cowper, whom Hayley had also patronised. Hayley wanted to help Blake improve himself in two specific ways: in his art, which Hayley saw as filled with genius, but technically defective; and in his worldly circumstances, which Hayley knew were severely straitened.

Butts, on the other hand, was gratified by Blake's move to Felpham because it separated him from London and Blake's radical urban world. Blake wrote to Butts on 23 September – shortly after he had begun his stay at Felpham – that he was very pleased with the prospect of the place: 'I have begun to Work, & find that I can work with greater pleasure than ever . . . Felpham is propitious to the Arts.' Butts's reply to this letter is more sober, and quite revealing:

Whether you will be a better Painter or a better Poet from your change of ways & means I know not; but this I predict; that you will be a better Man – excuse me, as you have been accustomed from friendship to do, but certain opinions imbibed . . . from reading . . . nourished by indulgence, and rivetted by a confined Conversation, and which have been equally prejudicial to your Interest & your Happiness, will . . . now I trust, disperse as a Day-break Vapour, and you will henceforth become a Member of that Community of which you are at present, in the opinion of the Archbishop of

Canterbury, but a sign to mark the residence of dim incredulity, haggard suspicion, & bloated Philosophy.[9]

Blake's reply to *this* is equally revealing. Addressing Butts as the 'Friend of Religion and Order', Blake writes that 'Your prediction will I hope be fulfilled in *me*, & in future I am the determined advocate of Religion & Humility the two bands of Society' (E711–12). The point is that Blake was fully conscious of what his move to Felpham entailed, and that he made the move in an effort to put his life under the instruction and direction of certain 'corporeal friends' who had nothing but his best interests in mind – according to their view of those interests.

As we know, his willing submission to the hopes of Butts and Hayley soon put him into conflict with his daimon. This conflict he at first described – in clear deference to the imaginations of Butts and Hayley both – as an inner struggle between his 'Abstract folly' and 'the world of Duty & Reality'. In the end he would decide that the struggle was *in itself* pernicious as it kept him trapped in 'the Doubts of other Mortals. perhaps Doubts proceeding from Kindness. but Doubts are always pernicious'.[10] Those doubts Blake, writing to Butts, chiefly associated with Hayley, who was far more concerned with Blake's commercial and technical success than with his visionary commitments. Indeed, the different interests which Butts and Hayley took in Blake only exacerbated Blake's uneasiness and sense of 'doubt'. Blake writes to Butts about his unhappiness at Felpham because he knows that Butts will sympathise with his feelings in a way that Hayley would not: for Blake had been continuing to do visionary paintings while he was at Felpham, and whereas Hayley condescended to this work, Butts encouraged and patronised it. This differential between Hayley's Blake and Butts's Blake was an index of the various conflicts Blake felt himself torn by. The poem Blake sent to Butts in November 1802, which he in fact had written the previous autumn, underscores the problem:

> 'Must the duties of life each other cross'
> 'Must every joy be dung and dross'
> 'Must my dear Butts feel cold neglect'
> 'Because I give Hayley his due respect'
> 'Must Flaxman look upon me as wild'
> 'And all my friends be with doubts beguild'
> 'Must my Wife live in my Sisters bane'

[9] G. E. Bentley Jr, *Blake Records* (Oxford, 1969), pp. 75–6.
[10] The crippling effect of a doubting mind is a recurrent preoccupation of Blake's, but it became a central topic in his work beginning around 1798.

'Or my Sister survive on my Loves pain'
'The curses of Los the terrible shade'
'And his dismal terrors make me afraid' (E721)

It is clear that his immediate life – including his visionary life – has become a pool of crosscurrents, with various conflicting interests and demands. It is equally clear, from his various Felpham letters, that he has been temporising with these conflicts; when he does confront them, he either speaks equivocally or he speaks in private, or he deals with them in partial terms, speaking in different terms and different tones, depending on his correspondent.[11] Blake only regains his famous candour at the end of his stay at Felpham, when the decision to leave has been made and openly sanctioned by everyone.

AM: What is the point of all that?

JJR: Simply to establish Blake's credentials with the most conservative flanks of the liberal and dissenting movements, and to indicate how various were the interests of these groups. We rightly associate Blake with the Friends of Peace, the Friends of Liberty, even the jacobinical Party of Humanity; what we do not so often remember is that he was equally capable of finding common ground with the Friends of 'Religion and Order', or that those friends of religion and order were themselves committed to a diverse set of predilections and goals.

Besides, many commentators have pointed out that Blake experienced a kind of spiritual renovation that swept him back toward an apparently more orthodox Christianity, and that this occurred around the turn of the century.[12] The intellectual change first appears in his late revisions and additions to *The Four Zoas*, where Blake attempts to solve the formal problems of that work by introducing his concept of the forgiveness of sins. Of course, Blake's interpretation of that concept is anything but orthodox – indeed, it lays down the apparently outrageous demand that 'the guilty' should 'go free' and the 'innocent' suffer. Blake's interpretation of 'Christian forgiveness' is an antinomian one which has its English roots in the seventeenth century, and which Blake himself calls by its traditional name: The Everlasting Gospel.

We have to remember these things because Blake's post-Lambeth repudiation of worldly politics is the consequence of the renewal of his antinomian Christianity.

AM: I am not sure what you mean to imply in all this. But I take it you are suggesting that Blake finally joined the antinomian wing of the 'Religion and Order' party of Southey, Wordsworth and Coleridge. And if this is what you *do* mean, I have to dissent in the strongest terms. I could remind *you*, of course,

---

[11] See especially his letter to his brother James of 30 January 1803. David Wells's *A Study of William Blake's Letters* (Stauffenberg, 1987) gives a shrewd reading of the Felpham letters (pp. 70–101).

[12] See Wells's discussion, *ibid.*, pp. 84–5, and Margaret Bottrall, *The Divine Image: A Study of Blake's Interpretation of Christianity* (Rome, 1950).

that Blake opposed the church, the king and the government to the end of his
life . . .

JJR: And I could remind *you* that for the last twenty-seven years of his life he cut
his radical London ties. More than that, he established his deepest personal
connections with a circle of pious, and mostly all very conservative, evangelical
Christians.

[Note: The typescript has an editorial note here indicating a hiatus in the
original conversation. Evidently the controversy grew so heated and *ad
hominem* at this point that it broke off entirely. The text resumes with a heading
that simply reads: 'The next day'.]

AM: All right, let's begin again by agreeing that the evidence in these matters is
strangely contradictory. Perhaps we can sort out some of the problems by
trying to clarify those apparent contradictions.

Let me start with your imagination of Blake as political quietist. When
people like you argue this position, they typically support it by drawing a sharp
contrast between the Blake of 1790–5, and the Blake of 1800 and thereafter.
Furthermore, they – you – represent the earlier Blake as a politically active
agent, one of the many Friends of Peace and of Liberty who – in the 1770s and
1780s – opposed England's war with America as well as her intermittent
imperialist conflicts with France; and who, in the 1790s, engaged in open
intellectual war with the policies and spokesmen of the English government.
Blake's supposed political backsliding, in this view, is based upon a prior
conception of the young Blake as a Jacobin and a Paineite.

Now that picture of Blake's career is certainly not false, but it *can be* taken in
misleading ways. Blake's illuminated Lambeth works of 1790–5 are eloquent
enough. Nevertheless, a work like *The French Revolution* should remind us
that Blake's political programme, in *that* work at any rate, was imagining an
outcome to the internal struggles in France along lines that would reconcile
various class positions. The fact that Blake saw very clearly the class-based
character of social exploitation does not mean that he therefore supported –
like the (secular) Jacobins and the (religious) Ranters – class conflict. *The
French Revolution* takes a relatively moderate political line, far indeed from a
jacobin position. Furthermore, we should remember that Blake never joined
any of the radical political associations, not the London Corresponding
Society, not even the relatively moderate Society for Constitutional Information; and – perhaps most telling of all – his name never appears in a single
police report of the period.

Blake's hostility to the government and its policies seems to have been most
deeply founded on a hatred of the worlds of violence and war which kings and

aristocracies seem always to create. Blake's first book of poetry, the *Poetical Sketches*, printed in 1783, is dominated by a self-conscious critique of the general ambition of kings and the violence that ambition engenders, as well as a specific attack upon the mytho-historical roots of England's violent political traditions.[13]

An important event in Blake's early life brings these issues into sharp focus. I mean the Gordon Riots of 1780 and Blake's involvement in them.[14] Alexander Gilchrist reports that 'In this outburst of anarchy, Blake long remembered an involuntary participation of his own' which occurred on the third day of the riots, Tuesday 6 June:

> That evening, the artist happened to be walking in a route chosen by one of the mobs at large . . . Suddenly he encountered the advancing wave of triumphant blackguardism, and was forced (for from such a great surging mob there is no disentanglement) to go along in the front rank, and witness the storm and burning of the fortress-like prison [i.e., Newgate], and release of its three-hundred inmates.[15]

Everyone agrees that this experience must have had a profound effect on Blake, and that the images of urban upheaval found their way into his later work. But Gilchrist's vision of 'triumphant blackguardism' is dismissed, for example, by David Erdman, as the reactionary vision of the pious biographer who even wanted 'to absolve Blake of sympathy with the French Revolution'.[16] Erdman knows that the Gordon Riots involved an 'obscure' 'mixture of motives in the rioters' minds',[17] but his desire to connect this experience with working-class and insurrectionist sympathies in Blake leads him to gloss the strong conservative elements in the anti-government riot. In fact, the Gordon Riots were carried out explicitly under the reactionary cry of 'Church and King',[18] and it is extremely unlikely that Blake would have been sympathetic to what he saw. The liberal-minded George Crabbe judged the events an unmitigated horror, and the radical Thomas Holcroft wrote an account which was anything but sympathetic to either the political goals or the actual deeds of the rioters.[19]

[13] Blake's anti-war views are also evident in his pictorial work of the early 1780s – for example in the picture *War Unchained* (see no. 186 in Martin Butlin, *The Paintings and Drawings of William Blake* (New Haven, Conn., 1981)).

[14] See George Rudé's classic essay 'The Gordon Riots: A Study of the Rioters and their Victims', in *Paris and London in the Eighteenth Century* (New York, 1970), pp. 268–92 and J. Paul de Castro, *The Gordon Riots* (Oxford, 1926). [15] *The Life of William Blake* (London, 1942), p. 30.

[16] *Prophet Against Empire*, p. 9. [17] *Ibid.*, p. 8.

[18] See Rudé, 'The Gordon Riots'; and George Rudé, *The Crowd in History. A Study of Popular Disturbances in France and England 1730–1848* (New York, 1964), chapter 9, and Carl B. Cone, *The English Jacobins. Reformers in Late 18th Century England* (New York, 1968), chapter 7.

[19] See *Thomas Holcroft's A Plain and Succinct Narrative of the Gordon Riots, 1780*, edited by Garland Garvey Smith (Atlanta, 1944); *The Life of George Crabbe, by His Son*, edited by Edmund Blunden (London, 1947), pp. 71–4.

Nor should we expect that Blake would have reacted very differently. Indeed, the conservative Gilchrist was himself aware that the riot only provoked further violence, in particular the government's subsequent acts of what he termed 'indiscriminate vengeance' carried out afterwards 'when strings of boys under fourteen were hung up in a row to vindicate the offended majesty of law'.[20] It is difficult to imagine Blake reacting to these horrible events with anything but disgust.

I rehearse these matters for the following reason. If the argument is that Blake's post-Lambeth years are politically passivist because of his new vision of Christianity, the position will not hold. Of course English government propaganda during the 1790s portrayed the dissenters as dangerous promoters of bloodshed and civic upheaval. The truth of the matter is, however, exactly the opposite – that is to say, the dissenters consistently took pacifist (not passivist) positions. The Gordon Riots were 'Church and King' riots, as was the Birmingham mob's attack on Priestley in 1793. The pacifist line was especially entrenched, moreover, among those groups Blake most identified with: that is to say, the heteroglot circle of urban intellectuals we now associate with the name of the publisher Joseph Johnson. This group ranged, on one hand, to the limit of Paine's relatively a-religious deism, and, on the other, to the unorthodox but passionate Christian nationalism of a man like Edward Williams (Iolo Morganwg), the Welsh poet and patriot.[21]

For all of these people, the onset of fire and blood in the human world was the result of what Blake himself exposed in his early dramatic fragment 'King Edward the Third' as the 'ambition' of kings and the powerful of the earth. When, in *Jerusalem*, Blake says that 'Luvah is France: the Victim of the Spectres of Albion' (66: 15), he continues to follow the ideological line which the Friends of Peace and the Friends of Liberty held in the 1790s, after England declared war on France.

But the position is funded at a deeper level, as we can see by recalling Blake's 'King Edward the Third': for there the king invades

> A country not yet sown with destruction,
> And where the fiery whirlwind of swift war
> Has not yet swept its desolating wing. (E424–5)

---

[20] *The Life of William Blake*, p. 30.

[21] Blake was probably well acquainted with Williams's 1794 poetic collection of poetry and associated mythographical lore: Edward Williams, *Poems, Lyrical and Pastoral* ... (Printed for the Author by J. Nichols, sold by J. Johnson, 1794), 2 vols. See also Williams's other book of the early nineties which he co-authored: *Llywarch Hen: The Heroic Elegies and Other Pieces of Llywarc Hen, Prince of the Cumbrian Britons: with a Literal Translation by William Owen [Pughe]* ... (London, Printed for J. Owen ... and E. Williams, 1792). Williams wrote the long introduction to the book, which gave a history of bardic lore in Britain; Pughe translated the poems and did the notes.

The king's destructive career merely follows a pattern which the play represents as a kind of ancient fate brought into England when the 'Sons of Trojan Brutus', 'Heated with war, fill'd with the blood of Greeks' (E437), destroy the Celts and their way of life. This is a victory which the English minstrel of such deeds represents as a victory of civilisation over 'savage monsters' (E437). Those savages, however, are called 'the Ancient Britons' by patriot mythographers and poets like Edward Williams, a phrase which Blake himself will later use as the title of one of his mytho-historical frescoes of 1809.[22]

The historical and political texts in *Poetical Sketches* thus outline England's peculiar 'circular of destiny'.[23] When Edward III tries to rouse his soldiers to battle with France, he appeals to 'Liberty, the charter'd right of Englishmen' (E424). The line glances back, of course, to the much celebrated source of English 'Liberty', the Magna Charta. But the word 'charter'd', for Blake, carries as well very different overtones, as we know best from Blake's spectacular use of the term in 'London'. To an eighteenth-century patriot, the Magna Charta was itself a highly equivocal achievement.

Edward III's immediate bequest to England and Europe is the Hundred Years' War, but he is only repeating the cycle begun when 'the detestable Gods of Priam' (*Milton* 25: 49) were brought to Britain. Blake's 'Prologue to King John' fills in another signal moment of this allegorical history: 'Justice hath heaved a sword to plunge in Albion's breast; for Albion's sins are crimson dy'd, and the red scourge follows her desolate sons' (E439). Blake's new production of these texts, in 1783, exposes both the latest turn of England's ancient historical destiny, as well as the 'Patriot' current which runs against that history:

Then Patriot rose; full oft did Patriot rise, when Tyranny hath stain'd fair Albion's breast with her own children's gore. (E439)

This is a dissenter's text, as the (all but technical) term 'Patriot' underscores. It is important to see, as well, that the text draws a distinction between 'Tyranny' and 'Albion': for the evil that has descended upon Albion and her children comes through a tyrannical line of warriors that stretches back to Troy, comes to England through Roman, Scandinavian and Norman invasion, and emerges at last in the form called 'England' (to Blake, this word is by no

---

[22] Blake's discussion of this work, in his *Descriptive Catalogue* (E542–5), is extremely important for indicating the depth of Blake's knowledge of patriotic antiquarian lore.

[23] The best discussions of Blake's *Poetical Sketches* are Margaret Ruth Lowery, *Windows of the Morning* (New Haven, Conn., 1946); Erdman, *Prophet Against Empire*, chapter 1, 2, 4; John Ehrstine, *William Blake's Poetical Sketches* (Pullman, Wash., 1967).

means to be equated with those other words he uses: Albion, Britain, Britannia).

The text itself therefore constitutes a kind of 'patriotic rising'. In the 'Prologue to King John' an immediate allusion is also being made to England's war with 'her own children' the Americans. 'King Edward the Third', on the other hand, primarily develops a general comment on a long stretch of European history.

J J R: I am sure your narrative must be leading somewhere, and of course I long to be led. But may I interrupt for a moment? Not to fight with you – on the contrary. What you are saying about Blake's early poetical work suddenly clarifies important aspects of his famous letter to Hayley of 23 October 1804:

> Now ... I have entirely reduced that spectrous Fiend to his station, whose annoyance has been the ruin of my labours for the last passed twenty years of my life. He is the enemy of conjugal love and is the Jupiter of the Greeks ... the ruiner of ancient Greece. I speak with perfect confidence ... Nebuchadnezzar had seven times passed over him; I have had twenty; thank God I was not altogether a beast as he was; but I was a slave bound in a mill among beasts and devils; these beasts and devils are now, together with myself, become children of light and liberty, and my feet and my wife's feet are free from fetters. O lovely Felpham, parent of Immortal Friendship, to thee I am eternally indebted for my three years' rest from perturbation and the strength I now enjoy.
> (E756)

Blake associates his new sense of freedom with being 'enlightened with the light I enjoyed in my youth, and which has for exactly twenty years been closed from me as by a door and by window-shutters'. The new liberty is also connected in Blake's mind with his recent visit to 'the Truchsessian Gallery of pictures', and to the work he is doing on some plates he is 'engraving after Romney, whose spiritual aid has not a little conduced to my restoration to the light of art' (E756)

A M: Well, the letter still seems a cryptic text. What are those 'twenty years', and what have they to do with Blake's 'conjugal love', George Romney and the visit to the Truchsessian Gallery?

J J R: I doubt that we shall ever sort it all out, but I think we can reconstruct some of what Blake was talking about. 'Twenty years' takes us back to 1784, the year that Blake and James Parker set up a print shop in London, the year after the publication of the *Poetical Sketches* where we trace the poetical form of the light Blake enjoyed in his youth. In this letter Blake sees his sojourn at Felpham as a 'three years' rest' from the years of 'perturbation' which, by this account, began 'exactly' in 1784.

Romney enters into this equation because in 1784, a few months before Blake decided to start his print-selling business with Parker, Romney was so enthusiastic about the young Blake's talents that he was working to raise money to send Blake to study in Rome.[24] At this juncture Blake's father died, leaving Blake with an inheritance of about £100. Instead of using the money to help finance a trip to Rome, however, Blake invested it in the print-selling business, which shortly failed. The Truchsessian Gallery of pictures brought Rome to London, and to William Blake, twenty years after these events.

In this enigmatic letter, then, Blake seems to be saying a number of related things. Romney's 'spiritual aid has not a little conduced to my restoration to the light of art' because Romney's 'spiritual form' has, as it were, reminded Blake of Blake's early commitment to the 'sublime allegory' of historical painting. In 1784 Romney was telling Blake and others that Blake's 'historical drawings rank with those of Mi[chael] Angelo'.[25] The *Poetical Sketches* exhibit, in verse form, analogous allegorical methods.

But in 1784 Blake decided not to pursue the line of work which Romney admired in Blake's historical drawings. He set up a print shop instead, and 'bound [himself] in a mill with beasts and devils'. Blake is surely referring to his subsequent years in London where he had to struggle for a living with other engravers and artists, all of whom had to compete with each other. Following the 'footsteps of the fiends of commerce' (E754), Blake scraped together a meagre subsistence.

When he returned to London from Felpham, he saw it as 'a City of Assassinations' (E751) where artists and artisans would do anything for worldly success and pre-eminence. It was, in this respect, worse than he had known it in the 1790s, and had become an emblem of a country in desperate need of spiritual renovation. That renovation would come from the clear symbolistic–historical vision that Blake, along with his beloved brother Robert, had 'enjoyed in [his] youth'.[26]

During the 1790s, and up to the Peace of Amiens, Blake clearly flirted with the idea that a political solution might be found for the evil events which had overtaken Europe. The breaking of that illusory peace was important for Blake

[24] See *Blake Records*, pp. 27–8, and Joseph Viscomi, 'The Myth of Commissioned Illuminated Books: George Romney, Isaac D'Israeli, and ONE HUNDRED AND SIXTY designs . . . of Blake's', *Blake. An Illustrated Quarterly*, 23 (Fall, 1989), 48–74. Viscomi's essay documents the Blake–Romney relationship, but its importance for Blake studies far transcends this local matter.
[25] Viscomi, 'The Myth of Commissioned Illuminated Books'.
[26] Robert Blake was also an artist. At his death in 1787 he left behind some allegorical paintings of Druid ceremonies – another indication that Blake was also learned in these matters at a very early period. Blake's early acquaintance with antiquarian mythography and Druid lore would have come through Jacob Bryant's *A New System; or, An Analysis of Ancient Mythology . . .*, 3 vols. (London, 1774–6); John Toland, *A Critical History of the Celtic Religion and Learning . . .* (London, 1718); and William Stukeley's two books *Abury . . .* (London, 1743) and *Stonehenge . . .* (London, 1740).

because it separated him for good from an imagination that anything but visionary art could halt the money-driven cycles of destruction. War and bloodshed were only the most spectacular signs of the evil that was at work. Equally significant was the dehumanising spirit of Mammon which Blake saw throughout his society. In the same letter where he speaks of London as the 'City of Assassinations', he mentions a *Life of Washington* which had been sent to him by Hayley:

I suppose an American would tell me that Washington did all that was done before he was born, as the French now adore Buonaparte and the English our poor George; so the Americans will consider Washington as their god. This is only Grecian, or rather Trojan worship, and perhaps will be revised [reversed?] in an age or two. In the meantime, I have the happiness of seeing the Divine countenance in such men as Milton and Cowper more distinctly than in any prince or hero (E749–50)

This equation of the debased imaginations of America, England and France with 'Trojan worship' is extremely significant. Blake here recurs to the antinomian forms of thought which figure so strongly in the *Poetical Sketches*, and which he kept in touch with during the Lambeth years by his Swedenborgian contacts, and his readings in religious and patriotic antiquarians like Williams.

Between the *Poetical Sketches* and 1804, however, Blake's work does not make much use of the mythographic materials that relate to the aboriginal histories of the British Isles. These influences appear in the *Poetical Sketches*, but they do not reappear until Blake starts writing *Milton* and *Jerusalem* twenty years later. When, in *Jerusalem*, Blake says that 'Luvah is France: the Victim of the Spectres of Albion' the allusion is only partly to England's hypocritical 'Crusade' against France. The line means as well that Napoleonic France is the monstrous *creation* of Albion's spectres (i.e. English militarism) – according to the mytho-historical logic of the *Poetical Sketches* as it would be formulated in the late epics: 'All things begin & end in Albions ancient Druid rocky shore' (*Milton* 6:25).[27]

Furthermore, the paintings Blake would exhibit in 1809 are dominated by

[27] For two good studies of Blake and early British mythologic history see Peter F. Fisher, 'Blake and the Druids', reprinted in *Blake: A Collection of Critical Essays*, edited by Northrop Frye (Englewood Cliffs, N.J., 1966), pp. 156–78; Ruthven Todd, 'William Blake and the Eighteenth-Century Mythologists,' in *Tracks in the Snow* (London, 1946), pp. 29–60. Blake of course would have been familiar with the mythic reconstruction of Irish history in the Ossian poems, and Lowth's *Lectures on Hebrew Poetry* (translated into English in 1787) was another important work he used. Marilyn Butler provides a good general introduction to these matters in her (unpublished) lecture 'Bards and Prophets: or Macpherson, Blake and the Poetry of Origins'; see also David Worrall, 'Blake's *Jerusalem* and the Visionary History of Britain', *Studies in Romanticism*, 16 (1977), 189–216; and Jerome J. McGann, 'The Idea of an Indeterminate Text: Blake's Bible of Hell and Dr Alexander Geddes', *Studies in Romanticism*, 25 (1986), 303–24.

this mytho-historical consciousness of civilisation and its discontents. Blake's paintings *The Spiritual Form of Nelson Guiding Leviathan* and *The Spiritual Form of Pitt, Guiding Behemoth* are 'compositions of a mythological cast, similar to those Apotheoses of . . . the ancient republics, monarchies, and patriarchates of Asia' (E530–1). Blake says the great Asiatic monuments, like the celebrated artistic works of the Greeks and other later periods, are in fact 'copies from some stupendous originals now lost or perhaps buried till some happier age'. Blake learned of these matters when he was 'taken in vision' to see the 'wonderful originals'. His paintings of Nelson and Pitt represent his attempt to reproduce the original visions in forms suitable for his own age and country.

Two matters are crucial here: first, that such visionary works 'contain . . . mythological and recondite meaning, where more is meant than meets the eye' (E531); and second, that Blake's paintings, like the 'grand works of ancient art', are copies made from original visions. These paintings do not ask the viewer to take the figures of Nelson and Pitt as worshipful heroes or gods. Blake called that kind of response to art 'Trojan worship':

but the Greeks, and since then the Moderns, have neglected to subdue the gods of Priam. These Gods are visions of the eternal attributes . . . which, when erected into gods, become destructive of humanity. (E536)

Figures like Pitt and Nelson 'ought to be the servants, and not the masters of man, or of society'. When they become masters they appear in the full truth of their perverted existences, that is, they appear as tyrants and warriors. The 'recondite meaning' of Blake's paintings is that these figures have to be understood in a double sense at all times: as emblems of humankind's 'eternal attributes', and as signs of how and when those attributes are perverted.

AM: And so Blake's Nelson is a demon, a satanic presence?

JJR: That is the Nelson of history, the 'hero' worshipped by Englishmen. Blake has perceived the eternal truth of the historical evil called Nelson. But Blake's *painting* of Nelson is not demonic, it is visionary – a 'recondite' image whose true meaning Englishmen must be brought to understand, however difficult it might be. When rightly understood even 'beasts and devils' like Pitt and Nelson, or like those other unnamed ones Blake speaks of in his letter to Hayley, can 'become children of light and liberty'.

AM: That seems to me correct. Blake's views here inevitably recall what he wrote much earlier, in Plate 11 of *The Marriage of Heaven and Hell*, where he denounced those who turned heroic and legendary materials into 'forms of worship'. But there *is* a difference between the two sets of texts, and the difference might come as a surprise – especially to you: *Blake's 1804–9 views are more fully and self-consciously political than the ones he formulated in 1790–3.*

JJR: What!?

AM: This conclusion shocks you because, as I said before, you have narrow ideas about what counts as 'political consciousness'. After England renewed her war with France in 1803, Blake was moved to 'mental fight' with the spectrous imagination that so dominated his own country's militarist policies. The collapse of the Peace of Amiens was crucial, but almost equally important were certain fortuitous publishing events. In the years immediately after the turn of the century Blake clearly renewed his contact with the traditions of religious and patriotic antiquarianism which had been so influential in his 'youth'. He was able to do so because a spate of new books began to appear which dealt with these subjects at length. Among other things, the Welsh Triads were published in 1801 in the *Myvyrian Archaiology of Wales*, Pughe's *Cambrian Biography* appeared in 1803 and Davies's *Celtic Researches* came out in 1804.[28]

The 'Spirit who lovst Brittannias Isle'[29] moves through texts like these, and it led Blake to the *political* acts of his mytho-historical paintings, and of his late epics *Milton* and *Jerusalem*.[30] He specifically invokes that spirit in a revealing set of unfinished Notebook verses (date *c*. 1808–11):

> Now Art has lost its mental Charms
> France shall subdue the World in Arms
> So spoke an Angel at my birth
> Then said Descend thou upon Earth
> Renew the Arts on Britains Shore
> And France shall fall down & adore
> With works of Art their Armies meet
> And War shall sink beneath thy feet
> But if thy Nation Arts refuse
> And if they scorn the immortal Muse
> France shall the Arts of Peace restore
> And save thee from the Ungrateful shore (E479)

The vision is the same: the intellectual war of the artist is opposed to the corporeal war of the nations; Blake is summoned from birth to this political mission of visionary art; and for the London-born Blake the struggle is to release the soul of 'Britain' from its 'English' enslavement.

[28] Iolo Morganwg (Edward Williams) introduced the Triads printed in the first (1801) volume of the *Myvyrian Archaiology*. The Triads were further discussed in Sharon Turner's *A Vindication of the Genuineness of the Ancient British Poems* (1803). Other important books so far as Blake is concerned were Richard Brothers's *A Description of Jerusalem* ... (1801) and Edward Davies's *The Mythology and Rites of the British Druids* (1809).

[29] Blake writes 'Brittannias', not 'England's', because the distinction between the terms is important.

[30] Blake's close connection with the Welsh nationalist movement has been recently underscored by the discovery that his monumental painting of *The Ancient Britons*, exhibited in 1809, was commissioned by William Owen Pughe. See G. E. Bentley Jr, *Blake Records Supplement* (Oxford, 1988), 65–8.

With respect to the Hayley letter I would add only one thing: that the visit to the Truchsessian Gallery figured more intimately in Blake's renovated insights than you suggest. This result comes about, I think, through Blake's peculiar reaction to a peculiar collection of paintings. The Truchsessian pictures were not in fact painted by the original masters Blake would have studied had he gone to Rome in 1784; they were all studio copies made after the originals. Blake's encounter with the Gallery's copies may well have helped him to formulate his theory of 'original vision' on one hand, and copywork on the other.[31]

JJR: Well, it is true that Blake followed the line of the antiquarian patriots in believing that poets were the unacknowledged legislators of the world. And it is also true that he did not follow the Lake Poets in their jingoist careers. Nevertheless, the religious ground of his politics – which you threw in my face some time back – strangled his hopes for social change. You yourself have pointed out Blake's conviction that 'Religion and Politics [are] the Same Thing' (*Jerusalem* 57: 10). As a result, his 'politics of vision' spun into another dance of those famous Shelleyan reciprocals, beauty and ineffectuality.

We see this throughout Blake's career, but nowhere more dramatically than in the work produced after the Peace of Amiens. In *Jerusalem* Plate 45/31, for instance, the prophet Los enters London to try to find out who is responsible for the fact that 'every Minute Particular of Albion [is] degraded & murderd'. But his quest to find the guilty is immobilised by his adherence to The Everlasting Gospel:

> What shall I do! what could I do, if I could find these
>   Criminals
> I could not dare to take vengeance; for all things are so
>   constructed
> And builded by the Divine hand, that the sinner shall
>   always escape,
> And he who takes vengeance alone is the criminal of
>   Providence (lines 29–32)

'The conclusion is that vengeance is futile and only compounds the crime, since individuals are not responsible for this state of affairs. Then who is? Blake

---

[31] For further discussion of Blake's visit see Morton D. Paley 'The Truchsessian Gallery Revisited', *Studies in Romanticism*, 16 (1977), 165–77; Wells, *A Study of William Blake's Letters*, pp. 105–9. Paley notes that some of the Truchsessian pictures were not copies, but the genuine ones were from the Dutch school ('Netherlandish'), which Blake scorned. In a private communication Robert Essick doubts that Blake's Truchsessian Gallery experience was 'a source for Blake's theories on the differences between an original and a copy . . . I think that the original/copy distinction (like the conception/execution non-distinction) has a much deeper source in Blake's activities as a printmaker – known in his own town primarily as a copy-engraver, but always striving to become an original printmaker like Durer.'

seems at this point to be hamstrung by his new liberal doctrine of compassion and the forgiveness of sins. If the sinner always escapes . . . social justice can never be implemented. (This is the very opposite of the violent retribution which the Messiah brings back in the Book of Revelation.) It is not unfair to conclude that the Divine hand has constructed things in this way in order to frustrate change and maintain the system – a kind of predestinarian pessimism Blake would have no doubt disclaimed, yet that is where his argument seems to lead.'[32]

A M: That is where the argument may be *taken*, but it is emphatically *not* where Blake himself took the argument. The devil can quote Scripture to his own purpose, and if later commentators have used Blake to support their political quietism, this is not a wickedness to be laid at Blake's feet. To Blake, 'vengeance' can have nothing to do with the active implementation of social justice. Indeed, preserving a clear distinction between vengeance and social justice is the ground on which, for him at any rate, a programme of fundamental social change would have to begin. Otherwise the 'circle of destiny' . . .

[Note: Here the dialogue ends, as it had begun: *in mediis rebus*.]

---

[32] Stewart Crehan, *Blake in Context* (Dublin, 1984), p. 81.

7

Presentation of the self in the composition of
The Prelude

ROBERT WOOF

Wordsworth takes the presentation of the self as poetic subject onto a higher level and into a longer narrative range than any previous poet. He seems indispensable to any book about the presentation of the poetic self and its role in the wider subject of the presentation of poetry. But what makes Wordsworth doubly interesting is not only that it is without precedent for a poet to write so much about himself, even in a long poem, but also because so much is now known about the early growth of *The Prelude*. Changes of connection and direction, some radical, some marvellously subtle, occurred between the composition of the earliest fragments of late 1798, the two-book *Prelude* of late 1799, the temporary design of a five-book *Prelude* of early 1804 and the poem as completed in 1805-6. Many of these changes reveal a different, often expanded and more deeply explored presentation of Wordsworth's experience as a boy, a young man, a political figure and a potential poet whose subject is haunted by the need to deepen his self-analysis.

The passage he gives us first is a cry of release and an exhilaration at some new freedom:

> Oh there is blessing in this gentle breeze,
> That blows from the green fields and from the clouds
> And from the sky: it beats against my cheek,
> And seems half conscious of the joy it gives.
> O welcome messenger! O welcome friend!
> A captive greets thee, coming from a house
> Of bondage, from yon city's walls set free,
> A prison where he hath been long immured.
> Now I am free, enfranchis'd and at large,
> May fix my habitation where I will.
> *(Prelude* (1805), Bk I. 1–10; p. 28)[1]

---

[1] Unless otherwise stated, all quotations from *The Prelude* are from the Norton Critical Edition, *The Prelude, 1799, 1805, 1850*, edited by Jonathan Wordsworth, M. H. Abrams, Stephen Gill (New York, 1979). The three Cornell editions (cited below) are indispensable guides to and presentations of the Wordsworth texts. I am grateful to the Trustees of the Wordsworth Trust, Dove Cottage, Grasmere, for permission to quote from their manuscripts.

At once we are in a world where Nature is not an object; the breeze 'seems half conscious of the joy it gives'; it is alive, and a little later its vitality is linked with the 'mild creative breeze' of poetic inspiration. A characteristic of Wordsworth's genius is a preference for metaphors that can be read literally. Thus he is able to make use of the conventional notion of inspiration coming like a breeze, or wind, or breath, but unlike most poets, he must first establish that there is a real breeze playing over him. So Wordsworth has us begin on this note of freedom where there is opened to him an immense potential for both living and writing. His words invite us to remember Milton's Samson coming from his dark prison, and moreover, with a phrase a few lines on, 'The earth is all before me', to remember Milton's words describing the departure of Adam and Eve into a new world at the close of *Paradise Lost*. So Wordsworth begins.

Was it from Goslar, a walled city in Germany, that he came in 1799, with so powerful a sense of release? He had gone there, with the anonymous *Lyrical Ballads* just out, in the October of 1798, and remained for more than eighteen weeks, immured by what he understood was the coldest winter of the century. He had gone with his sister, Dorothy, to make himself fluent in the language; in the event the two were left much alone and Wordsworth wrote a great deal in English and learnt very little German. They suffered from cold, lack of money and social ostracism, for a young man travelling with his sister was a notion as hard to take as a young man travelling with his mistress: Wordsworth wrote from Goslar in February 1799:

Goslar was once the residence of Emperors, and it is now the residence of Grocers and Linen-drapers who are, I say it with a feeling of sorrow, a wretched race; the flesh, blood and bone in their minds being nothing but knavery and low falsehood. We have met with one dear and kind creature, but he is so miserably deaf that we could only have with him games of cross-purposes, and he likewise labors under a common German infirmity, the loss of teeth, so that with bad German, bad English, bad French, bad hearing, and bad utterance you will imagine we have had very pretty dialogues but the creature is all kindness and benevolence, and I shall never forget him.[2]

It was during this cold winter in a strange country that Wordsworth, in the common way of exiled poets, recalled in verse his boyhood and schooltime among English hills. The memories are golden, though not sentimental, for Nature's severity is as moving as her kindness. These are the famous memories – the bathing of a summer's day in the mill race at Cockermouth, the plundering of snares set for woodcocks, the scrambling up to ravens' nests, the stealing of a boat, the skating, the schoolboy imitating the hooting of owls. These and some other such came out of Goslar, and formed the main part of those drafted passages called 'manuscript JJ'. Was it then – and I am conscious that different

---

[2] *The Letters of William and Dorothy Wordsworth*, second edition, edited by Ernest de Selincourt; second edition, revised by Chester L. Shaver, Mary Moorman, Alan G. Hill, 8 vols. (Oxford, 1967–93), I, 249.

views exist – having written these passages, and having got out of Goslar in the early spring of 1799, feeling understandably greater confidence in his own poetic powers, that Wordsworth wrote that exhilarated passage which became the beginning of the 1805 *Prelude*?

For myself, I think it was. Immediately after that beginning Wordsworth, in the 1805 version, goes on to comment on his own opening passage, the poem being now addressed to Coleridge:

> Thus far, O friend! did I not used to make
> A present joy the matter of my song,
> Pour out that day, my soul in measured strains,
> Even in the very words which I have here
> Recorded.
>
> (*Prelude* (1805), Bk I. 55–59; pp. 30, 32)

Of course, Wordsworth, not interested in editorial commentary, does not tell us which day 'that day' was, if indeed it was one single day; he does not tell us that release, 'from yon City's walls set free', was from Goslar – some scholars identify the city as London, others try Bristol.[3] But since the lines are in any case a proper

---

[3] Although most recent scholars accept John Finch's suggestion in his essay, 'Wordsworth's Two-Handed Engine' in *Bicentenary Wordsworth Studies in Memory of John Alban Finch*, edited by Jonathan Wordsworth (Ithaca, 1970), that the preamble (*Prelude* (1805), Bk I. 1–54) belongs to 18 November 1799, or thereabouts, one is reluctant to reject Wordsworth's own insistence that the 'glad preamble' (see *Prelude* (1805), Bk VII. 4) was an extempore effusion upon leaving 'yon city's walls'. Reasons for this reluctance include: the fragments of the preamble text in manuscript JJ (Z verso, reproduced and transcribed in *The Prelude, 1798–1799*, edited by Stephen Parrish (Ithaca, 1977), pp. 116–17) suggest Goslar; the notes to *The Prelude* (1850) and Christopher Wordsworth in the *The Memoirs* (1851) both confirm it; the spring-like feel in the preamble would better fit February 1799; Wordsworth's late amendment in the 1850 text, suggesting that it was *six* years, not *five*, from his writing the preamble, implies there is some particular occasion to which he is alluding. Lastly, the preamble is peculiar in that it is extempore – whereas the rest of the passages in manuscript JJ are recollections, or, as Dorothy put it to Coleridge, a description of William's 'boyish pleasures'.

The post-preamble itself seems to divide into two separate episodes. Lines 68–142 – with its two-day loitering journey – seems to refer to an autumnal event which may, or may not, belong to *c*.18 November 1799, but, if it should, since the episode is reported, it must have been written later than that experience; certainly, contrary to John Finch, it could have taken place at a time separate from *The Prelude*. One simply has to accept that there is no absolute historical basis for this seminal moment, but it is poetically and symbolically appropriate. Mark Reed, in his magisterial *Thirteen-Book Prelude* (Ithaca, 1991), pp. 3–6, thinks that 'some portions of the passage may have been in Wordsworth's mind as early as 1795' (which implies Wordsworth is remembering his leaving London or Bristol), but he concludes with a more sophisticated and less specific date – that the preamble was 'the first passage of *The Prelude* composed after the copying of manuscripts U and V.' Whatever dates are involved with the post-preamble, its later part, lines 143–271, must be at the earliest 1801 (see footnote 10 below); at their latest, 1804, for then they appear as the opening of *The Prelude* in manuscript M (Coleridge's copy taken to Malta in April 1804). The preamble and post-preamble do not fit into any known biographical facts, even though it all seems thematically effective and 'true'.

opening for a long poem, what matters is perhaps the metaphor of the city. Naturally such dangers and hazards of trying to date, or to place, lurk for the reader behind every bush and tree of *The Prelude*, confessedly, after all, an autobiographical poem. But we should keep Wordsworth's own warning in mind: when over seventy years old he spoke of his earlier poem, *An Evening Walk*: 'the plan of it has not been confined to a particular walk or an individual place; proof (of which I was unconscious at the time) of my unwillingness to submit the poetic spirit to the chains of fact and real circumstance'.[4]

The sense of release, the spring, or vernal promise, is followed in our 1805 text by a description of an autumnal walk that lasted two or three loitering days. Wordsworth lay on the ground – 'a day / With silver clouds, and sunshine on the grass.' He is warmed by the sun, confident in the future of his poetry, and then follows a seminal, and, I think, a symbolic moment:

> Long I lay
> Cheered by the genial pillow of the earth
> Beneath my head, soothed by a sense of touch
> From the warm ground, that balanced me, else lost
> Entirely, seeing nought, nought hearing, save
> When here and there, about the grove of oaks
> Where was my bed, an acorn from the trees
> Fell audibly and with a startling sound.
> *(Prelude* (1805), Bk 1. 88–94; p. 32)

Balanced by the earth, 'else lost entirely': this sums up much about Wordsworth. For one of his problems was a tendency to withdraw so completely into his mind, that he lost touch with tangible everyday reality. He once said: 'Many times while going to school have I grasped at a wall or tree to recall myself from this abyss of idealism to the reality.' His mind and imagination needed the balance of the earth: the great temptation that he constantly resists is that of being the blind poet – of writing from entirely within his head. Geoffrey Hartman may seem melodramatic on this point, but he is right that Wordsworth found the imagination a burden unless balanced by images from the everyday world.[5]

Then begins in the 1805 *Prelude* a troubled passage where Wordsworth describes his inability to write and to find a suitable subject for a long poem. In my own early reading of the poem – the first two books, set, as always, for a certain examination – I found this part difficult. The subjects Wordsworth brings forward for consideration seemed so unlike his own great themes. When I read Gerard Manley Hopkins's comment that Wordsworth's poetry could suffer from a certain 'Parnassian' quality, I felt I understood better; for Parnassian

---

[4] *The Fenwick Notes of William Wordsworth*, edited by Jared Curtis (Bristol, 1993), p. 7.
[5] *Wordsworth's Poetry 1787–1814* (New Haven, 1964).

verse is verse technically polished and well wrought, but without inspiration. Later, when the chronology of how Wordsworth wrote *The Prelude* became clearer, the passage seemed to have a thematic rightness. Perhaps it is Parnassian, but once one has its probable date – 1803 or 1804 – its kinship with the political sonnets of those years becomes clear. In those sonnets, Wordsworth's public voice – Juvenalian in its serious tone and its demand for moral rigour – has developed: 'Milton! thou shouldst be living at this hour', 'The World is too much with us, late or soon / Getting or spending, we lay waste our powers.' The theme of national independence and liberty, in part stimulated by the threat of invasion from France, had, in 1802–3, seized Wordsworth's imagination, and in this proposed list of topics for a poem, the theme gets a hearing even within *The Prelude*. Even though Wordsworth does not develop it in the autobiography, it is part of his agenda of concerns. Almost all the rest of that poem springs out of personal experience. The very canvassing of epic topics reminds us that the poem Wordsworth *is* writing must be taken seriously: and his first reference is to Milton:

> I settle on some British theme, some old
> Romantic tale, by Milton left unsung . . .
> (*Prelude* (1805), Bk I. 179–80; p. 38)

Then a chivalric theme is a possibility, and Wordsworth's phrasing suggests that Boccaccio's *Decameron* – which we know he read in Italian – is as much a model as Spenser himself. He goes on to pick out a few likely – and some unlikely – characters from history, and though they are not among the best known heroes, he retains a lofty allusiveness, which adds, at a first reading, to one's coldness towards the passage.

Lack of learning was never one of Wordsworth's faults; he had an excellent schooling at Hawkshead, at what was then a remarkable school (three boys who were his contemporaries there became Senior Wranglers at Cambridge; others were highly placed). Wordsworth's abilities were recognised: within a week of his arrival at Cambridge he was elected a Foundress scholar.[6] Of course, he was not eligible for a classified degree because he had dropped mathematics, but even from his schooldays, and certainly at Cambridge (where his private studies included Italian, in addition to his major readings of Latin and some further exploration of French, begun at Hawkshead with his dancing master), he read widely and seriously. In his list of possible subjects for heroic poems he is uncompromisingly allusive; certainly Ernest de Selincourt, arguably the greatest of Wordsworth's editors, felt the need to write long notes explaining who such

---

[6] Ben Ross Schneider in *Wordsworth's Cambridge Education* (Cambridge, 1957) thinks Wordsworth was a sizar, and therefore suffered from social slights and financial constraints, a view unsupported by *The Prelude* or other known facts.

men as Mithridates and Sertorius were, feeling perhaps that the twentieth-century reader did not know his Plutarch, or even his Gibbon, as well as Wordsworth. Yet it may be these straight historical notes misfire. By considering as poetic subjects men from past times who are not readily part of our common knowledge, Wordsworth was enabled in part to reinvent them. Mithridates, for instance, who was a first-century king from Asia Minor, Wordsworth (either by a sleight of hand, or misunderstanding Gibbon) identifies with the much later Odin, the presiding figure of Gothic mythology, and he attributes to this Mithridates/Odin the Goths' overthrow of tyrannical Rome. Again, perhaps taking a hint from the eighteenth-century English traveller, George Glas,[7] he suggests that the followers of that other great enemy of Rome, Sertorius, were the forbears of the natives of the Fortunate Isles (Canary Isles), and that while the usages, arts and laws that those heroic Romans brought with them gradually perished, the 'Souls of Liberty' did not:

> the soul
> Of liberty, which fifteen hundred years
> Survived, and when the European came
> With skill and power that could not be withstood,
> Did like a pestilence maintain its hold,
> And wasted down by glorious death that race
> Of natural heroes
> (*Prelude* (1805), Bk I. 195–202; p. 38)

This last is a reference to the fifteenth-century resistance of the Canary Islanders to the Spaniards. Thus Wordsworth can compress, and wield, history into images, and if the reader knows no Plutarch and little of the Fortunate Isles, he will gather sufficiently that these topics concern 'natural heroes', the spirit of liberty and a courageous man's continuing influence after his death. That the image matters more than the historical fact, or person, is clear from Wordsworth's inclusion of two unnamed heroes: first,

> some unknown man,
> Unheard of in the chronicles of kings,
> Suffered in silence for the love of truth
> (*Prelude* (1805), Bk I. 203–5; p. 38)

second,

> . . . that one Frenchman, through continued force
> Of meditation on the inhuman deeds
> Of the first conquerors of the Indian Isles,

---

[7] George Glas, *History of the Discovery and Conquest of the Canary Islands* (London, 1764), which, as W. J. B. Owen (*The Fourteen-Book Prelude* (Ithaca, 1985), p. 33) points out, 'cites Plutarch, contains all Wordsworth's facts and provides an occasional verbal parallel'.

> Went single in his ministry across
> The ocean, not to comfort the oppressed,
> But, like a thirsty wind to roam about,
> Withering the oppressor . . .
> <div align="right">(<i>Prelude</i> (1805), Bk 1. 205–11, pp 38, 40)</div>

That unnamed Frenchman is one Dominique de Gourges whose fierce vengeful action Wordsworth knew from the sixteenth-century Hakluyt's *Voyages* (1582): the Spaniards it seems had destroyed a French Protestant settlement in Florida in 1565, and had hanged many settlers – 'not', he said, 'as French men, but as Lutherans'. De Gourges, finding the French government indifferent to this atrocity, sailed as a private citizen to Florida, and with the help of the local 'savages', overcame a force of four hundred Spaniards in three forts. He hanged his prisoners, causing 'to be imprinted with a searing iron in a table of Firrewood, I doe not this as unto Spaniardes, nor as unto Mariners, but as unto Traitors, Robbers, and Murtherers'. He returned home to find his exploit ill received by the French court.

A bitter story for a possible epic poem. But it reminds us that there was a militancy in Wordsworth – a wish to scourge oppressors: he once said, had he not been a poet, he thought himself well fitted to be a general; and he admired resolution,[8] and those who voyaged in fact or (like Isaac Newton) in thought alone.

He turns then to two national heroes: first, Gustavus Vasa of Sweden, the 'deliverer of his country', as the subtitle of the eighteenth-century English play by Henry Brooke (read by Wordsworth by 1789)[9] has it; and second, Wallace of Scotland,[10] whose life, Wordsworth feels, shows fine human endeavour long after a man's death, imprinting itself even upon the landscape:

> How Wallace fought for Scotland, left the name
> Of Wallace to be found like a wild flower,
> All over his dear country, left the deeds

---

[8] Twelve years before 'Resolution and Independence' was published, and fifteen years before that title was used, Wordsworth uses this word emphatically of himself in his first surviving letter, 6 and 16 September 1790. Writing to Dorothy, he describes his journey through the Alps, and explains that the setbacks that he and Jones had suffered have only served to give them additional 'resolution and Spirits'.

[9] Duncan Wu, *Wordsworth's Reading 1770–1799* (Cambridge, 1993), p. 18.

[10] As Mark Reed points out (*The Thirteen-Book Prelude*, 2 vols. (Ithaca, 1991), I, 17), Wordsworth's phrases echo those of John Stoddart (*The Marks and Local Manners and Scenery in Scotland*, 2 vols. (1801), I, 163–5) in his notion that 'The name of Wallace is attached to every spot, with which there is a bare possibility of historically connecting it' and that 'if any man were really possessed with the spirit-stirring enthusiasm, of the true epic (the same which worked, from youth to age, in the breast of Milton) he could nowhere find a more noble subject than the life of this patriot warrior.'

> Of Wallace like a family of ghosts,
> To people the steep rocks and river banks.
> *(Prelude* (1805), Bk I. 213–17; p. 40)

But none of these stories of stoicism or liberty actually held his imagination – indeed, we have no evidence that he considered such topics outside the demands here in the *Prelude*. As he admits, it suits him better to shape out

> Some tale from my own heart, more near akin
> To my own passions and habitual thoughts.
> *(Prelude* (1805), Bk I. 221–2; p. 40)

Here we have indeed a pointer to a great part of Wordsworth's early work – a 'tale from my own heart'. The capacity to tell a story was above all Wordsworth's, and no intelligent reader will despise it. It was perhaps significant for his development that when his first books of poems were reviewed in 1793, when he was twenty-three, the critic in the most intelligent of the reviews, the *Analytical*, noted of *Descriptive Sketches of the Alps*: 'this poem is on the whole less interesting than the subject led us to expect; owing in part, we believe, to the want of a general thread of narrative to connect the several descriptions, or of some episodical tale, to vary the impression'. In most of the poems after 1793 there is an element of narrative: it might be as slight as the general anecdotal situation of *Tintern Abbey*, where Wordsworth discusses the feelings of a particular day, an actual visit, and gives the date, as though to emphasise that he is not generalising; or it might be a tale like *A Night on Salisbury Plain*, a version of which is published in his *Guilt and Sorrow*. It was his first long narrative, begun when he was twenty-four: there, two outcasts of society meet in a desolate spital and exchange stories of surpassing misery.[11]

Wordsworth intends to grieve the reader's heart, to make him consider what man has made of man. Wordsworth's narrative art became characteristically his own: he prefers a scheme where one speaker tells his tale to another, and thus a dramatic situation exists and the reader is invited to watch the hearer react to the tale he is told. This is familiar from Coleridge's *Ancient Mariner*, where the wedding guest is made to suffer the story, and to carry the burden of its meaning away with him. The wedding guest is not the reader, but he is kin to him. It is in the *Ruined Cottage*, later to be the first book of the *Excursion*, that we have a thoroughgoing Wordsworthian example of this narrative art: two friends, a pedlar and a poet, meet by chance at a ruined cottage; the pedlar tells the poet the story of Margaret, the last human tenant of these ruined walls, and the action, the shift in the poem, takes place in the listening poet's mind. At first he is indifferent

---

[11] *The Salisbury Plain Poems of William Wordsworth*, edited by Stephen Gill (Ithaca, 1975), presents from hitherto unpublished manuscripts the earliest and politically radical versions of the poem, written 1793–4.

to the cottage and to Margaret, but by the close of the tale he speaks of her as one with whom now he has a depth of contact: it is with a brother's love he 'blessed her in the impotence of grief' –

> At length towards the cottage I returned
> Fondly, and traced with milder interest,
> That secret spirit of humanity
> Which, 'mid the calm oblivious tendencies
> Of nature, 'mid her plants, her weeds and flowers,
> And silent overgrowings, still survived.[12]

Such an enlargement of sympathies is an act of Wordsworth in the imagination, and it is brought about by the artful tale of the pedlar. Thus the *Ruined Cottage*, early, before *The Prelude*, demonstrates, and with a nice clarity, the very centre of Wordsworth's concern, a concern not for the world or with Nature, but with them as they are apprehended in the mind, in the creative imagination. The place, the ruined cottage, is made significant through the telling of a human story. Man's capacity to make and enrich the universe becomes from 1797, when the *Ruined Cottage* was first written, a theme that Wordsworth is constantly brooding upon – it must later be connected with his concern for epitaphs, gravestones and his feeling for the richness of a village churchyard; much of the *Excursion* suggests that the dead inform the life of the living. Again, there is another notion along with the idea that the dead are a presence, a notion that a landscape that does not know or need man is perhaps a desolation; and presumably even a natural paradise, if a man or a consciousness has not been there, is but a desert. There is a fine passage that Wordsworth drafted for *Michael* in 1800, partially published by de Selincourt, but never published by the poet, in which he describes one of those concealed valleys that one can come upon in the English Lake District, a valley apparently not known to humans unless some shepherd such as Michael himself. There is desolation here until the human element intervenes: Wordsworth admits to that feeling of blankness, even terror – a modern enough feeling – in a nature that does not need man:

> Nor me,
> When it has chanced that having wandered long
> Among the mountains, I have waked at last
> From dream of motion in some spot like this,
> Shut out from man, some region – one of those
> That hold by an inalienable right
> An independent life, and seem the whole
> Of nature and of unrecorded time;
> If, looking round, I have perchance perceived

---

[12] *The Ruined Cottage*, edited by James Butler (Ithaca, 1979), Bk II. 500–6; p. 73.

> Some vestiges of human hands, some stir
> Of human passion, they to me are sweet
> As light of day break, or the sudden sound
> Of music to a blind man's ear who sits
> Alone and silent in the summer shade.
> They are as a creation in my heart;
> I look into past times as prophets look
> Into futurity, a stream of life runs back
> Into dead years, the porticos of thought.
> The Lyric spirit of philosophy
> Leads me through moods of sadness to delight.[13]

This is a plea for human history, a cry that meaning should be given to a void that could be Nature. Poems other than those actually entitled *Poems on the Naming of Places* do take a piece of the natural world – a ghyll, a heap of stones, in *Michael*; a thorn tree, a mound and a pond in *The Thorn* – and, by naming it, bring it into existence or recognition: by words alone, Nature is given meaning. The poet Wallace Stevens conveys something of this in his 'Idea of Order at Key West'; through the singing of a muse—woman, shape is brought even to the formless sea:

> tell me, if you know,
> Why, when the singing ended and we turned
> Toward the town, tell why the glassy lights,
> The lights in the fishing boats at anchor there,
> As the night descended, tilting in the air,
> Mastered the night and portioned out the sea,
> Fixing emblazoned zones and fiery poles
> Arranging, deepening, an enchanting night.
> (lines 43–50)[14]

Does the following phrase – hitherto unpublished – from the *Michael* fragment, 'The Lyric spirit of Philosophy', give us much help with Wordsworth's 'last and favourite aspiration' in that list of possible epic subjects?

> some philosophic song,
> Of truth that cherishes our daily life,
> With meditations passionate from deep
> Recesses in man's heart . . .
> (*Prelude* (1805), Bk I. 230–1; p. 40)

This high ambition, like all the others he brings forward in 1804, he claims he cannot manage; and with this statement of his own failure he is able to launch into those questions written years before (I suggest) in Goslar, beginning 'Was it for

---

13 Edited from the manuscript; see also *The Poetical Works of William Wordsworth*, edited by Ernest de Selincourt (Oxford, 1944), II, 479–80.
14 *The Collected Poems of Wallace Stevens* (London, 1955), p. 130.

this . . .', i.e. this failure, that he experienced all those splendours of his childhood. We have to look in some detail at what Wordsworth did with that poem drafted in Germany; but first, the Philosophic Song. Although Wordsworth in the list mentions such song separately, it is not probable that he meant by 'Philosophic Song' anything too different from 'tale from my own heart'. But did the phrase also mean for him the unwritten *Recluse*, the poem Coleridge kept demanding that he should write, that Coleridge said was to be the first philosophic poem in the language?

What was Coleridge asking Wordsworth to do, and what did Wordsworth think was being asked of him? A clue comes from a comment Wordsworth made about moral philosophers about 1798 when (as an unpublished manuscript[15] penned by De Quincey confirms) he was intending to write against the radical, William Godwin: he found modern thinkers such as Godwin (or even the more religiously orthodox William Paley) too abstract to be useful. 'Can it be imagined', he wrote in an essay he never published, 'can it be imagined . . . that an old habit will be foregone or a new one formed by a series of propositions . . . presenting no image to the mind . . . They contain no picture of human life; they *describe* nothing.' Coleridge, too, talked about 'the danger of thinking without images'. Certainly, Wordsworth at his characteristic best in *The Prelude* presents his thinking through images which have the particularity of the novelist's art. Surely *The Prelude* is Philosophic Song.

Yet the realism, the matter-of-factness, has curious blendings with a fantasy; this comes out strikingly in the first draft of the poem, the Goslar-written manuscript JJ, which developed during 1799 into the two-book *Prelude*. Here is the sense that the world is full of spirits. A helpful statement that explains Wordsworth's aims is that found in the Alfoxden notebook:

> There is an active principle alive in all things,
> In all things, in all natures, in the flowers
> And in the trees, in every pebbly stone
> That paves the brooks, the stationary rocks
> The moving waters and the invisible air
>
> (Edited from the MS)

There is not the grandeur here of *Tintern Abbey*'s:

> . . . Something far more deeply interfused,
> Whose dwelling is the light of setting suns,
> And the round ocean, and the living air . . .
> (*Poetical Works*, vol. II. 96–98; p. 262)

---

[15] The Wordsworth Trust, Dove Cottage: 22 August 1806. De Quincey, in his draft for an *Essay on Happiness*, discussing his first interest in *Political Science*, notes 'I recollect wondering that this science should ever have engaged the attention of W[ordsworth] when Mr Cottle told me that he had entertained thoughts of answering Godwin.'

but in both passages there is an exploring of similar notions. When Wordsworth in manuscript JJ first describes his boyhood, he introduces a very active Nature. First, as all must remember, the objects in the landscape do things, they act: the river Derwent, directly addressed, 'lov'd / To blend his murmurs with my Nurse's song'; when the boy steals woodcocks from the snares of others, 'low breathings' come after him; and the boy's presence is said 'to be a trouble to the peace' that was among the stars; when he is skating in a noisy, joyful throng and tumult, 'the distant hills' send 'a sound of melancholy'. The boy of book one constantly meets a cognisant Nature, and despite the adjustment of opinions and all the revisions from manuscript JJ to the two-book *Prelude*, to the 1805, 1818–20, 1832, 1839 (to name by date the full versions recently published by the Cornell editors) right up to the 1850, none of this is essentially altered. However, the second way in which an active Nature comes into JJ is in an incipient mythology, where local deities have their being within the elements of the landscape. I quote from JJ:

> Yes there are genii which when they would form
> A favor'd spirit open out the clouds
> As with the touch of lightning[16]

In the two-book *Prelude* Wordsworth has changed 'genii' to 'spirits', and some four years later in 1804 'spirits' is changed to 'Nature':

> But I believe
> That Nature, oftentimes, when she would frame
> A favor'd Being . . .

Here is another passage from the two-book *Prelude*:

> Ye powers of earth, genii of the springs
> And ye that have your voices in the clouds
> And ye that are familiars of the lakes
> And standing pools.
> (Parrish, p. 251; lines 186–9)

Is this the language of Prospero in *The Tempest*?

> Ye elves of hills, brooks, standing lakes, and groves:
> And ye that on the sands with printless foot . . .
> Do chase the ebbing Neptune.
> (v.1.33–5)

Yet Wordsworth's sense that the world is animated by spiritual presences differs somewhat from Prospero's: Prospero is the architect of what happens in the play, and his art is that of controlling all these minor forces – spirits, genii, presences.

---

[16] *The Prelude, 1798–1799*, edited by Stephen Parrish (Ithaca, 1977), p. 93.

But in *The Prelude* it is they who have the power to control the growing boy; in *The Tempest* the spirits seem smaller than men. For Wordsworth, the spirits as they really manifest themselves are much bigger, they are immense – like the cliff that upreared its head when the boy stole the boat – and thus Wordsworth's reminiscence of *The Tempest* does not quite seem to help this poem. The fanciful mythology of literary landscape sorts uneasily with real mountains, winds and rivers. Nor does the epic which also seems to lie behind Wordsworth's address to 'ye powers of earth, ye genii of the springs / And ye that have your voices in the clouds / And ye that are familiars of the lakes / And standing pools . . .' – I am referring to the Morning Hymn in the fifth book of *Paradise Lost*, when Adam and Eve call upon created earth to praise the Lord:

> Ye Mists and Exhalations that now rise
> From Hill or steaming Lake . . .
>   ye winds . . .
> Fountains and ye, that warble, as ye flow . . .
> (v.185–95)

For there is no evident Lord in book one of *The Prelude*: the spirits are the power: they do not praise Him. By the time the version of 1804 is reached the mythical spirits, though still lurking, are hidden in a newly coined terminology:

> Ye Presences of Nature, in the sky
> And on the earth! Ye visions of the hills!
> And Souls of lonely places!
> *(Prelude* (1805), Bk I. 490–2; p. 54)

Never again was Wordsworth to bring pagan genii or familiars into the English landscape. The new muted 'Presences', 'visions' and 'Souls' are neutral enough not to conflict with traditional religious attitudes. Indeed, the whole concept of an intensely active and animated Nature is of less importance to Wordsworth after book one is written in the form of manuscript JJ. Anyhow, in book one, since he deals with early childhood, it is psychologically appropriate that the boy be passive, acted upon, monitored by Nature; when he grows up his own imagination takes over something of the role of that first active Principle.

Manuscript JJ is in another way perhaps even more significantly different from *The Prelude* as it was to develop. Consider the following three lines in JJ:

> Then dearest Maiden on whose lap I rest
> My head . . . do not deem that these
> Are idle sympathies
> (Parrish, p. 79)

These occur among lines that start, animistically enough, 'I would not strike a flower', and they are rightly, I think, associated with the poem *Nutting*. Of this marvellous poem, Wordsworth said, 'Written in Germany: intended as part of a poem on my own life, but struck out as not being wanted there.' *Nutting*, after the description of the boy's cool sensual experience in ravaging the hazels for their nuts, ends with the address:

> Then, dearest Maiden, move along these shades
> In gentleness of heart; with gentle hand
> Touch – for there is a Spirit in the woods.
> (*Poetical Works*, vol. 11. 54–6; p. 212)

Thus, although much in J J is direct address to the elements – the Derwent, genii, familiars, spirits – it seems that Wordsworth also intended to turn to a human being: the maiden is someone very like Dorothy, and so we can see that the structure of this early poem, had it but developed, could have been like that of *Tintern Abbey*, where the poet in the last section turns to Dorothy, finding comfort in her being an image of his former self, whom the sounding cataract had once haunted like a passion. When, in September 1799, Wordsworth decided to make Coleridge the figure addressed in the poem, passages to the 'dearest Maiden' were clearly inappropriate; but it is worth remembering that the intimate tone of book one had perhaps Dorothy as its muse rather than Coleridge.

It seems that Wordsworth was prompted to bring Coleridge into the poem by the latter's famous letter of September 1799:

I am anxiously eager to have you steadily employed on 'The Recluse' ... My Dear friend, I do entreat you go on with 'The Recluse'; and I wish you would write a poem, in blank verse, addressed to those, who, in consequence of the complete failure of the French Revolution, have thrown up all hopes of the amelioration of mankind, and are sinking into an almost epicurean selfishness, disguising the same under the soft titles of domestic attachment and contempt for visionary *philosophes*. It would do great good, and might form a part of 'The Recluse'.[17]

The *Recluse* was of course the projected blank-verse poem that Coleridge always wanted Wordsworth to write: Wordsworth wrote little of it – except a thirteen-book *Prelude* to it and a nine-book *Excursion* from it. Coleridge, who had learnt more of the language than the Wordsworths had, returned from Germany some two months after William and Dorothy. He reached England at the end of July 1799, and some of his first visits were to the family of Josiah Wedgwood at Stoke Cobham, Surrey; this was the second Josiah, the son of the great potter, who, along with his unmarried brother, Tom, had a philanthropic urge to share inherited wealth with men of genius. Thomas Beddoes, the father of the poet and the energetic medical experimenter; Humphry Davy, assistant to Beddoes before moving to the Royal Institution; William Godwin, philosopher, author of the

---

17 *Collected Letters of Samuel Taylor Coleridge*, edited by Earl Leslie Griggs, 6 vols. (Oxford, 1956–71), 1 (1785–1800), 527.

influential *Political Justice* and the radical novel *Caleb Williams*; and Coleridge himself – these were some of those who received patronage from the Wedgwoods. It happened that Josiah Wedgwood and James Mackintosh, a Scottish lawyer whom Coleridge hated, married two sisters. A considerable orator, with a reputation from 1791 for his *Vindiciae Gallicae, A Defence of the French Revolution and its English Admirers*, against the accusations of Edmund Burke, Mackintosh was highly esteemed by the Wedgwoods, and there can be no doubt that they would tell Coleridge (if no one else did) of Mackintosh's great lecturing triumph.

These were lectures lasting from February to June 1799, and in them Mackintosh attacked all the progressive causes that he had once seemed to support. They were never published but Hazlitt describes them in his essay on Sir James Mackintosh:

The effect was ... electrical ... [Mackintosh] grew wanton with success. Dazzling others by the brilliancy of acquirements, dazzled himself by the admiration they excited, he lost fear as well as prudence; dared every thing, carried every thing before him. The Modern Philosophy, counter-scarp, outworks, citadel, and all, fell without a blow, by 'the whiff and wind of his fell *doctrine*', as if it had been a pack of cards. The volcano of the French Revolution was seen expiring in its own flames, like a bonfire made of straw: the principles of Reform were scattered in all directions, like chaff before the keen northern blast. He laid about him like one inspired; nothing could withstand his envenomed tooth. Like some savage beast got into the garden of the fabled Hesperides, he made clear work of it, root and branch, with white, foaming tusks –

'Laid waste the borders, and o'erthrew the bowers,'

The havoc was amazing, the desolation was complete. As to our visionary sceptics and Utopian philosophers, they stood no chance with our lecturer – he did not 'carve them as a dish fit for the Gods, but hewed them as a carcase fit for hounds'. Poor Godwin, who had come, in the *bonhomie* and candour of his nature, to hear what new light had broken in upon his old friend, was obliged to quit the field, and slunk away after an exulting taunt thrown out at 'such fanciful chimeras as a golden mountain or a perfect man.'[18]

It was against such attacks as this by Mackintosh, and perhaps also against the recent pessimistic account of the human dilemma by Malthus in his *Essay on Population*, 1798, that Coleridge wished Wordsworth to write something of comfort for those whom the French Revolution had disappointed, and who had sunk into despondency and selfishness.

Wordsworth replied to Coleridge's continued and urgent encouragement by suddenly turning the two-book *Prelude* into a poem addressed to him. He wrote no poem in blank verse specifically addressed to those who had lost faith in the

---

18 *The Complete Works of William Hazlitt*, edited by P. P. Howe, 21 vols. (London and Toronto, 1932), XI, 98.

amelioration of mankind, but he did preface the *Lyrical Ballads* (1800) with a motto 'Quam nihil ad genium, Papiniane, tuum!' ('How little to your taste, O lawyers!'), a reference presumably to Mackintosh, or again to the talkative and over-confident friend John Stoddart who (as Dorothy's *Journal* shows) had talked at length with Wordsworth at Grasmere at the end of October 1800. Wordsworth in the whole tenor of his verse, while avoiding political subjects, did show such concern for people as he thought might enlarge human sympathies and even challenge the thinking of politicians – witness his sending *Lyrical Ballads*, 1800, to Charles James Fox, the leader of the opposition, claiming in an accompanying letter,

... that men who do not wear fine cloathes can feel deeply ... [and hoping that his poems] may in some small degree enlarge our feelings of reverence for our species, and our knowledge of human nature. (*Letters*, I, 315)

Coleridge, then, in a slight and not too emphatic way, comes into the poem at the two-book *Prelude* stage, with one and a half of the two books already set down – and there is a manuscript surviving of book two (manuscript R V) which shows Wordsworth actually adding the passages addressed to Coleridge.[19]

The first result of Coleridge's presence was Wordsworth's adopting that rather full didactic tone in the latter half of book two, when he outlines the growth of the child's first notions at the loving mother's breast. Nothing here that Erasmus Darwin then, or our century's psychologists – such as Donald Winnicot – would not approve of. Indeed, Wordsworth's early sense that he needed to deal with the child's experience before memory actually began shows a remarkable psychological insight for his time. And so Coleridge remains fairly inert in the poem until the extensive development into the 1805 *Prelude*. By then he is indeed the muse behind the poem, and confers characteristic benefits, so that there is at once the intimacy of deep friendship and the fact that the poem is addressed to a great thinker; its style is neither high nor low but has the ruminating, exploratory manner of conversation where there is no need to simplify. Much of the new writing is particularly appropriate for Coleridge, such as Wordsworth's amused commentary on himself as a fashionable Cambridge undergraduate; the satirical account of preachers; the critical spirit towards compulsory attendance at college chapel; the dislike of those passions that are aroused by competitive examinations; the Juvenalian tones, now with a sense of anger and remorse, heightened with some awareness of tragedy, come when the City, or the Reign of Terror in the French Revolution, are described. Again, the poem is touched throughout with a certain loving-kindness for Coleridge – an awareness of his poor health; sorrow that they missed each other at Cambridge, with the wondering possibility

[19] Stephen Parrish, *The Prelude, 1798–1799*, pp. 168–71.

that perhaps, had they met earlier, Coleridge's disastrous undergraduate failure might have been avoided. Certainly true it is, that with Coleridge in mind as the receiver and listener of this poem, Wordsworth got it swingingly under way at the beginning of 1804; except for some linking in 1801, *The Prelude* had stood still for over three years. It was his friend's imminent departure for Malta that made Wordsworth expand with urgency.

Apart from the sheer expansion involved in taking the autobiographical exploration further for the complete *Prelude*, Wordsworth effected re-arrangements. First Wordsworth placed 271 lines before the original opening of the poem, 'Was it for this'; the first 54 of these lines seem to be a fragment written possibly on leaving Goslar in 1799; and, in the rest of them, Wordsworth later (possibly as early as 1801, perhaps as late as 1804) wrote of himself as a man, wanting and unable to write a long poem, and considering epic possibilities. Second – and most interesting here – he took three passages out of book one of the two-book *Prelude*, and one passage written in manuscript JJ, published them as four separate passages, although, like all the others in books one and two, they deal with 'Childhood and Schooltime'; these four he placed in later parts of the 1805 poem and it would be helpful, now, to consider how the passages were fitted into their new contexts, and how these have helped to shape a more developed poetic self.

These four passages are all concerned with people and with death. The first of them he took from JJ and *Lyrical Ballads*, 1800, into book five. It is that description of a boy, 'There was a Boy, ye knew him well, / Ye cliffs and Islands of Winander', who, with his hands 'as through an instrument, / Blew mimic hootings to the silent owls / That they might answer him.' They did, and in the silence after the shouts, while the boy 'hung / Listening, a gentle shock of mild surprize / Has carried far into his heart the voice / Of mountain torrents.' Then Wordsworth tells us that the boy died, not ten years old (though we suspect from parish registers that it was a boy of twelve who died) and that his grave was a familiar stopping place for Wordsworth, passing through the churchyard at evening. When this passage was first drafted it was Wordsworth himself, and not another boy, who blew mimic hootings to the owls – and – another peripheral historical detail – the boy among Wordsworth's schoolfriends who was really good at hooting was neither Wordsworth nor the dead boy, but one William Raincock.[20] However that may be, the poetic theme was one much brooded on by Wordsworth – the death of one favoured by Nature. Sometimes, as in the *Ruined Cottage*, he expressed its more bitter aspect – 'The good die young, and those whose hearts are dry as summer's dust burn to the socket.' The episode 'There

[20] See T. W. Thompson, *Wordsworth's Hawkshead*, edited by Robert Woof (Oxford, 1970), p. 56 and *passim*.

was a Boy' has much the same structure as the elegiac Lucy poems, also written in that Goslar winter in Germany, and part of Wordsworth's feeling seems to be that it is those left alive who suffer death, while the dead pass to the impersonal security of another order, another society, that of rocks, stones and trees.

Of the other three passages, even as he put them into the two-book *Prelude*, Wordsworth there remarked on their central importance: it is as though he well knew the darker power did not quite fit his major evocation throughout the first book, that of the intimate relation between the boy and the natural world.

So, the final episode of coming upon the drowned man during his first week at Hawkshead is now placed in book five – entitled 'Books and Nature' – where Wordsworth attacks educationalists who believed that children should be given only morally uplifting books to read. He finds a context for the early episode in support of his theory that indiscriminate reading is far better. He begins by saying that the episode took place during his first week at school.

> the calm Lake
> Grew dark, with all the shadows on its breast,
> And, now and then, a fish up-leaping, snapp'd
> The breathless stillness. The succeeding day,
> (Those unclaimed garments telling a plain Tale)
> Went there a Company, and in their Boat
> Sounded with grappling irons, and long poles.
> At length, the dead Man, 'mid that beauteous scene
> Of trees, and hills and water, bolt upright
> Rose with his ghastly face . . .
> (*Prelude* (1805), Bk v. 463–72; p. 176)

After this episode, as it stood in the two-book *Prelude*, Wordsworth said that this was one of the numerous 'tragic facts / Of rural history that impressed my mind / With images . . . with forms / That yet exist with independent life / And, like their archetypes, know no decay', and then he went straight on to a consideration of the notion of 'spots of time', those memories of such force that they always

> retain
> A fructifying virtue, whence depressed
> By trivial occupations and the round
> Of ordinary intercourse, of minds –
> Especially the imaginative power –
> Are nourished and invisibly repaired.
> (*Prelude* (1799), Bk i. 289–94; pp. 8–9)

In the 1805 version the famous meditation on the spots of time is reserved for the later eleventh book; but in his commentary in the fifth book, Wordsworth goes on in a passage clearly written in 1804 with a straightforward explanation for his lack of horror at the 'ghastly' corpse:

> for my inner eye had seen
> Such sights before, among the shining streams
> Of fairyland, the forest of romance –
> Thence came a spirit hallowing what I saw
> With decoration and ideal grace.
> (*Prelude* (1805), Bk v. 475–9; p. 176)

Jack the Giant Killer, Robin Hood, 'Tales that charm away the wakeful night', these had been of more value than tomes of morality and information; they had prepared his young imagination for anything, not excluding images of death.

Yet the next two episodes touched death and terror more closely within Wordsworth's personal experience; he moved them out of book one of the two-book *Prelude* into book eleven of the 1805, a book entitled 'Imagination, How Impaired and Restored', and they form one of the climaxes of the later part of the poem. Wordsworth by this point in the poem has described the dark areas of his experience – the City and the French Revolution – and he now turns to talk of the beneficent power of experiences that come to be seized and held in the memory. The experience he describes is one of terror. In the two-book *Prelude*, of course, significant experiences follow one after the other in an astonishing concentration, and this episode comes immediately after that of finding the drowned man in Esthwaite Water and the assertion that 'There are in our existence spots of time'. Wordsworth then begins, 'I remember well, / While I was yet an urchin': in the 1805 version he says he 'was then not six years old', but I am quoting the account from the early version in the two-book *Prelude*:

> While I was yet an urchin, one who scarce
> Could hold a bridle, with ambitious hopes
> I mounted, and we rode towards the hills.
> We were a pair of horsemen; honest James
> Was with me, my encourager and guide.
> We had not travelled long ere some mischance
> Disjoined me from my comrade, and, through fear
> Dismounting, down the rough and stony moor
> I led my horse, and, stumbling on, at length
> Came to a bottom where in former times
> A man, the murderer of his wife, was hung
> In irons. Mouldered was the gibbet mast,
> The bones were gone, the iron and the wood;
> Only a long green ridge of turf remained
> Whose shape was like a grave. I left the spot . . .
> (*Prelude* (1799), lines 299–313, p. 9)

For the 1805 version Wordsworth appears to have checked the facts, so that the murderer is not the murderer of his wife, but simply a murderer; and in fact we know from other sources that the hanged man was Thomas Nicholson of Penrith, executed in 1767 for the robbery and murder of Thomas Parker, some thirty years before Wordsworth was writing. It is of some side-interest to wonder why Wordsworth, in 1799, thought of a wife-murderer: he had written a fragment, called later by scholars *The Somersetshire Tragedy*, on a bitter tale he had heard from Thomas Poole, about a man called Jack Walford who had been forced by the parish officers to marry a simpleton because of a bastard child; he had then murdered the woman and been hanged near the spot. We know that Wordsworth had been thinking of Walford's story during his winter in Germany.[21] A second change is that by 1805 the 'long green ridge of turf' is gone, and Wordsworth has introduced the notion of the murderer's name being carved in the sod,

> and still from year to year,
> By superstition of the neighbourhood
> The grass is cleared away; and to this hour
> The letters are all fresh and visible
> 　　　*(Prelude* (1805), Bk XI. 295–8; p. 430)

Wordsworth never reveals the name; of interest is his notion that the man, by the events of some thirty years before, has literally named the place.[22]

> And, reascending the bare common, saw
> A naked pool that lay beneath the hills,
> The beacon on the summit, and more near,
> A girl who bore a pitcher on her head
> And seemed with difficult steps to force her way
> Against the blowing wind. It was, in truth,

---

[21] The so-called *Somersetshire Tragedy*, the manuscript of which was destroyed by Gordon Wordsworth (on learning from Tennyson that it did not enhance Wordsworth's reputation), was an attempt by Wordsworth while in Germany in 1799 to write a second story for *A Night on Salisbury Plain*, to replace 'The Female Vagrant' which he had extracted and printed in *Lyrical Ballads*, 1798. By 27 February 1799 he 'resolved to discard Robert Walford and invent a new story for the woman', which he never did (*Letters*, I, 256).

[22] Wordsworth alone reports that the name of the murderer was carved in the turf. It is possible that he (and others) misunderstood the origin of the carved letters, as did J. Walker, *History of Penrith* (1858), p. 100, who says they were 'T. P. M.'. The first edition of the Ordnance Survey map (Carlisle Record Office) marks the stones zigzagging on the fell-side from Cowrake Quarry up Penrith Beacon. These stones were introduced to establish the boundary between the Musgrave and Portland estates, disputed and finally arbitrated in 1766. Thus, the grass from these lettered stones was perhaps cleared not on account of superstition, as the poet has it, but in order to establish the rights of the owners. That the dispute was settled in 1766, the year in which Parker was murdered and the year before Nicholson was hanged, would lead to a popular confusion. The emphatic 'no' in the margin of Daniel Scott's copy of Walker's book (now in the Wordsworth Library, and reported by Helen Darbishire in her revision of Ernest de Selincourt's *Prelude*, 1959, p. 614) is almost certainly because Scott, an excellent local historian, knew of this boundary dispute.

> An ordinary sight but I should need
> Colours and words that are unknown to man
> To paint the visionary dreariness
> Which, while I looked round for my lost guide,
> Did at that time invest the naked pool,
> The beacon on the lonely eminence,
> The woman and her garments vexed and tossed
> By the strong wind.
> (Prelude (1805), Bk XI. 302–15; p. 432)

Towards the close of this incident, balancing the death of the murderer with its pagan mystery, is the whole picture of the firm sufficiency of the girl maintaining her hold on life; the lonely beacon, the pool, the upright figure with the vessel on her head, stoically moving against the wind, her steps difficult, her garments vexed and tossed. The term of power is 'visionary dreariness' – Wordsworth offers no reductive explanation of the moment. He now continues that it was in this same area around the Penrith Beacon that he came in 'the blessed time of early love',

> Long afterwards I roamed about
> In daily presence of this very scene,
> Upon the naked pool and dreary crags,
> And on the melancholy beacon, fell
> The spirit of pleasure and youth's golden gleam
> (Prelude (1805), Bk XI. 318–22; p. 432)

And, he goes on to claim, his childhood terror there at six years old has brought now a power and radiance to later and pleasurable experience. And from those two memories, one from childhood and one from his early manhood, Wordsworth moves into a meditation on that theme of loss which so powerfully informs the 'Ode: Intimations of Immortality'. He is writing now, not of the child, not of the lover in 'youth's golden gleam', but as one who at least feels old and realises that the visionary power does indeed ebb and perhaps fail:

> Oh mystery of man, from what a depth
> Proceed thy honours! I am lost, but see
> In simple childhood something of the base
> On which thy greatness stands – but this I feel,
> That from thyself it is that thou must give,
> Else never canst receive. The days gone by
> Come back upon me from the dawn almost
> Of life: the hiding-places of my power
> Seem open; I approach, and then they close;
> I see by glimpses now; when age comes on,
> May scarcely see at all; and I would give
> While yet we may, as far as words can give,
> A substance and a life to what I feel:

> I would enshrine the spirit of the past
> For future restoration.
>> (*Prelude* (1805), Bk XI. 328–42; pp. 432, 434)

Despite the stoical resolution to write as much as possible about the past, there is not that sense of reconciliation that comes at the end of the 'Ode', that comfort that comes from the years that bring the 'philosophic mind'.

At this point in book eleven Wordsworth puts another, indeed, the last section to be taken out of the two-book *Prelude*; and as in that early version, it follows immediately after the Penrith Beacon episode. This 'spot of time' is Wordsworth's description of waiting for horses at school to take him and his brothers home for vacation, the vacation in which his father died. The scene is of bleakness: the boy goes up to an eminence above the meeting point of two roads, along either of which the horses might come:

> 'Twas a day
> Stormy, and rough, and wild, and on the grass
> I sate, half-sheltered by a naked wall.
> Upon my right hand was a single sheep,
> A whistling hawthorn on my left, and there,
> With those companions at my side, I watched,
> Straining my eyes intensely as the mist
> Gave intermitting prospect of the wood
> And plain beneath.
>> (*Prelude* (1805), Bk XI. 355–63; p. 434)

This desire to go home was rewarded ten days later by the death of his father, and to Wordsworth this seemed a chastisement, and brought with its sorrow 'trite reflections of morality', but for the future it was the image of the place that haunted him:

> . . . the wind and sleety rain,
> And all the business of the elements,
> The single sheep, and the one blasted tree,
> And the bleak music of that old stone wall,
> The noise of wood and water, and the mist . . .
>> (*Prelude* (1805), Bk XI. 375–9; p. 436)

and these became images of restoration from which he could drink 'as at a fountain'.

So, Wordsworth at one of the climaxes of his poem is drawing on the 'spots of time' passages, written five years before, in order to establish that a healthy mind is nurtured by its earliest memories, and it is true that part of the brooding optimism of the *Prelude* comes from the placing of these passages towards the close of the poem. But there is more to the optimism than that. For he had also by him, as he wrote the last seven books between April 1804 and May 1805, at least another pair of great passages: the first is the description of crossing the Alps, and the second, that of climbing Snowdon. Evidence that these passages were already written is in Wordsworth's manuscripts; and not least is the important forty-page manuscript of *The Prelude* – manuscript w w – which, with the help of infra-red photography[23] (courtesy of the audiovisual centre at the University of Newcastle upon Tyne, 1969), it has been possible to read for the first time. This manuscript consists of small cardboard sheets razored out of a sketchbook. The sketchbook was once Dorothy's, and she used it for some notes and a drawing of a rather useful gate during the tour by herself and William in Scotland, in August and September 1803.

It seems that Wordsworth got the book after Dorothy had copied up her notes into that formal account, *Recollections of a Tour Made in Scotland*, which she also gave to her friends. Wordsworth's manuscript is not simple, either to decipher or to understand, but it does contain links with work that he was doing in February and March 1804, and it becomes clear that he had it in mind to finish *The Prelude* with the Snowdon episode, even before Coleridge left for Malta in April 1804 with the first five books of the poem. The evidence points to this: that in that very same month when he recognised that he must undertake another and larger expansion, he had, already prepared, the climax towards which he could travel – it was the technique of several other poems (such as *The Ruined Cottage* or 'The Idiot Boy'), the writing of the last passage before the composition of the beginning. That security, the having in hand the Snowdon passage (not to mention the 'spots of time'), meant that Wordsworth was able to explore without anxiety some of the great themes his poetry had avoided or at least evaded: the City (book seven), and above all, the French Revolution (books nine and ten), whose failure was the original cause of the despondency and cynicism among their contemporaries which Coleridge had wished Wordsworth to counteract. Wordsworth's commentary and meditation in those areas are rich and detailed confessions, but at this point I choose only to emphasise that, through the imagery, the place and events are set before us as spectacles, or as moments of theatre. Wordsworth makes us feel the vitality and bustle of the streets of revolutionary Paris on his first visit in 1791; he himself finds it difficult to play the part of the revolutionary enthusiast when he visits the Bastille, now a demolished building. He can make you feel the bliss of that dawn when he describes his walking with the soldier Beaupuis, an aristocrat but radicalised, in the woods surrounding Blois (he compares their discourse to the privilege of walking in conversation in the groves of Athens with Plato himself); but, at the same time, readers are made to recognise his sense that whatever exists of permanent value from those days, it is not in the deceptions of the revolutionary or the urban experience.

[23] These photographs are now reproduced in Mark Reed's *The Thirteen-Book Prelude*, I, 329–66, and are transcribed in II, 237–61.

In his account of his second visit to Paris, Wordsworth's imagery betrays his sense of tragedy. He calls upon Macbeth's nightmare phrase; 'Methought I heard a voice cry "Sleep no more, / Macbeth doth murder Sleep"' (II.2.35–6) and equally (though not hitherto observed), he draws upon two images of cruel Rome in *Titus Andronicus* when he talks of Paris being 'Defenceless as a wood where tigers roam' (*Prelude* (1805), Bk x. 82); in that play, Rome is a city of victims: the villainous Aaron urges Chiron and Demetrius to rape Lavinia in the Palace walks. 'The woods are ruthless, dreadful, deaf, and dull' (II.1.128): and Titus himself declares: 'dost thou not perceive / That Rome is but a wilderness of tigers? / Tigers must prey and Rome affords no prey / But me and mine' (III.1.53–6.)

When Wordsworth says of his radical youth, 'bliss was it in that dawn to be alive, / But to be young was very Heaven!', he is telling a truth as one confesses a folly. He was then, he now feels, in the charge of an enchanter – Reason; and he was long and deeply conscious (his play *The Borderers* – 1796/7 – is his first treatment of this) that Reason could always be used to justify violence and crime; that Reason had been Robespierre's justification for the Reign of Terror. Reason to Wordsworth was what we might call rationalisation. But in and beyond these darker areas of the experiences he records, he also had images of 'Crossing the Alps' and climbing Snowdon, both fine passages being composed in early 1804, both specifically leading to the term: the Imagination. In 1790, when Wordsworth did cross the Alps, he found the experience disappointing – he was over them without realising it. In *The Prelude*, in the very act of describing this disappointment, he breaks off with the sudden discovery that it was the Imagination that gave the experience a real importance for him, that it was only in the Imagination that he could have the full grandeur of the notion, 'Crossing the Alps'.[24] And having crossed, he then describes his walk as through a landscape of the Apocalypse; he draws upon imagery that would be fit for the Book of Revelation where all is permanent yet beautiful: both in time and yet timeless.

> Of woods decaying, never to be decayed,
> The stationary blasts of waterfalls,
> And every where along the hollow rent
> Winds thwarting winds . . .
> (*Prelude* (1805), Bk VI. 557–60; p. 218)

but finally, tumult and peace, the darkness and the light in balance.

[24] Though Wordsworth had no concept of the imagination in September 1790, it is clear from his letter to Dorothy that he had already registered that something extraordinary had happened in the Simplon Pass: 'At Brig we quitted the Valais and passed the Alps at the Semplon in order to visit part of Italy. The impressions of three hours of our walk among the Alps will never be effaced' (*Letters*, I, 33). Then he would have thought the landscape of the natural world had the inherent active power to affect him.

Robert Woof

The ascent of Snowdon is reserved as the final extended image, the only mountain experience in a poem full of mountains to take place on the top of one, and thus perhaps more archetypally convenient for the conclusion of a long poem. Wordsworth finds, at the top, not the expected dawn but something more interior — the moon and moonlight over a vast cloudscape. He stands with his friend and the shepherd-guide at the edge of the mist, the mist active and moving and with the homeless noise of waters, and interprets what he sees as an emblem of the single mind, not his, the poet's, but any man's. The clouds become form — like a mind creating order. It is Wordsworth's answer to despondency, whether a personal melancholy or a political dismay. It is one of those images that, perhaps, even yet remains shored against the ruins.

8

The epiphanic mode in Browning's poetry

ROBERT LANGBAUM

Some years ago I published an essay called 'The Epiphanic Mode in Wordsworth and Modern Literature'.[1] The essay essentially moves from what Wordsworth in *The Prelude* calls his 'spots of time' to what Joyce a century later called 'epiphanies'. Both were referring to imaginative transformations of realistic material by a sensitised observer, transformations that last only a moment but leave an enduring effect. I did not at the time deal with Browning, whose concept of 'infinite moment', often repeated in various ways, clearly puts him in the line of epiphanic writing. I would like to repair that omission here, since the application of the term 'epiphany' places Browning's 'infinite moment' in a large tradition.[2]

I did not deal with Browning because he seemed to present a special case – special because Browning developed the epiphany of character which does not, like the epiphany deriving from Wordsworth, depend upon a sensitised observer within the poem. Browning also wrote poems in the Wordsworthian manner that do depend on the sensitised observer. I shall discuss both kinds, showing along the way new modes in that fashioning of an author and a voice that has always figured in the presentation of poetry. In Wordsworth's poems, the author's self is clearly projected in the sensitised observer. In Browning's poems, the author seems to have disappeared; yet he remains present in the intellectual and spiritual force of the dramatised character.

Wordsworth's transformations are most often of natural objects, which carry inherent significance, or of human figures on landscapes carrying inherent significance. Joyce explains epiphany by saying that his method is to give 'my idea of the significance of trivial things'. Joyce found a 'resemblance between the mystery of the Mass and what I am trying to do . . . by converting the bread of everyday life into something that has a permanent artistic life of its own'.[3] In

---

[1] In Robert Langbaum, *The Word from Below: Essays on Modern Literature and Culture* (Madison, Wis., 1987).

[2] William O. Raymond first broached the subject in an essay, 'The Infinite Moment', which does not, however, use the term 'epiphany' (in *The Infinite Moment and Other Essays in Robert Browning*, second edition (Toronto, 1965)).

[3] Quoted in Richard Ellmann, *James Joyce* (New York, 1965), p. 169.

Joyce significance is detached from nature; it derives entirely from the imagination and art of the sensitised observer. Browning's epiphanies are mainly detached from nature, but there are poems as we shall see in which nature matters.

Browning made many remarks which taken together suggest a theory of epiphany. Writing to Elizabeth Barrett in 1845, Browning describes his poetry as momentary 'escapes of my inner power, which lives in me like the light in those crazy Mediterranean phares I have watched at sea, wherein the light . . . only after a weary interval leaps out, for a moment, from the one narrow chink'.[4] This imagery anticipates the Pope's description at the end of his monologue in *The Ring and the Book* of the epiphanic experience which will be Guido's only means of salvation. 'For the main criminal I have no hope', says the Pope,

> Except in such a suddenness of fate.
> I stood at Naples once, a night so dark
> I could have scarce conjectured there was earth
> Anywhere, sky or sea or world at all:
> But the night's black was burst through by a blaze –
> Thunder struck blow on blow, earth groaned and bore,
> Through her whole length of mountain visible:
> There lay the city thick and plain with spires,
> And, like a ghost disshrouded, white the sea.
> So may the truth be flashed out by one blow,
> And Guido see, one instant, and be saved.
>
> (x.2116–27)[5]

Sudden understanding, physically described – that is what makes this passage epiphanic.

In a letter defending his poetry against Ruskin's charge of obscurity, Browning explains that 'all poetry [is] a putting [of] the infinite within the finite', and for this reason poetry lies precisely in the jumps the reader is forced to make for himself.

You would have me paint it all plain out, which can't be; but by various artifices I try to make shift with touches and bits of outlines which *succeed* if they bear the conception from me to you. You ought, I think, to keep pace with the thought tripping from ledge to ledge of my 'glaciers' . . . in asking for more *ultimates* you must accept less *mediates*, nor expect that a Druid stone-circle will be traced for you with as few breaks to the eye as the North Crescent and South Crescent that go together so cleverly in many a suburb.[6]

---

[4] R. B. to E. B. B., (11 February, 1845), *The Letters of Robert Browning and Elizabeth Barrett Barrett 1845–1846*, edited by Elvan Kintner, 2 vols. (Cambridge, Mass., 1969), I, 17.

[5] Richard D. Altick, ed. Robert Browning, *The Ring and the Book* (New Haven and London, 1981), pp. 533–4.

[6] Quoted in W. G. Collingwood, *The Life of John Ruskin* (Boston and New York, 1902), p. 164.

Browning describes here what I call the Epiphanic Leap. The definition of romantic and modern poetry tends to merge with the definition of epiphany.

In his excellent book *Epiphany in the Modern Novel*, Morris Beja distinguishes modern epiphany from traditional vision by two criteria: the Criterion of Incongruity (the epiphany is irrelevant to the object or incident that triggers it) and the Criterion of Insignificance (the epiphany is triggered by a trivial object or incident). Dante in his vision at the end of *Paradiso* 'sees God in all His magnificence', but the modern epiphany, says Beja, is out of proportion to its cause.[7]

I would add four more criteria. The first is the Criterion of Psychological Association: the epiphany is not an incursion of God from outside; it is a psychological phenomenon arising from a real sensuous experience, either present or recollected. The second is the Criterion of Momentaneousness: the epiphany lasts only a moment, but leaves an enduring effect. The third is the Criterion of Suddenness: a sudden change in external conditions causes a shift in sensuous perception that sensitises the observer for epiphany. The fourth is the Criterion of Fragmentation or the Epiphanic Leap: the text never quite equals the epiphany; the poetry, as Browning put it, consists in the reader's leap. Hence the deliberate fragmentation of modernist literature, which blocks grammatical or logical organisation in order to enforce psychological organisation. All these criteria, Beja's and mine, are illustrated by the epiphany at the end of Joyce's 'The Dead', which derives from a sudden change in conditions: 'A few light taps upon the pane made him [Gabriel] turn to the window. It had begun to snow again.' All these criteria are strikingly illustrated by Wordsworth's Lucy poem 'Strange Fits of Passion Have I Known', in which the narrator's epiphanic intimation of Lucy's death derives from his hypnotic gaze upon the moon which suddenly drops behind her cottage roof. We will see to what extent these criteria apply to the Browning poems I will now discuss.

'Two in the Campagna' and 'By the Fire-Side' are two love poems which derive their epiphanies from involvement with nature. In the first the path to epiphany begins with the speaker's words to his wife or lover, 'I touched a thought'. 'Help me to hold it' (sts. II, III).[8] The elusive thought is compared, indeed transmuted, into a floating cobweb that leaves the 'yellowing fennel' to alight upon a weed, 'Where one small orange cup amassed / Five beetles, – blind and green they grope' (sts. III, IV): the beetles' groping corresponds to the speaker's groping for the 'thought'. It is a fertilising thought which spreads with the randomness of natural process: 'Everywhere on the grassy slope / I traced it.

---

[7] Morris Beja, *Epiphany in the Modern Novel* (Seattle, 1971), pp. 16–17.

[8] Browning's shorter poems will be quoted from Ian Jack, ed., *Poetical Works 1833–1864* (London, 1970).

Hold it fast!' (st. IV) The unconscious spontaneity of nature is beautifully evoked:

VI

Such life here, through such lengths of hours,
  Such miracles performed in play,
Such primal naked forms of flowers,
  Such letting nature have her way
   . . .

The epiphany emerges from this sensuous texture, as the speaker wishes they could give themselves to each other with the unconscious abandon of nature.

VIII

I would that you were all to me,
  You that are so much, no more.
Nor yours nor mine, nor slave nor free!
  Where does the fault lie? What the core
  O' the wound, since wound must be?

The fault lies in the self-consciousness that produces isolation. We are perfectly united, he realises, only for moments such as the following:

X

No. I yearn upward, touch you close,
  Then stand away. I kiss your cheek,
Catch your soul's warmth, – I pluck the rose
  And love it more than tongue can speak –
  Then the good minute goes.

There is a flaw even in this 'good minute' since the speaker's love is diverted to the rose. Nothing suggests that the rose symbolises the lady; the speaker does not say, 'I pluck thy rose'.

We see here the Criterion of Momentaneousness – in that 'the good minute goes' – except that the enduring effect is not beneficial but leads to frustration. The speaker is already 'so far / Out of that minute' as to have returned to his original randomness: 'Must I go / Still like the thistle-ball' (st. XI),

XII

Just when I seemed about to learn!
  Where is the thread now? Off again!
  The old trick!

He has even lost the elusive thought which finally found expression in stanzas VIII and IX. 'The old trick' of such fleeting epiphanic moments is to leave you barren.

Only I discern –
Infinite passion, and the pain
Of finite hearts that yearn.

166

He is left with the perception of the two elements – 'infinite passion' and 'finite hearts' – that are momentarily united in epiphany and are now rent asunder.

Although 'Two in the Campagna' is highly successful, indeed a masterpiece, it projects an unsuccessful or abortive epiphany. The poem provides a good example of Browning's innovatively modern, sophisticated style of love poetry – for one thing because the two lovers are of equal intelligence, which is why some critics think the woman is the speaker. There is also the sophisticated casualness of the diction and the broken metre: 'Where is the thread now? Off again! / The old trick!' And there is the remarkably original transmutation of the developing 'thought' into the remarkably original nature imagery of the Roman campagna, giving the poem a well-defined location. Precise location is important for development of the speaker's character, leading to epiphany, and for the author's localisation in the speaker.

Equally modern and sophisticated in style, the love poem 'By the Fire-Side' projects instead a successful epiphany of union. Early in the poem we are shown how the lovers, now husband and wife, sit by their fire-side (probably in Florence), still living in the recollected atmosphere of that 'moment, one and infinite!' (st. XXXVII) which occurred in an Alpine setting in November. Indeed in the opening stanzas, the husband looks forward to old age, 'life's November' (st. I), when he will sit by the fire in England, with his descendants around him, yet slip back in memory to Italy to 'Look at the ruined chapel again' (st. VII) where the epiphany took place.

He retraces a 'path grey heads abhor / For it leads to a crag's sheer edge with them' (sts. XXI, XXII), where youth ends. But it leads for him down a path of continuity to the fire-side where he sits with his 'perfect wife', Leonor, portrayed as Elizabeth Barrett Browning (sts. XXI, XXIII) – a sign of how the dramatic poem can through easily apparent biographical connection represent the author as person. This fire-side scene is the present from which the poem projects forward and backwards. The present shows that the union which began in an extraordinary moment has, unlike the moment in 'Campagna', become habitual.

XXVI

My own, see where the years conduct!
    At first, 'twas something our two souls
Should mix as mists do; each is sucked
    In each now: . . .

If we have come this far together in life, think how much farther we will go after death: 'when our one soul understands / The great Word which makes all things new' (st. XXVII).

So 'Come back with me to the first of all' (st. XXX), to that epiphanic moment which we finally reach through this path of recollection: 'Hither we walked then, side by side, / Arm in arm and cheek to cheek' (st. XXXIII). 'Silent the crumbling bridge we cross, / And pity and praise the chapel sweet' (st. XXXIV),

XXXVI

We stoop and look in through the grate,
 See the little porch and rustic door,
Read duly the dead builder's date;
 Then cross the bridge that we crossed before,
Take the path again – but wait!

XXXVII

Oh moment, one and infinite!
 The water slips o'er stock and stone;
The West is tender, hardly bright:
 How grey at once is the evening grown –
One star, its chrysolite!

The details are prosaic, the language restrained in the modern manner. What then causes the Epiphanic Leap to 'Oh moment'? Here we can invoke the Criterion of Psychological Association. The couple bring to the experience their love for each other, and their sense of holiness – in the silence ('the silence grows / To that degree, you half believe / It must get rid of what it knows' (st. XXXII)) and in the chapel ('And wish for our souls a like retreat' (st. XXXIV)). It is after they recross the bridge and retake the path that they encounter the moment as a recognition experience – the recognition of a spirituality they have brought there. The description of nature in stanza XXXVII gives duration to the moment.

Stanzas XLIV, XLV praise the lady for having given herself to him without reserve (unlike the lovers' reserve in 'Campagna'). 'I am named and known by that moment's feat', he says, as 'One born to love you, sweet!' (st. LI), 'And to watch you sink by the fire-side now' (st. LII). Thus we are brought back again to the present. And the poem with its cyclical pattern returns wittily in the last stanza to the intention expressed in the first to recollect the November epiphany and its enduring effect in some future November:

LII

. . .

And the whole is well worth thinking o'er
 When autumn comes: which I mean to do
One day, as I said before.

The poem's obscurity, which is its problem and its glory, comes from the deliberate blurring of time frames – from Browning's attempt to make time after the 'moment' stand still, while he also makes time move along.

Browning eternalises the moment with more concentration in the epiphany which concludes 'The Last Ride Together'. The speaker's lover, having announced their break-up, asks as a favour 'one more last ride with me' (st. i), and the last lines of the subsequent stanzas repeat as a refrain the bliss of riding together. The following lines point toward the epiphany. 'So, one day more am I deified. / Who knows but the world may end to-night?' (st. ii), 'Thus lay she a moment on my breast. / Then we began to ride' (sts. iii, iv). The riding is on horseback, but the bold reader may think also of riding in sexual intercourse.

This blissful riding compensates for the mistakes of the past. He thinks of other forms of compensation for human failure – the soldier's fame: 'My riding is better, by their leave' (st. vi). He thinks of the poet who for all his success does not in his personal life approach his 'own sublime' (st. vii), of the great sculptor, who having enslaved himself to Art, produces a Venus from 'whence we turn [in preference] to yonder girl' and of the musician's praise from a friend who points out how in music fashions change. 'I gave my youth', says the speaker, presumably to love and failed; 'but we ride, in fine' (st. viii).

In stanza ix we come to the point: 'Had fate / Proposed bliss here should sublimate / My being.' It is *earthly* bliss which spiritualises me. 'Earth being so good, would heaven seem best? / Now, heaven and she are beyond this ride.' They arrive at the epiphanic transformation of understanding in the next, which is also the last, stanza.

> X
>
> And yet – she has not spoke so long!
> What if heaven be that, fair and strong
> At life's best, with our eyes upturned
> Whither life's flower is first discerned,
> We, fixed so, ever should so abide?

With the lady's silence, the speaker can assume she shares his feelings when he goes on to ask whether heaven is not that moment when we first discern the best of life and remain fixed in that moment of perception:

> What if we still ride on, we two
> With life for ever old yet new,

it is the old life transformed by new perception, therefore

> Changed not in kind but in degree,
> The instant made eternity, –
> And heaven just prove that I and she
> Ride, ride together, for ever ride?

The speaker has arrived at a flash of understanding like Keats's when he speculates that 'we shall enjoy ourselves here after by having what we called happiness on Earth repeated in a finer tone'.[9] The transforming perception of

---

9 John Keats to Benjamin Bailey, 22 November 1817, *The Letters*, edited by Hyder E. Rollins, 2 vols. (Cambridge, Mass., 1958), i, 185.

heaven in earthly terms eternalises the moment of perception and the riding that led to it. 'The Last Ride Together' does not take into account, as does 'By the Fire-Side', the quotidian time surrounding the moment, or as in 'Campagna' the moment's passing, but leaves us fixed in the epiphanic moment.

In the early poems 'Cristina' and 'Porphyria's Lover' (1842), heaven is instead separated from the earthly 'moment'. 'Cristina' shows the moment of recognition between two lovers as frustrated by worldly circumstances, so that the speaker awaits fulfilment in the 'next life' (st. VIII). The speaker of 'Porphyria's Lover' strangles Porphyria in a failed attempt to eternalise 'That moment she was mine, mine, fair, / Perfectly pure and good' (lines 36–7).

The much later 'Abt Vogler' (1864) projects a musical epiphany through the hexameters corresponding to the music of a musician who, extemporising on an organ of his own invention, brings together heaven and earth. The obscure Abbé Vogler was chosen, according to W. C. DeVane, because among other things Browning 'needed a notable extemporizer'.[10] It is indeed true that extemporised music offers an immediate epiphanic experience, as written music, poetry and painting would not; for we see, says Abt Vogler, how they are made, how 'effect proceeds from cause' (st. VI).

In the palace of music reared by notes, heaven and earth yearn toward each other:

IV

. . .

And the emulous heaven yearned down, made effort to reach the earth,
　　As the earth had done her best, in my passion, to scale the sky:
Novel splendours burst forth, grew familiar and dwelt with mine,
　　Not a point nor peak but found and fixed its wandering star;
Meteor-moons, balls of blaze: and they did not pale nor pine,
　　For earth had attained to heaven, there was no more near nor far.

Note how this auditory experience is displayed through visual imagery. The speaker himself shares in the perfection of the epiphanic moment: 'I was made perfect too' (st. V).

The first line of stanza VII – 'But here is the finger of God, a flash of the will that can' – presents a problem. For according to my Criterion of Psychological Association, the epiphany is not an incursion of God from outside; it is a psychological phenomenon arising from a real sensuous experience. Certainly this epiphany arises from the sensuous experience of the music; but since music, especially extemporised music, is an expression of pure will, that expression can give the illusion of being God's will. As the musician modulates back to commonplace reality ('The C Major of this life' (st. XII)), he realises that the

---

[10] W. C. DeVane, *A Browning Handbook*, second edition (New York, 1955), p. 290.

vanished epiphany has left an impression of permanence and perfection: 'On the earth the broken arcs; in the heaven, a perfect round' (st. IX). Epiphanic poetry consists, if we recall Browning's letter to Ruskin, of broken arcs, requiring, according to my Criterion of Fragmentation, an Epiphanic Leap from inadequate text to meaning. Paradoxically the most fleeting, incomplete art provides the surest index to eternal perfection. 'Abt Vogler' differs from 'Cristina' and 'Porphyria' in that it shows the epiphanic moment as definitely over, but contact with heaven is nevertheless not lost. Browning's doctrine of imperfection supports his epiphanic art.

In order to understand what modern epiphany is, we must also understand what it is not. David's revelation in 'Saul' (revised version, pp. 727–30, sts. XVI–XVIII) is not epiphanic, for it is not projected through a visual reorganisation as David, speaking now and no longer singing to his harp, induces God's love from his own love for Saul and prophesies: ' "See the Christ stand!" ' It is only *after* David has doctrinally entered the New Dispensation that in the last stanza the world is sensually transformed for him, and he can be said to have an epiphanic experience: 'The whole earth was awakened, hell loosed with her crews; / And the stars of night beat with emotion' (st. XIX).

The ending of 'Cleon' is not epiphanic, for the intellectual Greek speaker backs away from his own logically derived understanding of need for a promise of immortality, when he hears that the doctrine is preached by Paulus, 'a mere barbarian Jew' (lines 340, 343). The moving outburst at the end of 'An Epistle . . . of Karshish' is, it seems to me, a borderline case; for while there is no visual reorganisation, there is the sensuous line, 'So, through the thunder comes a human voice', and the passion deriving from Karshish's inclination to believe in a loving God which he has been repressing throughout for the sake of science: 'The very God! think, Abib; dost thou think? / So, the All-Great, were the All-Loving too' (lines 304–6). This outburst seems epiphanic because it is concentrated within a moment that will pass, leaving Karshish his usual self but strangely disturbed. Working differently because of multiple epiphanies, Prince Hohenstiel-Schwangau's 'casuistic fantasy is,' as Thomas E. Fish shows, 'punctuated by moments of lyric epiphany' that illuminate his character[11] – showing how epiphanies are moments of character revelation.

Perhaps the purest example of epiphany is ' "Childe Roland to the Dark Tower Came" ', which takes off from an epiphanic line in *King Lear* Act III, scene 4 to end with just that line. Lear encounters Edgar, disguised as a naked madman, Poor Tom, in a storm on the heath when for Lear the whole moral order is cracking. Lear calls Poor Tom a 'philosopher', and Gloucester says to Lear, 'No words, no words! Hush.' It is then that Edgar, for no reason and as if to

---

[11] Thomas E. Fish, 'Questing for "The Base of Being": The Role of Epiphany in *Prince Hohenstiel-Schwangau*', *Victorian Poetry*, 25 (Spring 1987), 29.

utter the antithesis of words, sings out: 'Childe Rowland to the dark tower came' (lines 184–5).

Retaining the quality of song, the grotesque landscape and events quintessentialise all circumstances, turning them into a morally ambivalent pattern of quest – a 'landscape of estrangement', according to Harold Bloom.[12] Although Browning said that 'Childe Roland came upon me as a kind of dream',[13] the poem does not present itself as a dream or there would be no epiphany, since epiphany is a real transformation of a reality.

It is a 'hoary cripple, with malicious eye', who directs the knight 'Into that ominous tract which, all agree, / Hides the Dark Tower' (sts. I, III). The knight's first thought is that the cripple lies and sets a trap for him. But it turns out that the cripple has told the truth. Yet the knight's suspicion is justified, too. The cripple sends him to his doom and to the triumphant accomplishment of his quest.

The journey cannot be judged logically, because the details of it mark no sort of progress. To the extent that they mean anything, they mean the same thing over and over – sterility, death and the defeat of the knight's predecessors in the quest; and since the events are unaccounted for, they appear not as the expected development of a theme but as each time a shock, a unique experience.

When the Dark Tower is finally achieved, the knight does not go to it; it comes upon him suddenly, unaccountably, as an illumination, a visual reorganisation. Just when he thinks he is 'as far as ever from the end', the sudden passing of 'A great black bird' (st. XXVII) meets my Criterion for a sudden change of conditions. Then he somehow grows aware, in spite of the dusk, that the plain has given place all around to mountains; no progress this way, he thinks, then he hears the trap click shut – and he *sees*: 'Burningly it came on me all at once, / This was the place!' 'Dotard', he accuses himself as though the thing had been there before him the whole time, 'a-dozing at the very nonce, / After a life spent training for the sight!' (st. XXX).

XXXI

What in the midst lay but the Tower itself?
    The round squat turret, blind as the fool's heart,
        Built of brown stone, without a counterpart
In the whole world.

This might be called negative epiphany which then gets mixed inextricably with positive epiphany. What he sees is not his physical surrounding but a sensuous transformation of it, as darkness gives way to light and silence to noise, as the mountains turn into giant spectators of his destruction, and he hears in the tolling

[12] Harold Bloom, 'Browning's *Childe Roland*: All Things Deformed and Broken', *The Ringers in the Tower: Studies in Romantic Tradition* (Chicago and London, 1971), p. 162.
[13] Quoted in DeVane, *Browning Handbook*, p. 229.

of bells the names and stories of the friends who preceded him on the quest, and sees them in a sheet of flame ranged to meet him. 'Not see? because of night perhaps? – why, day / Came back again for that!' (st. XXXII).

XXXIII

Not hear? when noise was everywhere! it tolled
　　Increasing like a bell. Names in my ears
　　Of all the lost adventurers my peers, –
How such a one was strong, and such was bold,
And such was fortunate, yet each of old
　　Lost, lost! one moment knelled the woe of years.

XXXIV

There they stood, ranged along the hill-sides, met
　　To view the last of me a living frame
For one more picture! in a sheet of flame
I saw them and I knew them all. And yet
Dauntless the slug-horn to my lips I set,
　　And blew. '*Childe Roland to the Dark Tower came.*'

What is this but the experience of understanding as distilled from what is understood? The slug-horn blast is, I think, a blast of defiance and triumph, in that it contains both the knight's praise of himself for having endured and discovered and his dispraise of what has been endured and discovered. The negative and positive elements are so intertwined as to make music, epiphany, the appropriate final expression, eluding words. It is a condition of Wordsworthian epiphanies that they seem to reproduce experiences that really happened to the author as person. In Browning's poems with sensitised observers the autobiographical connection is less direct, but the poem's genuineness suggests that the experiences stand for similar experiences in Browning's life.

Most importantly, in his great dramatic monologues Browning developed epiphanies of character, which differ from the epiphanies we have been discussing in that they are not revealed to a sensitised observer within the poem. The auditors of these dramatic monologues do not arrive at a complete understanding of the speaker; their understanding is limited by their dramatic purpose. The count's envoy in 'My Last Duchess' is trying to understand how much dowry the duke will demand of his prospective duchess; he may also want to know, perhaps as a warning, what happened to the last duchess. Nor does the speaker, engaged in his dramatic purpose – to impress the envoy with the unfaithfulness of his last duchess and his expectation of dowry from the next – understand all that he is revealing about himself. Thus his last duchess's goodness shines through the duke's utterance despite his condemnation of her; he makes no attempt to conceal it, so preoccupied is he with his own standard of judgement and so oblivious of the world's. He is also oblivious of the irony involved in his turning back to the duchess's portrait, after having boasted of ending her life, to admire, of all things its life-likeness: 'There she stands / As if alive' (lines 46–7).

In 'Childe Roland' the epiphany of his own spiritual development breaks upon the speaker, but the epiphany of character breaks upon the reader. The reader picks up all the discrepancies and ironies, and sees the speaker move through constant intensification of what he is, until finally some all-revealing gesture transforms the character in the reader's perception. In 'My Last Duchess', it is after the above quoted lines, and after the duke waives his lordly privilege by saying 'Nay, we'll go / Together down sir', that he asserts his privilege again by choosing to stop to show off still another object in his art collection:

> Notice Neptune, though,
> Taming a sea-horse, thought a rarity,
> Which Claus of Innsbruck cast in bronze for *me*!
> (lines 54–6, my italics)

Everything the reader has been seeing in sequence is condensed and confirmed into a static moment of insight: the duke's aristocratic arrogance, his aestheticism which reduces the duchess's portrait with her sad story into an object in his art collection, and finally his maniacal possessiveness which explains why the duchess, whose 'looks went everywhere' (line 24) displeased him, and why 'none puts by / The curtain [covering the duchess's portrait] I have drawn for you, but *I*' (lines 9–10, my italics). Now he has the duchess where he can possess her completely, in a painting. The theme of Neptune's conquest underlies all the other themes, bringing them together in a retrospective flash of epiphanic characterisation, if the last line is read with a distinct pause after 'bronze' and a distinct emphasis on 'me.' The speaker is the poem, but a poem that exists in the reader's head; for it is only the reader who by relating all parts of the poem can admire the duke for his existential intensity while perceiving his villainy. This neither the envoy nor the duke himself can do. In the epiphany of character, the speaker's development not through conversion but through a steady line of self-intensification is perceived through the intensification and finally transformation of the reader's consciousness. This is a new technique in the presentation of poetry.

I will end with two more examples. In 'The Bishop Orders His Tomb at Saint Praxed's Church', the dying bishop's 'nephews', really sons, gathered around his bed, are certainly not capable of appreciating in him the qualities we, despite his venality, admire – qualities which we see as typical of the Italian Renaissance: the bishop's energy and zest for life, his love of fine materials and choice Latin, and the imaginative consistency which enables him to conceive of heaven as the immortality granted by a tomb made of the best marble. The sons, who have heard all this before and are thinking of how little expense they can get away with, are hardly responding to the utterance as we do. The bishop himself can hardly be aware of the Renaissance picture he presents, which accounts for the mixture in him of Christianity and paganism and his revelation, along with pieties and aestheticism, of baser motives. Near the end the bedridden bishop is already imagining himself as the recumbent statue upon his tomb, when he realises that his sons will not give him the marble tomb he has prescribed but will leave his soul to ooze out through inferior gritstone:

> There, leave me, there!
> For ye have stabbed me with ingratitude
> To death – ye wish it – God, ye wish it! Stone –
> Gritstone, a-crumble! Clammy squares which sweat
> As if the corpse they keep were oozing through –
>   (lines 113–17)

In still another reversal, one which displays in retrospect the bishop's most fundamental traits, he betrays his compulsive love of ritual, as he arranges the departure of the sons he has just dismissed:

> Well go! I bless ye. Fewer tapers there,
> But in a row: and, going, turn your backs
> – Ay, like departing altar-ministrants,
> And leave me in my church, the church for peace

from whence he proceeds without any sense of disjunction to the surprising revelation that his whole career, with its pieties and grandeurs, has been motivated by competitiveness and illicit sexuality:

> That I may watch at leisure if he leers –
> Old Gandolf, at me, from his onion-stone,
> As still he envied me, so fair she was!
>   (lines 119–25)

So his aim all along was to build a bigger, more expensive tomb than Gandolf's and thus confirm his right to his beautiful mistress, the mother of his sons. We had hints of this before, but the final lines cause in the reader a retrospective flash, rearranging the parts into the new static order that amounts to the epiphany of character taking place in the reader's mind.

In *Andrea del Sarto*, Andrea's wife and model Lucrezia is even less adequate as auditor than are the bishop's sons. Andrea and Lucrezia have just been quarrelling, and she puts up with his long, self-pitying reflection on his art, his successes and failures, and his subtle blame of her for the failures, just long enough to get his permission to join the 'Cousin', really lover, who is whistling for her below. But since the self-conscious Andrea seems to understand his situation

175

completely, the distinction between speaker and reader presents a more difficult problem than in 'My Last Duchess' and 'The Bishop Orders His Tomb'.

The discerning reader sees, however, that Andrea's pretence of understanding is self-deceptive. For Andrea does not understand that he cares less to make love than to indulge in self-pity – that he enjoys degrading himself before his wife, enjoys making clear his awareness of the 'Cousin' below and his awareness that she stays with him only for the money he promises, money with which 'To pay for this same Cousin's freak' (line 239). He does not realise that he enjoys playing her victim since it means that he has resigned his will to her and can blame her for his moral failure in art. Had she as his model enjoined upon him 'the play, the insight and the stretch', which his work for all its technical perfection now lacks, 'Had you enjoined them on me, given me soul, / We might have risen to Rafael, I and you!' (lines 116, 118–19).

Each time he makes the accusation, he withdraws it – 'Nay, Love, you did give all I asked, I think – / More than I merit' (lines 120–1), taking the blame upon himself but in such a way as not to invalidate the accusation and to make him feel self-castigating and injured, while depriving her of a chance to fight back. 'Beside', he says,

> incentives come from the soul's self;
> The rest avail not. Why do I need you?
> What wife had Rafael, or has Agnolo?
> (lines 134–6)

The question is ambiguous with at least one meaning unfavourable to Lucrezia. It is this meaning that Andrea takes up again at the end, where he fancies himself competing in heaven against Leonardo, Raphael and Michelangelo:

> the three first without a wife,
> While I have mine! So – still they overcome
> Because there's still Lucrezia, – as I choose.
>
> Again the Cousin's whistle! Go, my love.
> (lines 264–7)

'As I choose' goes farthest in a pretence of self-understanding, which remains self-deception. The shock of the last two lines causes the reader to review the poem, connecting the surrender at the end with the surrender at the beginning:

> But do not let us quarrel any more,
> No, my Lucrezia; bear with me for once:
> Sit down and all shall happen as you wish
> (lines 1–3)

to see how, as in all epiphanies of character, there has been no conversion but only a straight line of self-intensification. 'As I choose' keeps Andrea from seeing how much he really has chosen – that he has chosen to create, indeed compose as for a painting, the whole poem, as a 'twilight-piece' (line 49), as the elegiac vehicle for his self-pity. He does not see that in this composition of his own making, he is a voluptuary, creating the ideal conditions for his own pleasure. In such a picture, Lucrezia is 'My serpentining beauty', curled inside 'the man's bared breast' (lines 26, 22); while the 'Cousin', as sign of Andrea's degradation, is a not unwelcome figure who sets the seal upon the special kind of victory Andrea wins over Lucrezia in the end. All this the reader, in a retrospective flash, can realise as Lucrezia and even Andrea cannot. The reader emerges with admiration for the fine imagination that created the utterance and its finely expressed self-pity, and with condemnation for the moral weakness and secret manipulativeness in what is perhaps the most complex epiphany of character in Browning. One could hardly find a character more unlike Browning than Andrea; yet we discern Browning's sympathy for and judgement of him. Despite Browning's many dramatic disguises, we derive, if we read a lot of him, about as clear a picture of his authorial *persona* as we do of Wordsworth's.

In 'Transcendentalism: A Poem in Twelve Books', an epilogue to *Men and Women*, the older poet says finally to the younger poet: 'You are a poem, though your poem's naught. / The best of all you showed before, believe, / Was your own boy-face' (lines 47–9).[14] These lines apply in the poems I have discussed to the poet as projected in the speaker, who is the poem. Browning is related to his various speakers through the 'prismatic [or fragmented] hues' alluded to by Robert and Elizabeth.[15]

But the quotation which best expresses Browning's relation to the speakers of his epiphanic monologues is the one cited earlier, which I will now cite more completely than before, in which Browning describes his poetry as not yet composing ' "R. B., a poem" ', but as momentary

escapes of my inner power, which lives in me like the light in those crazy Mediterranean phares I have watched at sea, wherein the light is ever revolving in a dark gallery, bright and alive, and only after a weary interval leaps out, for a moment, from the one narrow chink.[16]

It is because of suppression and incompleteness, because each burst represents only one phase of Browning's authorial *persona*, that such energy emerges in the momentaneous explosiveness of epiphany.

[14] For an illuminating discussion of 'Transcendentalism', see Herbert F. Tucker, 'Epiphany and Browning: Character Made Manifest', *PMLA*, 107 (October 1992), 1216–17.
[15] See William O. Raymond, 'The Jewelled Bow: A Study in Browning's Imagery and Humanism', in Philip Drew, ed., *Robert Browning: A Collection of Critical Essays* (London, 1966), pp. 110–11.
[16] *Letters of Robert Browning and Elizabeth Barrett Barrett*, I, 17.

❧

PART THREE

Readerships inherited and invented

9

Newman's leading

ERIC GRIFFITHS

LXXXVI.

THE PILLAR OF THE CLOUD.

LEAD, Kindly Light, amid the encircling gloom,
    Lead Thou me on!
The night is dark, and I am far from home –
    Lead Thou me on!
Keep Thou my feet; I do not ask to see
The distant scene, – one step enough for me.

I was not ever thus, nor pray'd that Thou
    Shouldst lead me on.
I loved to choose and see my path, but now
    Lead Thou me on!
I loved the garish day, and, spite of fears,
Pride ruled my will: remember not past years.

So long Thy power hath blest me, sure it still
    Will lead me on,
O'er moor and fen, o'er crag and torrent, till
    The night is gone;
And with the morn those angel faces smile
Which I have loved long since, and lost awhile.

At Sea   *June* 16, 1833[1]

Kingsley thought he was asking a simple question when he asked, 'What, then, does Dr Newman mean?', but to judge by the answer – the *Apologia pro vita sua* – the question was less simple than he thought.[2] A reader of 'The Pillar of the Cloud' also may believe it a simple task to say what this poem means. 'At least', someone might urge, 'it must be easy to *sing* what the poem means, for generations have done that.' This encouraging notion supposes, though, that nothing much happened to the poem when it became a hymn; it also imagines

---

[1] I give the text of *Verses on Various Occasions* (London, 1868), the last which Newman saw through the press.

[2] The beginnings of the *Apologia* are best described in M. Svaglic's edition (Oxford, 1967).

that what many people manage to do must be easily done, which is not self-evidently the case (bringing up children, for instance).

An editor might approach this matter by asking, 'What, then, did Newman write?', for the text was not ever thus; it underwent revision over thirty-four years. The first publication in the *British Magazine* of February 1834 does not capitalise 'kindly', reads 'prayed' for 'pray'd', 'Shouldest' for 'Shouldst', and prints the ninth line as 'I loved to choose and see my path; but now'. No great need for an edition which prints all variants, then: accidentals are all that change, and of those changes only the repointing of the ninth line makes a difference; substantively, the text stays the same, if its body begins at 'LEAD', and ends at 'awhile'.[3] Yet 'THE PILLAR OF THE CLOUD' and '*At Sea*' and '*June* 16, 1833' may be dearer to the poem than a hat and a pair of shoes it happens on one occasion to be wearing; they might be its head and feet and, as such, ask for considerate treatment – 'Keep thou my feet'. Newman certainly paid the title attention; he changed it each of the four principal times he published the poem. It first appeared anonymously with the title 'Faith' as the second poem of the ninth instalment in the magazine serialisation of *Lyra Apostolica*; in the gathering of those pieces into one volume (1836), it changed its name to 'Light in the Darkness', gained Psalm 112: 4 as an epigraph, and was pseudonymously owned as by 'Delta'.[4] Years later, when Newman had gone over to Rome, the piece crossed the Irish Sea and figured in *Verses on Religious Subjects* (Dublin, 1853), a volume whose title-page declares no author, as 'Grace of congruity'. After the *Apologia* restored his good name with his countrymen, though the man known as 'Newman' had changed, for many readers beyond recognition, it was at last published over his name in *Verses on Various Occasions*, but this time the poem itself had a new name, 'The Pillar of the Cloud', shed its epigraph, and acquired those reminders of where and when it began which bring Newman's dealings with it to a close.

Owen Chadwick summarises this textual story as 'a playing, not for the better, with the title of the poem'. 'Not for the better' puts his vexation mildly; the same essay with franker testiness calls 'The Pillar of the Cloud' 'a very inappropriate title' because 'A pillar of cloud led the Israelites by day, a pillar of fire by night. The author of the hymn is in dusk. The original had no title but "Faith".'[5]

---

[3] The other editions which I mention also present no substantive variants. I have not been able to see *Verses on Religious Subjects* and rely for my knowledge of that volume on Vincent Ferrer Blehl, SJ, *John Henry Newman: A Bibliographical Catalogue of His Writings* (Charlottesville, Va., 1978).

[4] Both sympathetic and hostile reviewers at the time evidently knew Delta's identity; see *The Christian Observer* (1837), p. 469 and *The British Critic*, p. 138, though both conspired to pretend ignorance.

[5] See '"Lead, Kindly Light"' in his *The Spirit of the Oxford Movement: Tractarian Essays* (Cambridge, 1990), pp. 94, 86.

Professor Chadwick forgets that dusks can in English take place either when day turns to night or, as here, when night turns to day (*OED sb.* 2a); the poem starts in the dark but looks towards a 'morn', a 'morn' different from the 'garish day' of proud automotion, different just in making visible the need of such a guide as a cloud. (Not to mention that 'The Pillar of the Cloud' may or may not be the same as a 'pillar of cloud'; Professor Chadwick moves too fast over the divine signs in the Book of Exodus, where a cloudy pillar serves to illuminate some while perplexing others, as a 'STOP' sign as well as a beckoning.)[6] Still, there is something odd about a poem which sounds as if it addressed a pillar of the cloud as a 'kindly light', a trick of grammatical twilight like that played in Hardy's 'After a Journey' where we eventually find that what we had thought took place at day happens at night. But then there is something congruously odd about a poem which is all about walking and which yet says that it was written '*At Sea*'. An eye at twilight strives to determine quickly what is what, but there is more to the story of this poem than meets the eye of impatience, and that is partly because its subject is patience.

After he had converted to Rome, Newman was for obvious reasons particularly keen to date his Anglican writings, even a piece such as this which had been both welcomed and shunned because of its apparent lack of doctrinal content.[7] Pestered for years to say what it meant, Newman grew curt. The poem was an exercise 'in an art which is the expression, not of truth, but of imagination and sentiment', occupied with 'transient states of mind which come upon one when homesick or sea sick, or in any other way sensitive or excited'.[8] Several things won't do about this dismissal: the state of mind expressed may be 'transient' but it is also, as the poem's popularity attests, recurrent; a recurrent state of mind might be termed a 'habit', and 'habit' was not for Newman something on the side of 'imagination and sentiment' as sheerly opposed to 'truth'.[9] In 1869, Newman may find the 'art' of poetry only this touchy or febrile thing, but forty years earlier he had thought that a 'poetical view' of reality was for Christians 'a duty, – we are bid to colour all things with hues of faith, to see a Divine meaning in every event, and a superhuman tendency . . . It may be added that the virtues peculiarly Christian are especially poetical – meekness, gentleness, compassion, content-

---

6 See Exodus 14: 19–20, 40: 38, 13: 21–2, respectively.
7 Chadwick notes that complaints began early, ' "Lead, Kindly Light" ', p. 96. Compare Gordon S. Wakefield's discussion in *Kindly Light: Meditations on Newman's Poem* (London 1984), especially the remark, p. 48, 'This is a poem of personal faith; there is nothing of the objectivity of the church's creed about it.'
8 Letter to W. A. Greenhill, 18 January 1869, in *The Letters and Diaries of John Henry Newman*, edited by C. S. Dessain *et al.*, 31 vols. (London, 1961–), XXIX, 113 (hereafter referred to as *LD*).
9 On 'habit' and 'ethos' in Keble and Newman, see Stephen Prickett, *Romanticism and Religion: The Tradition of Coleridge and Wordsworth in the Victorian Church* (Cambridge, 1976).

ment, modesty, not to mention the devotional virtues . . .'[10] And though Newman may have been relieved to let people make of the piece what they wished by way of interpretation, he was not happy to let them make of it what they wished by way of interpolation, protesting in 1881 that 'Mr Bickersteth (I think) of Hampstead, without even asking my leave, added a stanza of his own, without notice to the public, to "Lead Kindly Light". No one likes interpolations in what he has written.' and adding tartly, 'It [interpolation] is one of the imputed crimes of Rome, which ought to have occurred to so good a Protestant.'[11] He would probably not have approved the substantive variant, introduced by Dr Horatius Bonar in the *Bible Hymn Book* (1845) where the first line reads 'Lead, Saviour, lead amid the encircling gloom.'[12]

The poem might make no doctrinal statement and yet be a doctrinally partisan utterance. The original version did not have 'no title but "Faith"', for it stepped out under the banner heading *Lyra Apostolica. No.* IX; the 'Advertisement' for the one-volume *Lyra Apostolica* has a definite idea what such a *Lyra* is tuned up to do: the poems are published 'in the humble hope that they may be instrumental in recalling or recommending to the reader important Christian truths which are at this day in a way to be forgotten'. Newman's 'Postscript' to the 1879 reprint of the *Lyra* is even more forthright; he couples his poems of that time with the *Tracts for the Times* as written 'with the simple purpose of startling, of rousing, or suggesting thought, and offering battle, in the cause of the Ancient Church'; he remembers having said 'to Froude or some other intimate friend at the time, "We must not mind roughness or awkwardness of versification; we are but bringing out ideas in metre."' These are the purposes to which he returns in his most interesting comments on the *Lyra* poems:

I wrote them in the Lyra just before the commencement of the Oxford Movement, while travelling, and during convalescence after fever, and in crossing the Mediterranean home. I have never had practice enough to have words and metres at my command. And besides at the time, I had a theory, one of the extreme theories of the incipient Movement, that it was not right 'agere poetam', but merely 'ecclesiasticum agere' – that the one thing called for was to bring out an idea; that the harsher the better, like wearing sackcloth . . .[13]

---

[10] 'Poetry, with Reference to Aristotle's Poetics', *London Review*, January 1829, reprinted in *Essays and Sketches*, edited by C. F. Harold, 3 vols. (London, 1948), I, 76.

[11] *LD*, XXIX, 359.

[12] See Chadwick, '"Lead Kindly Light"', p. 92 which gives the added stanza which, like Bonar's version, wants to find a 'Saviour' in the lines. Both re-writers are trying to make Newman's 'Faith' an Evangelical 'saving faith'.

[13] Letter to R. H. Hutton, March 1864, in *LD* XX, 69. Roger Sharrock points out the significant format of later editions of the *Lyra* with its 'pages designed like those of a devotional book with red and black lines and Gothic type for headings'. See his 'Newman's Poetry', in I. Ker and A. G. Hill, eds., *Newman after a Hundred Years* (Oxford, 1990), p. 50.

Readers of an Evangelical persuasion, for instance, heard quickly enough that the poem, call itself 'Faith' though it might, lacked a theologically desirable assurance of faith. Its very 'encircling gloom', which now seems so neutrally experienced, was then seen in doctrinal colours as 'the natural and necessary attendant on religious views such as those that are held by the writers of [this] school'; the *Christian Observer* went on to observe: 'It is from this most distressing mode of teaching, from this deep cloud – nay, rather, *night* – of doctrine, that we pray God to deliver our brethren. It is our strong, our fervent prayer, that God may yet make them pillars of the Apostolic Church, of which they are members . . .'[14] The Tractarians considered themselves the true 'pillars of the Apostolic Church' – that was why their 'lyra' was 'apostolica' – but were in turn considered as just under a 'cloud'; this is part of the irony of the poem's final title.[15]

At different times, Newman presents his verses as champions of 'important Christian truths' or as expressions 'not of truth, but of imagination and sentiment'. He might have changed his mind; after all, changing his mind was something Newman did extremely well. Yet he was usually more conscious of having done so than he appears to be here. As he was not a consistent poet, it comes as no surprise that he had no consistent grasp on what as a poet he was doing. This was not his predicament alone. Sure as they may have been of their doctrinal ground, all Tractarian versifiers were poetically at sea. They were trying to make Anglican music of a non-Evangelical persuasion, and this was something which had not been done for some time. Sung Eucharist, for example, had virtually died out in the Anglican communion during the seventeenth century and was revived by the Tractarians, one of the first occasions being at the consecration of Leeds parish church in 1841.[16] They laboriously sought pre-Reformation purity of doctrine in their patristic studies; they also tried to unearth a *Gregorian Hymnal* (in 1844); John Mason Neale researched for years to translate his *Medieval Hymns and Sequences* (1851) and *Hymns of the Eastern Church* (1862). Contributions to a *Lyra Apostolica* were a more ticklish business even than those attempted revivals of liturgy, for these were to be poems written in the English of their day that yet brought out into that English 'important Christian truths which are at this day in a way to be forgotten', made the current

---

[14] *Christian Observer*, July 1837, pp. 478, 479.

[15] The second stanza of the poem originally referred to what Newman had come to regard as the Evangelical vice of choosing some portions of Scripture to support tendentious interpretations of the whole. I discuss this briefly in my 'Newman: The Foolishness of Preaching' in Ker and Hill, *Newman after a Hundred Years*, pp. 88–91 but see Stephen Thomas's much fuller treatment in his *Newman and Heresy: The Anglican Years* (Cambridge, 1991).

[16] See Winfred Douglas, *Church Music in History and Practice* (London, 1937; revised by L. Ellinwood, 1963), p. 71.

tongue speak in behalf of 'the cause of the Ancient Church'. As in much Tractarianism, the enterprise is enmeshed in the paradoxes of a sectarian movement which yet claims to be itself *the* Church, paradoxes which Newman was to unfold with lethal gentleness and intimate humour in the *Anglican Difficulties*. The title of the volume already teeters under strain: *Lyra Apostolica* – as Newman noted 'Keble does not like the name – but I do'.[17] Keble's taste on this point was better than Newman's but that did not prevent a torrential fad for *Lyras* from bursting over the English-speaking world in the next couple of decades. There was a *Lyra Innocentium* (1846), a *Lyra Catholica* (1849), a *Lyra Sanctorum; Lays for the Minor Festivals of the English Church* (1850), a *Lyra Germanica* (1855) – a translation of Lutheran hymns to show that Papists and Tractarians didn't have all the good *Lyras*, a *Lyra Eucharistica* (1863), a *Lyra Messianica* (1864), a *Lyra Mystica* (1865), a *Lyra Americana* (1865), a *Lyra Liturgica* (1865), a *Lyra Consolationis; or, Hymns for the Day of Sorrow and Weariness* (1866), a *Lyra Sacra Americana; or, Gems from American Sacred Poetry* (1868), and a *Lyra Anglicana* (1873). David's harp went forth and multiplied with daunting brio.

The thought of this massed band of competing and disputatious lyres is sad as well as funny. The poignant absurdity is not specific to Victorian England but as wide and old as the Church. Though Eusebius of Caesarea rightly felt that 'The measure of God's acceptance of the singing of a Christian congregation, and of his delight in it, is the unanimity of mind, passion and sentiment, the unity of faith and piety with which we sing together the melodies of our praises',[18] the Church's song has long been marked by the facts of real disharmony: St Gregory Nazianzen wrote anti-Arian hymns and St Ambrose 'the real father of the liturgical hymn, was moved to write his truly popular songs during his critical persecution by the Arian Empress Justina'.[19] The Newman of the *Essay on Development* would have understood such phenomena as part of the arduous 'reality' of an idea, the protracted birth-pangs of its realisation or 'bringing home', but the Newman of the *Lyra* does not allow in his polemical poems that ideas need to be 'realised'; he thought they could be just brought out in metre, as when he wrote that it was 'not right "agere poetam", but merely "ecclesiasticum agere"' – that the one thing called for was to bring out an idea'. Concern for your own achievement as a poet – 'acting for the sake of poetry' or even 'acting the poet' – might be irrelevant or worse for the purposes of the *Lyra*, but the concern to achieve poems in which doctrine, sentiment and language were in accord was the ecclesial point of the enterprise. A theological definition is not a liturgical custom nor a devotional lyric, yet unless these and similar forms of religious

---

[17] 25 March 1833, in *LD*, III, 269.
[18] Erik Routley: *The Church and Music* (London 1950, revised edition 1967), p. 234.
[19] Douglas, *Church Music in History and Practice*, p. 131.

belief have some interdependence one on another, a Church, as Newman understood it, has not come into being. 'Let me write the hymns and I do not care who writes the theology' is not something we would imagine Newman saying (and not only because it is so cheery a remark); it is, though, a symmetrical converse of his attitude to the 'agere poetam' / 'ecclesiasticum agere' distinction.[20]

The instance matters not only because it shows elements of philistine shallowness in Newman's attitude to poetry. This is also a difficult case for the application of a set of general laws, a set described by J. L. Austin in his 'doctrine of the *Infelicities*'. Austin's work starts from a consideration of what makes an utterance successful. Philosophers long concentrated their minds on statements, and the question of what makes statements true, but Austin observed that we do many things with words as well as make statements: we promise, threaten, bequeathe and baptise in the name of the Father, Son and Holy Spirit. Such utterances, which Austin called 'performative', are not normally true or false but rather 'happy' or 'unhappy': if I bequeathe you my watch in ignorance of the fact that you are already dead, my bequest is infelicitous; if I attempt to define a dogma of the church *ex cathedra* even though I am not the Pope, I do not succeed in defining a dogma. As Austin writes: 'Besides the uttering of the . . . performative, a good many other things have as a general rule to be right and go right if we are to be said to have happily brought off our action . . . we call the doctrine of *the things that can be and go wrong* on the occasion of such utterances, the doctrine of the *Infelicities*.'[21] Amongst the things which need to be and go right are, roughly speaking: there must be an accepted procedure to be invoked and followed for performing the act; the person invoking the procedure and the circumstances of its invocation must be 'appropriate'; these conditions must be recognised as fulfilled by any other persons concerned if the invocation of the procedure is intended to be consequential for them. This need for a circumstantial appropriateness at various levels if an utterance is to be successful applies across a wide range of human practices; these practices include both lyric poetry and the teaching of doctrine. In Austin's words, 'infelicity is an ill to which *all* acts are heir which have the general character of ritual or ceremonial, all *conventional* acts';[22] both a sermon and a lyric poem are conventional acts. We may add: and so too is the making of a statement. I may tell you this or that in the sense that I may speak certain words in your hearing, but I do not teach you anything until I persuade you of the truth of what I say, bring you to realise what

---

[20] The remark is R. W. Dale's, who was a Methodist minister at Carrs Lane, Birmingham while Newman was at the Oratory there; see Gordon S. Wakefield, *Kindly Light: Meditations on Newman's Poem*, p. 53.

[21] *How to Do Things with Words*, edited by J. L. Urmson (London, 1962), p. 14.

[22] *Ibid.*, p. 19.

I am saying. Neither in the case of teaching nor of poetry does the sheer fact of statement constitute the happiness of utterance.

The poems of *Lyra Apostolica*, like many *Tracts for the Times*, suffer the infelicity of according themselves an authority which is not recognised and therefore not possessed. Their authors wish to speak not only for the Church but also *as* the Church, to act not only 'ecclesiasticum' but 'Ecclesiam'; in the circumstances, it would have been more apt to have settled for a mere 'agere poetam'. The 1836 'Advertisement' explains their originally anonymous publication as flowing directly from their magisterial ambitions; because they hoped to be 'instrumental in recalling or recommending to the reader important Christian truths', they had to be 'strictly anonymous'. 'We are not allowed to regard ourselves as individuals but as members of one body', as Newman said of eschatological hope.[23] Yet it was to become a pressing question for the Tractarian Newman whether he and his like were flesh of the flesh of the Anglican Church or just a thorn in her flesh. The *Lyra*'s confidence may have been in his mind when he wrote in his 'Preface' to the *Hymni Ecclesiae e Breviaro Parisiensi* of the cumulative and transpersonal character of the Paris breviary as contrasted with snappier and more self-determined productions:

The Roman Hymns, whether good or bad, were the work of no one generation, much less the outpourings of one mind. They were not the contents of one collection, published all new in a day according to the will of man. They were the gradual accumulation of centuries, bearing in old and new upon one treasure-house . . . Nay even such as the Parisian [hymns] . . . which have no equal claims to antiquity breathe an ancient spirit; and even where they are the work of one pen, are the joint and invisible contribution of many ancient minds.[24]

Thus, for example, though 'Lead, Kindly Light' said that 'I' now abstain from picking my own way and give myself up to divine guidance, its way of saying remained individualistic, self-assured, and this not because in it Newman too much acted the poet but because he did so too little, taking for granted that his words would be granted the status he himself accorded them. This is a matter insufficiently realised in the verses of *Lyra Apostolica*. The not realising it fully enough in the verses themselves lies at the centre of their poetic thinness which is at the same time their lack of power doctrinally to persuade (that they are unpersuasive does not entail that the doctrines of which they fail to persuade us are untrue), for the poetic thinness shows itself in features of the writing which mistake parochial, literary habits – genteel archaism, late eighteenth-century

---

[23] Sermon of 14 March 1830, reprinted in *John Henry Newman: Sermons 1824–1843: Volume I, Sermons on the Liturgy and Sacraments and on Christ the Mediator*, edited by Placid Murray, OSB (Oxford, 1991), p. 92.

[24] See Donald A. Withey, *John Henry Newman: The Liturgy and the Breviary* (London, 1992), pp. 151–2.

diction, lyrical declaiming which has never heard of Wordsworth – for the voice of the Primitive Church.

To explain how the failure 'agere poetam' was also a failure 'ecclesiasticum agere', I need to introduce a term of Newman's theological art, the word 'connatural'. This word is particular to him; he re-introduced it into English in a sermon of 1830 (the *OED* records no use in the relevant sense between 1711 and Pusey in 1860). The sermon, on 'Faith and Obedience', has it as follows in a passage on a doctrinal failing:

It is undeniable that there are multitudes who would avow with confidence and exultation that they put obedience only in the second place in their religious scheme, as if it were rather a necessary consequence of faith than requiring a direct attention for its own sake; a something subordinate to it, rather than connatural and contemporaneous with it.

When 'Lead, Kindly Light' was called 'Faith', it held such a view of obedient conduct as integral to, and not merely derivative of, faith (that is one aspect of its anti-Evangelical colouring); to those who asked what the 'Faith' was which the poem espoused, it might have replied that the faith was *in* the obedience, not a matter for propositional summary. Yet such a reply came to seem riskily pietistic to Newman. He returned to the word 'connatural' in his *Letter to Pusey* when considering how devotional excesses arise:

Religion acts on the affections; who is to hinder these, when once roused, from gathering in their strength and running wild? They are not gifted with any connatural principle within them, which renders them self-governing and self-adjusting.

This Catholic Newman suspects that even Tractarian reserve, patristic scholarship, and fear of innovation may be more unbridled than they thought themselves to be; the careful steps he takes in his poem were evidently not 'running wild' and yet might have been going astray. To see one's way clear in areas where inclination prompts and there is no certain rule is always difficult because, as the Angel explains to the Soul in *The Dream of Gerontius*:

> ANGEL   In thy trial-state
> Thou hadst a traitor nestling close at home,
> Connatural, who with the powers of hell
> Was leagued, and of thy senses kept the keys . . .

The centrality of the concept of 'connatural senses' for his manner of thinking is most manifest in the *Grammar of Assent* where he attempts to explain a quandary in which logic and poetry are akin:

The concrete matter of propositions is a constant source of trouble to syllogistic reasoning, as marring the simplicity and perfection of its process. Words, which denote things, have innumerable implications; but in inferential exercises it is the very triumph of that clearness and hardness of head, which is the characteristic talent for the art, to have stripped them of all these connatural senses, to have drained them of that depth and breadth of associations which constitute their poetry, their rhetoric, and their historical life . . .

Such are the characteristics of reasoning, viewed as a science or scientific art, or inferential process, and we might anticipate that, narrow as by necessity is its field of view, for that reason its pretensions to be demonstrative were incontrovertible. In a certain sense they really are so; while we talk logic, we are unanswerable; but then, on the other hand, this universal living scene of things is after all as little a logical world as it is a poetical; and, as it cannot without violence be exalted into poetical perfection, neither can it be attenuated into a logical formula.[25]

The logical and poetical, the tools of doctrine and the task of lyric, meet when they face 'the concrete matter of propositions'. For logic, this concrete matter in the form of the 'connatural senses' of words is an obstacle to be cleared; for poetry, it is a chaos which needs attuning. In both cases, the 'connatural senses' of words make up the 'concrete matter of propositions', make up, that is, the real circumstances in which utterances are issued and received.

Such 'connatural senses' appear, for instance, when David Daiches suggests that unbelievers may be best placed to understand devotional poetry: 'it would seem that far from the inability of a reader to share the author's beliefs preventing him from appreciating a poem, such an inability can liberate the reader to see the poem as something more than a document of faith . . . Perhaps it is the sceptic who is the one capable of the most generous response to poetry of different ages and cultures, the uncommitted open-minded eclectic observer of the varieties of human efforts to explain the contradictions and mysteries revealed by human experience.'[26] It is as hard to be truly sceptical as truly to resign one's self-will (perhaps the tasks are related). Professor Daiches has not doubted whether it is always a 'liberation' to be able to see a poem as 'something more than a document of faith': what might this 'more' mean – 'more than a *document* of faith' or 'more than a document *of faith*'? So too, it is open to doubt whether the uncommitted eclectic will always be 'generous' in his understanding of 'different ages and cultures', especially when those ages and cultures differ just by being doctrinally committed or disputatious, by having different notions of how good it is, whether it is good, to be 'open-minded'. It could be wondered if Professor Daiches has sceptically heard that the words 'eclectic', 'mysteries' and 'revealed' have, connaturally, more than one meaning, so that a believer might think the

[25] 'Faith and Obedience', in *Parochial and Plain Sermons* (London, 1868; reprinted in 8 vols., 1907–10), III, 87; *A Letter Addressed to the Rev. E. B. Pusey, DD, on Occasion of His Eirenicon*, in *Certain Difficulties Felt By Anglicans* . . . 2 vols. (London, 1879), II, 79; I quote *Gerontius* from the text of *Verses on Various Occasions*, p. 338; *An Essay in Aid of a Grammar of Assent* (London, 1870), I quote from the edition of I. T. Ker (Oxford, 1985), pp. 174–5.
[26] *God and the Poets* (London, 1984), pp. 211–12, 217.

mysteries revealed *to* human experience were more important than those revealed by it. Such divergent 'connatural senses' are a linguistically integral form of those 'appropriate circumstances' which Austin defines under his 'doctrine of the *Infelicities*'; they are bearers (often mute) of the procedures which we invoke, often tacitly, when we strive for successful utterance, and they are – both for doctrine and for lyric – what may most go wrong.

To return to Newman '*At Sea*' on June 16, 1833. He composed the doctrinal lyric, 'Lead, Kindly Light' in the darkness of many connatural senses of his own words. He sent his mother a batch of poems on the ninth of that month in the last letter he wrote before this poem. They include, to give them their eventual titles from *Verses on Various Occasions*, 'Sympathy', 'The Age to Come', 'Warfare', 'Relics of Saints', 'Liberalism', 'Day-labourers' and 'Declension' (along with 'There is one only bond in the wide earth' which was not republished there). In those poems we find the following phrases: 'the view / Of crag and steep ravine', 'the day / Which shall the lost unite' – that is, the 'crag and torrent' of 'Lead, Kindly Light' as well as the plangent cadence of 'those angel faces smile / Which I have loved long since, and lost awhile'. Given that 'The Pillar of the Cloud' was eventually to be the title of what he wrote on 16 June, much in these immediately preceding poems speaks aptly of a fire which leads, of Moses, of saving a people or a church lost in bondage. Almost every poem mentions fire – 'eyes of fire', 'the truths that in me burn', 'A sword to sever, and a fire to burn', 'Smouldering and struggling till the judgment day'. He had just recovered from his Sicilian illness. This imaginative complex of connatural senses in which a man may be said to be 'on fire' – extreme longing, missionary conviction, a fever at once prophetic and physical – forms the appropriate circumstance for understanding what the words of 'Lead, Kindly Light' mean. For some time before 16 June and for long afterwards, Newman was to be in a ferment of confidence, in his role of controversialist, champion, 'leading light', but 'Lead, Kindly Light' is becalmed, experiences a reversal of much within and everything around him.

How odd, for instance, that a poem written, according to his diary entry, 'In sight of Sardinia'[27] should have so un-Mediterranean a landscape, a landscape of gloom, moor and fen. So intense was his desire to be home that he writes as if he were already there, – indeed, north of Oxford; the poem remains, though, also expressive of longing for a virtual landscape, a look ahead into a promised land, but Newman didn't as he wrote know the relation of that home to the land that was to be promised him. He wrote to his mother from Lyons, 1 July 1833: 'Really it seems as if some unseen power, good or bad, was resisting my return. The thought of home has brought tears in my eyes for the last two months . . . So it is a simple trial of my patience. I am quite desolate. I am tempted to say, "Lord, heal

---

[27] Diary, Monday 17 June 1833, in *LD*, III, 322.

me, for my bones are vexed." But really I am wonderfully calm, and I trust from right principles. Thwarting awaits me at every step.'[28] The turns of urgency and resignation in this beautiful letter aptly comment on his poem. Thwarting awaited him at every step, as he was soon to find out and often to complain, but the poem thinks it will be enough to know 'one step' ahead, entrusts its pace elsewhere than in his plans. Its versification too is 'really . . . wonderfully calm', calm as he is amidst the impatience of his letter home; the wonderful calm which comes, for instance, when the last line of the poem resignedly inverts the shape of the last line of the first two stanzas: 'The distant scene, – one step enough for me.' / 'Pride ruled my will: remember not past years.' – both these lines break into a four-syllable unit followed by a six-syllable unit; they have the tone of knowing how to go on in verse at least. The poem ends 'Which I have loved long since, and lost awhile'- six syllables followed by four, a gentle acquiescence in loss as in the being led. The psalm he quotes to his mother has itself a composure like that of his letter and his poem: the psalmist's soul and bones are vexed; he cries out 'O LORD, how long?', like Newman fretting at the delay of his journey; the psalmist is figuratively 'at sea' as Newman was – 'all the night I make my bed to swim'. Yet he ends quietly: 'The LORD hath heard my supplication, the LORD will receive my prayer' (Psalms 6: 3.6.9). In the very interim of the psalm's lyric present, the poet knows that God has heard and will answer: 'hath heard' and 'will receive' over-arch the now of uncertainty. This is a poetic shape of hope, of 'patient subdued tranquil cheerful thoughtful waiting',[29] as it is in 'Lead, Kindly Light' which contains its present in which 'the night is dark' within a span which concludes 'the night is gone' and with a magnificently elliptical present tense which confidently lives in expectation of a future 'till / With the morn those angel faces smile'. The 'will' which had once been a faculty of the human soul – 'Pride ruled my will' – dissolves into the emphatically trusting and rhyming submission of 'So long Thy power hath blest me, sure it *still* / *Will* lead me on . . .'

The poem was written a month before Keble, on Bastille Day, 1833, preached his Assize Sermon on 'National Apostasy' and began the 'Oxford Movement'. It was to that city Newman, idling reluctantly in the Straits of Bonifacio, longed to be led. Oxford was then Newman's Canaan. Yet when Newman named the poem for the last time in 1868, he knew that the decisive movement he had made was away from Oxford, when, in the sad, punning words of the *Apologia*: 'I left Oxford for good on Monday, February 23, 1846', a move which he wrote to a friend was 'like going on the open sea', taking him back to the '*At Sea*' from which the kindly light was to have led him home, and did, but to a home he had not then imagined would be his.[30]

<hr/>

[28] *LD*, IV, 3.
[29] Sermon of 14 March 1830, in Murray, *Sermons on the Liturgy and Sacraments*, p. 90.
[30] The remarks about leaving Oxford are from the *Apologia*, edited by Svaglic, pp. 212–13.

The changing titles of the poem give Newman's sense of the changing pattern of connatural senses which came together in what he wrote then. At first, the lyric is un-occasioned and has no particular author, its 'I' just instances any member of the Church anywhere at any time. Though in fact the date of composition as eventually declared tells on the interpretation of what he meant at that date, that he reserved the date and his name tells more of what he thought he meant. We could say: the important thing is that he thought *he* didn't mean it. The poem faces a large task and asks to be helped through it by a 'kindly light' called 'Faith'. There is a Protestant nuance to that title, though Newman was to head a 'Catholicwards' movement. What he relies on is 'faith', *tout court*, though this is no longer the Evangelical saving faith he had once inclined to. The poem itself says: 'I was not ever thus' – he knows that he has changed his mind in the past but envisages the future as purely a regaining of a communion he had known, 'angel faces . . . / Which I have loved long since, and lost awhile'. All this biographical detail is but one possible example of experienced 'Faith'; the lyric transcends its setting. By 1836, the kindly light, though still the light of 'Faith', is also a 'Light in the Darkness'; it has become the beleaguered light of the true, primitive Tractarian Church which shone in the darkness of Anglicanism, and Anglicanism comprehended it not. The poem now has a pseudonymous declaration of authorship, a declaration forced on the poets of *Lyra Apostolica* by Hurrell Froude's death;[31] it also stands in a collection which has acquired a Homeric epigraph: 'Froude chose the words in which Achilles, on returning to the battle, says, "You shall know the difference, now that I am back again."'[32] Newman longing for Oxford, Moses in sight of the promised land, and Achilles, bereft of Patroclus, looking towards a Troy still unshaken in its ways after years of combat: as it ages, the poem draws to itself depths of experience not all harmonious with each other in implication or tone; its concrete matter grows dense with divergent connatural senses. (Achilles' wrath was, in some respects, divinely willed but then it was for anger that Moses was denied Canaan; the irate partisan does not speak with the voice of the universal Church.) The poem, like Newman's mission, had seemed so simple but, again like his mission, was developing a mesh of infelicities he had not foreseen or foreheard.

Within ten years, the thought of such a process of development in Christian doctrine and practice would so have grown in Newman that it took him out of the Anglican communion. When he next re-named the poem, he was no longer in Oxford but in Dublin, and he found for the ascertaining of true direction amidst obscure circumstance a technical and Catholic term: 'Grace of congruity'. The early 1850s were one of the darkest times in Newman's life: there were problems with the Oratory, with the hierarchy in Ireland, he had been found guilty (in a

---

[31] See the 'Advertisement' to the 1836 collection.
[32] Newman, in the 'Postscript' to the 1879 reprint of *Lyra Apostolica*, p. vii.

scandalously unfair trial, presided over by a Tractarian judge) of libelling Achilli. These gloomily encircling facts may explain the theological pugnacity of the new title. 'Congruous' grace is grace which is efficacious through 'its "congruity" or adaptation to the interior dispositions and exterior circumstances of time and place of the recipient of the grace'.[33]

This is grace which has defeated the 'doctrine of the *Infelicities*' but only by finding its way through the 'appropriate circumstances', the 'connatural senses' of its recipient. The poem's first title had said quickly what the poem meant; its second title admitted that the poet had spoken too soon. Having been led further and elsewhere than he had intended, 'Grace of congruity' became the proper name for a complex of self-assertion, relinquishing of will, certainty that one has relinquished one's will, discovering that even such certainty was self-willed, for the long process of vision and revision, of which the poem had always been speaking, though it only slowly made itself heard. The thing about God, he comes wrily to reflect, is that if you give Him an inch, He'll take you a mile. By 1868, things looked kindlier around him: the *Apologia* was out, he was rehabilitated in the imaginations of many of his countrymen, and could look back to the 'Faith' of 1833 with a mingled amusement and gratitude, such as is consummately and devoutly expressed in the phrase 'The Pillar of the Cloud'. The story of when and where it was written had been told in the *Apologia*; the published text now at last attached this utterance to its occasion '*At Sea*', '*June 16, 1833*'. Not that the meaning of the poem was tied to its occasion. On the contrary. Its occasion had been largely misunderstanding and for a long time misunderstood. The poem had done what all good lyrics must do; it had, not transcended, but survived its occasion, as it continues to survive its author. Over the years, it had become, like its author, subdued, so that there is a historical felicity in the fact that it was in the year of the *Apologia* that J. B. Dykes set the words to 'Lux Benigna' and thus at last made sure that its 'I' would be thereafter both J. H. Newman and nobody in particular.[34]

In my copy of *Verses on Various Occasions*, a previous owner has written beneath the text of 'The Golden Prison' ('Weep not for me, when I am gone') which Newman dates '1853': 'June 1943 – the high summer, with nature at its loveliest, all this and the death of our loved Peter. May the eternal loveliness of God fill his being for ever and ever.' This is touching but scarcely, it might be thought, relevant to editors or bibliographers. So much the worse for editors and bibliographers, if that is so. Fortunately, it is not. The anonymous reader in June 1943 re-applies Newman's lyric to a new occasion after a ninety-year interim; the capacity of the poem for re-application shows that it has the force of a rule, and that the relation of poem to occasion is that of rule to instance not that of effect to

---

[33] *A Catholic Dictionary of Theology*, 3 vols. (Edinburgh, 1962): 'Congruism', II, 95.
[34] See A. Haeussler, *The Story of Our Hymns* (St Louis, Miss., 1952), p. 350.

cause. Newman himself made similar re-applications of 'Lead, Kindly Light' when he changed its title and style of publication. A poem's title has the force of guidance for the application of a rule, as when we explain to someone that 'Women and children first' applies in emergencies and not to the adjudication of athletic events. The questions which matter in the establishing and interpretation of texts are mostly of the form:

> How does it come about that this arrow → *points?* Doesn't it seem to carry in it something besides itself? – 'No, not the dead line on paper; only the psychical thing, the meaning can do that.' – That is both true and false. The arrow points only in the application that a living being makes of it.
> This pointing is *not* a hocus-pocus which can be performed only by the soul.[35]

Editorial practice concerns not dead lines on paper but the application that living beings make of such lines, particularly the application made by the beings who drew the lines, though, as the case of 'Lead, Kindly Light' shows, it may be especially the author who has re-applied the rule he gave and was given, changed his sense of the direction in which he was being pointed.

To think of 'Lead, Kindly Light' as having a meaning which grows over thirty-five years, and so complicated a process of developed meaning, runs counter to the evident fact that the poem speaks, or sings, plainly. It is obvious, we might say, what the poem means, that the arrow points this way and not that. Just that obviousness is worth thinking about. The poem does not record one of Newman's 'transient states of mind', nor does it state 'important Christian truths'; that first account of what it does, relates it to its occasion only as effect to cause, and so cannot explain its staying-power; the second account fails to convey how rules are bound to their instances, taught only through their application, seized only by living beings. It is because, as Newman said, 'the Gospel is no mere philosophy thrown upon the world at large, no mere quality of mind and thought, no mere beautiful and deep sentiment or subjective opinion, but a substantive message from above, guarded and preserved in a visible polity'[36] that a logomachy which seeks either a 'quality of mind and thought' such as logic might state in its phantasmal purity or a 'beautiful and deep sentiment' such as poetry might revel in will never properly express the Gospel or what the Gospel can inspire in religious writings such as 'Lead, Kindly Light'.

The 'visible polity' in which the author of *The Dream of Gerontius* received 'a substantive message from above' was the Church of Rome as that existed in England while he wrote. That polity (the Church of Rome) was not easily

---

[35] Ludwig Wittgenstein, *Philosophische Untersuchungen* (1953), translated as *Philosophical Investigations* by G. E. M. Anscombe, second edition (London, 1958), No. 454.

[36] *A Letter Addressed to His Grace The Duke of Norfolk on Occasion of Mr Gladstone's Recent Expostulation*, in *Certain Difficulties . . .*, 11, 236.

attended to in that place (England). As John Coulson notes in his edition of Newman's *On Consulting the Faithful . . .*, Bishop Brown, when writing of Newman's work to Archbishop Bedini, secretary of Propaganda at Rome, translated from the original *Rambler* publication phrases such as 'the body of the bishops' as 'corpus Episcoporum' and 'general councils' as 'Concilia Oecumenica', translations which made Newman appear to have uttered 'statements which taken in their *Latin* sense could indeed be said to border on heresy'.[37] In those days, doctrine, like certain wines, did not travel well, was often '*At Sea*'. In 1874 Newman himself counter-expostulated against Gladstone for, amongst other things, mistranslating the word 'doctrina' from the *Pastor Aeternus* as 'rule'.[38] In *On consulting the faithful . . .*, he had needed to defend his use of words such as 'consult' in a 'popular and ordinary' or a 'vague, familiar, genuine' sense; he appealed from the phantasmal strictness of Roman parlance to Dr Johnson's *Dictionary*. Fifteen years later, he was journeying between connatural senses and defined logic in the opposite direction, warily conscious of how difficult it would be to get Mr Gladstone and the English 'to put off the modes of speech and language which are usual with them, and to enter into scientific distinctions and traditionary rules of interpretation, which as being new to them, appear evasive and unnatural'.[39]

Such reciprocal mis-takings are part of Gerontius' dream. The poem follows the *Apologia*, whose publication was completed in June 1864. Newman himself gave 17 January 1865 as the date in which 'it came into my head to write' and the poem was published in *The Month* of May and June of that year. Between its composition and its publication, Cardinal Wiseman died; shortly after its publication, Newman received from Pusey a copy of the latter's *Eirenicon, in a Letter to the Author of 'The Christian Year'*, his reply to which was to occupy him in November and December of 1865. The *Apologia* had been an attempt to describe the development of Newman's faith, considered principally as a matter of doctrine; *Gerontius* and the *Letter Addressed to the Rev. E. B. Pusey* concern the realisation of those doctrines in devotion, realised in as much of their connatural fullness as Newman was capable of as a poet. Some of Pusey's instances of Marian eulogy and devotional practice had 'seem[ed] to me like a bad dream' when Newman read them, but *Gerontius* was already written, his good dream of devotion, his true act of translation between England and Rome. For this is the subject of *Gerontius*, as of the *Letter . . . to Pusey*: 'English habits of belief and devotion' in relation to 'books of devotion of the Italian school', the finding of 'a character and tone of religion . . . suited for England',[40] in particular with relation to the figure of Mary and intercessory prayer – a finding which occupies so much

---

[37] *On Consulting the Faithful in Matters of Doctrine* (London, 1861), edited by John Coulson (London 1966), p. 38.   [38] *A Letter Addressed to his Grace the Duke of Norfolk . . .*, p. 233.
[39] *Ibid.*, p. 177.   [40] *A Letter . . . to the Rev. E. B. Pusey*, p. 21.

of the argument of the *Letter . . . to Pusey* and which punctuates the Soul's utterances from the first words of the *Dream . . .* – 'JESU, MARIA' – and repeatedly: '(Jesu, have mercy! Mary, pray for me!)', 'O Jesu, help! pray for me, Mary, pray!' Though Newman had felt it would be 'a simple purism' to 'insist upon minute accuracy of expression in devotional and popular writings',[41] even the Soul's outcries are instructively careful: it is Jesus who may 'have mercy', Mary is asked only to 'pray for' Gerontius.

The Dream of Gerontius strives not only at the level of such vigilance over terms to bring 'substantive message' and 'visible polity' into earshot of each other. The poem is throughout a work of refined and experienced macaronic. That is, it is written in two languages – in Latin *and* in English – two languages so often in Newman's day in fact unpersuasive of each other, but in this poem drawn near each other. It is not just that the poem quotes Roman Catholic liturgy in a passionate English lyric: the 'Sanctus fortis, Sanctus Deus' of the Good Friday service against and next the sturdy English words 'Firmly I believe, and truly'. Newman has also filled his poem with Latinisms, with words which have a new, vivid meaning in English by being old, disused Latin words. So, for instance, just before the Soul meets the Angel, he remarks:

> some one has me fast
> Within his ample palm; 'tis not a grasp
> Such as they use on earth, but all around
> Over the surface of my subtle being,
> As though I were a sphere, and capable
> To be accosted thus . . .

'Accosted' was not such a word as they used in this sense on English earth when Newman wrote the poem. He went back, behind senses which, according to the *OED*, were all obsolete by the mid-seventeenth century, to find a Latinate meaning for the word: 'to border, to lie alongside, to go along the side of, to coast'. Again and again, when the Soul speaks after death, he speaks in an English which is at the same time Latin – 'discriminant', 'apprehensive' (not in the current sense), 'elaborated' (in a Latinate sense), 'febrifuge', 'intemperate' as a term of praise, when the Soul flies to the 'dear feet of Emmanuel' 'with intemperate energy of love' (though the word had predominantly meant 'over-inclined to strong drink' since the seventeenth century in English). These old connatural senses, this Latin still harboured within English, are no more dead than the Soul is.

The Dream of Gerontius is an *eirenicon* in the English language itself, a peace offering made just by making English something other than itself. Given its manner of trying to link England to Rome, it is fitting that the most piercing

---

[41] Quoted in Ian Ker, *John Henry Newman: A Biography* (Oxford, 1988), p. 586.

allusions in the poem should be to two great Protestant figures. On the point of death, the Catholic Gerontius makes a last resolve: 'Rouse thee, my fainting soul, and play the man'. He speaks the words of Latimer to Ridley – 'Be of good comfort Master Ridley, and play the man. We shall this day light such a candle by God's grace in England, as (I trust) shall never be put out.' Latimer's terrifying wit in calling his own body to be burned 'a candle', but a candle of 'God's grace' for which he thought he stood against the Catholics and all their works (including their reliance on candles) – all this is pacifically acknowledged in Newman's allusion, brought to mind but without that factional spirit which raised the Martyrs' Memorial to spite the Tractarians in 1843.

The second allusion is to Milton, who latinised for reasons very different from Newman's, an allusion to the closing words of 'Lycidas'. Shortly before judgement, the Soul says:

> My soul is in my hand: I have no fear, –
> In His dear might prepared for weal or woe.
> But hark! a grand, mysterious harmony:
> It floods me like the deep and solemn sound
> Of many waters.

As 'fear' melts into 'dear' and into 'mysterious', so Newman melts into Milton. For this 'dear might' of Christ, about which the English have so quarrelled, is in these lines of Newman's voiced through Milton:

> Weep no more, woful Shepherds weep no more,
> For *Lycidas* your sorrow is not dead,
> Sunk though he be beneath the watry floar,
> So sinks the day-star in the Ocean bed,
> And yet anon repairs his drooping head,
> And tricks his beams, and with new spangled Ore,
> Flames in the forehead of the morning sky:
> So *Lycidas* sunk low, but mounted high,
> Through the dear might of him that walk'd the waves . . .

Newman's home-ward looking Angel's words of farewell, his 'penal waters', his 'Sinking deep, deeper, into the dim distance', constantly murmur that this Soul is not '*At Sea*' but purged, though purged through Milton's lines in which 'young *Lycidas*' was lost, through which old Gerontius will now be found, while the 'watry floar' and 'Ocean bed' and 'your sorrow' of Milton become the watery 'bed of sorrow' into which the Soul is dipped, though Milton would not have been pleased to find his words in Purgatory. So that the hope at the end of *The Dream of Gerontius* – 'And I will come and wake thee on the morrow' speaks for a moment the same language as Milton's last line: 'Tomorrow to fresh woods, and pastures new.'

Here what Hans Urs van Balthasar has called 'the two-in-oneness of *justice–justesse*',[42] the congruence of aesthetic and doctrinal rightness, happens briefly in Newman's verse. Such achieved convergence of connatural senses which for centuries have led in opposed directions points for a moment to an immense power of cultural reconciliation, of ecumenism realised in a living language with all its infelicities. Only for a moment, though, because poems such as 'Lead, Kindly Light' under any or all of its many names, or *The Dream of Gerontius*, speak well but always, as it were, too soon. Their perfectedness images a judgement which has not yet come even as their essential infelicity stands for, and squarely in, the imperfected world which will be brought to the judgement they prefigure, the attunement to which they partly give voice, for which they are all ears.

[42] Hans Urs van Balthasar *Herrlichkeit: Eine Theologische Ästhetik* (Einsiedeln, 1961–7), translated by A. Louth, F. McDonagh and B. McNeil as *The Glory of the Lord*, 6 vols. (Edinburgh, 1984–91), II, 14.

10

The politics of genre and audience in Yeats

SEAMUS DEANE

In Burke's *Reflections on the Revolution in France* (1790) two distinct vocabularies dominate at different moments in the argument. One is the vocabulary of sensibility; the other, of calculation. The famous passages which lament the fate of the French royal family, and most particularly, of Marie Antoinette, at the hands of the mob and as a consequence of the new 'barbarous philosophy', draw heavily on *King Lear* in their elaboration of the motifs of stripping, humiliation of royal, familial and political dignity, the reduction of traditional status to the nudity of the body and the arrival in the world of a fierce new animality before which the codes of chivalry wilt and disappear. Yet Burke's inflection of the Shakespearean text is gendered to such a pitch that the tragic status of the original passes from king to queen; Marie Antoinette becomes the Queen Lear of the text. The assault on her status and her person is imagined in luridly sexual terms as an attempted mob rape from which she scarcely escapes, in the physical sense, but to which she and all that she represents are figuratively subjected. Most important of all, for the present purpose, is Burke's incredulity that the two audiences who most naturally would have responded to the queen's plight have failed to hear or see what is happening. The French audience of chivalric men, sworded and protective, who would once not have borne to see their queen insulted even by a glance, now allow her to become a spectacle for the mob in the long rite of passage from Versailles to the Tuileries and in the subsequent assault of the night of 6 October 1789. (Burke himself had been part of the public audience or *levée* in Paris in 1773 when he first saw Marie Antoinette, then the dauphiness.) But it is the impassivity of the British audience that exercises him most. Had these events been witnessed in the theatre, any audience susceptible to natural feeling would have wept. But this is not theatre, not fiction. This is historical reality. The events in Paris have actually taken place – and there is no reaction that could be called 'natural'. This is all the more shocking since the British audience and tradition, as Burke goes on to argue, is as naturally allied to feeling as was the French audience and tradition to codes of chivalry. One of the aims of the *Reflections* is to reconstitute the traditional British audience; one of the means by which this is to be achieved is by the exploitation of the idea of the real, by insisting upon the historical reality of the present in the vocabulary of sensibility in order to elicit a sympathy for the French queen and for the royal family that would be greater than that accorded to a theatrical spectacle – like a Shakespearean tragedy. On the other hand, Burke wishes equally to provoke hostility to the revolutionaries by showing that, however real their actions are, these are founded upon fantasies. The vocabulary of calculation, extended through the long accounts of the actual state of the French finances before the Revolution, is deployed for two different purposes. One is to demonstrate that, by any real calculation of the French debt, income and the tax reforms inaugurated by Calonne and Necker, the French economy is not irretrievably ruined; quite the reverse: it is fundamentally stable. The other purpose is to show that the new economics, as practised by the revolutionaries, is a kind of inverted aesthetic practice. It converts something actual (land) into something fictive (assignats); it turns economics into theatrical farce; coin becomes paper; stability becomes bankruptcy; the real becomes the represented; intrinsic worth becomes ascribed value; the realities of the state are replaced by the phantasms of the revolutionaries. Finally, these phantasms themselves become realities. The natural order is inverted and the British audience, witnessing these things, has its natural instincts inverted also, welcoming the phantasm of revolution and ignoring the reality of what it is replacing.

Burke's rhetoric is resourceful in its pursuit of the distinctions as well as the similarities between what is 'real' and what is 'phantasmal', figuring these categories from fields as diverse as chemistry, theatre, economics, architecture, garden landscaping and political theory. Yet his fertility of invention in discovering analogues for the conversion of one into the other does not disguise – and in some respects enhances – the schism between the two vocabularies already mentioned, nor does it mask the force of the text's address to an audience that the text itself wishes to re-create. In a sense, the British (Whig) audience that welcomed the Revolution is itself a phantasm, a 'new' Whiggery that is out of line with the old tradition of Whiggery, a fictive and temporary substitute for what had been and what, in the aftermath of Burke's work, would be again. Such an audience would be 'natural' in its response to French events; in being natural, it would also be historical; in being both these things it would display feeling and sensibility, not vulgar calculation and heartlessness, most especially in relation to women and sexuality. Burke intensified the gendering of political discourse to such a degree that many of those who sponsored radical positions thereafter – Jeremy Bentham and William Godwin, for example – made a fetish of being both male and calculating, free of the distortions of sentiment in their estimation of political and historical material.

The history of Irish writing after Burke bears the impress of his emphatic rejection of the French Revolution although it is obviously the case that Britain is substituted for France in many instances, and is characterised as the dull, heartless country of Benthamite calculation while Ireland parades itself as the country of sentiment, natural affection, sensibility. There are many variations on this pattern, but it survives the century in its main outlines. Indeed, the Great Famine of 1845–50 was interpreted by many as a remarkable and horrifying instance of the homologous divisions between Britain and Ireland, political economy and natural charity, Saxon and Celt, coloniser and colonised. Lord John Russell's adherence to the principles of political economy was so strict in those years that the consequence was an intensification of the Famine's progress and an undying bitterness at the inhuman spirit with which economic laws had been pursued at the expense of all human feeling. Yet, while this interpretive frame remained in place and was sometimes potent enough, without modification, to govern responses to British–Irish relations, Irish writing frequently resorted to the other predominant elements in Burke's analysis – those in which the act of writing itself is construed as the act by which an audience is formed (or re-formed) and in which the success of such a formation depends upon the suasive powers of the author in discriminating between what is real and what is phantasmal. For it is in virtue of that distinction that the proper relation between feeling and non-feeling can be established. In turn, such a relation can be understood historically as a characteristic feature of the British or Irish nation's behaviour; and the historical argument, no matter how emaciated it might be on occasion, is then available as support to the notion of a national character, doubly operative as Fate and as History.[1]

Although it is beyond the limits of this essay to detail the struggle of Irish writers to form an audience (Irish and British) in the nineteenth century, some aspects may be mentioned. There are many occasions on which Irish writers appeal to their putative British audience to recognise that what passes for real in Ireland might appear phantasmagoric in Britain. Few of them, with the exception of writers of Gothic like Le Fanu or of genial 'Oirish' sketches, like Somerville and Ross, realised the formal implications of this position. It was not until George Moore and Joyce that Irish writers recognised the incongruity of realism as a mode for the representation of realities that were, from the outset, admitted to be beyond the horizon of a culture for which realism was 'natural'. In poetry, a similar unease with the lyric as a form concordant with Irish experience was articulated by Yeats in various ruminations about the linkage in Ireland between verse and music – inescapable in a country that had Moore's *Irish Melodies* and *The Spirit of the Nation*, with music added in some editions, as its most popular collections – and about the status of the ballad and the epic both in the Irish past and present. He frowned at the direction taken by English poetry in

---

[1] See S. Deane, 'Irish National Character 1790–1900' in *The Writer As Witness*, edited by T. Dunne, Irish Historical Studies XVI (Dublin 1983), 91–113. See also Ian Jack, *The Poet and his Audience* (Cambridge, 1984), pp. 144–68.

Tennyson, Browning and Swinburne and, along with George Sigerson, Thomas MacDonagh and many others, tried to recreate a version of the native literary tradition that would both explain and affirm the need for a generic hierarchy in poetry different from that established in England. The question of genre was deeply bound up with the search for modernity, in part because 'modernity' in Irish writing, especially in poetry, was interpreted as an ancestral condition. George Sigerson, in the Preface to the second edition of his important anthology *Bards of the Gael and the Gall* (1907; first edition 1897) claimed that 'the reason why the Celts did not compose rimed epics was because of their extreme mental modernity . . . The activity and restlessness of our own days were in their blood in all known time . . . They were, in truth, the Moderns of the Past – perhaps they are also fated to be the Moderns of the Future'. In addition, the different genres of the Irish tradition further indicated the difference between the chronologies of the two nations. In a lecture entitled 'Nationality and Literature' which he gave to the National Literary Society in Dublin in May 1893, Yeats claimed that the epic and dramatic periods in literature 'tend to be national' while 'the lyric age . . . becomes as it advances . . . more and more cosmopolitan'. He continued:

Look at our literature and you will see that we are still in our epic or ballad period . . . Our best writers, De Vere, Ferguson, Allingham, Mangan, Davis, O'Grady, are all either ballad or epic writers, and all base their greatest work . . . upon legends and upon the fortunes of the nation. Alone, perhaps, among the nations of Europe we are in our ballad or epic age.[2]

Nationality was attached not only to genre but also to gender, since the ballad and epic were regarded by Yeats as masculine forms, not etiolated like the lyric to that exquisite 'feminine sensitiveness' that he wrote of in 1909, when describing the young Oxford men influenced by the Paterian culture that 'can only create feminine souls'.[3] If ballad and epic were genres favoured by the Irish, the Irish were not at all like the Arnoldian Celt, all sensibility and no architectonic sense. Yeats agrees with Arnold that 'the characteristics he has called Celtic, mark all races just in so far as they preserve the qualities of the early races of the world'.[4] Beyond that point he does not go. He rewrites the feminised version of the Celt – the association with sensibility, with lyric, with lack of 'mastery' – in masculinist terms, claiming that in an epic or ballad age poets 'take their inspiration mainly from external activities and from what are called matters of fact' whereas in a lyric age, the poet is doomed to 'express every phase of human consciousness no matter how subtle, how vague, how impalpable'.[5] The interesting association

[2] Yeats, *Uncollected Prose*, edited by J. P. Frayne and C. Johnston, 2 vols. (London, 1970–5), I, 273.
[3] *Ibid.*, I, 159.   [4] *Ibid.*, II, 241.
[5] *Ibid.*, I, 271. See also Yeats's *Memoirs*, edited by D. Donoghue (London, 1972), pp. 159–60.

here is that of consciousness with femininity and of both with a subtlety that separates poetry from a general audience, turning it into 'a mysterious cult . . . an almost secret religion made by the few for the few.'[6] This shrivelled audience fed on a diet of exquisitely discriminated and esoteric forms of consciousness by an elite authorship is in loud contrast to the imagined national community that shares with its authorship – an authorship that is not highly individuated but more akin to the anonymous authorship of the ballad and some of the ancient epics – a recognisable, actualised world. Of course part of the irony of Yeats's early formulations of the contrast between a national and cosmopolitan audience consists in the fact that he came in the end to cater to both. For his poetry he still looked to the large communal audience, even though he found it impossible to imagine the Irish Catholics, especially those of them who had received a Catholic education, embodying that role.[7] For his plays, especially after the death of Synge, he came increasingly to depend on the cultivation of a select audience, both cultish and occultish. The nurturing of these two audiences went hand-in-hand with the revision of the 'cosmopolitan', 'feminine' lyric tradition of England and its conversion into the lyric with epic ambitions and national ballad-like resonance that Yeats set himself to write. The careful arrangement of poems within a volume and the linkages between the volumes themselves are so pronounced that the recurrent symbols and motifs – Irish and national, occult and universal – chime the more audibly together, producing a public resonance that Yeats considered far beyond the reach of the precious inwardness of the English lyric.

Although it is true that in his early work Yeats did attempt, either in his narrative poems like *The Wanderings of Oisin* (1889) or *The Shadowy Waters* (1906) to provide a version of what he considered to be Gaelic epic literature, and that he also, especially in that same period, produced a number of ballads or ballad-like verse, there is no question but that his most memorable poems deserve to be described as lyrics, no matter how loosely the term 'lyric' is used. The alliance between words and music rarely lapses; the ventriloquial adaptation of a voice that is at once solitary, marginalised in its source and communal, universalist in its address and appeal is a rhythmic feature in the composition of each volume, so that Yeatsean *personae* intermingle with the Yeatsean 'I', each inflecting the pride of solitude with its pain, each discriminating between versions of the audience as community and versions of it as mob or crowd. Thus the Irish Airman, Michael Robartes, Owen Aherne, Crazy Jane, Ribh, A Woman Young and Old, The Lady and the Chambermaid of *New Poems* (1938) are voices that are both generic and genred. Whole sequences – *Words for Music Perhaps* (1931), *A Woman Young and Old* (1933), *Supernatural Songs* (1934), *The Three*

---

[6] *Uncollected Prose*, I, 271.   [7] 'Journal' in *Memoirs*, p. 187.

Bushes (1938), *Three Marching Songs* from *Last Poems* (1938–9), at least aspire to music as one of their enabling conditions for voices that are both balladeering in their form of address and lyric solos in their form of intensity. Mythological, occult and historical figures are constantly recruited by Yeats to perform the double function of being both voices that address an audience and the voices of the audience that he himself wishes to address. He emphasises their provisional and fictive status; the Fisherman, Robert Gregory, Oscar Wilde, Cuchulainn and many others exist as formulations of a possibility, are 'but a dream'; yet, at the same time, Yeats exploits a certain queasiness in his own doubled function as author and as audience. In 'To Ireland in the Coming Times' he is at once asking and asserting that he 'accounted be / True brother of a company' of poets and no less so ('Nor I be any less of them'; 'Nor may I less be counted one') because he is a follower of 'the red-rose-bordered hem'. He is a follower of the tradition of magic and leader of the tradition of Ireland. The poem makes it clear that the plea to be no less considered is, under another aspect, a claim to be the more considered because the Irish audience is, through him, to be realised as the historical successors to those pre-historical communities with whom Yeats has communed – those whom he identifies in the immediately preceding poem, 'To Some I have Talked with by the Fire' as 'dark folk', as 'the wayward twilight companies' and 'the embattled flaming multitude'. That double allegiance, to history and to pre-history, to legend and actuality, provides the basis upon which Yeats is able to exploit the generic distinctions between epic and ballad on the one hand and the lyric on the other. For the exquisiteness and privacy of the lyric in its attenuated English form is now reinterpreted as the energy and occlusion of the pre-historical forces in which traditional wisdom and historical actuality have their source. The lyric is not the antithesis of the ballad or epic in Yeats; it is the stifled form that, in this new restoration, is attempting to give to these more impersonal genres a resonance that transcends the historical and yet retains the intensity of the personal. Yeats's often-repeated claim that Ireland was still 'Asiatic', in touch with the autochthonous forces of pre-history, reinforces the claims that are implicit in his recording of genre hierarchies and in his peculiar fusions of epic, ballad and lyric elements in the structuring of individual volumes and in the poems themselves.

All the collections of Yeats's poems define as 'Lyrical' those twelve volumes (including *Parnell's Funeral and Other Poems* (1935) and *Last Poems* (1938–9)) which, in various combinations with his plays and the so-called 'Narrative and Dramatic' grouping, constitute his Irish epic. It is quite in keeping with his addiction to formal experiment, most clearly manifest in the plays, that there should be such an appearance of paradox or even confusion in the ascription of the most appropriate genre name to much of Yeats's work. The poetry very often operates in the performative mode; the drama very often in the meditative mode. The plays provide many of the lyrics that are characterised as 'Additional Poems'; many of the great dialogue poems – 'Ego Dominus Tuus', 'The Phases of the Moon', 'Solomon and the Witch', 'A Dialogue of Self and Soul' – are like moments from a play. Similarly, the ballad sequences are highly performative lyric runs that depend for their voicing on an established 'character', Crazy Jane, Ribh, Owen Aherne. Yeats is not, of course, unique in his unease with the established genres, nor in his attempt to reorder these by a conscious attempt to reconstitute the idea of the ballad, the lyric, the drama or the epic. Thomas Hardy is an obvious comparison, the more so since he too was concerned with the recovery of an ancient territory and with the valorisation of its fading culture in the face of the 'modern world'. But Hardy's monotonous attempts to theorise the relation between Wessex and the cosmopolis in terms of an endlessly repeated tragic condition, that was always already there in the design of things and only the more pronouncedly visible in periods of transition, is entirely innocent of Yeats's political alertness to the significance of the ghostly conflict between 'tradition' and 'modernism'. For Yeats sees 'tradition', not 'modernism', as the new arrival on the cultural–political scene. Modernism, with its crowd, mob, demagogues, its gaunt intelligence, anaemic sexuality and kitsch art, has so far failed that it has entered into a dying convulsion that will produce its counter-image. But the counter-image has a dual aspect. It is both an after-image of what has been and a proleptic image of what will come to be. Tradition arrives as a new future but also as an old past – as the new Ireland of the twentieth century or the old Anglo-Ireland of the eighteenth or the older Gaelic Ireland of any century between the fifth and the seventeenth. The centuries are as zoned as the phases of the moon in *A Vision*. What is reborn within them is not civilisation as such but the energy for civilisation.

In *A Vision* Yeats wrote history in terms of aesthetics, using the categories of occult thought as his organising principle. Inevitably, in doing so, he also wrote aesthetics in terms of history. Both history and aesthetics are confined within the armature of oppositions – Phase One and Phase Fifteen, dark and light, subjective and objective, rhythm of violence, rhythm of elegance – that close in resolution and, simultaneously, reopen in conflict. The wheel of Becoming forever turns, yet at Phases One and Fifteen it has a paradoxical moment of poise, when Being is erased and realised respectively. In Phase One, aesthetics disappears; it is history, pure and concentrated, total darkness. In Phase Fifteen, history disappears; it is aesthetics, pure and concentrated, Beauty, total light. The subjective or aristocratic phase strengthens gradually from One to Eight, then intensifies; the objective, more banausic phase gradually strengthens from Sixteen to Twenty-two, then intensifies. In the earlier phase, the process of self-fashioning accelerates. It is the phase of the author, the genius, the creation of the

Self as a work of art, the production of art as a work of the Self. In the later phase, the audience predominates. It is the historical agency to which the Self is increasingly sacrificed, until all individuation disappears in a democratic rabblement. The contrast constitutes, for Yeats, the difference between 'tradition' and 'modernism'. Yet when individuality reaches its highest point of development, in Phase Fifteen, it becomes generic. Reverie becomes Vision just as, in Phase One, conviction becomes Opinion. Tradition and modernism outface each other across the wheel along one axis, while along the other intersecting axis the confrontation is between author and audience.

This representation of Yeats (by Yeats) has a conceptual clarity that is not reproduced in his poems, plays and essays, although I do not mean by that to say it is a wholly emaciated account. But to pursue the fragmentary versions of Yeats's reflections on genre and audience (and, eventually, on gender) is a more exigent task than to rehearse the Blakeian rewriting of his work that *A Vision* provides. It is certainly the case that Yeats admired the literary–aesthetic version of the self-made man. But the greatest self-makers were, like Dante, writers in whose work the historical and the aesthetic became one and in whom, in virtue of that achievement, mere individuality was overcome and replaced by a kind of iconic representativeness. The transition from individuation to representativeness is analogous, in terms of genre, to that from lyric to epic. That is to say it is an 'upward' movement, from local intensities to general comprehensiveness, a characterisation that owes a great deal to Matthew Arnold's well-known formulation of the difference between the romantic poets and the great universal geniuses like Goethe, Dante and Shakespeare. In terms of audience, though, the movement is reversed. Lyric, especially in its attenuated English form, has lost its audience; the poet has become the connoisseur of private, ever more refined sensation. To recover its audience, poetry must involve itself both in a genre-change and in a 'downward' movement towards 'the people'. They form a constituency very different from the crowd or mob, which is how the commercially minded middle classes are rendered when brought face to face with Art. Ireland still had, in Yeats's view, a 'people', a folk saturated in the memory of epic, of the heroic, needing now a great poet to make their legendary pantheon visible to the world at large. Specifically, the Irish folk were the already existing audience for the Yeatsean enterprise; in him, already historically completed, was the process of individuation that had been achieved by his Anglo–Irish ancestors. It was their authority that authored him to authorise the Gaelic past, the 'Asiatic' world that also happily contained the mysteries of the occult, to give to a figure like Cuchulainn an auratic quality that would ratify his Gaelic and Eastern lineage under western, modernist eyes. Yeats imagined several audiences for himself; it was a means of imagining and imaging himself. The original Abbey audience was of the 'folk'; after the rejection of Synge, he abandoned the Abbey to its plebified audience and sought for his small audiences in big houses that

Seamus Deane

would appreciate the experimental, impersonal form of theatre in which the historical and the aesthetic could achieve a reconciliation. Similarly, in his poetry, he created several figures to whom he could address himself, like the Fisherman, or more obviously, Maud Gonne and, equally, several figures, like Crazy Jane and the Wild Old Wicked Man, in whom the idea of the self-made author has been subsumed into the idea of the traditional, authentic audience. This pair addresses established convention in the voice of the traditional addressing the modern. The distinction between author and audience is nimbly revised by Yeats; the author is legitimised by the audience he creates; the audience is rediscovered by the author who addresses it. In accord with this mobility of relation the genre of poem and of play alters too. Yeats's poems, constituted as volumes, perform an epic, twelve-volumed gesture. His lyrics are solos, arias, in which there is established an aristocracy of feeling, from the ground floor of the most basic emotion spiralling up to the most esoteric and privileged; his hatred for the aging of his body becoming a celebration of spiritual intensities available only to the man who has forsaken the desire for the individuality that had stimulated the hatred in the first place. But the soaring, etherealising movement of the lyrics needs the rebuke of degradation in which they begin. In a comparable manner, in the ballad poems, the return to the voice or the beliefs of the people, the downward swoop, becomes itself the principle of invigoration, the movement towards pure energy, the force that inheres in the 'folk', the durability that is never fully recruited by history but belongs to myth. It was the capacity of the Irish people to mythologise historical figures like Swift or O'Connell that Yeats attempted to match in his various accounts of the Tragic Generation, of Synge, Robert Gregory, Parnell, Roger Casement and, with more unease, the men of 1916. In each case there was a crucial transaction between the grandeur of the individuals and the degradation of the world that destroyed them, even if the destruction was itself the determining element in raising them to the mythological level. Yeats's prose accounts of these and other figures are characterised by that genre blur that we find elsewhere in his work. They mix the address of the essayist with the address of the voice that speaks through the medium in a seance, worldly and other-worldly, individual and not-individual, a curious genre of writing that wants to make the most eccentric and individual of voices also the most generic and recognisable.

Debasement and transcendence, actions co-ordinated within lyric and ballad, reaffirm author-ity by co-opting the idea of an audience into the poem, so that the audience is a presence within it rather than an external agency that is addressed by it.[8] Yeats was aware that the question of author and authority had been

[8] See in this relation M. Bakhtin, *Rabelais and his World*, tr. H. Iswolsky (Bloomington, 1984), pp. 376–448; R. Gasche, 'Of Aesthetic and Historical Determinism' in *Poststructuralism and the Question of History*, edited by D. Attridge, G. Bennington and R. Young (Cambridge, 1987), pp. 139–61.

208

important in nineteenth-century Ireland, partly because of the vexed problem of translation and also because of the political status of many poems and songs that had become items in the popular repertoire, their authors forgotten. Writers as various as William Allingham and Thomas Davis welcomed the anonymity that followed upon the success of their most popular work. The translations and adaptations of James Clarence Mangan, the most important Irish poet of the century before Yeats, were variously ascribed by Mangan himself to various pseudonyms. He declared himself through pseudonymity and, like Yeats, exploited the genres of ballad and lyric in a search for a form appropriate either to his (sometimes non-existent) 'original' or to his own or his country's experience.[9] In addition, the practice, governed by British political censorship of 'seditious' journals, of using a pseudonym for the militant ballads published by the *Nation*, reinforced by the anonymity that had become a convention in the century's journals and reviews, made authorship a less secure assumption in periodical literature than in book publishing.[10] A great deal of Irish poetry of the nineteenth century had made its impact through its publication in popular journals. Yeats wanted to appropriate for himself that kind of popular appeal and the prestige of 'high' literature, book-culture. With him, pseudonyms became the names of adopted *personae* and the question of translation was revised to accommodate the enterprise of recovering for literature the lost vocabularies of mysticism and magic as well as the lost narratives of the Celtic past. The debasement of literature into political opinion by the Young Ireland movement would be overcome by the transcendence of opinion and politics into vision and myth.

Yet the one person to whom Yeats most famously addresses himself in his writings, and in whom the countermovement between debasement and various forms of idealisation is most repetitively embodied, is subjected to a critique that reveals another aspect of Yeats's strategies in his creation of an audience that is integral to his creation of his own authorship. Maud Gonne was, in one sense, highly disobedient to the status he authorised for her, the woman of heroic beauty, the aristocrat in a degenerate world, a Helen born to hellenise a province of imperial London–Rome. By committing herself to political action on behalf of Irish nationalism, she, like Constance Markievicz, refused the eternal shelf-life to which Yeats would have consigned her. But, of course, her disobedience is itself crucial to her role; even to think of her as disobedient or as worthy of blame, or even to forgive her as blameless, given the conditions she was born into, as Yeats does in 'No Second Troy', is both patronising and possessive.[11] In herself, she is an emblem of debasement; in Yeats's poetry she becomes an emblem of

9 D. Lloyd, *Nationalism and Minor Literature: James Clarence Mangan and the Emergence of Irish Cultural Nationalism* (Berkeley, 1987).

10 S. Deane, 'Poetry and Song 1800–1890' in *The Field Day Anthology of Irish Writing*, edited by S. Deane, A. Carpenter and J. Williams, 3 vols. (Derry, 1991), II, 1–9.

11 See T. Docherty, *After Theory: Postmodernism/Postmarxism* (London, 1990), pp. 177–90.

debasement and of recuperation from it. She serves to ground his idealisation of the Beloved, the Dantean Beatrice;[12] the idealisation is thereby affirmed as an energy that arises out of actuality, not out of stereotyped emptiness. The fact that Helen and Beatrice are her ancestors confers upon her a peculiarly literary nobility; she has been the occasion of epic achievement by Homer and Dante. But now there can be no second Troy, partly because this is the modern, not the ancient world – and therefore too degenerate and fragmented for epic treatment – but partly too because she has given herself to modernity and thereby robbed Yeats of an epic opportunity. In effect, he makes an epic out of having been so deprived, even if it is an epic composed of lyric sequences in which she is the subject of and the audience for the poem. Her self-betrayal is betrayed to herself. She has robbed history of its traditional link with aesthetics by refusing to give her Ledaean body to the violence of Yeats's imperious Zeus-like imagination. The charisma of the feminine has been surrendered to the dour actualities of a democratising politics.[13]

The distinction between the feminine and the effeminate, as operated by Yeats, is deeply embedded in earlier literary and political discourse, although in its nineteenth-century form it largely derives from Burke.[14] The effeminate is an enfeeblement of the virile; the feminine is the Other of the masculine. What Burke would have called 'manliness' is reduced in power by the first, empowered by the second term. The political charge in these terms is interfused with their erotic appeal, for effeminacy (in men) is a threat to the maintenance of civilisation in both Burke and Yeats while the preservation of the feminine is necessary for its stability. Maud Gonne and Constance Markievicz threaten that stability by refusing to participate in the construction of the feminine, while Lady Gregory and George Yeats do not since they fulfil their culturally appointed roles as enabling patron–matron and wifely medium. The refusal of femininity is a debasement. These rebellious women have ceased to be an audience for Yeats; they have created audiences for themselves at the political hustings. These audiences are also debased and debasing, unsexed and unsexing. In the case of the Gore-Booth sisters, aging, loss of sexual attractiveness and political commitment or political dreaming are allied:

> The older is condemned to death,
> Pardoned, drags out lonely years

[12] G. C. Spivak, 'Finding Feminist Readings: Dante–Yeats' in *In Other Worlds: Essays in Cultural Politics* (New York and London, 1988), pp. 15–29.

[13] See D. Lloyd, *Anomalous States: Irish Writing and the Post-Colonial Condition* (Dublin, 1993), pp. 59–87.

[14] See S. Deane, *The French Revolution and Enlightenment in England 1789–1832* (Cambridge, Mass. and London, 1988); D. Simpson, *Romanticism, Nationalism and the Revolt against Theory* (Chicago and London, 1993).

> Conspiring among the ignorant.
> I know not what the younger dreams –
> Some vague Utopia – and she seems,
> When withered old and skeleton-gaunt,
> An image of such politics.

In 'The Man and the Echo' the famous reference to his play *The Countess Cathleen* is followed by a less frequently cited but interlinked reference to Maud Gonne:

> Did that play of mine send out
> Certain men the English shot?
> Did words of mine put too great strain
> On that woman's reeling brain?

Although Yeats is here, as on other occasions, trying to claim a central role in the events that led to the foundation of the Irish state, the immediate point at issue is the characterisation of Maud Gonne as his incompetent audience. Yeats's cultural nationalism had issued, through a misunderstanding on the part of his audience, in a violent and disappointing politics. This is an expansion of a position announced early, as in the poem 'Under the Moon' from *In The Seven Woods* (1904):

> To dream of women whose beauty was folded in dismay,
> Even in an old story, is a burden not to be borne.

Thirty-four years later he is still so dreaming, but the dream has now ramified into a meditation on beauty, women, violence and a foundational moment in Irish political history. It is well known that in poems such as 'Leda and the Swan', 'The Second Coming', 'Blood and the Moon', and 'Nineteen Hundred and Nineteen' Yeats's ponderings on such questions turned time and again towards the question of human agency in history and most especially towards the connections between foundational violence and knowledge. He construes the opposition between action and contemplation in traditional ways, most especially in *The Wild Swans At Coole* (1919), a volume dominated by that opposition and by the question of the ideal audience, as in the sequence from 'The Fisherman' to 'Presences'. 'The Fisherman' is an ideal type of 'The People' to whom, in the poem of that name, Lady Gregory declares her fidelity and who, in the immediately preceding poem 'Her Praise', are correspondingly faithful to the memory of Maud Gonne's beauty. Yeats's address to Lady Gregory in 'The People' is couched in standard terms:

> '. . . You, that have not lived in thought but deed,
> Can have the purity of a natural force,
> But I, whose virtues are the definitions

Of the analytic mind, can neither close
The eye of the mind nor keep my tongue from speech.'

This constituency of the people is both traditional and powerless, definitively separated from the urban-Dublin middle classes that, in the aftermath of 1916, had taken over the Irish cultural revolution for a political one of their own. In this context, to have 'the purity of a natural force', to have the mythological status of having been beautiful and, in virtue of that, to be powerless, is a compliment. The Fisherman, the People and Lady Gregory are versions of his ideal audience and, as always, Yeats himself, the 'Hic' and 'Ille' of 'Ego Dominus Tuus', the Aherne and Robartes of 'The Phases of the Moon', self and anti-self communing. But in the poem 'Presences' there is yet another audience, those women who

> had read
> All I had rhymed of that monstrous thing
> Returned and yet unrequited love.

These women, dreamed as 'laughing, or timid or wild', are identified so:

> One is a harlot, and one a child
> That never looked upon man with desire,
> And one, it may be, a queen.

These women, it may be, are a composite of Maud Gonne in her Yeatsean mutations. Child, harlot and queen constitute a hierarchy of the feminine audience for 'that monstrous thing' which is, ambiguously, a love that is returned but not sexually gratified or a love that is refused and is still ('yet') unsatisfied. Of all the imagined audiences in this volume, this is the one that has read Yeats and refused him. Their refusal is, inevitably, a kind of response; but is this response characteristic of women or of Woman? Are they incapable of knowing, an incompetent audience? In the rape of Leda by the swan

> Did she put on his knowledge with his power
> Before the indifferent beak could let her drop?

In similar vein, the poem 'On A Political Prisoner', about Constance Markievicz, pits her political ignorance against the power of the 'rock-bred, sea-borne bird' to which, in her former beauty, she is assimilated. For such women, knowledge, especially foundational political knowledge, is a disaster. It deprives them of their beauty, their mythological regality and child-like innocence. Harlotry is the sexual analogue for political knowledge. In misreading Yeats, they have put too much strain on their reeling brain and rendered themselves incapable of requiting the love he offered in his poems. Why should not old men be mad who have known

> A Helen of social welfare dream,
> Climb on a waggonette to scream.

In 'The Second Coming' we meet another 'monstrous thing', the 'Rough Beast' that is released in a world where 'the worst / Are full of passionate intensity', a reference that has an inescapable application to Maud Gonne and her 'opinionated mind' in the succeeding poem 'A Prayer for my Daughter'. This is a poem about revolutions – the French and the Russian, about violence and the failure of the feminine principle in civilisation that has led to an effete and effeminate Christianity, emblematised in 'the rocking cradle'. Patrick Keane has demonstrated the Burkean background to this poem and the direct relation in its early drafts to Burke's lament for Marie Antoinette's downfall in that burst of atrocious and eroticised violence of 1789.[15] Finally, we have history without aesthetics, poetry without an audience. In place of the audience we have, as a shadowy presence, the woman who, like Marie Antoinette in Burke, is remembered as a child–dauphiness, is a queen in whom a whole civilisation has invested its concept of love, lineage and stability and is now, confronted by the mob, reduced to the threat of rape and treated as a harlot. Like Burke, Yeats asks for an audience, for someone who will recognise that this is not a phantasm, not a dream, but a historical reality in which civilisation has been put to death. Burke found his audience, in Yeats and in many others. Yeats found his audience in Burke. In the connection between them we see an anti-modernist, anti-intellectual version of national identity and tradition eroticised and aestheticised.

---

[15] See P. J. Keane, *Yeats's Interactions with Tradition* (Columbia, Miss., 1987), esp. pp. 72–105; S. Deane, '"The Second Coming": Coming Second; Coming in a Second', *Irish University Review* 22, 1 (Spring-Summer 1992), 92–100.

11

The shaping of D. H. Lawrence's *Look! We Have Come Through!*

MARK KINKEAD-WEEKES

How is one to look at this book of poems and its exclamatory title? At first this might seem a personal as much as a poetic question. Catherine Carswell, reading the manuscript by candlelight in February 1917, was impressed by the nobility of the heart it revealed. Cecil Gray dared to question the claim for the marriage, presuming perhaps on his own relationship with Frieda and tensions in Cornwall more recent than the poems. Bertrand Russell quipped that he was glad for the Lawrences, but didn't see why he should look – especially since they had quarrelled.[1] All obviously assumed the book to be straightforward personal expression, an assumption strengthened for Catherine Carswell by the inclusion in the manuscript of a love-letter, which she persuaded Lawrence to drop.[2] Yet the 'Argument' which replaced it summarises a situation that corresponds no less exactly with the Lawrences', for all its anonymity. Indeed even scholarly Lawrencians make the same assumption: that the poems date from the places and the periods assigned to them in the text (and hence are evidence which biographers can use). The rediscovery and publication of the second half of *Mr Noon*[3] appears to reinforce this, 'corroborating' and expanding the story of the early months in Bavaria and the journey to Italy across the Alps. Personal response, moreover, whether admiring a courage of self-revelation, or embarrassed at being made witness to such rawly private experience, naturally affects criticism too. Lawrence's poet friends 'H. D.' and Amy Lowell, who were sympathetic and admiring in general, were merely the first to feel that in this particular the poems were often too personally involved, 'too much body and emotions' to achieve true poetic form.[4]

---

[1] Catherine Carswell, *The Savage Pilgrimage* (Cambridge, 1932; rpt, 1981), p. 84; Lawrence to Gray (6 November 1917), James T. Boulton and Andrew Robertson, eds., *The Letters of D. H. Lawrence*, vol. III (Cambridge, 1984), p. 173 (hereafter referred to as *Letters*, III etc.); Harry T. Moore, *The Priest of Love* (London, 1974; rpt, Harmondsworth, 1976), p. 369.

[2] Carswell, *Savage Pilgrimage*, p. 85.

[3] *Mr Noon*, edited by Lindeth Vasey (Cambridge, 1984).

[4] Lawrence to Catherine Carswell (9 March 1917), *Letters*, III, 102: 'Hilda says they won't do at all; they are not *eternal*, not sublimated: too much body and emotions'; S. Foster Damon, *Amy Lowell: A Chronicle* (Boston and New York, 1935), p. 445: 'As a book the volume is a masterpiece; as poetry it is perhaps not quite that.'

Yet is the book a collection of insufficiently 'sublimated' autobiographical lyrics? – and how if the poems we read now, even when they date back to 1911–15 in some form, are not the poems that were written then? Sixty of the sequence we now read in *The Complete Poems*[5] appear to 'date' before 'Zennor' (i.e. 1916). Only twenty or perhaps twenty-one of these, however, exist in versions earlier than 1917;[6] and it ought to surprise no reader of Lawrence to discover that very nearly all have been not merely revised but substantially rewritten and in many cases transformed, in the light of a later vision. Even the few exceptions such as 'Green', 'On the Balcony', [and 'Bei Hennef', only added to *Look!* in *Collected Poems*, 1928][7] read differently, in their new context and relation to other poems in the sequence. Of the rest, we cannot be certain that any was 'written' when or where the sequence suggests, or even shortly afterwards.

A number, however, though we cannot tell how many, must have existed in early versions in the 'brown Tagebuch of Frieda's'[8] which Lawrence left behind in Fiascherino when he came to London in 1914, meaning to return after the summer. He had to retrieve this before *Look!* could be composed, but there has been no sign of it since 1918. Frieda told Edward Garnett in September 1912 from Lake Garda that Lawrence had written 'heaps nicer poems' since they had been together than those soon to be published in *Love Poems*, and Lawrence wryly confirmed her preference for poems 'concerning herself' and her eagerness

[5] *The Complete Poems of D. H. Lawrence*, edited by Vivian de Sola Pinto and Warren Roberts, 2 vols. (London, 1972).

[6] The twenty ⟨earlier titles thus⟩ [added later, thus]: 'Moonrise'; 'Martyr à la Mode'; 'The Sea'; 'Don Juan'; 'Ballad of a Wilful⟨Wayward⟩ Woman'; ['Bei Hennef']; 'On the Balcony' ⟨'Illicit'⟩; 'Green'; 'River Roses'; 'Gloire de Dijon'; 'Roses on the Breakfast Table'; 'A Youth Mowing' ⟨'The Mowers'⟩; 'Fireflies in the Corn'; 'Meeting Among the Mountains'; ['Everlasting Flowers' ⟨'From the Italian Lakes'⟩]; 'Giorno dei Morti'; 'Paradise Re-Entered' ⟨'Purity'⟩; 'Song of a Man Who is Loved'; 'People'; 'Street Lamps'. An earlier version of 'New Heaven and Earth' ⟨'Terranova'⟩ was given to H. D. for *Some Imagist Poets* in October 1916 (see note 41 below), but may well have been written at Greatham after 'a thousand nights' with Frieda, i.e. about mid-1915. Pending the publication of the new Cambridge edition, the early variants are to be found in Carole Ferrier, *The Earlier Poetry of D. H. Lawrence: A Variorum Text*, dissertation submitted to the University of Auckland, 1971 (University Microfilms International, 1974), vol. II. I am also very grateful to Christopher Pollnitz, joint Cambridge editor, for helpful comments and for a draft of his new cumulative list of manuscripts. Mistakes in the argument are mine.

[7] The use of square brackets indicates that a poem was not in the sequence as originally published in 1917, but was added later. Lawrence added three poems ['Bei Hennef', 'Everlasting Flowers', 'Coming Awake'] in the *Collected Poems* of 1928, and restored one of the two that the original publishers had demanded be left out ['Song of a Man Who is Loved']. The other ['Meeting Among the Mountains'] was restored by the editors of the posthumous *Complete Poems*.

[8] Lawrence to Thomas Dunlop, 16 December 1915, George Z. Zytaruk and James T. Boulton, eds., *The Letters of D. H. Lawrence*, II (Cambridge, 1981), p. 478, 511. The *Tagebuch* was left behind again in Zennor when the Lawrences were expelled in 1917. Lawrence asked Gray in March 1918 to retrieve it, *Letters* III, 229, but it has not been heard of since. Both the original typescript of *Look! We Have Come Through!* and its carbon have also disappeared.

to have them 'blossom forth', presumably in print.[9] Ten of the twenty which exist in pre-1917 versions do, indeed, deal with their first months together in Germany, (including 'Bei Hennef' which was the only 'Frieda' poem in *Love Poems*, 1913). There may well have been others which Lawrence decided not to copy out and submit for publication, perhaps because they were too intimate or sexually explicit, or might compromise Frieda – who was not divorced until 1913. The first version of the 'Ballad of a ⟨Wayward⟩ Wilful Woman' must have seemed disguised enough to be submitted,[10] yet it alone of these ten was not accepted, perhaps because it appeared to condone the 'waywardness'. The notebook probably went on being used for poems set in Gargnano and San Gaudenzio, some of which Frieda might not have been so anxious to see in print. Indeed only 'Giorno dei Morti' from that part of the sequence was published earlier than 1917,[11] though others seem innocent enough to have been printed had they existed at the time. Early versions of two of the '1913' poems, 'Song of a Man Who is Loved' and 'Paradise Re-entered' ⟨'Purity'⟩, were fair-copied in October 1913,[12] but neither was published. Indeed Chatto and Windus forced Lawrence to exclude the former from the first edition of *Look!*, and it was restored only in 1928. There certainty ends. One might have a subjective 'feeling' that some poems are 'close' to the experience they 'express' – but a feeling is all it can be. Moreover *Mr Noon* turns out to be dubious help in fact, since it is both a fiction, written in 1920, and one that bears a suspiciously close relation to the poems of *Look!*, as against (sometimes) the evidence of Lawrence's letters, which of course were unavailable to him afterwards. The new Cambridge biographers have decided to be cautious about using either the poems with no early version, or the novel apparently based on them, as reliable biographical information, unless supported by other evidence. For even if some, many, or most of these poems *did* exist in early versions in the *Tagebuch*, albeit passed over by Lawrence as unpublishable then, the evidence of those he did choose suggests how different those early versions may have been from the poems we now read.

The 'rose' poems for example, labelled 'Icking' (where Lawrence and Frieda lived in Alfred Weber's flat from 1 June to 5 August 1912) and Kloster Schaeftlarn nearby, might serve as a miniature of the making of the whole. Frieda

[9] James T. Boulton, ed., *The Letters of D. H. Lawrence*, I (Cambridge, 1979), pp. 449, 454.
[10] Sent to Edward Marsh on 28 October 1913, see *Letters*, II, 94; MS 20b in the Ferrier designation/ MS 27a in the new Cambridge; Warren Roberts, *Bibliography of D. H. Lawrence*, second edition (Cambridge, 1982), E320.6.
[11] As ⟨'Service of All the Dead'⟩, copied and sent to Marsh about the same time, (MS 27b in the new Cambridge designation), see *Letters*, II, 106. Sent by Marsh to the *New Statesman* and published there on 15 November 1913; also in *Georgian Poetry 1913–1915* (London, 1915).
[12] Also included in MS 20b/27a, sent to Marsh 28 October, see note 10 above. For 'Purity' see also *Letters*, II, 104.

lovingly preserved a set of four, titled 'All of Roses', and printed them much later in *Not I, but the Wind*.[13] These were clearly among the 'heaps nicer poems' of her letter to Garnett. They must also surely – along with 'Green, On the Balcony' ⟨'Illicit'⟩, and the early versions of 'A Youth Mowing' ⟨'The Mowers'⟩ and 'Fireflies in the Corn' – have been in the *Tagebuch*, from which Lawrence chose them all to be the first to 'blossom forth' when he made fair copies and sent them, on 7 August 1913, to be typed by Douglas Clayton.[14] 'The Mowers' appeared in *The Smart Set* of November 1913, and Harriet Monroe accepted the others for the January 1914 number of *Poetry*. When Lawrence came to compose *Look!* in 1917, however, he dropped the fourth rose poem, rightly, and so transformed the other three that even in themselves (let alone by their placing in the whole sequence, of which more later) they became essentially different poems. Sentimentalities are banished; the confidence of love becomes transfused with intimations of transience and mortality; but these also heighten the warm and tender apprehension of beauty, affirmed in the face of time.

The first poem, now titled 'River Roses', is virtually unchanged for its first happy and vital stanza, but then 'our warm wild roses' in line 9 become 'the dark wild roses', and the new version takes on a new and darker note. The rose-scent becomes icy, and fear replaces the original rosy kisses.[15] The fear is of more than public opinion. As the twilight darkens, the snake and the marsh of 'The Crown' and *Women in Love* speak now of having to come to terms with what Birkin called the dark river of corruption, as well as green water and rosiness. (Snake and marsh are recombined again in the 'Reality of Peace' essays, within a month of the completion of *Look!* in manuscript.) A somewhat sentimental lyric has become a much more complex poem by the author of *Women in Love*; and the new 'experience' has only initially and superficially to do with an experience of 1912.

The second poem is even more tellingly transformed in the light of a later vision. A change to the beginning merely specifies that the woman is preparing to sponge herself. Then, however, there follows a marked improvement in the swung-rhythm and emphasis which enacts the (painterly) movement of light down the body, warmed by her skin into glow, and then fuller glow as it coincides with the sway of her breasts – just as the fully open 'Gloire' rose warms from pink through pale yellow to yellow–gold.

> She spreads the bath-cloth underneath ⟨stands in silhouette against⟩ the window
> And the sunbeams catch her
> Glistening white on the shoulders, ⟨:⟩

[13] Frieda Lawrence, *Not I, but the Wind* (London, 1935), pp. 45–6.
[14] MS 16 Ferrier/MS 23 Cambridge, Roberts E318, see Lawrence to Clayton, *Letters*, II, 55–6.
[15] '. . . and over the river closes / Was scent of roses, and glimmering / In the twilight, our kisses across the roses / Met, and her face, and my face, were roses.'

While down her sides the mellow ⟨sides, the mellow⟩
Golden shadow glows as ⟨glows, and her breasts⟩
She stoops to the sponge, and her swung breasts ⟨Swing like full-blown yellow⟩
Sway like full-blown yellow ⟨Gloire de Dijon roses.⟩
Gloire de Dijon Roses.

As the woman washes herself in the second stanza however, the poem is transformed.

She drips herself with water, and her shoulders ⟨water, / And her shoulders⟩
Glisten as silver, they crumple up
Like wet and ⟨shaken⟩ falling roses, and I listen
For the ⟨rustling⟩ sluicing of their ⟨white, unfolding⟩ rain-dishevelled petals.
In the window full of sunlight
Concentrates her golden shadow ⟨She stirs her golden shadow⟩
Fold on fold, until it glows as ⟨And flashes all herself as sunbright⟩
Mellow as the glory roses. ⟨As if roses fought with roses.⟩

Now it is something deeper than the interplay of light and 'crumpling' shoulders that catches the attention, at first unawares. For where before the water merely shook and freshened, soon outshone by the assertive vitality of the body, now the metaphoric emphasis is on roses *falling*, rain-*dishevelled* by the seasonal change that will soon destroy their beauty. As golden light and shadow now *con*centrate (beautifully exact word) into a glow "*as* mellow as the glory roses", the fanciful conceit of rivalry between woman–beauty and rose–beauty is replaced by a moving sense of richness-in-transience. "Mellow" and "golden shadow" are deepened, not merely repeated, as their paradox opens out. It becomes a love-poem to a woman already passing her best, and to a body seen as all the more beautiful because on the point of change from ripeness to overripeness and inevitable decay. (Frieda turned 33 in 1912, 38 in 1917.) Once again, this has become a poem of 1917, as *opposed* to the poem of 1912.

The 'Roses on the Breakfast Table' are similarly freed from sentimental fancy, as the poem re-sees playfulness and youth. The fallen petals, originally little boats 'waiting / For a fairy wind to wake them from their sloth', become harbingers now of the fall of the roses that haven't fallen yet. The kiss-beladen petal–boat, sent across the cloth by the lover's breath,[16] is replaced by a new perception, as sharp as it is tender, of the transience of her sense of his beauty, too. Yet this is fused with acceptance, as he looks at the "rumpled young roses" whose transience he shares: 'How lovely is the self this day discloses.' 'Day' acquires its full resonance as it qualifies 'lovely', both in revelation, and in acute temporariness.

---

[16] 'She laughs at me across the table, saying / She loves me, and I blow a little boat / Rocking down the shoals between the tea-cups / And so kiss-beladen that it scare can float.'

Now, however, two more poems complete this mini-sequence, and it is impossible to believe that they could have been passed over by Lawrence in favour of 'All of Roses' IV, which he now cuts altogether. None of the reasons for not risking early versions could possibly apply to these. Had they existed in August 1913, he would certainly have sent them for publication along with the others. 'I am like a rose' is a poem of joy: 'I am myself at last; now I achieve / My very self. I, with the wonder mellow, / Full of fine warmth, I issue forth in clear / And single me, perfected from my fellow.' 'Rose of All the World' explains the consonance of this selving with the natural force in 'Rose-leaves that whirl in colour round a core / Of seed-specks'; but goes on to an argument strongly reminiscent of the 'Study of Hardy' of late 1914[17] – itself the product of a first attempt to formulate a 'philosophy' out of *Sons and Lovers*, and of the eighteen months' struggle with two different versions of 'The Sisters' which culminated, after another six months, in the completion of 'The Wedding Ring', the predecessor of *The Rainbow*. 'He' now maintains, against 'her' idea that it is the seed that is the purpose of the rose, that (as in the 'Study's poppy) 'the seed is just left over / From the red rose-flower's fiery transience'. So 'he' urges 'her' to blossom 'for rosiness only', more than justified in and by the instant of unclosing. The simple 1912 love poetry has been first deepened and then supplanted by later understanding, in (probably) the author of *The Rainbow* and *Women in Love*, of the relation of beauty, individuation and transience for them both, and every living thing. Of the five poems we read now, three have become poems of 1917, and the other two, though they might conceivably have been drafted sometime after January 1914 (when 'All of Roses' appeared), are much more likely to have been newly written in 1917 as part of a process of revision and dramatisation – and at any rate not in Icking, 1912.

It seems likely therefore that if we could discover what poems did exist in early versions in the *Tagebuch*, we might find much the same proportion of transformation (as with most of the twenty) in 1917, and new composition. We have moreover yet to enquire, however summarily, into the effect of placing even exceptions like 'Green' and 'On the Balcony', which (almost) satisfied Lawrence as they were, into a sequence where they would be acted upon by other poems. And how was the sequence as a whole shaped, out of 'life'?

It begins ('Moonrise' to 'Hymn to Priapus') with poems about states of the self after a number of failed love affairs and just before the meeting with the 'Woman'. In the shaping, Lawrence's double purpose becomes clear. He aims

---

[17] *Study of Thomas Hardy and Other Essays*, edited by Bruce Steele (Cambridge, 1935), *cf.* pp. 12–13, 18, 52–4. In the 'Foreword' of January 1913, *Sons and Lovers* edited by Helen Baron and Carl Baron (Cambridge, 1992), p. 240, the emphasis is on the Woman, and hence the Seed as starting-point.

Mark Kinkead-Weekes

both to be faithful to an earlier self, and to stage it, with later understanding, to foreshadow a later meaning. The first part of 'Moonrise' is extracted from the middle of an early and unpublished poem, probably indeed composed in Bournemouth, which has survived because it was sent to Edward Garnett[18] – but to it is added, in not inappropriate style, a confidence that the Lawrence of January 1912 had not felt, but which is a suitable prologue to the sequence as a whole: that despite the flux of time no consummated beauty of relationship passes away. The other half appears later as 'The Sea', after a Schopenhauerish poem 'placed' in Croydon but now tartly labelled 'Martyr à la Mode', as (revised) expressions of still immature states of loneliness and *weltschmertz* – together with an 'Elegy' for a dead mother, unpublished before, which captures the feelings and imagery of the end of *Sons and Lovers*, whenever it was written. 'Don Juan' has almost certainly been back-dated, though true enough in mood to early 1912 and deftly functional in rakish summary, striking an attitude. It was certainly written before October 1913 when it was sent to Marsh,[19] but the imagery of mountains and rivers suggests that the insouciance was in fact post-'elopement' rather than the Lawrence of early 1912. While the refusal to feel guilty for the 'mistresses' remains true to the young man who so coldly observed Louie Burrows in the Castle Art-gallery, and told Jessie she would have to forgive 'Paul Morel', the pride in being beloved of 'Isis the Mystery' will also be destabilised within the sequence, as we shall find, by rather greater unease at being 'driven'. The remaining two poems, for which no early version survives, show the same blend of recall with dramatisation in the light of later knowledge. 'Nonentity' seems at first to be just another expression of longing for non-being after the mother's death. It is only after we have read the sequence through that we realise how this poem sounds thematic keynotes for the whole – as well as being an ironic reversal of 'The Wild Common', rewritten in Cornwall for *Amores* nine months before the manuscript of *Look!* The longing for non-entity, experiencing a dissolution of the self into the cosmos, will turn out to anticipate not death but renewal, and relate closely to poems that lie ahead. Similarly the 'Hymn to Priapus' which ends the sequence is archetypal more than autobiographical. We need no more posit another seduction, of a country lass after a dance,[20] than try to identify the seven mistresses of Don Juan; the poem is less confessional than thematic. The celebration of man the hunter and of sexual desire is a proleptic

[18] MS 19 Ferrier/MS 16 Cambridge, ⟨'An Address to the Sea'⟩, Ferrier, *Earlier Poetry*, Poems 147 and 152. See *Letters*, I, 346–7 and other letters of January 1912.
[19] MS 20b Ferrier/MS 27a Cambridge, the same batch as ⟨'Ballad of a Wayward Woman'⟩, ⟨'Purity'⟩, 'Song of a Man Who is Loved' and ⟨'Illicit'⟩, see notes 10, 12. Back-dating to before the meeting with Frieda has moreover changed the original implication in '. . . Isis the Mystery / Herself in love with me?'
[20] For the incident with the 'country lass' perhaps fictionalised here, see *Letters*, I, 369.

turning-point, requiring us to re-see the mother-complex and the Don Juan cynicism which have left a young man 'worn and careful' or despairing. It is priapic desire, recurring, that can save and make debonair and free, beyond grief: 'To be faithless and faithful together / As we have to be.' No early version exists. So this first section – shall we call it a chapter? – has both represented and re-presented the 'self' Lawrence had been at the beginning of 1912, using insight that the young man did not have, yet not falsifying the essence of what he then felt. If it be autobiographical, it is autobiography dramatised with some licence, and made (in yet another sense) representative.

The second much richer chapter ('Ballad of a Wilful Woman' to 'A Doe at Evening') deals with the months with Frieda in Germany in 1912. Once again the opening poem is altered with a new sense of meaning and prophecy that had not been available in 1912. While the original had sought to come to terms, in ballad and serious fairytale, with a 'wayward' woman's previous love-affairs, and her hesitating even now between husband and lover, the emphasis had fallen at the end on her many-sided vitality and life-giving, on the 'beggar's need of her healing and comfort, and on the production of 'stars' – like this poem – of *her* joy and pain.[21] Now, in 1917, the emphases shift. The pull between opposite yearnings for self-fulfilment remains, though the new title turns us away from any lingering moral question about abandoning husband and child, and towards a psychological ambiguity between a will-to-fulfilment, and a contrariness refusing commitment. Now, too, the beggar becomes a much stronger, more creative, and more ruthless figure – the leader – and the prophecy of the road ahead is much harsher, with a certainty of pain, though she dreams 'she is brewing hope from despair'. The ballad-form also helps establish a significance more representative than autobiographical – as in the fictive monologue of the pregnant woman in 'A Youth Mowing' later in the sequence, its original dialect softened. The early versions of both these will have been in the *Tagebuch*, and so will 'Illicit', retitled 'On the Balcony' now, but otherwise, and exceptionally, almost unchanged. Yet this points up all the more strongly how a mere change of title and the positioning of a poem in a sequence can change its meaning. By originally calling it 'Illicit' Lawrence had made the storm symbolise the world's hostility to the adulterous couple, and the vanishing boat on the river a mark of their isolation. But by now placing it after poems that bring out the tensions between the lovers themselves, as well as before one which shows them dancing *Rainbow*-like between sun and darkness, the storm and rainbow happen inside as well as out there. For the lovers, the 'Balcony' (an ironic allusion perhaps to *Romeo and Juliet*) is no security; 'what have we but each other?' becomes less

[21] Ferrier, *Earlier Poetry*, Poem 154. See also note 10 above.

complacent; and the boat that vanishes in the storm creates a greater tremor of unease. For now we are reading in the light of 'First Morning', 'And Oh – That the Man I Am Might Cease to Be', and 'She Looks back', which immediately follow the 'Wilful Woman' – and, from 1928, 'Bei Hennef' too, where the flux of the river in the background, and the final cry of suffering also undercutting the confidence of love, are given new point in the new context.[22] No poem in *Look!* stands by itself, since all are modified by the poems that surround them.

Moreover, there is a deeper and thematic reason too; for now ceaseless flux, announced in the 'Ballad', becomes a major theme, structurally enacted in the dramatic experience. No poem *can* stand alone, for 'the journey ends not anywhere', hence any 'stance' is temporary. And whether there were early versions or not of the first three 'Beuerberg' and 'Wolfratshausen' poems, the pointing-up of flux is a mark of the later Lawrence who announced it as a principal feature of the revolutionary art and characterisation of 1914–17.[23] The experience, as before, may be 'true' to 1912: to the first joyous confidence in the *Gasthaus* (though their first night together was in fact in Munich), the first battles over Frieda's yearning for her children, and her first running off to her sister's at Wolfratshausen – yet the structured sequence bears the imprint of an understanding that could not have been mustered at the time. Ostensibly, 'failure' is taken up into a wonderful sense of balance in the first poem, but in sequence the failure to stand clear of the past is as ongoing and mutual (hence the ironic 'And' of the second title) as the triumphant love, which gives way in him to Hamlet-like longing for annihilation, and to bitterness because 'She looks Back' to her lost children, Lot's wife rather than his. So the balance of togetherness 'On the Balcony', and in the dance between opposites in 'Frohnleichnam', becomes more perilous than if these were poems-in-themselves, before it tips downwards 'In the Dark' to 'Mutilation', 'Humiliation', and the 'compleynte' of 'A Young Wife', before tipping up again in 'Green', Lawrence's aubade. Conversely, in looking continually backward and forward the 'dark' poems also get modified. In harking back to 'Nonentity' (beyond even the 'sleep' of 'Martyr à la Mode') the nihilism flickers with an undermining of its exclamatory extremism – since the last fall into nonentity *was* a 'death, which quivers with birth'. The curse on motherhood is only partial, even at the time; the 'salt burns' held in fusion with the 'lymph' (frog-song, globe flowers, glow-worms) associated with moments of certainty in love. The poems begin to dance between the light and the dark before

[22] Lawrence changed trains at Hennef on 11 May 1912, *Letters*, I, 398, to which the poem is closely related. The poem was probably written then or soon after, and was published in *Love Poems and Others* in February 1913; but its irony 'sounds' louder when placed in this sequence in *Collected Poems*.
[23] See the denial of 'the old stable ego of the character' and the defence of the new kind of 'allotropic' characterisation in 'The Wedding Ring', Lawrence to Garnett 5 June 1914, *Letters*, II, 183.

the lovers do – and before the dance turns into explicit dialectic, between the sunshiny 'she' who fears his darkness will destroy her life, and the 'he' who wants them to be quite gone in the dark. Then 'he' *is* altogether in the dark, feeling 'Mutilation' without her, and 'Humiliation' that she should have become so '*necessary*' and he so choiceless and dependent; while 'she' laments that he has made her *see* 'The shadows that live in the sun!' Still, however, that pain of loving is only 'almost' more than can be borne; and it is out of the new sense of opposites fused into the very source of light and growth that 'Green' comes, significantly colouring up between dark and gold – and the roses which flower into new selfhood, for a transient moment, which is enough. But the 'mellow' fusion of beauty and mortality, gold and shadow, in the rose poems is also even *more* temporary in the full sequence than in the five poems themselves. For there comes again the experience of being 'Quite Forsaken'; indeed 'Forsaken and Forlorn' on the balcony, wondering 'where / Ends this darkness that annihilates me'. 'Fireflies in the Corn' are no longer signs of love but have become the medium of contempt because he is no proud soul-rider off to battle, but a poor thing 'Moaning for me to love him'. Yet, again, there will be the moment of transformation by the 'Other': the certain knowledge of relationship, not dead like the shot deer in the false dawn of 'Quite Forsaken', but suddenly revealed in the wild free life of 'A Doe at Evening', discovering selfhood in and through the recognition of another utterly strange being, other-and-opposite.

No earlier version is known for thirteen of the twenty-two poems in this chapter, and in the others, as we have seen, the hand of 1917 is clear, very often in rewriting rather than revision, and always in new meaning through positioning within the sequence and multiple cross reference. Some may be altogether new in 1917. Of the thirteen, indeed, there may be none that certainly and purely expresses the Lawrence of 1912 – even those that seem the most spontaneous, to their 'poetic' peril. No poem seems more nakedly personal, more rawly the feeling of the moment (when Frieda ran off to Wolfratshausen again) than 'Mutilation'. Yet what are the Tuatha de Danaan doing in Bavaria in 1912? The suspicion that the old Celtic gods are being invoked in Cornwall in January 1917 is reinforced by Lawrence's memory, in the 'Nightmare' chapter of *Kangaroo*,[24] of calling on them a month before. Even so (it might be said) the poem 'expresses what he felt', like 'Frohnleichnam' (say), and other poems which equally if not as frequently 'express what Frieda felt'? Or is that to praise a power of dramatic imagination working on memory? – and combined with post-*Rainbow* understanding of dance, battle, the marriage of opposites (particularly dark and light) and the experience and mutual accusation of characters in the fictions? 'In the Dark' is not only dramatised in dialogue, but also strongly reminiscent of Anna

---

[24] *Kangaroo* (London, 1923), rpt, Harmondsworth, 1950, 1954, pp. 250–1. (Lawrence has, however, misremembered Asquith's resignation which was in winter, 5 December 1916).

telling Will why she must sleep alone. 'She Looks Back' not only has the corrosive salt imagery of a scene between Ursula and Skrebensky, but is significantly retrospective. If Lawrence did visit Irschenhausen in 1912 with Edgar Jaffé as *Mr Noon* suggests,[25] he may have seen a doe at evening and have written a poem about it later (though the fiction may derive from the poem). But could it in any case have been *this* poem? – so finely balancing femaleness and motherhood with maleness all made 'strange', in opposition and relation? Would *The Rainbow* (and the *Prussian Officer* ending of 'Odour of Chrysanthemums') have taken so long to get hold of if he had seen so clearly in 1912? In one tiny case, moreover, theme can be shown to have been more important than autobiography. 'Fireflies' in its pre-October 1913 version already reverses the facts of the quarrel in 1912, in which Lawrence upheld fireflies and Frieda glow-worms. But now Lawrence cuts both the charge that 'he' can never say he loves her, and 'his' voice denying that; which gives the whole poem to 'her'. So it is *Women in Love*, in that tiny detail, that is the more autobiographical, and the poem that takes the liberty of dramatic fiction.[26] One begins to see that 'he' and 'she' are half way between the 'real-life' lovers and fully dramatised characters; and that the criteria for style and form may be dramatic rather than lyric also, placing and using 'immature' stances and rhetorics within a context of development.

Yet without biographical knowledge the next short chapter about the journey through the mountains towards Italy remains a little opaque. Chatto and Windus would publish only on condition that 'Meeting Among the Mountains' and 'Song of a Man Who is Loved' were left out; two other poems were retitled; and some verbal changes were made.[27] Lawrence restored the 'Song' in 1928, which he had been the more anxious to keep in the sequence. (The other had been printed twice already, notably in *Georgian Poetry*.) It was, however, left to the editors of the posthumous *Complete Poems* to put 'Meeting' back in; and they misplaced it. It is only when the poem is returned to its *chronological* position that the ironic positioning of the four poems in relation to one another becomes clear. More significantly still, the bitter contrast between the sense in which the man in the 'Song' in this chapter 'Is Not Loved', and the 'Misery' of the fourth poem, is diminished if we do not know what has happened in between. It was not until *Mr Noon* in 1920 that Lawrence was able to re-imagine how Frieda told him she had

---

[25] *Mr Noon*, pp. 105–9, the stag p. 109. In 1912, Lawrence only spent one weekend in Edgar Jaffé's Munich flat. Frieda and he were, however, lent Edgar's wooden bungalow in Irschenhausen in 1913, and stayed there from 19 April–1 June and 9 August–17 September. But if this poem was written before 28 October 1913, why was it not sent to Marsh then?

[26] See *Letters*, I, 420; MS 16 Ferrier/MS 23 Cambridge; Ferrier, *Earlier Poetry*, Poem 174; *Mr Noon*, pp. 213–14; *Women in Love*, edited by David Farmer, Lindeth Vasey and John Worthen (Cambridge, 1987), p. 251.

[27] Letters from Chatto and Windus are reproduced in *Letters*, III, 145 n.1, 148 n.1.

slept with Harold Hobson near the Dominikushütte (of which we do have other evidence).[28] This seems to be one place where reference to biography enriches dramatic point – a reminder that the tact we are looking for is one that mediates continually between both genres, never letting go of either.

'Song of a Man Who Is Not Loved', labelled 'Glashütte', refers primarily to a common experience in the mountains rather than to a personal quarrel (though in 'life' they had got lost and vexed before they found the chapel and the hayhut in the mountains, and climbed down to Glashütte the next morning). The poem moreover leads on from the 'fear' of the previous one; but the terror is not now of any threat from an 'other', but of being alone in an immensity of space, and helplessly 'driven' – Don Juan's word – by forces beyond the self. It is the horror of space which Paul Morel felt after the death of his mother and Gerald Crich after the death of his father, brought home by the absence of love, which alone can stay the self against the sudden knowledge of its tininess. Either character might have cried 'So much there is outside me . . . I am too / Little to count in the wind that drifts me through'. Yet if the poem, whenever written, 'remembers' a horror of feeling lost in space, with Frieda locked unlovingly into herself – that too was/is temporary, for 'Sinners' is a love poem of happiness in Mayrhofen (where they waited for Bunny Garnett and his friend Harold to arrive). Here, in renewed confidence of love, the mountains have no shadow and the physical and creaturely world is full of rich vitality. The idea that they are 'Sinners' would be pure foolishness were there no 'Swarms of mankind in the world, and we were less lonely'. Yet the inadequacy of *that* becomes apparent immediately – once the poems are properly placed – in the 'Meeting in the Mountains' which Frieda's version labels Tuxtal, before the big pale Christus. For there imagination, secretly aware of the injury the lover has done, suddenly realises the abandoned husband's despair and hate; and the passing mule-driver's eyes are suddenly the husband's, hating him, crucified and crucifying. And then (though only biographical knowledge will bring out the full bitter irony of having the tables turned), direction and relationship are lost again, in such 'Misery' that all ways out become equally pointless; and a beautiful world becomes an 'oubliette', a pit-dungeon for the forgotten, with no escape. This man is 'unloved' with a savagely ironic difference.[29]

In the next long chapter set on Lake Garda ('Sunday Afternoon in Italy' to 'Wedlock'), the relationship finally 'comes through'; but before it can do so there

---

[28] *Mr Noon*, pp. 276–8; David Garnett, 'Frieda and Lawrence' in *Great Friends* (London, 1979), p. 80.

[29] For Tuxtal, see *Not I, but the Wind*, pp. 48–9. The use of 'oubliette' in Lawrence to McLeod 2 September 1912 from Sterzing (to which they had inadvertently returned), *Letters* I, 445, suggests that 'Misery' may have been written soon afterwards.

are two related battles to be won, to free both lovers from the past. (In 1928, Lawrence made this clearer by adding 'Everlasting Flowers',[30] that dubious love-offering to a 'darling' dead mother, which then harks all the way back to 'Elegy'. If 'he' were to remain so everlastingly mother-fixated, could he ever really become lover and husband?) 'Sunday Afternoon', on the other hand, insists on the no less everlasting sex-war of Man and Woman. The first part describes the behaviour of courting couples in the descriptive vein of 'Italian Sketches' (1912); but in final strophe and antistrophe all women and all men cry their champions on, with the post 1914/15 understanding of eternal and inevitable conflict between Opposites. Problems both representative and personal have come with the lovers into Italy.

So the next three poems hark back sardonically to Icking. Two aubades subvert the vital green-to-gold of 'Green'. In 'Winter Dawn' the 'Green star Sirius' may herald the need to begin again, but it has been a dog-fight star; and to wash himself clean from hatred of the sleeping woman is to find that no feeling at all is left. In the next poem the sunrise 'falters', 'A Bad Beginning'. The lovers are 'bruised'; but when she opens her arms he feels that *she* should come to *him*, and not as visitor, winsome child or insolent mistress. (The idea of remarriage gave the Frieda of 1912 'creeps'.) And if she still weeps at night, 'Why Does She Weep?'[31] Is she afraid of God in the dark? If so, let God be the one to hide, for it is they that are – albeit only now – in the right. Here begins a chain of rewritings of the story of Adam and Eve. If she must weep for what is past and done with, let it be for 'the abomination of our old righteousness'. Whenever written, these poems faithfully reflect Lawrence's worst moments on Lake Garda, (though in concentrating only on these they also distort, for biography, the full impact of his experience there).

However, if the tensions of Icking continued to trouble Lawrence and Frieda in November 1912, the finishing of *Sons and Lovers* with its (probably new) mercy-killing of Mrs Morel marked a turning-point in Lawrence's mother-fixation. So, here, 'Giorno dei Morti', ostensibly a straightforward evocation of the All Souls procession to the cemetery in Gargnano, gains another dimension in 1917 by its placing in the sequence, where it becomes also a personal laying to

[30] As ⟨'From the Italian Lakes'⟩ in MS 26 Ferrier/MS 39 Cambridge, Roberts E320.2, a notebook containing 'Accounts at Portcothan' where Lawrence lived from 30 December 1915 to 29 February 1916. It occurs among revisions of earlier poems in 1918, all of which however date from before Portcothan. It may have been copied from the *Tagebuch* after Gray returned both notebooks. It was further revised for *New Poems* (October 1918), see *Letters*, III, 229.

[31] '. . . fancy marrying again, it gives me creeps', Frieda to Edward Garnett 29 December 1912, *Letters*, I, 498. In her later *Memoirs and Correspondence* (London, 1961), pp. 97–8, Frieda recalls how she wept for three days when she realised that Weekley could keep her from the children, and how she felt almost suicidal. Lawrence breaks with biography in order to pursue the structural theme of 'sin' and Eden. Would he have done so at the time?

rest. For in the next poem – of which no early version exists – the Italian custom of placing a lighted candle on the grave of one's dead becomes a reconciliation of contradictions. Lawrence had written that a man's life should be flame-like. Now the son's flame, still drawing from its dead 'source', becomes also a forgetting and a busyness with life. There is lasting connection, but (reversing the end of 'Everlasting Flowers' when that was added) there is liberation also.

Nine poems then bring the battle of the sexes to crisis at the year's end, followed by a kind of rebirth. 'He' is not grateful for the condescension of his 'Lady Wife' as angelic visitor, with 'blithe, glad mien'; and mounts a hurtful counter-attack on the value of her wedding-ring. She should put on sackcloth and ashes and learn to 'serve', since he must struggle priestlike with 'the mystery'. (The beggar has developed a new sense of vocation.) 'Both Sides of the Medal' brings into the open the hatred that surely exists in her love as in his. There is sardonic reference to Hobson's Christmas visit – even 'in my own house' she may want to 'enlarge' herself 'with this friend of mine, / Such a friend as he is, / Yet you cannot get beyond your awareness of me' – but the imagery of *orbiting* stars in the last two stanzas strongly suggests the author of *Women in Love*.[32] 'Loggerheads' shows 'him' 'quite indifferent' to 'her' uncertainty 'As to whether you've found a fortune / In me, or a flea-bitten fate' (the beggar again). But in 'December Night' he invites her out of the cold to warm herself at his 'innermost hearth', where no woman has been. On 'New Year's Eve' instead of the sojourning of a lady wife there is a coming to terms, naked, with the great extremities of darkness and fire. Afterwards, 'New Year's Night' can begin: 'Now you are mine, to-night at last I say it.' It is an extraordinarily paradoxical poem since the experience makes him both lover and priestly slayer. What must be 'killed' and offered in sacrifice to a mysterious God is what is most precious to both lovers; yet it is through the death in sex of winged freedom and purity, 'pride, strength, all the lot' (dove, and doe at evening), that all become renewed. So 'Valentine's Night' hails new being through the marriage of opposites, 'The Flower in the bud / Again, undefiled', beyond good and evil. 'New Year's Night' was originally titled 'Eve's Mass'; and 'Valentine's Night' ('you are a maid again') 'Candlemass', the Festival of the Purification of the Virgin. Chatto and Windus objected to what they feared would be seen as blasphemy. It was in fact a mark of the newly 'religious' view of sex which began in the 'Foreword' to *Sons and Lovers* and culminated in the vision of *The Rainbow*, which has certainly influenced this sequence. For after the death of old selves and their past comes 'Birth Night'; finally re-shaping the Book of Genesis as Eve is re-born, not from the rib but through exchange of blood with Adam, related in intercourse as

[32] Though stars had often imaged separateness and steadfastness earlier, the important image of two stars orbiting each other, separate still, yet bound to each other, was newly written into *Women in Love* several times over, in the 1917 revision. See also 'One Woman to All Women', below.

closely as parent and child in the womb. 'This is Noel for me, / Tonight is a woman born / Of the man in me'. (This reverses the 'Foreword's rewriting of the Fourth Gospel to proclaim how Man is born of Woman before he can utter his Word; and again might suggest a later date for the sequence, though not the experience.)

By 1917 moreover it had become very clear that however Lawrence may have felt in 1913 that he and Frieda were coming through to new life, their battle was by no means over, since growth through conflict is a never-ending process. This is why immediately after the triumph comes 'Rabbit Snared in the Night', a poem of violence which is not only the impulse of a violent man, but is called forth also by an apparently passive victim. It seems most unlikely to be a poem of early 1913 by the author who signalled the humanity of the lad in the 'Burns novel' fragment by his freeing of a rabbit caught in a snare.[33] Rather it relates to the rabbit scene in *Women in Love*, and Birkin's argument that there are murderees as well as murderers. The poem is disturbing enough when, sent separately in 1917 to Harriet Monroe, it appears to be about a man holding a rabbit. It becomes far more so when it is placed in a sequence about the sexual relationship of men and women, and exposes the potential for murderous violence in that relation.[34] If blood-desire can create rebirth, blood-lust can urge to throttle and destroy. Yet the very next poem is 'Paradise Re-Entered', in which violence purifies hate and liberates from fear. Here a 1913 version has survived, but a much less violent one called 'Purity'. It recognised fierceness in desire, even a 'cleansing hate', but passion quickly purifies them into 'beautiful candid lovers . . . like stars in our steadfast being'. The revision is much fiercer. In the flames of sex the mind fuses like a bead – the furnace image of *The Rainbow* – though incandescence is taken calmly, and death is approached and passed without fear. Moreover, though they could have been rosy and starry, they have no such wish in this version. As they dare the flaming angels at heaven's gate, roses seem withered, stars sun-dimmed, and they have no desire to be candid and beautiful, nestling together. Rather, they storm the Gates, beyond God and Devil, to the true Eden where Eve may dance, dishevelled, yet primally blissful. ('Frohnleichnam' and 'Gloire de Dijon' come into new relationship.)

'Giorno dei Morti' and 'Purity' are the only 'Gargnano' poems known to have existed before 1916; though Frieda claimed much later that 'While we were at Villa Igea Lawrence wrote also "Twilight in Italy" and most of the poems from

---

[33] See *Love Among the Haystacks*, edited by John Worthen (Cambridge, 1987), pp. 206–7.
[34] Ferrier, *Earlier Poetry*, Poem 194. The typescript sent to Harriet Monroe in August 1917 lacked lines 37–9. In the proofs of *Look!* Lawrence wrote in lines 34–6 and 40–2, omitted by printer's error because of similar openings to the three stanzas, see Chatto's apology, *Letters*, III, 165 n.1.

"Look! We Have Come Through!"[35] The first claim, however, is inaccurate, and the second likely to be no less so. It is true that (if what we read now *are* basically 'Gargnano' poems) many may have seemed too nakedly compromising for publication at the time – though that argument could not apply to 'Sunday Afternoon in Italy' or that fine poem 'All Souls'. On the other hand, the strong structuring and sequencing and the continual cross-reference to other poems in theme and image strongly suggest the hand of 1917. It is quite likely that the intensity of hate and violence, as well as the confidence of rebirth, were dramatically *heightened* from early versions as in 'Purity'; and poems may again have been newly written in 1917.

In 'Spring Morning', placed at San Gaudenzio,[36] the lovers have at last 'come through' to new life and happiness, have died to old selves, and can start again with no need to fight any more – for the moment. ('Coming Awake', to sunshine without memory, was added by Lawrence in 1928.) Finally, the six sections of 'Wedlock' transform the candle image of 'All Souls'. Now it illuminates sexual relationship, a marriage of opposites, two-in-one. 'He' is flame to 'her' candle as he embraces and warms her while she is the core of his fire. This is also to recognise his utter dependence on her as 'the very quick of my being'. Yet there is no humiliation or diminution now in knowing what it would mean Not to be Loved; for he can both feel tenderly protective while she cherishes him, and admit also that his strength comes from her, so the candle is like a tower. But now he too is 'full strong and certain', wondering what will issue from them, and sure that it will come not from either but from both (as he told Garnett 'The Wedding Ring' would do). Something will come forth, 'children, acts, utterances, / Perhaps only happiness'. All he wants is newness and they are sure of that; since (most important of all) she is 'other' on a deeper level now than 'Doe at Evening'; for she is both 'with' him, finally, *and* 'always beyond my scope'; 'Something that stands over' to be wondered at, yet making him new because she is near.

The next short chapter might have been a triumphant conclusion. 'History' – 'set' at Garnett's house The Cearne, i.e. summer 1913, whenever written – looks back over their whole relationship with a sense of how pathlessness (all the way

---

[35] *Not I, but the Wind*, p. 52. She placed *Movements in European History*, written in 1918–19, in 1915, see Cambridge edition, edited by Philip Crumpton, p. XIX, n.11. Moreover, on 17 December 1912 Lawrence wrote that he was '*resisting* too hard to write poetry – resisting the strain of Weekley, and the tragedy there is in keeping Frieda. To write poetry one has to let oneself fuse in the current – but I daren't' (*Letters*, 1, 488).

[36] The first three lines echo a poem by Ernest Collings which Lawrence quotes in a letter to him, 14 November 1912, *Letters*, 1, 472. This makes it likely that the poem may indeed have been written the following spring.

from 'Misery') has become accomplishment. 'Song of a Man Who is Loved', revised and improved from a 1913 version, proclaims new security, between her breasts, from the horrors of space when unloved; while 'Song of a Man Who Has Come Through', probably the finest poem in the book and the best known, reverses the earlier sense of being too 'Little to count in the wind that drifts me through'. (It is also the best poetic answer to Russell's jibe.) Lawrence had been reading Whitman again in early 1917 and this is his most powerful and sensitive use so far of the Whitmanesque breath-line, finding its own length and emphasis, a medium perfectly apt to the theme of 'Not I, not I, but the wind that blows through me.' It both proclaims and demonstrates a newly confirmed certainty, also, about the kind of poetry Lawrence most wanted to write: where the effort he had spoken of to Marsh in 1913 'to get an emotion out in its own course, without altering it',[37] has now also to be 'Like a fine, and exquisite chisel, a wedge blade inserted', if the inspiration or fountaining from sources beyond the self is not to be blocked. Wonder, also, at being made new by what is beyond oneself, is as vital for Lawrence's poetry as for his idea of relationship. 'What is the knocking at the door in the night? / It is somebody wants to do us harm. / No, no, it is the three strange angels. / Admit them, admit them.' The tartness of the biblical allusions in 'She Looks back' and 'Lady Wife' is lost in wonder now. Moreover, as 'One Woman' speaks 'to All Women', it seems that all this is true for 'her' too: 'How happy I am, how my heart in the wind rings true'. 'She' even captures what Birkin had been trying to say he wanted from 'love' – unsuccessfully in the 1916 *Women in Love*, and clarified only in the 1917 revision after this poem[38] – something quite different from sexist domination. 'There's the beauty you cannot see, myself and him / Balanced in glorious equilibrium . . . There's this other beauty, the way of the stars . . .' So, though the poem is 'dated' from Kensington at the time of their marriage in summer 1914, it either is, or has become, a poem of 1917. There remains the ruthlessness Frieda herself spoke of: he can be 'different . . . dangerous, / Without pity or love', and the relationship must be 'human inhuman'; yet 'his separate being liberates me / And gives me peace!', and what used to be feared has become beautiful, 'to be lifted and gone'.

Again, the sequence might have ended triumphantly there – but that would have been false both to life-experience and to Lawrence's post-1914 dialectic art, where relationship cannot conclusively stabilise if it is not to die. New conflict not only will but must begin again if growth is to continue. The lovers may be

[37] *Letters*, II, 61; also on the voicing of rhythm II, 102–4. See also the relation of this poem to the 'Preface' to the 1918 American edition of *New Poems* in *Phoenix: The Posthumous Papers of D. H. Lawrence*, edited by Edward D. McDonald (London, 1936; rpt, 1961), pp. 218–22, which, Lawrence concludes, 'should have come as a preface to *Look! We Have Come Through!*'
[38] On this 'star-equilibrium' in relation to *Women in Love*, see note 31 above.

triumphant, but they are also cut off from their society – already implicit in the rejection of 'You other women'. In 'People' and 'Street Lamps' now, we see the Unreal City of which Lawrence spoke to Russell in 1915 (though they are made out of a poem of Croydon days before 1912, now split in two).[39] People are 'a ghost-flux of faces' drifting meaninglessly; London is a City of Dissolution, its lamps like burst suns or seed-pods drifting into the dark. So it becomes necessary to 'cross into another world', to find 'New Heaven and Earth'. However, both this poem and 'She Said As Well To Me' show that the certainties of the previous chapter had come too easily. There is still conflict between the 'characters' after marriage and their whole world is now at war. Moreover, one realises now that 'the author' of these poems is 'unreliable'; *himself* a developing 'I' and imaginer, not at all omniscient. One should have realised before, of course, since the point of view has been shifting in a dynamic process throughout the sequence. But now 'the author' of 'One Woman to All Women' can be seen to have been over-optimistic, to say the least, in so assimilating 'her' to 'his' vision. A moment of comedy enters, if we read aright. What 'She' has now said 'As Well' seems at first only additional assurance and compliment, poking gentle fun at his physical shyness, and showing loving wonder at the functional beauty, the clean straight body of a man that only God could have made; 'so that I began to wonder over myself, and what I am'. But Lawrence the dramatist had a fine ear for tone, and there is something wrong in what 'She said', which makes him feel 'trammelled and hurt', not free, and which the poem goes on to pin down. (Most of the trouble with Frieda, including the rows when she lamented her lost children, had come from her refusal, as he saw it, to commit herself to him. Now they were married, but the difficulty had not ended, for something inside her apparent commitment and love left him uneasy.) In the poem, now, it is too easy for 'her' to 'love' without true respect. 'He' is not an 'instrument' – her tone was Gudrun's, looking at the sleeping Gerald. He is not to be used, still less possessed. She would not dare to speak of or touch a wild creature so, a weasel, an adder, a bull (or a Tyger, since the hint of Blake was ironic, or even a stag at evening). She does not see him as truly 'other' or singled out. The sense of him as strange and dangerous, put into her mouth in 'One Woman to All Woman', was wishful thinking. The poem is 'dated' to 'Greatham', i.e. 1915, but the adder and Gudrun's attitude suggest Zennor again.[40]

Most of 'New Heaven and New Earth', however, originally 'Terranova',

---

[39] Russell to Ottoline Morrell, 11 July 1916 (University of Texas) quoted in Paul Delany, *D. H. Lawrence's Nightmare* (Hassocks, 1979), p. 117. For ⟨'The Street Lamps'⟩ see Ferrier, *Earlier Poetry*, Poems 203 and 204.

[40] For the adder see *Letters*, 11, 599 (April 1916). For Gudrun looking at Gerald as 'instrument' see *Women in Love* (Cambridge, 1987), pp. 417–18.

probably does date from Greatham.[41] The sense of landing on a new shore might have been Ursula's at the end of *The Rainbow*. The old world is looked back on with double horror, for 'everything was tainted by myself' and hence *known* (Ursula's trouble); and moreover the world of 1915 has become a hell of death, mutilation and corruption in which he is implicated, since he too is murderous and deathly. Yet 'it is good to have died and been trodden out . . . absolutely to nothing', for with death comes resurrection of a self 'the same as before, yet unaccountably new'. More than ever this depends on experiencing the otherness of the Other: touching the flank of the absolutely unknown, suddenly aware that for 'over a thousand nights' beside his wife he had still failed to realise *her* true separateness and otherness, so that the 'she' he touched had been a projection of himself. Only at the hands of the truly Other can the self die to new life; but now he has been carried 'by the current of death' to a new shore, 'a new I'. There the 1915 poem ended, but a 1917 conclusion adds a descant on the greenness of the new world, like her eyes – linking back through 'Winter Dawn' to 'Green', each coming only now into its full reading – and like *Typee* (recently read), with fresh streams and 'white sands and fruits unknown and perfumes'. Now he knows that the current will have to drown him again, holding him down to mysterious depths, that he may be kindled to life again in never-ending process. So Zennor, with which the sequence has caught up now, is an 'Elysium', 'lovelier than Lyonesse' where the woman's hands have 'found the source of my subjection / To the All, and severed the connection', setting him free.

'Manifesto', in a long summary, explains how. The subjection had not come from hungering after the various needs of body or mind. He has found the one woman who can satisfy the deepest of these, and the rich man hungers no more. Above all he has discovered how to die and be re-born. But now the condition for making him finally detached, completed, free, is that she should 'take the same from me', should realise 'that I am that fearful thing . . . the other' and 'perish on me as I have perished on her'. Only then can they 'have each our separate being', free, pure, complete, distinct, yet in 'unutterable conjunction'. After that 'there will only remain' (a typical optimism, showing how much Lawrence wanted *not* to be isolated from his society) 'that all men detach themselves and become unique', for then, in love or hate, their 'utterance' will be music 'straight out of the unknown'.

However, all life is cyclical, seasonal. At this terrible point in history and in the soul (late 1916), 'Autumn Rain' in the city falls like tears, on a world whose painful harvest is 'the sheaves of dead men', on the Somme. In winter the crowds of bright young women on the pavements seem 'Frost Flowers' whose beauty is

---

[41] See note 6 above; *Letters*, 11, 664; Ferrier, *Earlier Poetry*, Poem 205; and Amy Lowell, ed., *Some Imagist Poems, An Annual Anthology* (Boston and New York, 1917).

scented with a wintry 'corruption', necessary (as 'The Crown' had explained) yet repellent. The sequence ends 'Craving for Spring' (1917):[42] a rhythm of longing whose intensity is both evocation – embodiment after embodiment of springing life – and invocation, since the intenser the clearer that what is longed for has not come, yet. 'He' speaks as for a world of longing: for those who have never flowered, for the winter-weary, for vindication 'against too much death'. Finally the voice is that of the prophet who represents the people, but whose greatest prayer is not to be like Moses, and 'die on the brink of such anticipation' – or worse, deceived.

So, how are we to 'look'? Perhaps the first conclusions seem negative ones – merely by way of clearing the ground for criticism, since I have had space only for survey. The poems are not to be seen as single lyrics, personal and confessional (if imperfectly 'sublimated'), dated and placed between 1912 and 1917. The book is not an anthology but an organic sequence; and no poem stands alone. Each is also a 'moment' in a structured process; related to what has been; about to be refocussed by what is to come; and finally securing its 'significance' only when the whole sequence is complete, in relation to all the others. Yet that 'also' is important. For once we are *seeing* process, we can also see, for the first time, the fullness-and-fragility of the instant, the poem, within the sequence. The 'best' poems are often moments of resolution, but we learn to see that as only momentary, gone through – any final 'perfection of form' a delusion. Yet the tact we need is never to let go of either 'opposite' in the fusion which is Lawrence's originality, both in form and theme; the moment, as in the rose poems, is all the more precious for being caught out of time. A similar tact must meet the challenge of the 'Kind'. Ian Jack taught us to look to this, and to how new Kinds grow out of established ones by creative 'invention'. What we see here is drama, in several acts, growing out of autobiography into something which is no longer either because it is both. The grounding in personal experience, for Lawrence, guarantees courageous, even embarrassing authenticity; the freedom to dramatise or even fictionalise a later vision makes it representative.[43] The 'We' of the title bears the same sort of relation to Frieda and Lawrence that 'Stephen Hero' had to Joyce: at once lifelike 'younger selves' and developing characters on a

---

[42] Lawrence to Catherine Carswell (13 February 1917), *Letters*, III, 93–4, 'I have finished it today. It has meant a great deal to me. And I feel more inclined to burst into tears than anything . . . I loathe it to go to a publisher.'

[43] Ballad, dramatic dialogue or monologue and chorus are all means to this end. The references to Adam and Eve, the angelic visitation to the Cities of the Plain, and Lot's wife, also suggest a 'mythic' dimension. (Lawrence's thought of using 'Iamque vale' as ironic epigraph might have increased this, inverting the Orphic tragedy too.) Amy Lowell thought it a 'novel . . . for all that it is written in a rather disconnected series of poems'.

journey imaginatively staged. Ian Jack has also emphasised the ambiguity of the 'I' in dramatic lyric: protagonist–subject, unreliable narrator, ostensible 'author', authorial semblance even at the end. All in turn become dramatised stages in the Lawrenceian sequence and its process of change, development, transformation, but *never* final identity, stable ego. The sequence is a chorus of voices, a spectrum of styles which evoke feeling dramatically, so that we should no more expect well-wrought urn-speech at certain moments than we should from characters on the stage; though that does not preclude criticism of how well poems are dramatically done. The privacies at which we are 'entitled' to 'look', if embarrassing in their naked explicitness, are also partly staged (and deliberately intensified from life) for dramatic purposes. The embarrassment is because we never lose awareness of relation-to-life; the developing drama is to make us look for more, for insight into what it might mean to 'come through'.

12

Presentation and self-presentation in *In Parenthesis*

COLIN WILCOCKSON

Of all Jones's works, it is *In Parenthesis* which contains the most complex and fascinating of his self-presentations. His most obvious method is through authorial association with particular characters in the narrative. Primarily, this is through Private John Ball, and this results in the predominant (though not exclusive) use of the pronoun 'he'; though at the same time he naturally uses the first-person pronoun 'I' in the footnotes – which he regarded as integral to the text.[1] Clearly Jones is unwilling to use the first person in the narrative itself, because 'I' would be too restrictive, would make unduly subjective the author's concerns about the moral dilemma of a war where German and British 'brothers' are at strife. Though Ball may physically, sometimes emotionally, represent Jones, however, he is not given the imaginative and intellectual ability of the poet – the narrator (e.g. in the meditation on Beiz Wood) takes over and moves beyond Ball's thoughts. The Welsh soldier Aneirin Lewis is nearer to Jones's mentality, and indeed the two characters may loosely correspond to Jones's English–Welsh ancestry. Far more complex is the topic to which I shall return later: the consistent representation of Jones's mind through the evocation of the moral dilemmas in Malory's *Le Morte d'Arthur*, where, again, the voice of an individual often represents the collective view of the group.

Jones's unwillingness to present himself *in propria persona* can be seen throughout his works and, before analysing the methods of self-presentation in *In Parenthesis*, I think it may be illuminating to compare his use of the authorial pronouns in this work with those he uses in some of his other poetry. The most obvious pronoun for an author to use in expressing himself in his work is 'I', but Jones's use of this first-person singular is rare, and therefore strikingly direct in

I am grateful to the following: for many helpful suggestions, Professor Thomas Dilworth, University of Windsor, Ontario; Professor Rudolf Germer, University of Cologne, particularly for insights into T. S. Eliot; Messrs Robert Douglas-Fairhust and Nicholas Perkins, research students of Pembroke College, Cambridge; Nigel Wilcockson; and for many points of fact and interpretation, Mr Derek Shiel. I have drawn on ideas from all of these and trust that this general acknowledgement will be accepted as a token of gratitude for considerable debt.

[1] See Preface to *In Parenthesis* (London, 1937), p. xiv.

235

A, a, a, Domine Deus,[2] a short poem which laments the sterility of twentieth-century technology. In Jones's other great visionary poem, *The Anathemata* (published some fifteen years later than *In Parenthesis*), even though Jones occasionally uses 'I', the usual pronoun for the authorial voice is the first person plural 'we'. Characters within the text (such as the spirit of London. 'The Lady of the Pool') speak *in propria persona* and naturally use 'I', but there is no one particular character in *The Anathemata* who is the consistent mouth-piece of the author.[3] Because the plural form 'we' is dominant, the effect is, paradoxically, a retreat towards anonymity. The poem opens and closes with the priest at the Mass. Between, is a recognition through all known time of the pattern which would be engaged and fulfilled in Christ's sacrifice (which is a sign), and man's attempts to express his awe through sign, through art:

We already and first of all discern him making this thing other. His groping syntax, if we attend, already shapes: ADSCRIPTAM, RATAM, RATIONABILEM ... and by preappli-cation and for *them* [author's italics], under modes and patterns altogether theirs, the holy and venerable hands lift up an efficacious sign.

Here we have three pronouns, 'we', 'he' and 'they'. All have the effect of depersonalisation. On these lines René Hague remarks, 'D[avid] frequently, particularly when beginning a passage, uses "he" or "his", "him" etc., to show that, while he has an individual in mind, that individual is to be regarded as typical'.[4] In other words, though it may be of biographical interest to know that he was watching a particular priest at the Mass, such knowledge adds nothing to the meaning of the poem. Jones himself remarks in the Preface to *The Anathemata* that a number of influences on the life of 'a Londoner, of Welsh and English parentage, of Protestant upbringing, of Catholic subscription' have dictated the nature of his poem but, importantly, he goes on to say, 'While such biographical accidents are not in themselves any concern of, or interest to, the reader, they are noted here because they are responsible for most of the content.' Just as the particular priest loses individuality as he assumes the priestly role and becomes the type of priesthood, so the 'we' becomes inclusive. 'We' represents the congregation, and the congregation is the human race. Occasionally the poet's voice is heard but even then in a collective context, sandwiched between 'our', so that the poet and his readers are considered to be a group of whom the poet is the representative: '. . . all our easting waters . . . I speak of before the whale-roads . . . our dear West' (pp. 114–15).

[2] Jones dates the poem 'c.1938 and 1966'.

[3] Of course, the name 'David' in the epigraph to *The Anathemata*, '*Teste David cum Sibylla*', though a quotation from the *Dies Irae*, is a personal signature, too. It thus acts differently from T. S. Eliot's epigraph to.*The Waste Land*, '*Nam Sibyllam quidem Cumis, etc.*' This *Waste Land* epigraph had doubtless been the germ of that of *The Anathemata*.

[4] René Hague, *A Commentary on the Anathemata of David Jones* (Wellingborough, 1977), p. 11.

There is, then, in *The Anathemata* a sense of collective national identity, an assumption of shared traditions, yet simultaneously of a distance between poet and text because the 'voice' is impersonal, often using the interrogative like an incantation ('What did he do other / recumbent at the garnished supper?'). This 'objectivity' of *The Anathemata* has, however, been called in question, because the very specificity of reference Jones makes to the traditions of these islands – Celtic legend, Welsh language, Roman history, Catholic ritual, and so on – could be considered to run counter to impersonality, to be 'a lapse from objective to subjective'.[5] This was certainly not his intention. Jones frequently explains that he can write only from what he knows, from what he has experienced. 'The imagination takes off best from the flight-deck of the known, from the experiential and the contactual.'[6] He is also, like Ruskin and Morris, conscious of the long continuity of man's artistic culture from its earliest manifestations in cave-dwellings to the present; these two writers see the 'artless' manufacture of artefacts in the aftermath of the Industrial Revolution as a 'break in the continuity of the golden chain' that links us with artists of the past, a tragic lesion which must be repaired.[7] The criticism that *The Anathemata* is so personally involved with the inner world of Jones's mind that the collectivism at which he aimed degenerates into the product of a mind 'turned inward and dreaming in the dark'[8] was totally at variance with his intention of reinstating 'man the maker of signs', the artist, with his art-creating ancestors throughout all time. A letter to Vernon Watkins (11 April 1962) takes up the topic: 'So far Classical allusions & Biblical ones and (in my case) Catholic liturgical ones still *more or less* work – but only more or less because the whole bloody past is more or less down the drain, as far as I can make out. The civilisational change in which we live has occasioned this and it's no use cracking on about it . . . People think one is being deliberately "obscure" or affected but the fact is that one "thinks" in these obsolete or becoming obsolete terms . . . This all sounds as though I thought that "poetry" could not be written . . . without this reference back – I don't think that at all, I mean only that *for me* it gets difficult if chaps don't know what Aphrodite, let alone Rhiannon (!) *signify*.'[9]

---

[5] John Holloway, *The Colours of Clarity. Essays on Contemporary Literature and Education* (London, 1964), p. 116. Discussed in David Blamires, *David Jones: Artist and Writer*, second edition (Manchester, 1978), pp. 196–7.

[6] See 'An Introduction to the *Rime of the Ancient Mariner*', Clover Hill edition of Coleridge's poem (1964), in which David Jones's engravings of 1928 are reproduced; reprinted in *The Dying Gaul and Other Writings*, edited by Harman Grisewood (London and Boston, 1978), p. 208.

[7] I discuss this in some detail in 'David Jones and "The Break"', *Agenda*, 15, 2–3 (Summer–Autumn, 1977), 126–31.

[8] See Colin Wilcockson, ed., *David Jones: Letters to William Hayward* (London, 1979), p. 16.

[9] Ruth Pryor, ed., *David Jones: Letters to Vernon Watkins* (Cardiff, 1976), p. 61. Similarly, Wilcockson, ed., *David Jones: Letters to William Hayward*, p. 17 and p. 18 n. a.

The regular occurrence of 'I' in Jones's works is, as I mention at the beginning of this essay, in the textual notes. In the notes to *In Parenthesis*, there is a tentativeness that strongly contrasts with the authoritative voice of the text. This tentativeness often accompanies an excuse – 'I quote from memory, and may be inaccurate' (p. 208); 'I cannot find the passage I had in mind' (p. 213); ' I have somewhere read a letter (which I associate with Francis Drake) . . .' (p. 218); 'In some battle of the Welsh, all reference to which escapes me . . . Also somewhere in Malory . . .' (p. 221), etc. At other times the tentativeness is a peculiarly nervous tactic so that Jones will not appear to be knowledgeable in areas where he feels himself to be amateur. He accurately paraphrases the well-known Welsh song 'Sospan fach', but feels bound to say, '. . . which implies, I think, that the little saucepan, etc . . .' (p. 201); or, later in the same note and on a different topic, we find the parenthetic '(that may be quite inaccurate)'. But by the time we get to the 'I' of the notes of *The Anathemata*, Jones has spelt out other reasons for tentativeness. Modesty certainly makes him fearful of appearing learned (in his letters and private conversations he constantly restated his lack of formal learning). More important, however, is his awareness of the limitation of human knowledge. A long footnote to *The Anathemata* (p. 82) states this clearly. The nub of it is: 'The findings of the physical sciences are necessarily mutable and change with fresh evidence or with fresh interpretation of the same evidence . . . But the poet, of whatever century, is concerned only with how he can use a current notion to express a permanent mythus.' This gives rise to the regular occurrence in the footnotes of words that express reservation: 'appears to be' (p. 159), 'it appears' (p. 168), 'appears to have become' (p. 178), 'it seems not improbable' (p. 198). I have mentioned elsewhere that in conversation he often ended a discussion, in which his considerable knowledge of archaeology, or history, or etymology had been abundantly evident, with the throwaway, 'But nobody knows anything about anything.'[10] This was modesty, but modesty which owed its origin not just to his consciousness of his lack of formal scholarship, but more importantly to his conviction of what might be called the 'chronically temporary' state of human knowledge.

There are moments in *In Parenthesis* when the author is concerned with memories so acutely felt that the third person 'he' gives place to a complex use of pronouns. The closing paragraph of part one may serve as an example:

Towards evening on the same day they entrained in cattle trucks; and on the third day, which was a Sunday, sunny and cold, the French women in deep black were hurrying across flat land – they descended from their grimy, littered, limb restricting, slatted vehicles, and stretched and shivered at a siding. You feel exposed and apprehensive in this new world.

[10] 'Notes on Some Letters of David Jones', *Agenda*, 14, 2 (Summer, 1976), 67–87, particularly pp. 67–71.

'They', 'you' and 'this' are strangely concatenated. 'They' distances as the narrator observes the soldiers. But in the final sentence the experience is personalised and immediate. The pronoun 'you' appears in its impersonal usage as a synonym for 'one', yet the 'this' makes it clear that the pronoun refers to the narrator himself. Through this trick, Ball and Jones are both the observed and the observers, and fuse. Concatenation, for similar effect but with different pronouns, appears on pages 53–5 where Ball, the night-sentry, is watching in the cold. 'He grips more tightly the band of his sling-swivel . . . You draw out warm finger-tips . . . You can hear [the rat] . . . at night-feast on the broken of us.'

In general, however, thoroughout *In Parenthesis*, Jones uses the third person 'he' to refer to 'Private John Ball' who (with whatever reservation one might want to make because Ball is himself a 'creation', a caricature at times, and who lacks the imaginative subtlety of the narrator) represents some aspects of the author. In no other work of Jones is that pronoun 'he' used in a way that is, albeit only partly, self-referential. The use of pronouns in *In Parenthesis* is discussed in interesting detail by Janet Powers Gemmill. She notes that,

The epic first person takes the form of an omniscient narrator who reserves the right to enter the mind of any character and to comment on the scene before him. There are moments, however, when the presence of the narrator interferes with the communication of highly personal or sensitive impressions. At those times, the narrator may either withdraw and present objectively what Private Ball hears and thinks or withdraw and allow his chief character to take over the job of narration.[11]

Beyond this, however, as I have already mentioned, there is a further projection of the authorial 'self' in this poem through the subtext of *Le Morte d'Arthur*, a work much 'in my head', Jones says, during the time when he was composing *In Parenthesis* (see note 33, below).

Indeed, twenty years after the publication of *In Parenthesis*, David Jones wrote, 'I should have thought that *if* a past literary source were to be sought for in *In Parenthesis*, the works of Malory would be perhaps most noticeable in that allusions to passages of Malory are pretty frequent in parts, I noticed when last I looked at it.'[12] I recognise that one should not lose sight of the integration of other works about war, such as are outlined in a brief, but convenient, summary by Janet Powers Gemmill: 'Utilising *anamnesis*, a kind of remembrance in which the individual's private stock of data is linked with the common stock of human memory, Jones draws upon ancient and medieval heroic myth to strengthen the ultimate meaning of Private John Ball's experience in battle. Thus through many

---

[11] '*In Parenthesis: A Study of Narrative Technique*', *Journal of Modern Literature*, 1 (March, 1971), 311–28.

[12] David Jones's letter to Harman Grisewood, 12 August 1957; reproduced in *Dai Greatcoat*, edited by René Hague (London, 1980), p. 174.

allusions this Anglo–Welsh soldier is simultaneously a hero of the *Mabinogion*, the *Chanson de Roland* and Aneirin's medieval Welsh epic *Y Gododdin*.'[13] Nevertheless, as Jones remarks, it is especially to Malory that he was drawn because, one reasonably infers, it was in his works that Jones found particularly apt parallels to his own experience of war. I shall, therefore, analyse the references to Malory to demonstrate how they are used by Jones to present himself via the subtext of Malorian association.

At this point, however, Gemmill's 'John Ball . . . this Anglo–Welsh soldier' calls for amplification. To what extent is Ball a substitute for the 'I' of a conventional autobiography, or to what extent is he a fictionalised approximation to Jones? As Colin Hughes has illustrated, the events described in *In Parenthesis* follow closely the actual events of the campaign Jones was engaged in on the Western Front offensive.[14] Furthermore, Jones remarks in a letter to Hughes, 'One of my rules is that when one uses some quotation or even a name that evokes some past author or event or some past literary association one *must* have an experiential, concrete, contactual matter in the narrative that corresponds in some way or other with the quoted situation or name.'[15] Thus, in some respects, John Ball, the untidy private, whose friendships and antipathies are observed (and in many cases traceable to actual soldiers with whom Jones served), who is wounded in the leg, coalesces with David Jones. More complex is the gauging of simultaneity, the co-incidence, of 'experiential, concrete, contactual', elements when Jones makes 'some past literary association'.

Most obviously, there are some amusing connections between Jones and particular soldiers who are given Malorian or actual and historical medieval names. For example, Ball mentions a number of his comrades whom he can observe. One is a character called Dai de la Cote Male Taile (p. 70). His mention is largely for its comedy.[16] The knight in Malory (*Le Morte d'Arthur*, book nine, chapter 1) wears his murdered father's ill-fitting coat as a token of his vow of revenge. His name is Breunor le Noire, but is mockingly nicknamed La Cote Male Taile by Sir Kay. Jones adds the name 'Dai' so that John Ball, the sad-clown soldier who coalesces with Jones, is further comically linked with Dai de la Cote Male Taile through the actual name of the author, *David*. In the Preface to *In Parenthesis*, Jones confesses that as a soldier he was 'the parade's despair', and one of the first references to Private Ball depicts him with 'pack ill adjusted and

[13] In *Encylopædia of World Literature in the Twentieth Century*, edited by Leonard S. Wilson; revised edition (New York, 1967), p. 521.
[14] In a talk given at the David Jones Society conference held at Pembroke College, Cambridge, 30 June – 2 July 1978, and subsequently published by the David Jones Society: Colin Hughes, *David Jones, the Man Who Was on the Field: 'In Parenthesis' as Straight Reporting* (1979).
[15] Hughes, *David Jones, the Man Who Was on the Field*, p. 22.
[16] Blamires, *David Jones: Artist and Writer*, p. 183.

without form'.[17] But the association with the Malorian character is superficial and jokey: the ill-fitting coat as a symbol of Breunor's revenge is not carried across into *In Parenthesis* because such a sentiment would be out of keeping in a poem of regret. 'Dai's boast', a passage that occurs later, is, however, with its many references to great epic poems, of a serious quality, linking the soldiers of all time through courage and pride in achievement. Similarly, Private Walter Map appears at Company HQ before the battle. The historical aptness of the man at Henry II's court, in a position that enabled him to observe, has been pointed out by David Blamires; and Colin Hughes suggests that, as Jones was for a while attached to Company HQ as a cartographer, and as his first name was in fact Walter, there may be a connection.[18] There can be little doubt that Hughes is correct, particularly as it is a typically Welsh custom to designate (often with humour) someone's trade as a distinguishing element of his name: thus 'Owen Bellows' might be a blacksmith, and Walter Map could certainly be a cartographer. Nevertheless, there are perhaps further reasons for Map's appearance in *In Parenthesis*. Map, in his *De Nugis Curialium*, ii.20, says that he is of Welsh descent, and he therefore links with Jones. More importantly, the authorship of the thirteenth-century French *Vulgate* (or *Lancelot-Grail*) *Cycle* of Arthurian romance was traditionally, though erroneously, attributed to Walter Map; half of the *Cycle* is made up of the immensely influential *Lancelot*-section, and the significance of the Jones/Lancelot association will be discussed in detail during the course of this essay. Thus these personal links between Jones and characters in *In Parenthesis* become highly complex, and – to revert to the 'untidy Jones/Dai de la Cote Mal Taile' link discussed above – even dependent on a probably exaggerated self-portrait (given to us in the Preface to *In Parenthesis*) of Jones's soldierly inefficiency.[19]

David Jones's attitude to the Great War is complex. He is aware of (and powerfully describes) its horror. Many passages are unforgettable: the description of the first shell explosion placed emphatically as the last paragraph of part two; the night-sentry's fear of death in the cold and the darkness (in part four); the terror of the invisible enemy snipers in the wood (in part seven), where John Ball is wounded. Such passages emphasise the unparalleled ghastliness of trench-warfare. Yet simultaneously there is the discovery of intense friendship where 'Roland could find, and for a reasonable while, enjoy, his Oliver'[20] (see Fig. 9), and of powerful empathy with 'the enemy front-fighters who shared our pains against whom we found ourselves by misadventure.[21] War is seen as treachery,

---

[17] Preface to *In Parenthesis*, p. xv; *In Parenthesis*, p. 2.
[18] Hughes, *David Jones, the Man Who Was on the Field*, pp. 22–3. Tom Dilworth informs me that this was Jones's job at battalion HQ in November 1916, and from March to August 1917.
[19] Hague, *Dai Greatcoat*, p. 58.   [20] Preface, p. ix, lines 11–12.
[21] Dedicatory page, preceding page 1.

9 David Jones, drawing of two soldiers in the trenches (*c*. 1928).

where the British soldier is pitted against his German brother,[22] where the work of the Creator is displaced by the 'all unmaking' explosion of a shell,[23] where Christ is re-crucified.

Christ, the *Christus miles*,[24] betrayed and sacrificed, is immanent throughout the poem, as the soldiers relive the emotional experience of Jesus – just as in *The Anathemata* where Jones's climactic illustration is the painted lettering of a passage from the Old English *Dream of the Rood*, where the poet describes Christ as 'the young warrior' going to his death 'proud in the sight of many'.[25] John Ball, before the terrifying attack on the wood (p. 158), prays as at Gethsemane:

> you can't believe the Cup wont pass from
> or they wont make a better show
> in the Garden.

This is, of course, an imaginative association in the minds of the soldiers, and not a suggestion that they 'become' Christ. In a letter written to Hague in 1973, Jones clarifies the concept: '. . . in writing "In Paren." I had no intention whatever in presuming to compare the various maims, death-strokes . . . etc. of the two contending forces . . . with the Passion, Self-Oblation & subsequent Immolation & death of the cult-hero of our Xian tradition for that is a unique and profound Mystery of Faith'.[26] For this reason I suggest above that the pains of the soldiers

---

[22] I agree with Thomas Dilworth, *The Shape of Meaning in the Poetry of David Jones* (Toronto, 1988), p. 141, 'German Hansel and Welsh Gronwy, who died fighting each other, lie together like Malory's Balin and Balan "beneath their single monument" [see *In Parenthesis*, p. 163].' It is this powerful feeling of ethnic and spiritual brotherhood that lies behind Jones's selection of Malory's description of the accidental mutual slaying of the brothers Balin and Balan as representative of the essence of Malory's writing: see 'The Myth of Arthur' in *Epoch and Artist* (London, 1959), p. 246. Jones specifically draws attention to the story by selecting Balin's slaying of King Pellam (the 'dolorous stroke') for the title of part four of *In Parenthesis*. The tragedy of war in spite of German/English brotherhood is taken up again in *The Anathemata*, p. 115, '(O Balin O Balan! / how blood you both / the *Brudersee* . . .)'. See Blamires, *David Jones Artist and Writer*, chapter 8, 'The Arthurian World', (particularly p. 179), which has many interesting comments on Jones's use of Malory. So also has Jonathan Miles in *Backgrounds to David Jones: a Study in Sources and Drafts* (Cardiff, 1990), chapter 5. See further Xavier Baron, 'Medieval Arthurian Motifs in the Modernist Art and Poetry of David Jones', *Studies in Medievalism*, 4 (1992), 247–69. The Balin/ Balan story was particularly in Jones's mind through Eric Gill's reading aloud of the passage at Capel y Ffin; see René Hague, *David Jones* (Cardiff, 1975), p. 26.

[23] The explosion of the destructive shell (p. 24) is described as a perversion of the creative sexual act: 'Then the pent violence released a consummation of all burstings-out.'

[24] For discussion of the 'Christ the Soldier' motif in medieval literature, see J. A. W. Bennett, *Poetry of the Passion* (Oxford, 1982), chapter 3. Jones also saw in the Malory text this Pauline vision of the Christian knight (Ephesians, 6: 12–18): he describes how in Malory men do things 'to the uttermost', and notes that this probably connects with the conception of the Christian armed man, 'and having done all, to stand' ('The Myth of Arthur', p. 247). *Cf.* also Thomas Dilworth, *The Liturgical Parenthesis of David Jones* (Ipswich, 1979), p. 10.

[25] Illustration facing p. 240 of *The Anathemata*.   [26] Hague, *David Jones*, p. 48.

are seen by them as reliving those of Christ, and thus the reference to Gethsemane can be included.

The painting Jones makes for the frontispiece of *In Parenthesis* (see Fig. 10) is of an almost naked soldier, arms spread; the helmet-strap could perhaps be seen to be halo-like.[27] The camouflage twigs on the helmet look like thorns. In the original drawing for this picture there is a reddish wash over the left leg, which seeps into the ground.[28] Jones himself was wounded in the left leg and describes the incident in part seven.[29] All become simultaneously the sacrificers and the sacrificed in grim 'misadventure'.[30]

The aptness of the parallels in one of our greatest English epics, *Le Morte d'Arthur*, were obvious to Jones, and doubtless made him choose the word 'misadventure' for the climactic word of the dedicatory note of *In Parenthesis*. *Le Morte d'Arthur* is a story where integrity and deceit, trust and treachery, passionate love and passionate hate, courage and cowardice, constantly intertwine and make the lines between moral absolutes impossibly blurred and confusing. The leitmotif, sounded many times, is precisely that of *In Parenthesis*, the lament over misadventure and regretted enmity: 'Alas, said the king, that ever this unhappy war was begun';[31] 'Ah Sir Lancelot, said King Arthur . . . alas that ever I was against thee';[32] 'O Balan, my brother, thou hast slain me, and I thee, wherefore all the wide world shall speak of us both. Alas, said Balan, that ever I saw this day, that through mishap I might not know you.'[33]

Within *Le Morte d'Arthur*, the character who pre-eminently represents moral confusion is Lancelot. Not only the reader, but also the characters within the fiction, cannot decide whether he is hero or villain. Even Arthur himself,

---

[27] See also Hague, ed., *Dai Greatcoat*, p. 238. Christopher Neve in 'Journey of a Soul', *Country Life*, 13 August 1981, p. 571, remarks of the picture, 'That he is naked and putting on an army jacket may equally suggest that he is Christ putting on human flesh.'

[28] Nicolete Gray, *The Paintings of David Jones* (Hatfield and London, in association with the Tate Gallery, 1989), plate 44. Briefly discussed in Paul Hills, *David Jones*, Catalogue for the Tate Gallery Exhibition (London, Tate Gallery publication, 1981), p. 59.

[29] Hills, *David Jones*, catalogue, p. 50.   [30] See Bennett, *Poetry of the Passion*, pp. 198–9.

[31] Book twenty, chapter 22. All references are to the edition David Jones used, namely, Malory, *Le Morte d'Arthur* with an introduction by John Rhys (Everyman's Library, London and New York, 1906). For evidence that he used this text see 'The Myth of Arthur', p. 245.

[32] Book twenty-one, chapter 5.

[33] Book two, chapter 18. See also note 21, above. See his letter written in 1929 about reading *From Ritual to Romance*, 'it's very interesting to me at the moment, with this Arthur business in my head'. Hague remarks that this 'could refer in some general way to the drawing upon Malory for some of the imagery of *In Parenthesis*', *Dai Greatcoat*, p. 46. I think, however, that the thematic importance of *Le Morte d'Arthur* to *In Parenthesis* was more fundamental than this suggests. For the recurrence of 'adventure' in Malory, see for example Jill Mann, 'Knightly combat in "Le Morte d'Arthur"', *New Pelican Guide to English Literature*, edited by Boris Ford, vol. 1 (London, 1982), pp. 332–5.

10 David Jones, frontispiece to *In Parenthesis* (1937).

wronged by Lancelot's affair with his queen, is confused and prefers to turn a blind eye. When the king is compelled to sanction Lancelot's exposure, it is only because the degenerate Agravaine and Mordred force him to do so, against the wishes of the other knights. Finally, Mordred kills Arthur, his uncle–father, before Lancelot can return from exile to save his king.

It is evidently because of his embodiment of moral dilemma that Jones empathises with Lancelot.[34] When presented in schematic form in Table 3 the distribution of references to Malory in *In Parenthesis* (*IP*) makes clear not just the frequency of allusion to *Le Morte d' Arthur* (*MA*), but also an interesting pattern. It will be seen that, even when the Malorian references are not specifically to Lancelot, they are almost always to characters whose lives are closely involved with his.

The first Malorian reference (p. 31) takes us to the movement of the platoons up to the front line. John Ball is the 'he' of the passage:

> Past the *little gate*.
> Mr Jenkins[35] watched them file through, himself following,
>   like western-hill shepherd.
> Past the *little gate*,
> into the field of *upturned defences*,
> into the *burial-yard* –
> the *grinning and the gnashing* and the *sore dreading* –
>   *nor saw he any light* in that place [my italics].

The Malory passage to which this refers is book six, chapter 15, Lancelot's visit to the Chapel Perilous. Lancelot tied his horse to 'a little gate' and as he passed through the churchyard he saw many shields which knights had previously carried 'turned up so down', 'and many of the shields he had seen knights bear beforehand'. Thirty knights, who were giant-like in build, barred his way and 'grinned and gnashed' at him, so that Lancelot 'dread him sore'. I have indicated in italics in the *In Parenthesis* passage above the phrases that occur identically, or very similarly, in Malory. There are two main changes. First, the symbolic record of the death of previous knights in the quest of the Chapel Perilous (the upside-down shields) is replaced by the havoc the defences have suffered under bombardment. The defences are, of course, 'shields'.[36] But the reference to the subtext is more specifically retained in the semantic range of 'field'. Its primary meaning in the *In Parenthesis* context is 'field of battle'; but Lancelot's encounter

---

[34] That Jones was seeing parallels with Lancelot when writing to Harman Grisewood even seven years later (23 June 1939) about his personal emotional anxieties may be inferred from: 'I also think all the time about Prudence but don't get any clearer how to face up to it. O dear, this old romantic love, the only type I understand, does let you down. I do see why Lancelot ran "wood mad" in the trackless forest for four years so that no man might know him is easily understandable.' Hague, *Dai Greatcoat*, p. 93. See also p. 248, below.

[35] Mr Jenkins is the platoon commander.

[36] *Cf.* the corrugated iron used as a shield in the picture discussed in note 48, below.

Table 3

IP Part	DJ's notes to *IP* in which he draws attention to *MA* passages referred to in his text	Subject matter and location in *Le Morte d'Arthur*
1		
2		
3	Note 10	Lancelot at the Chapel Perilous: bk VI, ch. xv (cf. part 7, note 33, below).
4	Title and note 1	Balin fights with King Pellam: bk II, ch. xv.
	Note 2	Lancelot: bk XIII, ch. XIX.
	Note 12	Lancelot by a trick of enchantment lies with Elaine and is rebuked by Guinevere: bk XI, ch. viii [for misprint 'chapter iii' in *IP*].
	Note 22	Dai de la Cote Male Taile: bk IX, ch. i.
	Additional note F	the adder: bk XXI, ch. iv. A knight lifts his sword to slay the adder and, unintentionally, starts the battle between Arthur and Mordred, about which Arthur laments (ch. v), 'Ah Sir Lancelot', said King Arthur, 'this day have I sore missed thee; alas that ever I was against thee.'
	Additional note K	Agravaine and Mordred betray Lancelot: bk XX, chs. i–iv (*cf.* part 6, note 9, below).
5		
6	Heading	Bk I, ch. i: Uther Pendragon.
	Note 2	(a) Bk XXI, ch. i [for misprint 'ch. ii' in *IP*]: Mordred's attempt to capture and marry Guinevere who is sheltering in the Tower of London.
		(b) Lancelot fights with Gawain: bk XX, ch. xii.
	Note 4	Tristram: bk X, ch. xxix. But the reference is primarily local to Jones's regiment, 'So on the morn Elias the captain came.'
	Note 9	Agravaine and Mordred attempt to stir up the other knights of the Round Table to disclose the Lancelot and Guinevere affair to Arthur. Gawain attempts to dissaude them, but they persist. Gawain and Gareth predict, 'now is this realm wholly mischieved, and the noble fellowship of the Round Table shall be disparply': bk XX, ch. i (*cf.* part 4, additional note K, above).
7	Note 14	(a) story of Galahad about the tree: bk XVII, ch. v.
		(b) Dolorous stroke; Longinus: bk II, ch. xv.
	Note 33	Lancelot at the Chapel Perilous (*cf.* part 3, note 10, above): bk VI, ch. xv [for misprint 'bk IV' in *IP*].
	Note 36	Tristram: bk X, ch. xxix (*cf.* part 6, note 4, above).
	Note 37	Mordred attacks Tower of London in his attempt to capture Guinevere: bk XXI, ch. i (*cf.* part 6, note 2(a), above).

with the disgraced relics of those who had failed in the quest is retained because 'field' contains simultaneously the heraldic sense of the surface of the shield or escutcheon on which the charge (design) is displayed. Second, for *Le Morte d'Arthur*'s 'churchyard', *In Parenthesis* has the far more grim 'burial-yard'.

Analysis of particular words and phrases should not distract our attention from their more general context. In the chapter on the Chapel Perilous, Lancelot is presented with two temptations: the first is the fearsome sight of the thirty knights, but they do not deter him and they initially scatter. Lancelot then finds in the Chapel a dead knight and takes a piece of the silk in which the corpse is wrapped, and also the sword lying next to it, and 'it fared under him as the earth had quaked'. The knights reassemble and, 'with a grimly voice', threaten him with death if he keeps the sword. Lancelot refuses to part with it, and the knights retreat. The second temptation is in the Chapel yard: a beautiful woman commands him to relinquish the sword. He refuses, and she tells him that, had he done so, he would never have seen Guinevere again. Next she demands a single kiss, and when again refused she tells him that it would have brought about his death. She had, she says, built the Chapel for Gawain and Lancelot. When Gawain had come, he had slain the knight, Sir Gilbert the Bastard, and cut off his left hand. Lancelot leaves the Chapel, and within two weeks the lady (Hellawes the sorceress) dies of unrequited love. Lancelot finds a knight dying of his wounds, touches him with the sword and the cloth, and his life is fully restored.

The notes to *In Parenthesis* make reference to Malory at part three (note 10). But the text may be more throughly permeated with *Le Morte d'Arthur* than would appear from the references in the notes. The passage quoted above is on p. 31. On p. 34, the soldiers fear that Mr Jenkins, who is leading them, may have lost his way:

'. . . do we trapse dementedly round phantom mulberry bush . . . can the young bastard know his bearings. Keep well to the left – take care with these messages.'

First, the mulberry-bush reference emphasises their fear of wandering, like lost children, in circles. But then come 'bastard', 'bearings', 'left'. Jenkins, the officer beloved of his men, will eventually die – the incident is tenderly told in part seven (p. 166). The idea of the mutilated knight, the Bastard Gilbert, is kept alive when we find Jenkins described as a 'young bastard', followed by 'bearings' and 'left'; we see yet again the familiar pattern in Jones's wordplay: bearings = (1) compass directions, and (2) armorial bearings on the escutcheon. A bastard would have on his escutcheon a bar-*sinister*, and the subtext is kept resonant in our minds by, 'Keep well to the *left*'; and finally we are directed to make these connections, 'take care with these messages'.

Almost at the end of *In Parenthesis* (p. 180), and without any further references in the notes, we have circled back to the Chapel Perilous:

When they put up a flare, he saw many men's accoutrements medleyed and strewn *up so down* and service-jackets bearing below the shoulder-numerals the peculiar signs of their battalions.

> *And many of these shields he had seen knights bear beforehand.*
> And the severed head of '72 Morgan,
> its visage *grins* like the Cheshire cat
> and full *grimly*.
> *It fared under him as the earth had quaked.* [My italics]

The idea of the curative power of a bloodied weapon, which we have seen in the Chapel Perilous story, emanates from the legend of the blind warrior Longinus, who, commanded by the Roman soldiers, unwittingly pierces with his spear the side of Christ on the cross. The blood runs down the spear and restores his vision.[37] To be touched with a holy relic has the same curative power. This theme of the warrior unwittingly killing the Soldier Christ and deriving through his spilt blood the power to restore, figures again in Jones's second main reference to *Le Morte d'Arthur* in the title ('King Pellam's Launde') to part four, and he is specifically named in Dai's Boast (p. 83), where Dai admits to complicity in Longinus' wounding of the body of Christ, and connects this deed with that of the soldiers at the cross:

> 'I served Longinus that Dux bat-blind and bent;
> the Dandy Xth are my regiment;
> who diced
> Crown and Mud-hook
> under the Tree,
> whose Five Sufficient Blossoms
> yield for us.'

The link is that each deed (contributing to the Five Wounds: hands, feet and side) was a *felix culpa*, resulting in the vision-restoring blood from the spear of Longinus and the redeeming death of Christ. Before discussing the reference to King Pellam's Launde, however, it is of interest to see the subtle interweavings of the Malory and Jones texts: Table 3 gives the appearance that every now and then Jones finds a Malory reference apt. That is misleading. *Le Morte d'Arthur* is so consistently running in his mind that the threads of the one text are constantly making connections in the other. Furthermore, if the author is present as a character (Lancelot) in the Malorian text as well as, simultaneously, the Private Ball of the main text, the allusion to *Le Morte d'Arthur* must be constantly alive.

[37] The story comes from the apocryphal *Gospel of Nicodemus*, and is popularised in the Middle Ages in the *Legenda Aurea*. David Jones probably knew the story from several sources; one of the most dramatic accounts occurs in his favourite medieval poem *Piers Plowman* (Passus XVIII). For Jones's enthusiasm for the poem see Colin Wilcockson, 'Notes on Some Letters of David Jones', pp. 67–87, particularly pp. 71–2.

To take a complex example: the last two pages of part three (pp. 54–5) describe 'the rat of no-man's land' carrying portions of the bodies of the dead through the weeds:

You can hear his carrying-parties rustle our corruptions through the night-weeds – contest the choicest morsels in his tiny conduits, bead-eyed feast on us; by a rule of his nature, at night-feast on the broken of us.[38]

The Christ–soldier association I mention above is inherent in the eucharistic connotation 'this is my body which is broken for you'.[39] There is black comedy in the rat's 'carrying-parties'. In military terms, 'carrying-parties' are the stretcher-bearers taking the wounded to safety on their litters (cf. In Parenthesis, p. 175). For the rat, however, the broken body will simply be consumed; the words are to us a surprising evocation of the eucharistic feast. A few lines later, the last lines of this part, we find Ball admonished by the relief-sentry: 'All quiet china? – bugger all to report? – kipping mate? – christ, mate – you'll 'ave 'em all over.' The mind moves with the 'kipping/christ' association to Gethsemane: 'What, could ye not watch with me one hour?' It is just before Christ's betrayal to the soldiers and his execution (Matthew, 26: 40). At the same time, underlying all this is Le Morte d'Arthur, book thirteen, chapter 18, line 1: 'And so he [Lancelot] fell on sleep; and half waking and sleeping he saw come by him two palfreys all fair and white, the which bare a litter, therein lay a sick knight.' The knight has a vision of the Grail, kisses the cup and is healed. He sees Lancelot who slept in a trance when the Grail appeared; his squire tells him that doubtless the knight 'dwelleth in some deadly sin whereof he was never confessed' – Lancelot's illicit affair with Guinevere. He takes away Lancelot's sword, helmet and horse.

The literal danger of Ball's falling asleep is, as the relief sentry had warned, that the section would be overrun. Perhaps in Jones's mind (though not specifically in the text) is that he would have been instantly disarmed. There is a more complex strand, however, that binds all these incidents. The reason that Lancelot arrives at the ruined chapel where the grail was kept is that he has been attacked by a disguised knight and gives chase. We know the knight is Galahad. Only later, however, is it revealed to Lancelot that he is the father of Galahad.

---

[38] The verbal compounds are probably suggested by the style of Old English epic poetry; from those works, too, are probably derived the ravenous scavengers over the corpses of warriors – the 'beasts of battle' topos, e.g. 'earn æses georn' (the eagle eager for carrion) of The Battle of Maldon, line 107. The rather grander eagle, wolf and raven of these old epics are, in the squalor of the trenches, reduced to the rat. For discussion of the Old English trope see Francis P. Magoun Jr, 'The Theme of the Beasts of Battle in Anglo-Saxon Poetry', Neophilologische Mitteilungen, 56 (1955), 81–90.

[39] Paul Fussell suggests that the link is with Eliot's 'I think we are in rat's alley, / Where the dead men lost their bones' in The Waste Land. That work is constantly in Jones's mind, and the allusion is probably there. Paul Fussell, The Great War and Modern Memory (New York and London, 1975), p. 149.

When we turn over the page of *In Parenthesis* to find the heading 'King Pellam's Launde', the same oblique connection is there: Balin has killed King Pellam's brother, and will eventually be killed by his own brother. He smites Pellam with a spear (Longinus' spear, it is later revealed) and only much later is Pellam cured by Galahad with the blood of Christ. Because Balin had given the 'dolorous stroke' three kingdoms are cursed, as is Balin who will eventually die in mutual fratricide with Balan. Jones's surrogate, Ball, is racked with this horror. The German front-line fighters, to whom Jones dedicates the poem, are involved with the slaughter of their British kinsmen (just as he is involved with the slaughter of German kinsmen) against whom they are pitted 'by mischance'. Only the healing blood of Christ can redeem the consanguineous soldiers in their murderous actions.

The first line of part four brings us back to the Lancelot story: 'So thus he sorrowed till it was day, and heard the fowls sing: then somewhat he was comforted.' In Malory the sentence is framed thus: 'I see and understand that mine old sin hindreth me and shameth me, so that I had no power to stir nor speak when the holy blood appeared before me . . . But when Launcelot missed his horse and his harness then he wist well God was displeased with him.'[40] The guilt of the first statement is transmuted in Ball's mind to the general guilt of betrayal that permeates the war. If I am right in supposing that the first deed of the overrunning troops would have been to disarm the sleeping sentry, the second statement about the 'displeasure' attending the loss of one's weapons becomes grimly comic, and such an idea may well have been in Jones's mind because of a personal incident.[41]

The climax of *In Parenthesis* is the attack on the wood, held by the enemy and the immediate objective of their campaign. The wood is first described on pp. 65ff. and the notes make specific reference to the Malorian origin of the phrase 'or run want-wit in a shirt for the queen's unreason' on p. 66. But I suggest that the whole grove description is more generally suffused with reference to *Le Morte d'Arthur* and that through the suffusion Jones makes his comment on the incident:

---

[40] Jones may have been prompted to think of this passage of partial vision of the Grail by the actual episode of his first sight of a Roman Catholic Mass through the crack in the wall of a farmyard outbuilding on the Somme in 1916. See his letter to Hague in *Dai Greatcoat*, pp. 248–50.

[41] When stationed in Ireland, immediately prior to his demobilisation, he left his rifle unattended and it was stolen. A court martial, with dire consequences, would have followed. Jones told no one. A few days later, however, he returned to an army camp in England to receive his 'demob' papers. The camp was in chaos, with many soldiers being instructed to dump their rifles in a heap as soon as their paper-work was complete. Jones 'borrowed' one of the rifles, and passed it off as his own. For months afterwards, he feared that the original weapon would be recovered with its individual number stamped on it, showing it to be his. I have this anecdote from Stanley Honeyman to whom Jones told the story with much amusement.

To groves always men come both to their joys and their undoing. Come lightfoot in heart's ease and school-free; walk on a leafy holiday with kindred and kind . . . Or come in gathering nuts and may.

Although the actual time of the episode is 'Saturnalia, when men properly are in winter quarters' (p. 65), the men's thoughts stray to summer, the 'leafy holiday'. The confusion between frosty winter and leafy summer is cunningly continued in 'Here we come gathering nuts and may', with its (here unstated) continuation, 'On a cold and frosty morning'. The leafy season and may/May fuse, and as the poem is so redolent of the Arthur and Guinevere story, could well connect in Jones's mind with Guinevere's fatal May Day rituals. She had commanded her knights to prepare themselves to ride 'on Maying' bedecked with flowers and carrying no weapons. She falls easy prey to Meligraunce, who had hitherto been unwilling to attack her because of his fear of Lancelot. I am the more inclined to believe this link because Jones follows 'nuts and may' immediately by another reference to Guinevere where Lancelot is suspected of willingly sleeping with Elaine, whereas in fact he was tricked into the situation. The queen refuses to believe him and he runs mad in his shirt only, tearing himself on bushes and briars. This reference is specifically noted by Jones to gloss the quotation 'or run want-wit for the queen's unreason'. The contrast between May with its burgeoning of 'every lusty heart', and the jarring treason and mishap occur both here, and in the episode of Lancelot's betrayal by Agravain and Mordred, and in the passage that immediately follows on p. 69 where the style becomes strongly Malorian.[42] The subject is the reaction of the soldiers to the front-line trench in which they find themselves and their thoughts turn to loved ones at home:

Their loves whose burgeoning is finery trickt-out, who go queenly in soiled velveteen, piled puce with the lights' glancing.

The line is not easy to interpret. It is, we are told, day-break and the light is uncertain. Perhaps the khaki uniforms remind the soldiers of the velvet of their loved one's dresses. It would be in keeping with Jones's fascination with etymology to select 'puce' as the colour, since its etymological meaning is 'flea-coloured' and there is a grimly humorous contrast between the velvet of ladies' dresses and the verminous state of the soldiers.[43] This would explain 'soiled'.

[42] Jones makes specific reference to Malory's description of the betrayal of Lancelot by Agravaine and Mordred in part four, additional note K, and in part six, note 9: In May when every lusty heart flourisheth and burgeoneth . . . So in this season, as in the month of May, it befell a great anger and unhap that stinted not till the flower of chivalry of all the world was destroyed and slain.' (*Le Morte d'Arthur*, book twenty, chapter 1.)

[43] His mind constantly reverberated to the history implicit in etymology. See for example, Thomas Dilworth, ed., *Inner Necessities: the Letters of David Jones to Desmond Chute* (Toronto, 1984), p. 63; Wilcockson, 'Notes on Some Letters of David Jones', pp. 76–8, etc.

Perhaps, too, the May Day revels of Guinevere are ironically immanent in 'queenly': 'So as the queen had Mayed and all her knights, all were bedashed with herbs, mosses and flowers, in the best manner and freshest. Right so came out of a wood Sir Meligrance with eight score men well harnessed, as they should fight in a battle of arrest.' The lyrical passage in *In Parenthesis* is immediately brought back to the present, where Ball is observing through a periscope: 'From where John Ball sat and did his brother-keeping, mirror-gazing, in the corner of the fire-bay, he could easily observe the dispositions of his companions.' Ball's watching the German front-line soldiers recalls fratricide in Cain's words, 'Am I my brother's keeper?' – the Cain and Abel story is picked up again as the troops advance towards the Germans in part seven (pp. 162–3). All these connections vanish into the harshness of here and now, '. . . the nature of the place the fully-come day had now exposed, and robbed of mystery.'

The theme of misadventure and treachery continues in the passage called 'Dai's boast' (pp. 79–84), which imitates the challenging boasts of the poets who attended battles (Taleisin, Widsith etc.). Dai 'boasts' he was 'the adder in the little bush'. The reference is to the adder that came out of 'a little heath bush and it stung a knight [in Arthur's army] on the foot'. The knight drew his sword, Mordred's men saw the apparently aggressive action, and the last, fatal battle is joined. The connection is by now the familiar one – Caxton's chapter heading underscores it: 'How by misadventure of an adder the battle began, where Mordred was slain, and Arthur hurt to the death.' Dai, the poet who will record these things like his bardic predecessors, himself wounded in the leg, sees himself as an instrument in a battle of misadventure and the slaying of kinsmen. The Agravaine reference in a later passage of Dai's boast is to his plot to overthrow Lancelot and disgrace Guinevere, already discussed; Dai's plea ('confuse his tongue') is that Agravaine will not be heard.

Part five, as the platoon moves up the line, contains no references to *Le Morte d'Arthur*, but these are picked up again in part six. First in the heading 'Pavilions & Captains of Hundreds', for which Jones supplies no specific reference, other than that it is from Malory. Perhaps it is generalised, though book 10, chapter 58, has similar phraseology and would aptly describe the fear of the opposing armies before the battle in the wood: 'And then they were ware of four hundred tents and pavilions, and marvellous great ordinance'. In this passage Tristram recalls the prowess of Lancelot.

A glance at Jones's references to *Le Morte d'Arthur* in Table 3 will show how the remaining quotations in *In Parenthesis* for the most part return circularly: Mordred and Agravaine's plot against Lancelot; the 'Dolorous Stroke' and the story of Longinus; Lancelot at the Chapel Perilous. Among those who fall prey to the 'appetite' of 'sister death' (in part seven, pp. 162–3) are 'the sweet brothers

Balin and Balan'. I have discussed their constant presence in Jones's mind (see note 22, above). No one has satisfactorily explained why Jones adopts the name of the fourteenth-century revolutionary preacher Ball as his *alter ego* in *In Parenthesis*: it may be that that name, being the common element in the names of the brother–destroyers, *Bal*in and *Bal*an, suggested the pseudonym, and emphasised his simultaneous empathy with both the German and the British front-line soldier. The fullest of these final Malory quotations in *In Parenthesis* is, however, from the Chapel Perilous scene. It is significant that the first and last substantial quotations from *Le Morte d'Arthur* are from this passage. From the Chapel Lancelot takes a cloth drenched with the blood of Sir Gilbert – blood with which Lancelot miraculously cures the dying Sir Meliot, making him 'an wholer man'. The motif of the sacrifice of the warrior Christ is pre-eminently emphasised.

Perhaps I may be allowed some biographical speculation here. Jones had begun *In Parenthesis* in 1927–8, and it was published in 1937. The wonderful flowering in the media both of literature and of art in the mid- to late twenties gave place to the self-doubts and intolerable tensions that led to his nervous breakdown of 1932. I hope I have shown the powerful subtextual association in *In Parenthesis* with Lancelot, the man whose celestial vision is glimpsed at but flawed. The texture of Lancelot's life is woven of tense threads of glory, yet of consciousness of the horror of war, of guilt over the death of kinsmen and of conflict between clandestine love and friendship. Perhaps some of these tensions could be seen to be reflective of Jones's own complex emotional difficulties at this period; among other pressures may have been his grief over the British–German conflicts,[44] and possibly the fact that his engagement to Petra Gill in 1924, at the Eric Gill community in Ditchling, was broken off in 1927 when she decided instead to marry another member of the community.[45] Paul Fussell (while admiring the 'humanity that seizes the reader' of *In Parenthesis*) objects.

The poem is a deeply conservative work which uses the past not, as it often pretends to do, to shame the present, but really to ennoble it. The effect of the poem, for all its horrors, is to rationalize and even to validate the war by implying that it somehow recovers many of the motifs and values of medieval chivalric romance . . . The trouble is that the meddling intellect, taking the form this time of a sentimental Victorian literary Arthurianism after Tennyson and Morris, has romanticized the war.[46]

---

[44] For a contrasting view see Hague, *Dai Greatcoat*, pp. 58–9. Hague dismisses as 'completely untrue' any suggestion that the breakdown was due to Jones's war experiences; in his opinion the causes were 'the difficulties he met in his work, and the accompanying at times paralysing mental and spiritual stress'.

[45] See Fiona MacCarthy, *Eric Gill* (London, 1989), pp. 203 and 226.

[46] Fussell, *The Great War and Modern Memory*, p. 147.

Agreed, Jones, in the Preface to *In Parenthesis*, sees a change from the earlier to the second half of the Great War, when the increasing efficiency of chemical weaponry, obliterating hundreds of soldiers at a time, left little space for individual heroism or intimate comradeship. But Jones's 'Arthurianism' was not the sanitised vision of war of Tennyson, who omits such passages as Sir Lucan's presence at Arthur's death, evidently because in Malory he had died 'foaming at the mouth, and part of his guts lay at his feet'. When Jones makes the association with *Le Morte d'Arthur* it is not only with its brutality alongside its heroism, but also with its complexities of love and hatred and, supremely, its consciousness of remorse, even of despair. The Arthurian references are not superficial romanticising; rather, they impregnate the work with that tradition of moral dilemma which is to be found in many of the greatest epics.

An apt parallel can, I think, be seen in Eliot's *The Waste Land*, a poem deeply influential on Jones. The protagonist meets a friend, who presumably fought in the 1914–18 war, but addresses him as if he had fought in the Punic War, and there is a hint at the paradoxical kinship of ordinariness and heroism, and, simultaneously, as Cleanth Brooks remarks on this passage, that 'all wars are one war; all experience, one experience'. Furthermore, allusion to the buried god of old fertility rites chimes in exactly with the Sacrifice theme which is at the heart of *In Parenthesis*:

> There I saw one I knew, and stopped him, crying: 'Stetson!
> You who were with me in the ships at Mylae!
> That corpse you planted last year in your garden,
> Has it begun to sprout?'

Stetson is to the protagonist his *alter ego*, 'mon semblable, – mon frère!'[47] In *In Parenthesis* the subtextual Lancelot fuses with Ball, who fuses with Jones. Thus on the autobiographical level Jones becomes 'the soldier' of all times and of all campaigns through 'experiential, actual, contactual association'. Through the insistent reference to Lancelot, Jones spells out the personal anguish which he had already signalled when he dedicated the poem both to the British soldiers and to the German front-line soldiers 'who shared our pains against whom we found ourselves by misadventure'. Unwilling to present himself *in propria persona*, because that would create a personal lament, not a universal elegy, it is, nevertheless, his voice that calls out 'over the *Brudersee*': 'O Balan, my brother,

---

[47] See Cleanth Brooks, 'The Waste Land: An Analysis', *Southern Review*, 3 (Summer, 1937), 106–36; reprinted in Brooks, *Modern Poetry and Tradition* (Chapel Hill, N.C., 1939), pp. 136–72; reprinted in C. B. Cox and Arnold P. Hinchliffe, ed., *The Waste Land*, Casebook Series (London, 1986), pp. 128–61 (see particularly p. 136). In Brooks 'The "Waste Land": A Prophetic Document', *Yale Review*, 78, 2 (Winter, 1989), he mentions Eliot's approval of this interpretation.

thou hast slain me, and I thee, wherefore all the wide world shall speak of us both.'[48]

[48] Some years later (1941), shortly after the beginning of the Second World War, Jones made two paintings which indicated his grief that Britain and Germany were again engaged in combat. One is entitled *Sisters Two*, or *Britannia and Germania Embracing*. The two sisters are helmeted and hold broken spears. Behind them are scenes of destruction. Reproduced in Gray, *The Paintings of David Jones*, plate 51. The other picture, *Aphrodite in Aulis* (reproduced in Gray, plate 49), is far more complex. Aphrodite is shackled on a column engraved with the Paschal Lamb. Two semi-naked soldiers stand in admiration: the soldier on the left wears a British helmet and holds a sheet of corrugated iron as a shield. He carries, at the slope-arms position, a long spear (Longinus' spear). The soldier on the right wears a German helmet. Both these pictures are discussed in Hills, *David Jones*, pp. 59–60, 108, 109; and in Blamires, *David Jones, Artist and Writer*, pp. 67–8. Behind, a medieval knight carries his helmet; the blazon on his shield is the kai-rho (the Shield of Faith?). Horses to the left run wild. They appear to me to be very like the horses in the picture *Vexilla Regis*, painted in 1947, and reproduced in Gray, *The Paintings of David Jones*, plate 49; of the latter, Jones remarks: 'This idea, probably in turn, comes from something in Malory's *Morte D'Arthur* when right at the end, after the death of Guenevere and the break-up of the Round Table, Lancelot and other knights let their horses free to roam where they will – for the riders have now finished with the tournaments, display etc. and gone off to be hermits and the like.' *Dai Greatcoat*, p. 150. See also Baron, 'Medieval Arthurian Motifs in the Modernist Art and Poetry of David Jones', pp. 254–5, and the illustration reproduced in that article of a picture by Jones for a proposed edition of Malory.

Select bibliography of the work of Ian Jack

The only reviews included are front-page and middle-page pieces in the *Times Literary Supplement*. Unless otherwise indicated, they were anonymous.

1949

'The Case of John Webster.' *Scrutiny*, 16, 38–43.

'Laurel and Rue.' *TLS*, 12 August, 520. (Review of *Tennyson Sixty Years After*, by Paul F. Baum, sub-editor's title.)

1950

'The "Choice of Life" in Johnson and Matthew Prior.' *The Journal of English and Germanic Philology*, 49, 4 (October), 523–30. (The influence of *Solomon* on *Rasselas* and *The Vanity of Human Wishes*.)

1951

'Pope and "The Weighty Bullion of Dr Donne's Satires".' *PMLA*, 46 (December), 1009–22.

'John Dryden, Poet.' *TLS*, 16 February, 93–5. (Review of *The Poetical Works of Dryden. A New Edition Revised and Enlarged*, by George R. Noyes.)

'Poet and Preacher.' *TLS*, 20 July, 452. (Review of *The Monarch of Wit: An Analytical and Comparative Study of the Poetry of John Donne*, by J. B. Leishman.)

1952

Augustan Satire: Intention and Idiom in English Poetry 1660–1750. Oxford: at the Clarendon Press. Pp. x, 1–163. Issued in Oxford Paperbacks, 1966.

'Salute to a Poet.' *TLS*, 28 November, 776. (Review of *Collected Poems 1934–1952*, by Dylan Thomas.)

1953

'Fielding the Novelist.' *TLS*, 23 January, 56. (Review of *Henry Fielding His Life, Works, and Times*, by F. Homes Dudden.)

'The man without Secrets.' *TLS*, 11 December, 800. (Review of *The Letters of Sydney Smith*, edited by Nowell S. Smith.)

1954

Pope. Writers and their Work: no. 48. Published for the British Council and the National Book League (London). Pp. 36.

'Early Victorian Novels.' *TLS*, 23 July, 472. (Review of *Novels of the Eighteen-Forties*, by Kathleen Tillotson.)

1955

'Milton without the Epic.' *TLS*, 2 September, 501–2. (Review of *The Poetical Works of John Milton*, volume 11, edited by Helen Darbishire.)

1956

'Critical Opinions'. *TLS*, 10 February, 77–8. (Review of *A History of Modern Criticism: 1750–1950*, by René Wellek: volume 1, *The Later Eighteenth Century*, volume 11, *The Romantic Age*.)

'Shelley the Poet of Liberty'. *TLS*, 23 November, 696. (Review of *Shelley at Work: A Critical Inquiry*, by Neville Rogers.)

1957

'De Quincey Revises his *Confessions*'. *PMLA*, 72 (March), 122–46.

1958

Sir Walter Scott. Writers and their Work: no. 103. Published for the British Council and the National Book League (London). Pp. 40.

1959

'"The Realm of Flora" in Keats and Poussin.' *TLS*, 10 April, 212, with illustration on 201. (A signed article as a prelude to *Keats and the Mirror of Art*, 1967.)

1960

'"The True Raillery".' *Cairo Studies in English*, edited by Magdi Wahba (Cairo), pp. 9–23.

1961

'The Epistolary Element in Jane Austen'. *English Studies Today, Second Series. Lectures and Papers read at the Fourth Conference of the International Association of University Professors of English held at Lausanne and Berne August, 1959*, edited by G. A. Bonnard (Berne, 1961), pp. 173–86.

1963

English Literature 1815–1832 (The Oxford History of English Literature, volume x). Oxford: at the Clarendon Press. Pp. x, 643. Reprinted in 1990 as *English Literature 1815–1832: Scott, Byron, and Keats*, and renumbered as volume xii.

1965

'Two Biographers: Lockhart and Boswell'. *Johnson, Boswell and their Circle. Essays presented to Lawrence Fitzroy Powell in Honour of his Eighty-Fourth Birthday*, Oxford: at the Clarendon Press, pp. 268–85.
'Gray's *Elegy* Reconsidered'. *From Sensibility to Romanticism: Essays Presented to Frederick A. Pottle*, edited by Frederick W. Hilles and Harold Bloom (New York) pp. 139–69.

1966

'Poems of John Clare's Sanity'. *Some British Romantics. A Collection of Essays*, edited by James V. Logan, John E. Jordan, and Northrop Frye (Ohio University Press), pp. 191–232.

1967

Keats and the Mirror of Art, Oxford at the Clarendon Press. Pp. xxiii, 309.
'Edwin Muir'. *Filologia Moderna*, 25–6, October 1966–January 1967 (Madrid) 101–14.

1968

Laurence Sterne. *A Sentimental Journey Through France and Italy. By Mr Yorick To which are added The Journal to Eliza and A Political Romance*. Edited with Introductions. Oxford English Novels. Pp. xxvi, 241. Reprinted as a World's Classics paperback, 1984.
Robert Browning. Warton Lecture on English Poetry. British Academy, 1967. Proceedings of the British Academy, volume liii, pp. 219–41.

1969–92

General Editor of The Clarendon Edition of the Novels of the Brontës, published at The Clarendon Press, Oxford, as follows:

Charlotte Brontë, *Jane Eyre*, edited by Jane Jack and Margaret Smith, 1969.

Emily Brontë, *Wuthering Heights*, edited by Hilda Marsden and Ian Jack, 1976.

Charlotte Brontë, *Shirley*, edited by Herbert Rosengarten and Margaret Smith, 1979.

Charlotte Brontë, *Villette*, edited by Herbert Rosengarten and Margaret Smith, 1984.

Charlotte Brontë, *The Professor*, edited by Margaret Smith and Herbert Rosengarten , 1987.

Anne Brontë, *Agnes Grey*, edited by Hilda Marsden and Robert Inglesfield, 1988.

Anne Brontë, *The Tenant of Wildfell Hall*, edited by Herbert Rosengarten, 1992.

From 1980 onwards the successive volumes have formed the basis of editions in the World's Classics series, with new critical introductions but with abbreviated notes and apparatus.

1970

Browning, *Poetical Works, 1833–1864*. Oxford University Press; 1975, 1980. Reprinted as a World's Classics paperback, 1975.

'Physiognomy, Phrenology and Characterisation in the Novels of Charlotte Brontë'. *Brontë Society Transactions* (Keighley).

1971

'Laurence Sterne'. *Dryden to Johnson*, edited by Roger Lonsdale (*Sphere History of Literature in the English Language*, volume IV), pp. 302–19.

'The Clarendon *Jane Eyre*: A Rejoinder'. By I. J. and Margaret Smith. *Nineteenth-Century Fiction*, 26, 3 (University of California Press, December), 370–6. (A reply to a review by Bruce Harkness in the number for December 1970.)

1973

Browning's Major Poetry. Oxford: at the Clarendon Press. Pp. xiv, 308.

1974

'Gray in his Letters'. *Fearful Joy. Papers from the Thomas Gray Bicentenary Conference at Carleton University*, edited by James Downey and Ben Jones (McGill–Queen's University Press, Montreal), pp. 20–36.

1976

Emily Brontë, *Wuthering Heights*, edited by Hilda Marsden and Ian Jack (The Clarendon Edition of the Novels of the Brontës). Pp. xl, 513. (See above, 1969–92. See too 1981.)

1978

'"A Notion of the Troubadour's Intent": Some Reflections on the Words in *Sordello*'. *Browning Institute Studies*, volume v, edited by William S. Peterson (The Browning Institute and City University of New York), pp. 63–85.

'The Elegy as Exorcism: Pope's "Verses to the Memory of an Unfortunate Lady"'. *Augustan Worlds (Essays in Honour of A. R. Humphreys)*, edited by J. C. Hilson, M. M. B. Jones and J. R. Watson (Leicester University Press), pp. 69–83.

'Grammar and Graciousness'. *TLS*, 3 November, 25–6. Signed review of *The Brownings' Correspondence: A Checklist*, compiled by Philip Kelley and Ronald Hudson (The Browning Institute and the Wedgestone Press). (Sub-editor's title.)

1979

'Pope and his Audience: from the *Pastorals* to *The Dunciad Variorum*'. *Studies in the Eighteenth Century IV. Papers presented at the Fourth David Nichol Smith Memorial Seminar*, Canberra 1976. Edited by R. F. Brissenden and J. C. Eade (Australian National University Press, Canberra), pp. 1–30.

The Nature of Satire. A Lecture Delivered at the Fiftieth General Meeting of the English Literary Society of Japan on 27 May 1979. (Tokyo), pp. 5–30.

1980

'Tess of the D'Urbervilles'. *Tess of the D'Urbervilles with Essays in Criticism. Annotated with Critical Introduction*, by Byong-cho Chung (Seoul), pp. 494–508.

1981

'"Commented it must be": Browning Annotating Browning'. *Browning Institute Studies*, volume IX, edited by N. John Hall (The Browning Institute and City University of New York), pp. 59–77.

Emily Brontë, *Wuthering Heights*, edited with an Introduction by Ian Jack; The World's Classics. (The Introduction is not to be found in the Clarendon Edition: see 1969–92 above).

1982

'Browning on *Sordello* and *Men and Women*: Unpublished Letters to James T. Fields'. *Huntington Library Quarterly*, 45, 3 (Summer), 185–98.

'Byron Refreshed'. Review–article on *Byron's Letters and Journals*, edited by Leslie A. Marchand, 12 volumes, 1973–82, and of *Lord Byron: The Complete Poetical Works*, edited by Jerome J. McGann, volumes I–III. *Review*, volume IV, edited by James O. Hoge and James L. W. West III (University Press of Virginia: Charlottesville), pp. 1–17.

1983

The Poetical Works of Robert Browning, volume I: *Pauline, Paracelsus*, edited by Ian Jack and Margaret Smith. Oxford: at the Clarendon Press. Pp. 581. Ian Jack is the General Editor of the edition. (See also 1984, 1988, 1991.)

1984

The Poetical Works of Robert Browning, volume II: *Strafford, Sordello*, edited by Ian Jack and Margaret Smith. Oxford: at the Clarendon Press. Pp. 531.

The Poet and His Audience. Cambridge University Press. Pp. viii, 198. (The poets considered are Dryden, Pope, Byron, Shelley, Tennyson and Yeats.)

1985

'A Choice of Orders: The Arrangement of "The Poetical Works"'. *Textual Criticism and Literary Appreciation*, edited by Jerome J. McGann (University of Chicago Press), pp. 127–43. (An errata slip in later copies corrects many of the gross errors in the original printing, for which neither the editor nor the contributors were responsible.)

1987

'Browning's *Dramatic Lyrics* (1842)'. *Browning Institute Studies*, volume XV, edited by Adrienne Auslander Munich and John Maynard (The Browning Institute and Southwestern College), pp. 161–75.

1988

The Poetical Works of Robert Browning, volume III: *Bells and Pomegranates* I–VI (including *Pippa Passes* and *Dramatic Lyrics*). Oxford: at the Clarendon Press. Pp. xiv, 542.

1991

The Poetical Works of Robert Browning, volume IV: *Bells and Pomegranates* VII–VIII (*Dramatic Romances and Lyrics, Luria, A Soul's Tragedy*) and *Christmas-Eve and Easter-Day*, edited by Ian Jack, Rowena Fowler and Margaret Smith. Oxford: at the Clarendon Press. Pp. 531.

'Elizabeth Barrett and Browning's "Dramatic Romances and Lyrics" (1845)'. *Browning e Venezia*, a cura di Sergio Perosa (Florence: Leo S. Olschki), pp. 125–35.

1995

The Poetical Works of Robert Browning, volume V: *Men and Women*, edited by Ian Jack and Robert Inglesfield. Oxford: at the Clarendon Press.

Index